AMERICAN
FAITH

"American history overflows with rip-roaring, chestthumping, and tear-jerking adventure stories. It is a romantic moral drama. Thus, it most assuredly should be told with a measure of passion, unction, and verve. It is, after all, the story of remarkable heroes—heroes of faith, courage, and vision. This wonderful new survey of the American story is everything an historical narrative ought to be: in it you'll encounter all the blood and thunder, faith and chivalry, pluck and fury, mystery and intrigue of God's good providence as it is worked out in the lives of more than two dozen heroes. Kudos!"

— **George Grant**, Pastor, Parish Presbyterian Church

"As educational elites strive to deconstruct American history—calling good evil and evil good—Kevin and Generations produces the superlatively excellent volume, American Faith. While our "beautiful inheritance" is being perverted by the fake-history spin of the prophets of falsehood, Generations tells us the truth, and in such an engaging and winsome volume!"

— **Douglas Bond**, author of numerous books and director of the Oxford Creative Writing Master Class

AMERICAN FAITH

27 | SKETCHES FROM WINTHROP TO WILKERSON

Kevin Swanson

with Joshua Schwisow

Daniel Noor, and Peter Bringe

Generations

PASSING ON THE FAITH

Cover Design: Justin Turley
Interior Layout & Design: Rei Suzuki Design

Published by:
Generations
19039 Plaza Drive Ste 210
Parker, Colorado 80134
www.generations.org

For more information on this and
other titles from Generations,
visit www.generations.org or call 888-389-9080.

Contents

Introduction vii

UNIT 1: SPIRITUAL ROOTS (1600-1760)

Unit 1 Introduction 2

1 ★ John Winthrop: America's Founding Father 7

2 ★ William Bradford: Governor of Plymouth 33

3 ★ Anne Bradstreet: America's First Published Poet 55

4 ★ John Eliot: America's First Missionary 77

5 ★ Increase Mather: Rooting a Nation in Faith 95

6 ★ David Brainerd: A Life on the Altar 123

7 ★ Jonathan Edwards: A Passion for God's Glory 143

UNIT 2: FOUNDATIONS OF FAITH (1760-1800)

Unit 2 Introduction 164

8 ★ Patrick Henry: Lighting the Flame for Liberty 169

9 ★ Samuel Adams: Founding Father of American Independence 191

10 ★ Phillis Wheatley: First African-American Writer 215

11 ★ George Washington: The President Who Feared God 231

12 ★ Noah Webster: Christian Educator and American Patriot 253

13 ★ Daniel Boone: American Pioneer 271

UNIT 3: PRIDEFUL EXPANSION AND INTERNAL TURMOIL (1800-1865)

Unit 3 Introduction 294

14 ★ John Quincy Adams: Keeping Faith During the Decline 299

15 ★ Adoniram Judson: A Living Sacrifice...............317

16 ★ Asahel Nettleton: America's Forgotten Evangelist 337

17 ★ Lemuel Haynes: First African-American Minister 359

18 ★ Jedediah Smith: The Best Explorer of the American West 375

19 ★ Thomas "Stonewall" Jackson: A Godly Soldier...............391

UNIT 4: NATIONAL PROSPERITY AND SECULARISM (1865-1920)

Unit 4 Introduction 412

20 ★ Charles Hodge: Contending for the Truth...............417

21 ★ George Washington Carver: A Scientist in Awe of God...............435

22 ★ Dwight L. Moody: Evangelist and Entrepreneur 455

23 ★ William McKinley: Humble President, Faithful Husband...............475

UNIT 5: REMNANT REVIVALS AND SPIRITUAL DECLINE (1920-PRESENT)

Unit 5 Introduction 494

24 ★ J. Gresham Machen: Valiant for Truth...............499

25 ★ Elisabeth Elliot: A Life of Gospel Sacrifice 517

26 ★ Henry Morris: Father of Modern Creation Science...............533

27 ★ David Wilkerson: Spiritual Revival During an Age of Apostasy....553

Conclusion 575

Endnotes 579

List of Images 599

Introduction

*We will not hide them from their children, telling to
the generation to come the praises of the LORD, and
His strength and His wonderful works that He has
done. For He established a testimony in Jacob, and
appointed a law in Israel, which He commanded
our fathers, that they should make them known to
their children; that the generation to come might
know them, the children who would be born, that
they may arise and declare them to their children,
that they may set their hope in God, and not forget
the works of God, but keep His commandments.*

—Psalm 78:4-7

For far too many students, history turns out to be the most boring of
subjects. Squeezing a 500-year history into 500 pages usually results in
a long series of seemingly random dates, names, and places devoid of
any true application to the student's life. With an emphasis on abstract facts,
the knowledge of history often becomes superficial and meaningless, if any
information is retained at all. The goal of most studies is to ensure that the student
retains key names and dates at least until the examination is over. Afterward, the
student often walks away and forgets almost everything learned in class.

American Faith aspires to a different goal. This "unusual" introduction to

American history strives to provide a survey of important events while delving deeply into the real lives of the people who lived them. It strives to offer meaning and purpose as well as names and dates. The editing and writing team have endeavored to offer both breadth and depth in this brief study of American history. It is our hope that these twenty-seven vignettes of great American lives, all portraits of American faith, will provide a better overall understanding of American history.

After all, history should never be boring because it is "His Story." Truly, when we examine what is happening and what has happened in the world, we are seeing the very works of God. Though evil works are evident and God's judgment revisits the American nation over and over again throughout the centuries, yet glimpses of repentance and redemption are visible as well. Even in the midst of man's depravity and disobedience, the Kingdom of Jesus Christ emerges, and it is our duty and joy to take note of it and record these amazing events.

In God's good providence, He uses men and women of faith to accomplish remarkable things. Thanks to this godly heritage, America carved out liberties unlike many other nations. While colonialism and imperialism often mishandled indigenous peoples in many nations around the world, it was faith-filled American missionaries that took the gospel to Native Americans and to others in the far off reaches of the earth.

Where true faith exists in history, it is for us to recognize it and point it out to our children. The Lord God includes a list of the great men and women of faith in Hebrews chapter 11, "of whom the world was not worthy." These were true heroes of the faith. Since the writing of the Book of Hebrews, this heritage of faith, this cloud of witnesses, continues to grow as it extends its march through history. Others are added to the number, and it is for us to recognize them. They are examples for us, and we will do well to learn from them (Rom. 15:4; 1 Cor. 10:6).

Finally, history will become most relevant to our children only when they realize that they play a part in it. History is not merely an exercise in learning *about* the past. Our children must also learn *from* the past and must apply that knowledge to their own role in extending Christ's Kingdom through the ages. They must grasp the baton and continue the race. They must take their turn as they fight "the good fight of faith." Future history books will be written concerning the life of faith they lived as they follow in this procession of faith— looking to Jesus, the author and the finisher of our faith.

> *Therefore we also, since we are surrounded by so great a cloud of witnesses, let us lay aside every weight, and the sin which so easily ensnares us, and let us run with endurance the race that is set before us, looking unto Jesus, the author and finisher of our faith, who for the joy that was set before Him endured the cross, despising the shame, and has sat down at the right hand of the throne of God. (Hebrews 12:1-2)*

UNIT 1

Spiritual Roots (1620-1760)

*Blessed is the nation whose God is the LORD, the
people He has chosen as His own inheritance.*

—Psalm 33:12

The first American colonies were largely founded by godly Christian men and women. They wanted to bring the gospel to the New World. The first seals and charters indicated a commitment to this task of extending Christ's kingdom around the world. Churches were built in the colonies before the colonial governments built their own meeting halls. Regularly, colonial pastors would preach entire sermons in the presence of the governors and legislatures. Though not all colonists were Christians, many of the first roots of this nation sprang from persecuted Reformed Christians in Britain. The devil and his minions always desire to persecute true Christians wherever they may be found. During the reigns of James I, Charles I, James II, and Charles II in England, persecutions broke out against many godly families. Pastors were often the first victims of persecution and so many of these men fled to America between 1620 and 1688. During periods of British apostasy and persecution, America received Britain's best.

Naturally, some colonies received a stronger Christian foundation than others. By far, Massachusetts and Virginia were the largest colonies by the time of the War for Independence. Massachusetts, New Hampshire, and Connecticut were mainly settled by Puritans of Congregational background. Pennsylvania had a strong Quaker influence and New York was settled by the Dutch Reformed. Virginia and other colonies were mostly settled by members of the Anglican Church.

During these early years a tug-a-war was played out over the heart of America. Of course the evil one would not sit back and watch an experiment in godly leadership continue without interference. Spiritual forces were active during the time of the Salem Witch Trials in the 1690s. While the leaders in Massachusetts Bay did not handle the problem rightly or justly, some pastors (like Increase Mather) possessed better sense in these spiritual conflicts. It was the pastors who saw through the deceptions of the evil one and brought an end to the trials.

The American colonies functioned well under the charters they received from the kings of England. They governed themselves with a surprising level of independence from the Mother Country. However, as with all powerful men, it wasn't long before the king and parliament attempted to exercise undue power over the colonies. This created tension between nations that would eventually lead to war.

Bad teaching was also creeping into Harvard College from Europe during the formative years of the colonies. Men like Increase Mather tried to fight it off but eventually failed. By 1710 Harvard was controlled by liberal thinkers, but that was not the end of the American Christian heritage. In the merciful providence of God, He stirred up a Great Spiritual Awakening during the 1730s and 1740s, which served to fortify the foundations of a nation soon to form.

The Great Awakening also produced more missionary fervor to reach the Native Americans with the Gospel. David Brainerd was one of the more well-known missionaries who gave his life for the Indians whom he loved. Soon after his death, Dartmouth College was established as a training school for missionaries to the Indians.

Several motives worked in the hearts of the first colonials. Some came to America for religious freedom. Some came to protect their families from the evil influences arising in Europe. Some came to preach the gospel to the settlers and the Indians. Others came to enrich themselves. Though America was not a perfect nation, the Christian influence was strong in the foundations and this would serve as a blessing for the nation in the centuries that followed.

Rescue me and deliver me from the hand of foreigners,
Whose mouth speaks lying words,
And whose right hand is a right hand of falsehood—
That our sons may be as plants grown up in their youth;
That our daughters may be as pillars,
Sculptured in palace style;
That our barns may be full,
Supplying all kinds of produce;
That our sheep may bring forth thousands
And ten thousands in our fields;
That our oxen may be well laden;
That there be no breaking in or going out;
That there be no outcry in our streets.
Happy are the people who are in such a state;
Happy are the people whose God is the LORD! (Psalm 144:11-15)

Timeline of Important Events

1620	The Pilgrim expedition lands on Cape Cod.
1621	The first Thanksgiving celebration held by the Pilgrims.
1626	Peter Minuit buys Manhattan island for $24 in trinkets, the start of the New York Colony.
1630	The first vessels of John Winthrop's fleet depart from England for Massachusetts Bay.
1636	Harvard College founded in Cambridge, Massachusetts.
1636	Providence, Rhode Island founded by Roger Williams.
1640	The *Bay Psalm Book* becomes the first book printed in North America.
1675	King Philip's War begins in New England. Twelve towns are destroyed.
1692	The Salem Witch Trials begin.
1702	The Royal Colony of New Jersey is formed by Queen Anne.
1702-1713	Queen Anne's War
1718	Pirate Blackbeard is killed off the coast of North Carolina.
1738	George Whitefield begins preaching for the first time in North America.
1754	The French and Indian War begins.

John Winthrop (1587-1649)

CHAPTER 1

John Winthrop: America's Founding Father

Praise the LORD!
Blessed is the man who fears the LORD,
who delights greatly in His commandments.
His descendants will be mighty on the earth.
The generation of the upright will be blessed.

—Psalm 112:1-2

If historians were to choose five men as the earliest Founding Fathers of America, no doubt they would include John Smith (Virginia Colony), William Bradford (Plymouth Colony), William Brewster (Plymouth Colony), John Endecott (Salem Colony), and John Winthrop (Massachusetts Bay Colony). But if we were pressed to reduce the list to a single person, America's Founding Father would have to be John Winthrop. No other leader sacrificed so much, contributed so much, and exerted so vast an influence in the early years of America. Part Separatist and part Puritan but rejecting the immoderate extremes of both parties, he was all Christian all the way. John Winthrop exemplified genuine Christian faith better than many if not most of the early settlers in

America. He was a great leader and a humble Christian. The first roots of this country are found in the Puritans, and John Winthrop was the true Puritan exemplar.

The English Reformation and the Roots of the British Empire

On October 6, 1536, William Tyndale was burned at the stake in Vilvoorde, Belgium. His crime was translating and printing of the Bible in the English language. Tyndale's last prayer was for the King: "Lord, open the King of England's eyes!" Three years earlier King Henry VIII had appointed Thomas Cranmer Archbishop of Canterbury in hopes that Cranmer would annul the king's marriage to Catherine of Aragon. Reformation was on its way to England.

During this time Lutheran ideas from Europe were seeping into England's colleges and churches. The Reformation in England solidified under the reign of Henry's son, Edward VI, who ruled from 1547 to 1553. But, tragically, this young king did not survive his 16th year. Following Edward came Queen Mary (daughter of Henry VIII), a zealous Roman Catholic. During her reign from 1553 to 1558 "Bloody" Mary had her own cousin Lady Jane Grey executed, along with almost 300 other Protestants. In 1558 Mary's sister Elizabeth I assumed the throne and reigned for forty-five years. These were glory years for England, in which the roots of the British Empire formed. As God's providence played out, England would defeat the Spanish Armada in 1588 and put an end to the threat of a Roman Catholic army conquering Protestant England. Queens Mary and Elizabeth began promoting the colonization of Ireland (by the English) in the mid-1500s, and it

William Tyndale

was the Englishman Humphrey Gilbert who attempted the first colonization of Newfoundland in 1578. Then the English attempted a colony in 1585 on Roanoke Island. However, the colony disappeared mysteriously, probably due to disease or Indian attack. Finally, the English managed to pull off a successful colony in Virginia in 1607 under Captain John Smith's leadership at Jamestown. These were the rustic beginnings of the British Empire.

Portrait of Henry VIII

The Puritan Conflict

It was the relationship of church and state in England that crippled the Reformation from the outset. Although a Roman Catholic, King Henry supported the Reformation for personal and political reasons. He sought an escape from his marriage to Catherine, and the pope refused to approve the annulment. Henry's only alternative was to repudiate the pope and embrace the Reformation.

Henry VIII was a tyrannical king. Estimates vary, but historians say this king killed thousands of his political and religious opponents. The church in England was placed under the control of the king. Archbishops and heads of the church were appointed directly by the crown. State control of the church is unbiblical and is always unhealthy both for the church and the state. During and after Henry's reign, the British universities and seminaries were also corrupted by humanist thinking and state control. The English monarchs following Edward

Annulment: A legal act which cancels a marriage. An annulment voids a marriage and declares it to have been invalid from its beginning. Annulled marriages are treated as though they had never legally existed.

VI were not enthusiastic about the life-transforming teachings of men like Martin Luther and John Calvin. With such authorities exercising control over the Church of England, it was only natural that the church would slouch into moral and theological corruption.

Despite this decline, God mercifully raised up a remnant within the churches of England. In the 1570s and 1580s. Puritanism formed among the young students attending Cambridge University, under the tutelage of men like Laurence Chaderton and William Perkins. The life and writings of William Perkins were hugely important among the first American Puritans including Thomas Hooker, William Brewster, and John Winthrop.

In 1584 Puritan leaders in Parliament tried to change the form of church government in England to a Presbyterian model. However, the attempt failed and actually made for trouble between the Puritan faction and the monarchy. Queen Elizabeth now came to view the Puritans as a threat to her authority over the church. So she began persecuting the more radical of the Puritans and Separatists.

In 1593 Elizabeth's Star Chamber sentenced three Separatists to death by hanging—John Penry, Henry Barrow, and John Greenwood. The three men had "separated" themselves from the Church of England and they had urged others to do the same.

Puritans and Separatists: Puritans sought to reform and purify the Church of England from within. Separatists shared many beliefs with the Puritans but decided to separate from the Church of England and form their own churches. This was illegal, and many Separatists were arrested or fled England to the Netherlands.

John Winthrop's Uncle William

It was John Winthrop's Uncle William who led the family into the reforming church. After moving his residence in 1553 at the beginning of Bloody Mary's reign, William Winthrop began meeting secretly with other like-minded believers. He would join fellow Christians for worship in private homes and sometimes on ships in port. William may have provided some of his own merchant ships for this purpose. Uncle William was personally acquainted with some of the martyrs who lost their lives under Queen Mary. He kept in close contact with John Foxe and provided important first-hand information about some of the martyrdoms recorded in Foxe's *Book of Martyrs*.

Later in the 1560s William served as a lay elder in a church called St. Michael's in Cornhill, London. The church purchased copies of John Foxe's *Book of Martyrs* and John Calvin's *Institutes of the Christian Religion* to make available to the congregation. It was clear that these people were serious about reformation. The church also encouraged congregational singing at this time, using psalms adapted to music in Calvin's Geneva.

Uncle William also sponsored and funded several foreign Protestant churches in London. Two of his sons migrated to Ireland and helped lead the Irish Reformation (which in some respects was stronger than England's). Although operating somewhat in the background, William Winthrop was a major player in the English Reformation. His devout commitment to the reformation of the Christian church had a profound influence on his younger brother Adam (John Winthrop's father), nineteen years younger. While Adam admired his older brother's courage and faith, it would be Adam's son John who would take the reformation vision to the most radical conclusions.

Early Years

I charge you therefore before God and the Lord Jesus Christ, who will judge the living and the dead at His appearing and His kingdom: Preach the word! Be ready in season and out of season. Convince, rebuke, exhort, with all longsuffering and teaching. For the time will come when they will not endure sound doctrine, but according to their own desires, because they have itching ears, they will heap up for themselves teachers; and they will turn their ears away from the truth, and be turned aside to fables. (2 Timothy 4:1-4)

John Winthrop was born in 1588 to Adam and Anne Winthrop in

Edwardstone (located about sixty miles northeast of London). John's father did not start out rich, but he worked his way into England's upper middle class. In a day when books were considered a luxury, Adam Winthrop managed to collect a library of eighty-seven volumes. He was both a lawyer and a farmer in a time when a single source of income was insufficient to provide for a large family. John was the second child born to Adam and Anne. His sisters, Anne, Jane, and Lucy were born in 1586, 1592, and 1601.

John grew up in the Stour Valley in Essex, England. Beginning in 1563 the valley received two godly, Calvinist pastors: Henry Browne and William Bird. It was the preaching of these men that lit a fire under the families in the valley. And Stour Valley became known as the godliest commonwealth in any part of England.[1] Largely through the influence of a godly bishop (pastor) named Edmund Grindal, reformation swept through Essex. Two important elements came to characterize these Puritan churches:

1. Evangelical preaching.

2. "Prophesying" or Scripture-based, Spirit-filled encouragements and exhortations from ordinary men in the congregations or pastors gathered in small groups.

Puritan preachers preferred the powerful proclamation of God's Word to empty rituals and outward ceremonies. Typically people favored outward ceremonies when they did not want to be convicted of their sin or be subjected to the powerful truths of Christ's redeeming gospel. The devil does not like unfettered Gospel preaching and this was certainly the case in 16th century England.

John Winthrop's mother, Anne Browne Winthrop, was the daughter of Pastor Henry Browne. As a child she had been well discipled in the reformation faith in her father's home. Pastor Browne taught her, "A minister must tell the people of their sins," and "we must remember the law of God continually."[2]

In his youthful days John played football (soccer) with his friends and hunted rabbits with his musket and bow, although he was never a good shot. His father taught him to fish in the manor pond and streams. Each Sunday his parents took him to hear two sermons at the church in Groton or Boxford. Often his parents invited the pastors to their home for more fellowship in Christ.

John's father taught him a basic Christian catechism called "Principles of the Christian Religion." When his dad asked him, "What sure ground do we have to build our religion upon?" John would answer, "The Word of God contained in the Scripture."[3] The catechism taught him that God really does "ordain whatsoever comes to pass."[4]

Young John Winthrop was a sinner, and he came to be sharply aware of this truth about himself early on. When still a lad he stole two little books he found left in the house. Later in his life he wrote that, "ever since, when they have come to my mind, I have grieved at it, and would have gladly made restitution."[5] As early as twelve years of age John began struggling with sexual temptation. He admitted to having "attempted all kinds of wickedness."[6] He was, in his own words, "very wild and dissolute."[7]

At fourteen, John went off to Trinity College, Cambridge. At this time Cambridge was a seedbed of a robust, reforming faith. The young men rose early and assembled at chapel by 5:00 a.m. for early morning prayers and a sermon. Each student was assigned a tutor who held him to spiritual accountability and discipled him in the faith. Tutoring was a vibrant college ministry in the 1590s. During these years young John sat under the evangelical preaching of the most famous Puritan of the day, William Perkins. John Cotton was one of his classmates, a young man who would become the most famous pastor in the early days of America.

> **Calvinism**: Calvinism is the term used for those who generally accept the doctrines of the Swiss Reformer, John Calvin. Usually, Calvinists emphasize the doctrine of predestination — that God determines who will be saved and who will not be saved.

Nevertheless, the college scene was still not perfect in Cambridge. Tales of drunkenness and fornication among the student body were common. John Winthrop's days at college were marked by strong temptations to sexual sin. After barely two years at Trinity College John quit school never to return.

Immediately afterward, at only seventeen years of age, he married Mary Forth.

To the unmarried and the widows I say that it is good for them to remain single, as I am. But if they cannot exercise self-control, they should marry. For it is better to marry than to burn with passion. (1 Corinthians 7:8-9)

Adult Life

Repent therefore and be converted, that your sins may be blotted out, so that times of refreshing may come from the presence of the Lord . . . (Acts 3:19)

By his own admission, the first years of John's first marriage were marked by impatience, self-centeredness, and quarrels with his wife. At times John gave himself to "negligence and idleness."[8] He hunted birds along the creeks, but at times he would participate in illegal poaching. It was around this time that Winthrop began to pray that God would give him "a new heart, joy in His Spirit; that He would dwell with me, that He would strengthen me against the world, the flesh and the Devil, and that He would forgive my sins and increase my faith."[9]

Trinity College, where Winthrop attended from fourteen years of age.

John committed himself to fighting against the sins of "pride, covetousness, love of this world, vanity of mind, unthankfulness, sloth (both in my service and in my calling), and not preparing myself with reverence and uprightness to come to His Word."[10] John's faith now had a seriousness about it. He was assured of God's love at this time, even to the point that he "dreamed that I was with Christ."[11] He fell on his face and wept for a very long time, sensing the love of Christ like never before.

Six children were born to the couple—John Jr., Henry, Forth, Mary, and two daughters who died at birth. John's relationship with Anne was marred by his pride but improved as he grew closer to God. He committed himself to family worship both morning and evening. He wanted to "have a special care for the education of my children and to banish profaneness from my family." He committed every morning to "private prayer, meditation, and reading," and to "pray and confer privately with my wife."[12] These commitments turned out to be life-transforming for John Winthrop.

John made the entry in his journal at this time: "I will always walk humbly before my God, and meekly, mildly and gently towards all men . . . to give myself, my life, my wits, my health, my wealth to the service of my God and Saviour."[13] His commitment to the Lord solidified during his marriage with Mary.

Between 1605 and 1613 John and Mary lived in Southeast Essex with Mary's family. This part of the country was less committed to the reformation faith. Upon returning to the Stour Valley in 1613, John began meeting with a "covenanted group"—an accountability group of pastors and committed Christian men and women. They met every Friday for prayer and to discuss sermons. This provided a pattern for John Winthrop's spiritual walk in the years that followed.

On the birth of a seventh child, Anne, John's wife Mary died. A year later John married again. His second wife Thomasine died in childbirth in November 1616.

John Winthrop's third wife Margaret was a true jewel. Never was a relationship so sweet and so tender as that of John and Margaret. One historian described Margaret as "one of the most appealing women in American history."[14] Her husband called her "a very gracious woman,"[15] probably an underestimation of her character. Margaret's letters to John were filled with kindness, tenderness, concern, and love, as were his to her. He referred to her as his "sweet spouse," "most sweet heart," or "most loving and dear wife," and ended his letters with phrases like "the sweetest kisses and pure embracings of my kindest affection."[16] In her letters Margaret wrote him, "I have no way to manifest my love to you but by these unworthy lines, which I would entreat you to accept from her that loveth you with an unfeigned heart."[17] When she heard that he had injured his hand, Margaret wrote in the most tender, affecting language, "I will not look for any long letters this term because I pity your poor hand if I had it here I would make more of it than ever I did, and bind it up very softly for fear of hurting it."[18] In response John affirmed his appreciation for her and her letters as "the true image of thy most loving heart, breathing out the faithful desires of thy sweet soul towards him that prizeth thee above all things in the world."[19] Such records utterly dispel the myth that Puritans were a cold, emotionless, and hard-hearted people.

For his life's calling John Winthrop pursued the legal field. At 21 years of age his father appointed him as magistrate in a local court at Groton Manor. He continued to work as a local county judge from 1617 onward. Each day before he entered the court he prepared his heart "by earnest prayer."[20] Few men had a clearer view of the decline of English society in the 1620s than John Winthrop from his seat as judge. Crimes of murder, theft, witchcraft, and infanticide were not unusual in that part of the country. Local preachers called attention to the moral slipping, especially on the part of the civil leaders. Pastor Bezaleel Carter in particular preached against the extortion and bribery that was increasingly common in the Stour Valley.

By 1615 King James I began appointing men to positions of authority in the church who had little interest in reformation. Anglican bishops like William Laud discouraged the preaching of the Word by reforming, Holy Spirit-filled men of God. Under these new leaders the Winthrops had less access to preaching during the week than they had enjoyed for some forty years prior. In 1622 King James tried to stop preaching that addressed controversial matters. This included the teaching that God is in control of man's salvation. Humanist

kings like James believed that man should
be sovereign instead of God. When King
Charles I took the throne in 1625, matters
got even worse. Pastors who did not
conform to the new rules enforcing certain
ceremonies in the church were dragged into
court. Later, in 1629, the king shut down
all Sunday afternoon sermons in the land,
a devastating blow to the Puritans. As late
as 1633 Charles I insisted that pastors read
The King's Book of Sports from the pulpit on

King James I

Sundays. Such regulations imposed on the churches were deeply disturbing for
the Puritan congregants.

During the decade of the 1620s some of the faithful pastors began leaving
Stour Valley for Ireland. Puritans like John Winthrop feared that England was
returning to the old Roman Catholic tyranny over the church. At first, John
considered migrating to Ireland but decided against it. He wondered if God's
judgment would descend upon England. Winthrop soberly noted in his journals:

> *"We have humbled ourselves not, to turn from our evil ways, but have provoked
> [God] more than all the nations round about us; therefore he is turning the cup
> towards us. I am verily persuaded that God will bring some heavy affliction upon
> this land, and that speedily."[21]*

The cultural situation continued to degenerate in the Stour Valley where
the Winthrops had lived and prospered for generations. Violent crime was
on the rise. Roman Catholicism gained popularity in the valley. During the

The King's Book of Sports: King James I issued his "Book of Sports" for national
distribution in 1618. It was intended to encourage Englishmen to participate in
certain sports on Sundays, including archery, dancing, "leaping, vaulting, or any
other such harmless recreation" as permissible sports, together with "May-games,
Whitsun-ales and Morris-dances, and the setting up of May-poles."

election cycle of 1626, John Winthrop was rejected for the position of Member of Parliament representing the borough of Sudbury. The Puritans had committed themselves to laws prohibiting adultery and fornication, and these positions were unpopular at the time.

As tensions grew between the king and parliament, John Winthrop and other local magistrates were forced by law to collect illegitimate taxes for the king. John resisted, along with several of his Puritan friends. Some were sent to jail, although in God's good providence Winthrop escaped this treatment. John presented a bill to his friends in Parliament that would have prevented "the loathsome vice of drunkenness and other disorders in Alehouses [bars]," [22] but this effort failed.

In early 1629 Parliament attempted to pass two bills, one that discouraged the reverting to "papacy" and another that would have prevented anyone from raising taxes for the king. Charles quickly dissolved Parliament, imprisoned nine members, and shut down the people's government for eleven years. This was the last straw. It was clear to these Puritans that the tyrant in London was determined to create a tyrannical state, destroy representative government, and put an end to the Protestant Reformation in England. Seeing where his nation was headed, John Winthrop had very little hope for the future of his mother country. Its colleges were corrupt, its churches were compromised, and its civil government had become tyrannical. As far as he could see, the judgment of God was closing in on England. It was time to begin seeking a haven elsewhere. In his own words:

> All other churches in Europe are brought to desolation . . . and who knows but that God hath provided this place [America] to be a refuge for many whom He means to save out of the general calamity, and seeing the Church has no place left to flee into but the wilderness . . . The fountains of learning and religion are so corrupted as most children are perverted, corrupted, and utterly overthrown by the multitude of evil examples and the licentious governments of those seminaries. [23]

Moving to America

Seek you the LORD, all you meek of the earth, who have kept his commands; seek righteousness, seek meekness: it may be you shall be hidden in the day of the LORD'S anger. (Zephaniah 2:3)

Three small settlements had already found their way to Massachusetts Bay on the new American continent—Plymouth (1620), Cape Ann (1623), and Salem (1626). Cape Ann had failed, but the other two were still breathing as John Winthrop made plans for a larger settlement in the Bay.

All three of his older sons, John (24 years old), Henry (22 years old), and Forth (20 years old) agreed to join their father on the venture into the wilderness of America. Henry had already attempted his own plantation on Barbados at the age of 20, but the endeavor had failed. Now this adventurous (and somewhat rebellious) young man was ready for a new venture with his father.

By August 1629 John Winthrop was the primary visionary among the Puritans for settling New England. Publishing a document called "General Observations," he laid out to his countrymen his reasons for going to the New World. These reasons included the following:

1. Protestants have a commission to carry the Christian gospel to America and to "raise a bulwark against the Kingdom of Antichrist which the Jesuits labor to raise in all parts of the world."[24] Despite Scripture's clear injunction, Protestants in the 17th century were still slower to engage in mission work than their Roman Catholic contemporaries.

2. The judgment of God was hanging over Europe. America was a land that God had prepared "for a refuge for many whom he meaneth to save."[25]

3. England was overpopulated, in Winthrop's view. Moreover the European population had grown "vile and base."[26]

4. Economically, England was facing a terrible inflation which made it difficult for the middle class to succeed in business.

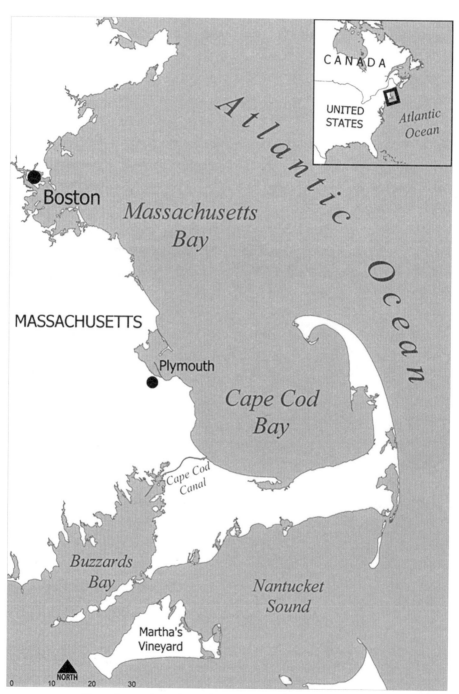

Massachusetts Bay where John Winthrop helped found a colony

> **Jesuits**: Called "The Society of Jesus," formed by Ignatius Loyola in 1540 who intended a Counter-Reformation (within the Roman Catholic Church) to the Protestants. This was a movement committed to high discipline, contemplative mysticism, and foreign missions work.

5. Oxford and Cambridge universities had become corrupt.

6. Opportunities were available in America to take dominion over lands which had never yet been cultivated.

7. The Reformation church was still in its infancy, and Winthrop felt that a fresh start would help the Protestant church develop in this new land.

8. If wealthy Christians were willing to give up their comforts to build the church in New England, they would follow through on Christ's exhortation to take up the cross and follow Him (Luke 9:23). Sacrifice is part of the Christian life, and this sort of strenuous application of faith played strongly in Winthrop's mind.

The risks of Winthrop's venture were enormous—far beyond what most modern Christians would ever consider. The death toll of the endeavor was staggering. Between 1605 and 1625, 80% of new arrivals to the Virginia Colony died within fifteen years of their arrival.[27] Yet these harsh facts did not deter such staunch Puritans. On March 4, 1629, the king issued a charter to the Massachusetts Bay Company which permitted them to begin a settlement. John Endecott, already leading the Salem Colony, was made the first governor. On July 28, 1629, John Winthrop called a meeting with pastors John Cotton, Thomas Hooker, and Roger Williams to discuss the objective of planting a "godly commonwealth" in New England. Then, on October 29, 1629, John Winthrop was elected governor by the court or board of the Massachusetts Bay Company.

Preparations were made for the first voyage, which would sail in late 1629, and another in early 1630. Provisions included eighty muskets, six long fowling pieces, 100 swords, and sixty pikes. Food supplies included forty-five large casks of beer, six casks of water, twenty-two hogsheads of beef, forty bushels of peas, twenty bushels of oatmeal, candles, beer vinegar, mustard seed, oil, soap, butter, and cheese. Over seventy of John's Puritan neighbors in Groton accompanied him on the first voyage. Because of the many dangers inherent in the new venture, John left his wife and young children at home until he was well settled in the new land. John's two younger sons, Stephen (11 years old) and Adam (10 years old) went with their father aboard the *Arbella*. He reported to his wife that the boys slept well on the ship, wrapped in a rug, "for we have no sheets here."[28]

As he prepared to leave England, John Winthrop preached his famous sermon called "A Model of Christian Charity," in which he outlined his vision for America. He wanted this new commonwealth "to improve our lives, to do more service to the Lord," and "to increase the body of Christ whereof we are members, [so] that ourselves and our posterity may be the better preserved from the common corruptions of this world" and might "serve the Lord and work out our salvation under the power and purity of his holy ordinances."[29] Ultimately Winthrop desired more obedience to God among the people of God.

John described the form of government of the new commonwealth as a "Covenant with God for this work."[30] The covenant was a "near bond of marriage" between God and the colony.[31] John hoped this would be the highest example and the very citadel of Christian virtue and influence in the world. Foremost, he wanted the members of the community to love one another. He desired a society knit together in love.

John Winthrop hoped that God would make this new settlement "a praise and a glory."[32] He envisioned that future colonies planted around the world would say, "The Lord make us like that of New England."[33] He wanted New England to be a true "City upon a Hill."[34] This was a reference to Jesus' words in Matthew 5:13-16:

> *You are the salt of the earth; but if the salt loses its flavor, how shall it be seasoned?*
> *It is then good for nothing but to be thrown out and trampled underfoot by men. You*
> *are the light of the world. A city that is set on a hill cannot be hidden. Nor do they*
> *light a lamp and put it under a basket, but on a lampstand, and it gives light to all*
> *who are in the house. Let your light so shine before men, that they may see your good*
> *works and glorify your Father in heaven. (Matthew 5:13-16)*

Suffering and Tragedy

The first church meetings in the Massachusetts Bay Colony were held outdoors under a tree. Nearly one hundred members formed the first church, including the leaders John Winthrop, Thomas Dudley, Isaac Johnson, and Pastor John Wilson. They swore to a covenant, "solemnly and religiously promising and binding ourselves to walk in all our ways according to the rule of the Gospel and in all sincere conformity to [God's] holy ordinances, and in mutual love and respect each to other, so near as God shall give us grace."[35]

Tragedy marked the first months in the new land for John Winthrop. In July 1630 one of the colonists noticed a canoe on the far side of the river and John's son Henry volunteered to swim over to fetch it. The boy never made it across the river, probably because the water was colder than he had anticipated. Of the first 1,000 members of the first settlement, some 200 had died by the first winter. Winthrop himself lost twelve members of his household, including a number of hired servants. That first cold winter was particularly hard on those who were living in tents or carved-out caves in the hillsides. Wolves picked off the livestock. The situation was so dangerous that John dared not venture away from his home without a gun in hand. One evening he lost his way in the wilderness and spent all night by a fire, singing psalms. By God's grace he found his way back home the following morning.

During the first difficult year, Winthrop exhibited the highest caliber of leadership which can only be demonstrated under the most severe circumstances. Despite the numerous hardships, John wrote to Margaret, "I like so well to be here . . . and if I were to come again, I would not have altered my course, though I had foreseen all these afflictions."[36] He wrote to his friend Sir William Spring that "these afflictions we have met with need discourage none, for the country is exceeding good."[37]

Few political leaders are willing to give up their own power or possessions for the sake of others. John Winthrop exhibited the best of Christian leadership in hard times. Using his own resources, he traded with the natives for corn to feed the colony. He funded more shipments of goods out of England. He dipped

Portrait of Cotton Mather

into his own supplies to keep the other members of the colony alive during that first winter. Cotton Mather reports in his history of early America that Winthrop was in the act of reaching into a barrel for the last handful of grain for a poor starving man when a ship "arrived at the harbor's mouth, laden with provisions for them all."[38]

In the spring of 1631, John Winthrop wasted no time in setting his household and hired servants to work. The team, himself included, set out to cultivate 600 acres of land. Right away John built a large house for Margaret (who joined him later that year). It was a two-story house with a kitchen, pantry, buttery, a large meeting hall, and bedrooms upstairs for the children. The meeting hall was used for the gathering of the local government as well as for the first church in Boston.

The first judicial cases taken up by Winthrop and his small court included fining Nicholas Knopp for selling plain water as a "cure" for scurvy. They forbade the use of dice and cards and instituted punishment for those who went hunting on the Sabbath (Sunday). For serious crimes like adultery, the first government required the death penalty.[39] A man named John Dawe was punished for seducing a Native American woman into sexual sin. The trading of guns and alcohol with the natives was also prohibited. The first court of New England protected the rights of the Native Americans as well as the British colonists, and an important leader in the colony was fined for burning down two Indian wigwams.

In May 1631 the government held another election, the first in Massachusetts. Only men who were members of Protestant churches were permitted to vote. A total of 116 freemen voted, and John Winthrop was reelected governor.

Meanwhile back in England things weren't getting any better for Winthrop's Puritan friends. As the decade progressed, more pastors were imprisoned. King Charles I and Archbishop Laud were working systematically to dismantle biblical theology in the churches and reintroduce Roman Catholic practices. Between

1630 and 1642 at least 13,000 immigrants moved into the Massachusetts Bay area. The population of New England reached 22,800 by 1650.

In-fighting within the Colony

And the Lord's servant must not be quarrelsome but kind to everyone, able to teach, patiently enduring evil. (2 Timothy 2:24)

John Winthrop and the colonial court ran into a little trouble when Watertown (one of the towns over which John governed) resisted an imposed tax. The colony was collecting the tax to construct fortifications to provide a defense for the towns against attacks from the surrounding native tribes. Eventually the town agreed to pay the tax.

The first major political quarrel in the new colony occurred between Winthrop and his deputy governor, Thomas Dudley. This fight would continue for over a decade. Basically, John Winthrop was hoping to maintain unity with those Christians who disagreed on minor doctrinal issues. On the other hand, Thomas Dudley was a hard man and best known for his hatred of "heresy." While Winthrop would freely give away his goods to help the poor and starving, Dudley would lend food to the poor and require a large repayment at harvest time. Although Dudley would raise a number of false charges against Winthrop, none of them stuck. By the grace of God the two were eventually reconciled and Winthrop's daughter Mary married Dudley's son Samuel.

Controversy again arose with Roger Williams, who had embraced a more complete separatism. Roger eventually left the colony and made his way down to the Plymouth settlement, but wasn't happy there, either. Although the Plymouth colonists were Separatists, some still attended Anglican churches when visiting England. This leniency was intolerable for Roger. The greatest point of contention for these hyper-separatists was a purely regenerate church membership. They wanted to know the condition of every person's heart. They carried this belief to such an extreme that they refused to baptize or receive anyone into church membership unless everyone else in the church was absolutely convinced that the new member had genuinely experienced the new birth. As Scripture clearly reveals, it is impossible for man to infallibly know the condition of another person's heart. Regeneration is a secret, mysterious work that the Holy Spirit produces in people's hearts, and the true effects of this mysterious work may take a long time to be outwardly visible.

> *Do not marvel that I said to you, "You must be born again." The wind blows where it wishes, and you hear the sound of it, but cannot tell where it comes from and where it goes. So is everyone who is born of the Spirit. (John 3:7-8)*

To attempt to infallibly judge another person's heart is to attempt to usurp the role of God Himself. It would be good for all to remember that the Lord Jesus received Judas into the membership of His group of disciples even though He knew that Judas was "a devil" (John 6:70).

As time went on Roger Williams became even more rebellious against the whole social order and began to call the colonists to reject the king's patent, dissolve the colony, and send everyone back to England. A generally unstable man, Roger invented increasingly wild ideas. He moved into Salem and caused more trouble there. Almost every leader in the colony vehemently opposed Williams, except John Winthrop. By this time Winthrop had proved himself to be a remarkably patient and tolerant leader in the colony. Hoping to avoid a clash between Roger and the town leaders, John advised Williams in a letter to quietly "steer his course" to the more remote Narragansett Bay. Roger Williams later wrote, "I took his prudent notion as a hint and a voice from God."[40] Their friendship continued to be affectionate and respectful as the years progressed, though John expressed a deep concern for Roger's spiritual condition in his letters. Roger accepted the letters as truly loving and caring, but in the end he rejected John's advice.

John Winthrop's moderation was also revealed in how he handled the problem of witchcraft. As early as 1638 Salem encountered the problem of demon possession. A certain Dorothy Talby suffered from spiritual delusions and "was so possessed by Satan" that she committed infanticide.[41] The first recorded execution for the crime of witchcraft in Massachusetts happened in Charlestown in 1648. Winthrop was not involved in the trial. However, it was Winthrop's son, John Jr., who helped to put a halt to the witchcraft trials in the 1650s.

In 1635, an attempt was made to produce a body of laws "in resemblance of the Magna Carta" for the colony. This failed largely because Winthrop desired more flexibility for future legislatures and judges to determine laws and implement them. A year later a committee produced a code based largely on John Cotton's *Moses His Judicials*. This was almost a word-for-word copy of God's law in the Mosaic code. Winthrop continued to question the wisdom of implementing this code. However, he did not believe that the church should control the "judicial proceedings in any court of civil justice." Neither did he want to dismiss the tradition of English Common Law. Yet, he still wanted each magistrate to "search the Scriptures for the proper rule in each case."[42] He realized that God's law still provided the perfect standard, yet the application of God's law to each particular case is not always cut and dried. While accepting the principle or "general equity" of the Old Testament civil law, he insisted on flexibility in the application of it. Winthrop understood that no person and no society could perfectly live up to God's laws. Common Law represented the outworking of the morality of a society, and it is not to be neglected by judges who want to make wise application of God's law.

Finally, in 1648, John Winthrop supported the Massachusetts Laws and Liberties document issued with a full preface authored by his pastor, John Cotton. A portion of this historical document is included at the end of this chapter. In all, John Winthrop served as governor of Massachusetts for about fifteen years over four terms: 1629-1634, 1637-1640, 1642-1644, and 1646-1649.

A Great Godly Example in Leadership

The Spirit of the LORD spoke by me, and His word was on my tongue. The God of Israel said, 'The Rock of Israel spoke to me: He who rules over men must be just, ruling in the fear of God.' (2 Samuel 23:2-3)

In many ways John Winthrop was an ideal Christian leader for a flawed and sinful world. He understood the limitations of sinful human nature. He realized the limitation of political government. His willingness to sacrifice his own resources will forever stand as a remarkable example for those who serve in civil government. Most political leaders reach into other people's pockets for government resources. They want to take other people's money and use it for their projects, but John Winthrop did just the opposite at the founding of this nation. As governor of the Massachusetts Bay Colony, his actions encapsulated the truth of Paul's words: "I seek not [what is] yours, but you" (2 Cor. 12:14).

John Winthrop was a humble man, sensitive to his own failings and sins. He gave glory to God for his successes and took full responsibility for his own failures. This enabled him to maintain a good balance and wise judgment in governance over Massachusetts during those first critical years. Other Puritan leaders often seemed to give way to a hypocritical ideal by attempting to hold the political system to a higher standard than the standards they would apply to themselves.

Governor Winthrop feared God. As Scripture dictates, this is the first requirement for any decent government leader (Exod. 18:21, 2 Sam. 23:3). He was a man of deep piety and personal integrity.

It would be hard to find anyone in history who communicated more love for his wife and children in his diary and letters than John Winthrop. His only published sermon was a call for Christian charity and taught that we must "love one another, with a pure heart fervently" (1 Pet. 1:22). This is the only way for a happy community to exist. Such a thing rarely happens in churches and civil communities, yet John was a good example of this. He loved his enemies, almost never held a grudge, and constantly forgave those who ruthlessly maligned and attacked him.

Last but not least, John Winthrop was a man of courage. He did not give way to discouragement in the face of unspeakable tragedy. He inspired courage and steadfastness in others, characteristics upon which nations are built. It was the Puritan ethic and attitude that built the nation, and John Winthrop was the prime example of Puritanism in the first generation.

America's first native historian, Cotton Mather, called Winthrop the

"American Nehemiah." John Winthrop was a visionary but not a man who sought a utopia. He was a reformer but not a revolutionary. He was a humble man, a godly man, and a repentant sinner. God chose to use this Puritan leader in a most remarkable way to build a remarkable nation.

— ★ ★ ★ —

Massachusetts Laws and Liberties, 1648

It is ordered by this Court and authoritie thereof, that there shall never be any bond-slavery, villenage or captivitie amongst us; unless it be lawfull captives, taken in just warrs, and such strangers as willingly sell themselves, or are solde to us: and such shall have the libertyes and christian usages which the law of God established in Israell concerning such persons doth morally require, provided, this exempts none from servitude who shall be judged thereto by Authoritie. [1641] ...

Capital Lawes.

1. If any man after legal conviction shall have or worship any other God, but the lord god: he shall be put to death. Exod. 22. 20. Deut. 13.6. & 10. Deut. 17. 2. 6.

2. If any man or woman be a witch, that is, hath or consulteth with a familiar spirit, they shall be put to death. Exod. 22. 18. Levit. 20. 27. Deut. 18. 10. 11.

3. If any person within this Jurisdiction whether Christian or Pagan shall wittingly and willingly presume to blaspheme the holy Name of God, Father, Son or Holy-Ghost, with direct, expresse, presumptuous, or highhanded blasphemy, either by wilfull or obstinate denying the true God, or his Creation, or Government of the world: or shall curse God in like manner, or reproach the holy religion of God as if it were but a politick device to keep ignorant men in awe; or shal utter any other kinde of Blasphemy of the like nature & degree they shall be put to death. Levit. 24. 15. 16.

4. If any person shall commit any wilfull murther, which is Man slaughter, committed upon premeditate malice, hatred, or crueltie not in a mans necessary and just defence, nor by meer casualty against his will, he shall be put to death. Exod. 21. 12. 13. Numb. 35. 31.

William Bradford (1590-1657)

CHAPTER 2

William Bradford:
Governor of Plymouth

He calms the storm,
So that its waves are still.
Then they are glad because they are quiet;
So He guides them to their desired haven.
Oh, that men would give thanks to the LORD for
His goodness,
And for His wonderful works to the children of men!

—Psalm 107:29-31

A mong the early colonial efforts in North America, the planting of Plymouth Plantation in modern-day Massachusetts is one of the most important. It is the story of God's remarkable providence. Indeed, the Lord mercifully preserved this small colony amidst severe trials. Many consider Plymouth Colony one of the key birthplaces of the United States. William Bradford, who served as governor of the colony for many years, was the chief chronicler of this early history. Therefore, the story of Plymouth Plantation is best told from the perspective of William Bradford.

Early Years in England

William was born in the small town of Austerfield around the turn of the 16th century. The exact date of his birth is unknown, but his baptism was recorded in the parish church on March 29, 1590.[1] The Bradford family was considered wealthy in that region of England. For four generations, the Bradfords had built a family legacy of property and business that passed down through each succeeding generation. Eventually, William would leave that wealth behind as he joined ranks with the Separatists, whose interest it was to guard the purity of God's worship.

For the first seven years of his life, young William worked on the family farm. From his daily chores, he learned many valuable skills, including milking the cows, brewing beer, cooking, and tending sheep. However, William's younger years were met with tragedy upon tragedy. When he was a mere sixteen months old, his father, William Bradford Sr., died. Then, in his seventh year his mother Alice also passed away leaving William an orphaned child. He went to live with his two uncles, Robert and Thomas. After the death of his mother, William also endured a long and difficult sickness, which prevented him from attending to many of the household chores. But this difficult trial afforded him the opportunity to learn reading and writing, a skill that would become vitally important for him in later years.

In addition to self-study, William received his early education from the local pastor, as was common for many in his day. As a boy, he read the Scriptures in the translation known as "the Geneva Bible." This edition of Scripture was unique because it contained marginal notes that explained the meaning of the text from a Reformation perspective. As the name suggests, the Geneva Bible was produced in Geneva, Switzerland. In the mid-1500s, many English scholars fled persecution in England under Queen Mary and joined John Calvin and his successor Theodore Beza in Geneva. During their time in Geneva, these learned men produced a new English translation of the Bible with explanatory notes at the bottom of each page. The Geneva Bible would become the Bible of the Pilgrims and many other English Christians of the time. William also read the highly influential book by John Foxe, later known as Foxe's *Book of Martyrs*. Foxe's book recorded many of the martyrdoms that took place during the reign of Queen Mary (known to history as "Bloody Mary").

Queen Elizabeth, the successor to Queen Mary, reigned from 1558 to 1603. She did not persecute the Protestants as her sister Mary had done, but Elizabeth still required conformity to the regulations set out by the Church of England. The Queen would not allow freedom for those Christians who objected to the worship of the Church of England. As William studied the Geneva Bible and its explanatory notes, he began to question whether the worship of the English church was faithful to the Word of God. At age twelve, he began to attend the preaching of Rev. Richard Clyfton who preached regularly a few miles down the road from Austerfield. Pastor Clyfton was convinced that the Church of England was holding on to unbiblical elements of church worship and practice inherited from Roman Catholicism, and he preached for reform.

In his younger years, William Bradford met another reforming brother named, William Brewster. They became fast friends, and Brewster would mentor the younger William by loaning him books on biblical doctrine and church practice. This cemented William's doctrinal convictions, eventually resulting in his joining the other Separatists who had left the Church of England to form a new congregation.

Life in Amsterdam and Leyden

These all died in faith, not having received the promises, but having seen them afar off were assured of them, embraced them and confessed that they were strangers and pilgrims on the earth . . . But now they desire a better, that is, a heavenly country. Therefore God is not ashamed to be called their God, for He has prepared a city for them. (Hebrews 11:13, 16)

Queen Elizabeth died in 1603 and King James I assumed the throne. Initially, the Puritans and Separatists were hopeful that James' reign would produce greater religious freedom and that the Church of England would be further purified. However, they were soon disappointed with the new king. James set himself against the Puritans and the Separatists and vowed that he would "make them conform, or . . . harry [harass and drive] them out of the land."[2] This promise was fulfilled in the case of William Bradford and his Separatist brothers and sisters.

King James' oppression of the Puritans and Separatists continued to increase in the early years of his reign. At first, the Separatists were constrained to meet secretly in order to avoid detection by local authorities. As the risks of arrest heightened, the Separatist group meeting in Mr. Brewster's home (Scrooby Manor), resolved to leave England covertly. The plan was to make a new home in the Netherlands. William recorded the personal challenge that faced each of the Separatists as they contemplated a move to this foreign country:

> For these reformers to be thus constrained to leave their native soil, their lands and livings, and all their friends, was a great sacrifice, and was wondered at by many. But to go into a country unknown to them, where they must learn a new language, and get their livings they knew not how, seemed an almost desperate adventure, and a misery worse than death.[3]

Separatist: A name applied to those English Christians who left the Church of England to form separate congregations. Separatists believed that the English church was still corrupted by many unbiblical and idolatrous practices. They argued that the church needed to be further reformed. They gathered in their own assemblies for worship and regulated their worship strictly according to what they understood the Bible to prescribe.

During this time, the small group of Separatists came to understand what the Bible teaches about the Christian life: we are all pilgrims and sojourners in a foreign land, looking for a heavenly country. The departure from England was only their first earthly sojourn. In the providence of God, the Netherlands would serve as a training ground for an even more difficult pilgrimage to the wilderness of North America. It was William Bradford who first applied the word "Pilgrims" to the little band. The term stuck and Brewster's little church has come to be known ever since as "the Pilgrims".

Getting out of England was no easy task for this small group of Pilgrims. The tyranny of England was far-reaching. On their first attempt to leave, William Brewster, John Robinson and the others hired a ship in the Lincolnshire town of Boston, but the captain turned them in to the authorities. Several of the leaders were arrested and thrown in jail. On the second escape attempt, they found a trustworthy Dutch captain to take their families to Amsterdam. As the men were sneaking on the ship on the southern bank of the Humby River, the local militia showed up to arrest them. The captain decided to push off to avoid arrest, leaving the women and children on the shore. Finally, the women and children were able to join the men in Holland some months later.

Leaving England was a major commitment for young, seventeen-year-old William Bradford. He would have collected his inheritance if he had waited until he was twenty-one. However, this young man held a commitment to Christ and to His church as a higher value than all of that which the world promises.

Since he was still a youth and single, William chose to stay with the Brewster family while living in Amsterdam. The Separatists found life in the Netherlands to be a difficult adjustment. William noted that the language barriers made it difficult for the Separatists to integrate into Dutch culture. But the Separatists also found it difficult to find profitable labor. Most of them were farmers in England, and Amsterdam was a large city of industry containing some 240,000 people. The Pilgrims were not skilled in many of the industrial labors of Amsterdam and thus were forced to take low-paying, low-skill jobs in order to put food on the table. William described their plight, saying, "it was not long before they saw the grim and grisly face of poverty coming upon them like an armed man, with whom they must buckle and encounter, and from whom they could not fly."[4] But God, who never leaves nor forsakes His people (Heb. 13:5), provided for William Bradford and his Separatist friends.

Pilgrims Looking for a New Country

But seek first the kingdom of God and His righteousness, and all these things shall be added to you. Therefore do not worry about tomorrow, for tomorrow will worry about its own things. Sufficient for the day is its own trouble. (Matthew 6:33-34)

After nine months of living in Amsterdam, the Separatists decided that Leyden would be a better place to settle. So once again, they moved their families with all their possessions to the much smaller town. Over the next few years, William learned the Dutch language and became a skilled tradesman in Leyden. In 1612 he married a young English woman in Amsterdam named Dorothy May. Their first son, John, was born in 1614.

Although the Netherlands had proven to be a haven of freedom for the Separatists, it wasn't long before the congregation began considering another move. After ten years, the families still found it difficult to make ends meet and many were still in poverty despite their hard labors. The Pilgrims were also concerned about the negative influence of Dutch society upon their children. William explained that many of the Pilgrim children were led astray by the foolish behavior of the Dutch youth: "Many of the children, influenced by these conditions, and the great licentiousness of the young people of the country, and the many temptations of the city, were led by evil example into dangerous courses, getting the reins off their necks and leaving their parents."[5] Yet another reason motivating the Pilgrims to make a move was a desire to see the gospel of Jesus Christ spread into the remote parts of the world. William Bradford writes of this motive:

Last and not least, they cherished a great hope and inward zeal of laying good foundations, or at least of making some way towards it, for the propagation and advance of the gospel of the kingdom of Christ in the remote parts of the world, even though they should be but stepping stones to others in the performance of so great a work.[6]

By their courageous sacrifice, the Pilgrims would do exactly what William described. They became stepping stones, laying a foundation for the establishment of the Christian faith in North America. All Americans must remember that the Pilgrims' main goal was to see the advance of Christ's kingdom. The Pilgrims already enjoyed religious freedom in the Netherlands; it was these additional reasons which motivated them to seek out a new country.

As the Separatist congregation gathered to discuss where to go, several different places were considered. The Pilgrims knew about the Jamestown Colony established in Virginia in 1607. But that colony had suffered many hardships in its first years—hundreds had already died. The conditions in Jamestown were so difficult that King James would send convicted criminals there as an alternative to the death sentence in England.[7] The Pilgrims also feared that they would lose their freedom to worship freely in Jamestown, as this colony had submitted itself to the Church of England. Guiana on the northern coast of South America was another possibility, but the Pilgrims thought that the Spanish might take over this colony by force. Finally the Pilgrims decided they would settle in Virginia, by carving out a piece of land separate from the Jamestown Colony.

They applied for a charter from the English king to establish a colony, and permission was granted. However, they had no means to finance the voyage. In God's good providence, a London merchant named Thomas Weston agreed to provide the resources to help the first group of Pilgrims reach the New World. It was an investment for Weston and his company of "Adventurers," and they expected to be paid off from profits taken from fishing and trapping. Historian Nathaniel Philbrick explained the agreement this way:

> The Adventurers would put up most of the capital with the expectation that, once they were settled in America, the Pilgrims would quickly begin to generate considerable profits, primarily through codfishing and the fur trade. The Pilgrims would each be given a share in the company valued at ten pounds. For the next seven years they would work four days a week for the company and two days a week for themselves, with the Sabbath reserved for worship. At the end of the seven years, the capital and profits would be divided among all of them, with the Pilgrims owning their houses and home lots free and clear.[8]

The *Mayflower's* Atlantic Crossing

Some of the Separatists decided to stay in Leyden, including the Pilgrim's faithful pastor, John Robinson. This pastor played a pivotal role in guiding the Pilgrims by letter writing for a number of years after they had settled in the New World. Although it was his intention to join the rest of the Pilgrims, Robinson never reached the shores of North America—he died in 1625.

The Pilgrims returned to England to meet up with Weston and his "Adventurers". After many delays the group left the shores of England in the *Mayflower* on September 6, 1620. Initially, the Separatist congregation planned to make the journey in two ships: the *Mayflower* and the *Speedwell*, but the smaller *Speedwell* leaked so badly that they were forced to abandon it. Those who were still committed to the journey packed into the *Mayflower* and off they sailed.

The *Mayflower*, though a fine ship and capable of making the potentially treacherous Atlantic crossing, was far too small for such a large number of people. All 102 persons were crowded into a space of 24 feet by 58 feet under the deck. Gary Schmidt explains what it was like to spend over two months on the *Mayflower* for William and his fellow shipmates:

> *In the area between decks, 102 souls tried to be comfortable. It was not easy. In fact, there was not enough room for all the passengers to lie down together; some may have slept in the shallop, the small boat aboard the Mayflower. The space allowed for no beds, so the passengers must have slept on hammocks or on the deck itself, perhaps on pallets they had brought along. There were few "cabbins," and probably these private places went to the married couples, including Bradford and Dorothy.*[9]

It was a slow journey across a vast ocean. The Mayflower only averaged about two miles per hour.[10] After sixty-six days of slow and hazardous travel, land was sighted on November 11, 1620. Although excited at the sight of land, the Pilgrims were also a bit troubled when they realized they were much further north than originally planned. They had arrived at Cape Cod, (in present day Massachusetts), hundreds of miles north of their original destination. The patent or land grant secured by the Adventurers was located near the mouth

Mayflower in Plymouth

of the Hudson River, the northernmost part of what was considered Virginia at that time.[11] At first the captain tried to navigate the ship south to the mouth of the Hudson, but the weather made the journey unsafe. So, the Pilgrims and Adventurers finally agreed to settle in the region of Cape Cod instead. William recorded the great joy and thanksgiving experienced by the little group as they stepped out upon solid ground.

> *Having found a good haven and being brought safely in sight of land, they fell upon their knees and blessed the God of Heaven who had brought them over the vast and furious ocean, and delivered them from all the perils and miseries of it, again to set their feet upon the firm and stable earth, their proper element.[12]*

William had now experienced personally what Psalm 93 declares: *"the LORD on high is mightier than the noise of many waters, than the mighty waves of the sea" (Ps. 93:4).*

Arrival in Cape Cod and the "Mayflower Compact"

Let every soul be subject to the governing authorities. For there is no authority except from God, and the authorities that exist are appointed by God. (Romans 13:1)

In order to form a government for the preservation of the colony, the Pilgrims and the other colonists drafted and signed an agreement known today as the "Mayflower Compact." This historic document is one of the most foundational texts in American history, ranking with the Declaration of Independence and the US Constitution in its importance.[13] The words of the Mayflower Compact read as follows:

In the name of God, Amen. We whose names are under-written, the loyal subjects of our dread sovereign Lord, King James, by the grace of God, of Great Britain, France, and Ireland King, Defender of the Faith, etc.

Having undertaken, for the glory of God, and advancement of the Christian faith, and honor of our King and Country, a voyage to plant the first colony in the northern parts of Virginia, do by these presents solemnly and mutually, in the presence of God, and one of another, covenant and combine our selves together into a civil body politic, for our better ordering and preservation and furtherance of the ends aforesaid; and by virtue hereof to enact, constitute, and frame such just and equal laws, ordinances, acts, constitutions and offices, from time to time, as shall be thought most meet and convenient for the general good of the Colony, unto which we promise all due submission and obedience.

In witness whereof we have hereunder subscribed our names at Cape Cod, the eleventh of November, in the year of the reign of our sovereign lord, King James, of England, France, and Ireland, the eighteenth, and of Scotland the fifty-fourth. Anno Dom. 1620.[14]

The Mayflower Compact begins with the words "In the Name of God,

Signing of the Mayflower Compact

Amen." Historian Daniel Ford notes that the Mayflower Pilgrims began the compact in this way in order to "place themselves steadfastly under the highest possible authority."[15] The Pilgrim settlers knew that all authority was given by God in both the church and the civil government.

The Compact also explained the purpose of the voyage. The Pilgrims undertook this hazardous expedition for the glory of God and for the advancement of the Christian faith among the native peoples of North America. These were some of the roots of the new country we call "America."

The First Winter and Spring

This is My commandment, that you love one another as I have loved you. Greater love has no one than this, than to lay down one's life for his friends. (John 15:12-13)

The Pilgrims arrived in Cape Cod in November. The weather was very cold and was growing colder as winter set in. Some of the men explored the inland territories, hoping to find an appropriate location for the colony. William Bradford joined the party of men in their hunt up and down Cape Cod, and after six weeks a location was chosen. Tragedy struck early in the Winter, when William's wife Dorothy fell over the side of the *Mayflower* and drowned.

Dorothy's death would not be the last of the tragedies suffered by the Pilgrims that first winter. William recorded that about half of the Pilgrims perished due to starvation and sickness. On certain days, as many as three people would die. According to Bradford's account, there were at times only six or seven healthy persons "who, to their great commendation be it spoken, spared no pains night or day, but with great toil and at the risk of their own health, fetched wood, made fires, prepared food for the sick, made their beds, washed their infected clothes, dressed and undressed them; in a word did all the homely and necessary services for them."[16] William and the other Separatists had many opportunities to show the selfless love of Christ to one another in the cold months of that first winter.

In March 1621, the Pilgrims were able to make friends with some of the natives near Plymouth Plantation. The Wampanoag tribe lived close by and one of them, Samoset, spoke English, and he turned out to be friendly towards the colonists. He introduced them to another Indian named Squanto, who spoke even better English than he did. And it was through Squanto that the Pilgrims came to know the leader of the Wampanoag tribe, Massasoit. In God's mercies, the Pilgrims and the Wampanoag Indians entered into a peace treaty which would last for over fifty years. Bradford called Squanto a "heaven-sent gift" to the struggling community.

At one point in his account, William recorded how Squanto's gifts were used to preserve the sick and starving Pilgrims:

Squanto stayed with them, and was their interpreter, and became a special instrument sent of God for their good, beyond their expectation. He showed them how to plant corn, where to take fish and other commodities, and guided them to unknown places, and never left them till he died.[17]

After the first difficult winter, the spring came along bringing warmer weather, and William recorded in his journal: "The spring now approaching, it pleased God the mortality began to cease among them, and the sick recovered apace, which put new life into them all."[18] The *Mayflower* then set sail for England on April 5, 1621, leaving the colonists to continue building and farming on their own.

As the Mayflower Compact was signed, John Carver was chosen as the first governor. But Carver died in the spring of 1621. At this point, the colonists turned to William Bradford as their leader, and he was elected as the second governor of Plymouth Colony. William was thirty-two years old. Throughout the early period of the colony, from 1621 until his death in 1657, William held the office of governor of Plymouth Colony.

The First Thanksgiving

Enter into His gates with thanksgiving, and into His courts with praise. Be thankful to Him, and bless His name. For the LORD is good; His mercy is everlasting, and His truth endures to all generations. (Psalm 100:4-5)

In the fall of 1621, the Separatists gathered for a time of thanksgiving, inviting the local Natives to join them in the celebration. This historic gathering came to be known by Americans as the first Thanksgiving. The exact date of the celebration is not known, but it probably occurred in late September or early October.[19] William Bradford asked Squanto to bring Sachem Massasoit (the tribe's leader) and his other companions to join them for the feast. William's fellow Pilgrim Edward Winslow described the first thanksgiving as a time of feasting and celebration similar to English harvest festivals complete with food, ale, and games.[20]

Massasoit and a hundred other Natives arrived, bringing five freshly-killed deer to share. The Pilgrims and Indians together enjoyed a great feast of plenty including deer, duck, wild turkey, corn, squash, beans, barley, and beer.[21] By God's mercy the colony had survived through much hardship. Edward Winslow, in a letter he wrote to friends in England two months later, explained: "although

The First Thanksgiving

it be not always so plentiful as it was at this time with us, yet by the goodness of God, we are so far from want [need] we often wish you partakers of our plenty."[22]

In November 1621 a ship called *Fortune* arrived unexpectedly from England, carrying more of the Separatist congregation from Leyden and some of Thomas Weston's Adventurers. The Plymouth colonists were overjoyed to see their friends and family, but the newly-arrived settlers on the *Fortune* were shocked by what they saw. William wrote that the new colonists "saw nothing but a naked and barren place. Then they began to wonder what would become of them, should the people be dead or cut off by the Indians."[23] Settling a barren wilderness was no easy undertaking.

William was glad to receive others from Leyden and England, but he was concerned about the food supplies of the colony. How would they provide for so many more through the second winter; and where would they be housed? The Plymouth colonists had only built seven houses thus far, and many single persons were already staying with families. Regrettably, Weston did not send the *Fortune* stocked with supplies, either. Bradford journaled his disappointment; "They brought not so much as biscuit-cake, or any other victuals with them, nor any bedding, except some poor things they had in their cabins; nor pot nor pan to cook any food in; nor many clothes, for many of them had sold their coats and cloaks at Plymouth [England] on their way out . . . The plantation was glad of this addition of strength, but could have wished that many of them had been of better class, and all of them better furnished with provisions."[24]

The Growing Years of Plymouth Colony

With the second winter setting in, both the original colonists and those newly-arrived set out to prepare for the cold weather. Shortly after the *Fortune* departed, an Indian from the Narragansett tribe walked into the colony with a bundle of arrows from the Sachem or tribe leader, Canonicus. Squanto explained to the Englishmen that this wordless message was an insult from the chief. This revelation convinced William Bradford that the colony needed a stronger defense. Together with a military captain named, Miles Standish, William tasked the colony with building a wall that would encircle the entire colony.

For a month, the men and boys worked to build a log palisade around the colony. Miles Standish was put in charge of the defense of the colony. He ran military drills and trained the men on what to do in case of an emergency. Each of the men was given a role to play in the event of an Indian attack or a fire.

On Christmas Day 1621, William faced a challenge to his authority when some of the Adventurers living among the Separatists asked for a day off from normal work in order to celebrate Christmas. William and the other Separatists did not celebrate Christmas; they sanctified Sunday as the Sabbath day, but did not consider any other holidays sacred. However, the Adventurers insisted that they could not in good conscience work on Christmas Day. William initially allowed the men to take the day off while the other Pilgrims continued their labors. But, things didn't go as he had anticipated. He recorded the incident, noting that, "on returning from work at noon he found them at play in the street, some pitching the bar, some at stool-ball, and such like sports. So he went to them and took away their games, and told them that it was against his conscience that they should play and others work. If they made the keeping of the day a matter of devotion, let them remain in their houses; but there should be no gaming and reveling in the streets."[25] William would have allowed the men to observe the day if they would have kept it as a sacred observance. He was concerned that they were turning the holiday into a time of partying, instead of keeping it as a time of sacred remembrance of the birth of Christ.

The summer of 1622 brought more changes to the colony. Two more ships from Weston's Company of Merchant Adventurers

Miles Standish

arrived: the *Charity* and the *Swan*. As was the case with the *Fortune*, these two ships carried no supplies with them. Yet, Weston still insisted that William and the colonists house and feed the new arrivals. At this point, the relationship between the Separatists and Thomas Weston was breaking down. In addition, these colonists did not come to join the Plymouth Colony but rather to set up a rival colony under the oversight of Weston's Adventurers company. This further upset the Plymouth colonists, who felt betrayed by their financier. In spite of the tense relations, William agreed to house and feed the new arrivals temporarily. He wrote, "they decided to give the men friendly entertainment, partly out of regard for Mr. Weston himself, considering what he had done for them, and partly out of compassion for the people, who had come into a wilderness."[26]

In 1622 the young colony encountered a severe setback when Squanto died. This young Indian had played a vital role in maintaining good relations for the colonists with other local tribes. He had been Plymouth's translator and guide from almost the beginning. William recorded details of his death:

> *Here Squanto fell ill of Indian fever, bleeding much at the nose, which the Indians take for a symptom of death, and within a few days he died. He begged the Governor to pray for him, that he might go to the Englishmen's God in heaven, and bequeathed several of his things to some of his English friends, as remembrances. His death was a great loss.*[27]

Despite this setback for the colonists, the Lord provided other means by which the colony could maintain friendly relations with the Indians for decades to come. This was a unique blessing enjoyed by the Pilgrim settlement. Others of the young colonies in North America did not experience this kind of peace with the local Native tribes. Nonetheless, this long-term concord came to an end in 1675 with the outbreak of King Philip's War.

Labors as Governor of Plymouth Plantation

William Bradford continued serving as governor of the Plymouth Colony intermittently through 1657. He was beloved by the other colonists because of his faithful servant leadership. His duties as governor of the colony were considerable, according to historian Gary Schmidt:

> *He was responsible for all the supplies of the colony: trading for them, overseeing them, arranging for rationing if necessary. He was the colony's accountant . . . the secretary of state, who made treaties and received visitors; the head of the military in charge of defense . . . He was judge and jury, the one who interpreted the law and saw that it was carried out. In addition, he took his turn in the fields and in the forests, hoeing and sawing with all the other colonists.*[28]

Given these extensive responsibilities, William Bradford could easily have become a dictator of sorts and lorded it over his fellow colonists. However, that was not his nature. Although he was no perfect governor, the colonists greatly respected him for his servant leadership. Often, he would work side by side with

Modern recreation of the original Plymouth Plantation, Plymouth, Massachusetts

the colonists out in the fields. His was the kind of leadership modeled and taught by our Lord Jesus Christ.

> *But Jesus called them to Himself and said, "You know that the rulers of the Gentiles lord it over them, and those who are great exercise authority over them. Yet it shall not be so among you; but whoever desires to become great among you, let him be your servant." (Matthew 20:25-26)*

William also demonstrated a remarkable wisdom when he reorganized labor and production in the colony. Under the original agreement with Weston's Adventurers, everyone in the colony was required to work and contribute to a common storehouse of food. Over time, this communal experiment didn't work out, and Bradford quickly realized this to be a demonstration of the folly of Plato's views of economics. This economic theory is better known today as communism, in which private property is abolished and the community holds all things in common. William wrote:

> *The failure of this experiment of communal service, which was tried for several*

years, and by good and honest men proves the emptiness of the theory of Plato and other ancients, applauded by some of later times, that the taking away of private property, and the possession of it in community, by a commonwealth, would make a state happy and flourishing; as if they were wiser than God. For in this instance, community of property (so far as it went) was found to breed much confusion and discontent, and retard much employment which would have been to the general benefit and comfort. For the young men who were most able and fit for service objected to being forced to spend their time and strength in working for other men's wives and children, without any recompense.[29]

So, William set out with his assistant council to assign parcels of land. Each family would now manage their own land and produce their own food. This change brought about better results for the entire colony.

So every family was assigned a parcel of land, according to the proportion of their number . . . This was very successful. It made all hands very industrious, so that much more corn was planted than otherwise would have been by any means the Governor or any other could devise, and saved him a great deal of trouble, and gave far better satisfaction. The women now went willingly into the field, and took their little ones with them to plant corn, while before they would allege weakness and inability; and to have compelled them would have been thought great tyranny and oppression.[30]

Later Years

Upon leaving England in 1620, the Bradfords had left their three-year-old son John behind. In 1627, the young boy arrived on a ship in Plymouth where he was finally reunited with his father. There he met his new mother, as William had remarried a woman named Alice Southworth in 1623. By this time, Plymouth had grown to a small town of 180 persons with thirty-two houses and numerous other structures as well.[31]

In the years that followed, William and the other Plymouth colonists found themselves surrounded by more colonies. The Massachusetts Bay Colony came about in 1629. Through the years, William enjoyed friendly relationships with the various governors of the Massachusetts Bay Colony, including John Winthrop.

Colonists from Plymouth would move around to other colonies, or they would form new colonies along the coastline. Thus, the population of the original Plymouth town actually declined in the 1640s. By the middle of the 1640s, only about 150 people lived in Plymouth town—the same number of residents the town contained in 1623.[32]

In 1643 William's close friend William Brewster died. Brewster had served for decades as one of the main leaders of the church in Plymouth, and his passing was a blow to the colony. Several different ministers had served in the church from 1620 to 1640, but William Brewster was a steady anchor and elder for the church over these years.

As numbers moved away to other parts, William Bradford could see the original vision for the colony wane. Had the kingdom of God and the glory of God been extended into this new land? Somewhat discouraged by the changes taking place, he ended his records of the history of Plymouth Colony in the late 1640s. Bradford died in 1657, a truly heroic leader who salvaged religious liberties and helped to form the foundations of a new nation.

The Legacy of William Bradford and Plymouth Plantation

In the providence of God, the Pilgrim Separatists of Scrooby Manor and Leyden established one of the first English-speaking colonies in North America. Despite the many changes that came about in this little colony of Plymouth, the vision of the Pilgrims had a profound influence on the shaping of American history. *The Mayflower* Pilgrims wanted to see the gospel of Jesus spread to the eastern shores of North America. By God's grace, that vision continued to grow as the Christian faith would work its way across the continent. The Pilgrims desired a place where they could worship freely without the civil government binding their consciences to forms they did not believe to be honoring to God.

Since the founding of America, the United States has become a bastion of liberty in the world. Although challenges to freedom will always come by tyrannical governments, may the vision of the Leyden Separatists continue to burn brightly in the hearts of this generation and the next, everywhere around the world.

Anne Bradstreet (1612-1672)

CHAPTER 3

Anne Bradstreet: America's First Published Poet

Charm is deceitful and beauty is vain, but a woman
who fears the Lord she shall be praised.

—Proverbs 31:30

Anne Bradstreet was one of the first of the Puritans who left the shores of England for the New World. She would become one of the most well-known American colonists of the 1600s. Anne holds the distinguished title of being the first published American poet. Her writings make up part of the corpus of American literature, and have been studied by historians and students of the English language for centuries. Yet Anne's writings cannot be rightly understood or appreciated without recognizing how her Christian faith served as the pillar for all that she wrote.

America During the Life of Anne Bradstreet

When Anne arrived on the shores of New England in 1630, other English settlements had already been founded along the Atlantic seaboard. After the first

English colony was attempted and had failed on Roanoke Island in the 1580s, another attempt was made to establish a permanent English colony in Virginia some twenty years later. On May 14, 1607, the colony of Jamestown was planted on the James River. Though the colony would face serious trials in the years that followed, it did survive and remained the first permanent English settlement in North America. Further north the Pilgrim separatists arrived on the *Mayflower* in 1620 at Cape Cod, Massachusetts. These settlers encountered many trials as they formed fledgling colonies. Extreme weather (both heat and cold), hostile natives, and disease all laid their heavy hand upon the colonists. Yet, a permanent English settlement in the New World would be the fruit of their labors.

Early Years

Anne was born in the year 1612 to Thomas and Dorothy Dudley in Northampton, England. As a child Anne never received a formal education, but she picked up a great deal of useful knowledge in her homeschool and supplemental reading she pursued at home. She had access to the Bible, ancient poetry, and a number of historical and scientific works. By God's providential workings, Anne's father Thomas became the steward of the Earl of Lincoln in 1620. That is what brought Thomas Dudley and his family to Lincolnshire, where Anne spent much of her childhood. With free access to the earl's extensive library, she could now read as much as she wished. It was a unique privilege for an eight-year-old child in England. In addition to the educational opportunities afforded at the earl's estate, Anne also sat under the preaching of the famous Puritan preacher John Cotton. Pastor Cotton served at St. Botolph's Church in old Boston, England before he was forced to flee to the New World.

This Puritan's preaching played an important role in Anne's faith. In a short autobiographical summary of her life that she penned for her children, she describes her spiritual struggles in early childhood years:

> *In my young years, about 6 or 7 as I take it, I began to make conscience of my ways, and what I knew was sinful, as lying, disobedience to parents, etc., I avoided it.*

If at any time I was overtaken with the like evils, it was as a great trouble, and I could not be at rest until by prayer I had confessed it unto God. I was also troubled at the neglect of private duties though too often tardy that way. I also found much comfort in reading the Scriptures, especially those places I thought most concerned my condition, and as I grew to have more understanding, so the more solace I took in them. [1]

Further in the autobiographical sketch she tells of how her heart was drawn away by the world at 14 or 15 years of age. Anne wrote, "I found my heart more carnal, and sitting loose from God, vanity and the follies of youth take hold of me."[2] At this time in her life the Lord in His wisdom chose to bring Anne a severe affliction in the form of smallpox. Anne explained the effect this illness had upon her. "About 16, the Lord laid His hand sore upon me and smote me with the smallpox. When I was in affliction, I besought the Lord and confessed my pride and vanity, and He was entreated of me and again restored me."[3] Smallpox was a deadly disease and often left life-long scars on the victim. No doubt Anne faced fears that her face might be permanently disfigured by the disease, in which she would lose some part of her natural beauty before marriage.

During these years the political situation was becoming more difficult in England for those with Puritan convictions. King Charles I came to the throne in 1625 and he proceeded to impose more regulations on the church. This was difficult for those with Puritan leanings to receive, as the Puritans were committed to a simplicity and purity in God's worship. They did not want extra-biblical traditions; in particular, they were concerned about "high church" practices in the Church of England that resembled those of Roman Catholicism. They feared that some of these practices were idolatrous.

Leaving Old England for the New World

Life in England became difficult for the Dudley family in 1626. When the earl was ordered by the king to make a loan to the crown, he refused. For one thing, Theophilus was not convinced that Charles I would repay the debt. Consequently, the Earl of Lincoln was thrown into the Tower of London. Here

King Charles I

was just one example of King Charles' tyrannical abuse of power. Although religious freedom was a primary motive for those Puritans leaving England, there were other instances of tyranny like this which led the Dudley family and other Puritans to make plans to leave.

By God's mercies, Anne was married to a Christian man named Simon Bradstreet in 1628. She was only sixteen years old at the time, and Simon was twenty-four. It was shortly after this happy union was formed that the young family began to consider the possibility of leaving their home in England for a new life in the wilderness of Massachusetts. A number of Puritan leaders met together to make plans for the journey. These included Isaac Johnson, Anne's father Thomas Dudley, Thomas Hooker, Roger Williams, and John Winthrop. In God's good providence, King Charles granted permission for the group to form a new settlement just north of Plymouth Colony, in what would come to be known as the Massachusetts Bay Colony. It was April of 1630 that Anne Bradstreet, in company with her husband, the Dudley family, and other Puritans, set sail on the *Arbella* for the Atlantic coast of North America.

Arriving in the New World

The Bradstreets endured three long months at sea. Travel across the Atlantic in the 17th century was difficult and dangerous. Storms, accidents (sometimes fatal), and illness often affected those on board such crossings. But the Lord protected the passengers of the *Arbella* and the ship arrived safely in Salem Harbor on June 12, 1630. Facing Anne and the Puritan families as they set foot on the soil of North America was a largely unexplored wilderness filled with imminent dangers and disease. The colonists had to relocate several times as they sought suitable land upon which to build, and also in response to the threats of Indian attacks. Within seven months over 200 colonists had died. The sacrifices these Puritans offered in order to pursue the vision of "a city on a hill" were staggering.

Eventually the colonists settled in a place they called "Boston," named after the English town of Boston where the Puritan pastor John Cotton had ministered. Like many of the other settlers, Anne would sometimes struggle with illness in the early years of her arrival in the New World.

In one of her earliest poems Anne provides a realistic and biblically-accurate portrayal of life in a fallen world, a life she knew well from her own experience in those first years in New England. She wrote:

> *Twice ten years old not fully told [19 years old]*
> *Since nature gave me breath,*
> *My race is run, my thread is spun,*
> *Lo, here is fatal death.*
> *All men must die, and so must I;*
> *This cannot be revoked.*
> *For Adam's sake this word God spake*
> *When he so high provoked.*
> *Yet live shall I, this life's but small,*
> *In place of highest bliss,*
> *Where I shall have all I can crave,*
> *No life is like to this.*
> *For what's this life but care and strife*
> *Since first we came from womb?*
> *Our strength doth waste, our time doth haste,*
> *And then we go to th' tomb.*[4]

Family Life

So Hannah arose after they had finished eating and drinking in Shiloh. Now Eli the priest was sitting on the seat by the doorpost of the tabernacle of the LORD. And she was in bitterness of soul, and prayed to the Lord and wept in anguish. Then she made a vow and said, "O LORD of hosts, if You will indeed look on the affliction of Your maidservant and remember me, and not forget Your maidservant, but will give Your maidservant a male child, then I will give him to the LORD all the days of his life, and no razor shall come upon his head." (1 Samuel 1:9-11)

Adding to the many other afflictions that Anne experienced in the rugged wilderness of Massachusetts, she was also childless after four years of marriage. She desperately wanted a child, and she feared that her childlessness might be permanent. Like Hannah in the Old Testament (1 Sam. 1), Anne poured out her heart's desires before the Lord with many tears. She wrote of these trials in her autobiography:

It pleased God to keep me a long time without a child, which was a great grief to me and cost me many prayers and tears before I obtained one, and after him gave me many more of whom I now take the care, that as I have brought you into the world, and with great pains, weakness, cares, and fears, brought you to this, I now travail in birth again of you till Christ be formed in you. Among all my experiences of God's gracious dealings with me, I have constantly observed this, that He hath never suffered me long to sit loose from Him, but by one affliction or other hath made me look home, and search what was amiss.[5]

And so Anne realized that the Lord loved her in these trials, and it was the afflictions that kept her close to Him, training her in humility and dependence upon Him. If our lives were filled with only success, prosperity, and ease, we would begin to rely upon ourselves. In the Apostle Paul's letter to the Corinthians, he explained how the Lord wisely uses trials to break us of our self-dependence.

For we do not want you to be ignorant, brethren, of our trouble which came to us in Asia: that we were burdened beyond measure, above strength, so that we despaired even of life. Yes, we had the sentence of death in ourselves, that we should not trust in ourselves but in God who raises the dead. (2 Corinthians 1:8-9)

Surely, our God is One who hears the prayers of His people, and He provided Anne with the gift of a baby boy. She named him Samuel after the child who came in answer to Hannah's prayers. The Lord not only gave her Samuel but, like Hannah of the Old Testament, she was blessed with many more children besides—eight in total.

In 1636 the Dudleys and Bradstreets moved north to a coastal strip of land called "Aggawam" by the Indians. The colonists renamed the new settlement Ipswich. Here Simon and Anne's second child, Dorothy, was born. During these years Anne had been quietly writing poetry in her spare time. In Ipswich Anne chose to share some of her writings with her pastor, Nathaniel Ward. Pastor Ward met with Anne, counseling her through various spiritual challenges and sharing his library with her, and thus Anne Bradstreet continued to develop her writing skills.

Anne Bradstreet's Early Work

For I say, through the grace given to me, to everyone who is among you, not to think of himself more highly than he ought to think, but to think soberly, as God has dealt to each one a measure of faith. (Romans 12:3)

Many of Anne's earliest poetic works were influenced by the French Huguenot poet, Guillame Du Bartas (1544-1590). This influential poet from the 16th century wrote many important works of poetry on biblical history and doctrine. Anne acknowledged the influence of Du Bartas in her poetry, praising this French poet in her poem, "In Honour of Du Bartas:"

Among the happy wits this age hath shown,
Great, dear, sweet Bartas, thou art matchless known;

My ravished eyes and heart with faltering tongue,

In humble wise have vowed their service long,

But knowing th' task so great, and strength but small,

Gave o'er the work before begun withal.[6]

French Huguenots: French Protestants who followed the teachings of the Protestant Reformation and John Calvin in particular. The Huguenots faced much persecution in their home country of France, and in many cases immigrated to other lands, including other parts of Europe, Africa, and North America. The persecution of the Huguenots in France reached its highest point in the bloody "St. Bartholomew's Day Massacre" in which tens of thousands of French Protestants were murdered. Persecution against the Huguenots diminished following the Edict of Nantes, issued in 1598 by King Henry IV of France.

Du Bartas' influence on Anne is evident in much of her early literary creations. She wrote a number of complex poetic works that dealt with various themes including the natural elements (in "The Four Elements"), world history (in "The Four Monarchies"), nature (in "The Four Seasons" and "Contemplations"), and English history (in "A Dialogue between Old England and New"). Anne would often confess her own weaknesses in her poetry, demonstrating a unique humility. She did not think "too highly" of her poetry. For example, at the end of "The Four Seasons" she includes this short apology for her work, rich in character and honest humor:

My subject's bare, my brain is bad,

Or better lines you should have had:

The first fell in so naturally,

I knew not how to pass it by;

The last, though bad I could not mend,

Accept therefore of what is penned,

And all the faults that you shall spy

Shall at your feet for pardon cry.[7]

Anne kept her poetry mostly private and had no intention of publishing it. But, as God directed, the work was published in 1650 without her knowledge or permission. Anne's brother-in-law John Woodbridge was called to England after Civil war had broken out between the Parliament and the King in 1642. A variety of armed conflicts followed until Charles I was executed for treason in 1649. It was under these circumstances that John Woodbridge traveled to England to help in the negotiations. Before John left Massachusetts, recognizing genius for what it was, he convinced his sister-in-law Anne to share some of her writings with him. While in England doing his political business, John decided to seek out a publisher for Anne's writings. Anne's former pastor, Nathaniel Ward, had recently published a book in 1647 through the publisher Stephen Bowtell, and it was to this publisher that John took his sister-in-law's work.

To print a collection of writings from a woman's pen would have been perceived as strange and unconventional in the 17th century. Nevertheless, in July 1650 Anne Bradstreet's first collection of writings was published by Stephen Bowtell in London under the title *The Tenth Muse – lately Sprung Up in America*. Anne's brother-in-law John Woodbridge wrote the opening letter in the published work, admitting that his readers might find it hard to believe that a woman could have penned such outstanding verses. He had nothing but public praise for his sister-in-law, writing:

> I doubt not but the reader will quickly find more than I can say, and the worst effect of his reading will be unbelief, which will make him question whether it be a woman's work, and ask, is it possible? If any do, take this as an answer from him that dares avow it: it is the work of a woman, honoured, and esteemed where she lives for her gracious demeanour, her eminent parts, her pious conversation, her courteous disposition, her exact diligence in her place, and discrete managing of her family occasions, and more than so, these poems are the fruit of but some few hours, curtailed from her sleep and other refreshments.[8]

The Tenth Muse became a remarkably popular work in England. Meanwhile Anne remained completely unaware that her private writings were being read and treasured by thousands. Soon however, Anne began receiving letters from many of her readers thanking her for her work. Then one day, she was greatly surprised to receive a copy of the published work itself. One can only imagine Anne's astonishment when she found her private poetry published, and without her consent! It is a testimony to Anne's humility that she never sought publication herself. Later she expressed her embarrassment at the first publishing in a series of verses appended to subsequent editions of *The Tenth Muse*. She called the publication "my rambling brat"[9] that had been set loose into the world before the right time.

Anne Bradstreet's writings became known to the world under circumstances outside of her control. And the influence of these writings upon future writers and upon American history would be of great consequence. Anne's final place of residence was not Ipswich but Andover, Massachusetts. Here she gave birth to her last two children and spent the rest of her life until she died on September 16, 1672 at the age of 60. She died of "consumption" (tuberculosis), a common illness in Puritan New England.

Anne Bradstreet's Poetry to Her Family

Anne's earliest poems were written as larger, more complex works influenced in particular by the French poet Du Bartas. However she was also writing a great deal of poetry for her family at this time. Some of Anne's most well-known poems are her beautiful works written to her husband Simon and to her eight children. In these we find an intimate, detailed look at a Puritan marriage and family. The recovery of these beautiful portrayals has shattered the false picture which 19th and 20th century historians painted of the Puritans as a dour and unemotional people.

In the following short poem, quoted in its entirety, Anne wrote these loving words to her husband Simon:

To My Dear and Loving Husband

If ever two were one, then surely we.
If ever man were loved by wife, then thee.

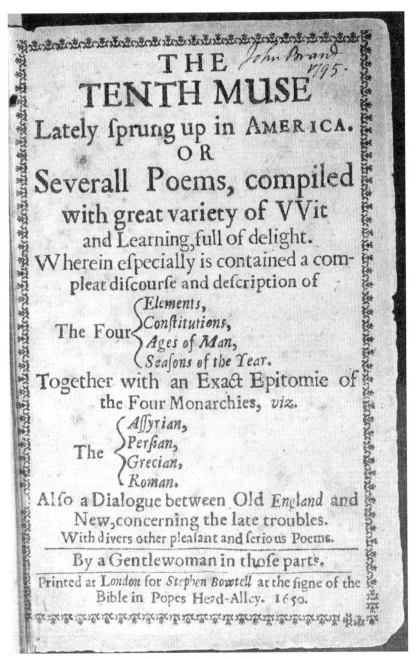

THE *John Brand*
1795.

TENTH MUSE

Lately sprung up in AMERICA.

OR

Severall Poems, compiled

with great variety of VVit

and Learning, full of delight.

Wherein especially is contained a com-
pleat discourse and description of

The Four {
Elements,
Constitutions,
Ages of Man,
Seasons of the Year.

Together with an Exact Epitomie of
the Four Monarchies, viz.

The {
Assyrian,
Persian,
Grecian,
Roman.

Also a Dialogue between Old *England* and
New, concerning the late troubles.

With divers other pleasant and serious Poems.

By a Gentlewoman in those parts.

Printed at *London* for *Stephen Bowtell* at the signe of the
Bible in Popes Head-Alley. 1650.

Title page of The Tenth Muse

If ever wife was happy in a man,
Compare with me, ye women, if you can.
I prize thy love more than whole mines of gold,
Or all the riches that the East doth hold.
My love is such that rivers cannot quench,
Nor ought but love from thee give recompense.
Thy love is such I can no way repay;
The heavens reward thee manifold, I pray.
Then while we live, in love let's so persevere,
That when we live no more, we may live ever.[10]

In language partly drawn from the Song of Songs, Anne describes the beauty and richness of her marriage to her dear husband Simon. She values Simon's love above mines of gold. Rivers cannot quench her love for him (Song of Songs 8:7). She in fact finds herself unable to repay Simon for the love he has shared with her. Anne then closes this brief poem with an encouragement to both of them to persevere in love, and a reminder of the hope of heaven.

Simon Bradstreet

In 1660 Charles II ascended to the throne in England. Since his father's execution in 1649, the country had been under the rule of the English Parliament and the Lord Protector Oliver Cromwell. After Cromwell died he was succeeded by his son Richard. But, due to various national events, the Commonwealth came to an end and the monarchy was restored under Charles II. This political shift in England placed the independent status of the Massachusetts Bay Colony in jeopardy. As an important magistrate in the colony, Anne's husband Simon joined a delegation to petition Charles II for a new charter. On the occasion of her husband's departure, Anne penned these beautiful lines as a prayer to God for protection:

> *O thou Most High who rulest all*
> *And hear'st the prayers of thine,*
> *O hearken, Lord, unto my suit*
> *And my petition sign.*
> *Into Thy everlasting arms*
> *Of Mercy I commend*
> *Thy servant, Lord. Keep and preserve*
> *My husband, my dear friend.*
> *At Thy command, O Lord, he went,*
> *Nor nought could keep him back.*
> *Then let Thy promise joy his heart,*
> *O help and be not slack.*
> *Uphold my heart in Thee, O God.*
> *Thou art my strength and stay,*
> *Thou see'st how weak and frail I am,*
> *Hide not Thy face away.*[11]

Thus, Anne commends the life of her husband to the protection of the Lord. She acknowledges that God is the one who rules over all and she is confident that God hears the prayers of His servants. In the closing lines of this poem Anne asks the Lord to return Simon to New England so that "we together may sing praise forever unto Thee."

> *Lord, let my eyes see once again*
> *Him whom Thou gavest me*
> *That we together may sing praise*
> *Forever unto Thee.*

And the remainder of our days
Shall consecrated be
With an engaged heart to sing
All praises unto Thee.[12]

In her autobiographical narrative, Anne registered a tremendous burden for her children's "rebirth" and salvation. Also, in her poetry she poured out her love as a mother upon her children, whom she recognized as God's gifts to her. In one of her most well-known poems about her children, Anne likens herself to a mother bird caring for "eight chicks."

I had eight birds hatched in one nest,
Four cocks there were, and hens the rest.
I nursed them up with pain and care,
Nor cost, nor labour did I spare,
Till at the last they felt their wing,
Mounted the trees, and learned to sing;[13]

In the closing lines of this poem, Anne encourages her children to tell her grandchildren of her love and guiding hand in her children's lives.

When each of you shall in your nest
Among your young ones take your rest,
In chirping language, oft them tell,
You had a dam that loved you well,
That did what could be done for young,
And nursed you up till you were strong,
And 'fore she once would let you fly,
She showed you joy and misery;
Taught what was good, and what was ill,
What would save life, and what would kill.
Thus gone, amongst you I may live,

And dead, yet speak, and counsel give:
Farewell, my birds, farewell adieu,
I happy am, if well with you.[14]

Anne's poetry on marriage and family describes the delight and blessings of family life lived according to the Word of God. She wrote poems about her father and mother, honoring them for their faithful parental guidance. She wrote poems extolling the love of her husband and poems about the love she had for each of her children. These poems not only provide an accurate historical picture of family life in early New England but they also offer future generations with God-glorifying, biblically-saturated verses of truth. Such writings truly help Christian families to more appreciate and savor the God-ordained relationships of marriage, parents, and children.

Anne's Poetry on Suffering

Anne Bradstreet's life was never easy. She constantly encountered trials, including the death of loved ones, the death of friends, the absence of her husband and children in different periods of life, the death of numerous grandchildren, the loss of a home to fire, and many illnesses, culminating in her final battle with tuberculosis. Anne often reflected on the vanity of this life, the importance of setting our hearts on eternity, and on holding fast to the goodness of a sovereign God through many adversities.

As she prepared for the birth of one of her children, Anne composed these lines on the shortness of life:

All things within this fading world hath end,
Adversity doth still our joys attend;
No ties so strong, no friends so dear and sweet,
But with death's parting blow is sure to meet.
The sentence past is most irrevocable,
A common thing, yet oh, inevitable.[15]

Upon the death of her grandchild (who died at only three months old), Anne articulated her grief with these words:

With troubled heart and trembling hand I write,
The heavens have changed to sorrow my delight.
How oft with disappointment have I met,
When I on fading things my hopes have set.
Experience might 'fore this have made me wise,
To value things according to their price.
Was ever stable joy yet found below?
Or perfect bliss without mixture of woe?[16]

Anne understood the futility of setting her heart on this fallen world. Eternity lay before her, and she was firmly convinced that her future life with God would be one of endless delight. On the one hand, she expressed a brutal realism about the pains of this present life. Yet, on the other hand, she speaks of the eternal hope in Christ Jesus promised to those who serve Him.

A notable tragedy in the life of the Bradstreet family occurred in 1666. One summer night the home of the Bradstreets in Andover caught fire and burned to the ground. Anne lost all of her earthly possessions, including her beloved library in the fire. She wrote the following words recounting the devastating experience:

In silent night when rest I took
For sorrow near I did not look
I wakened with thundering noise
And piteous shrieks of dreadful voice.
That fearful sound of "Fire!" and "Fire!"
Let no man know is my desire.
I, starting up, the light did spy,
And to my God my heart did cry
To strengthen me in my distress
And not to leave me succorless.

Then, coming out, beheld a space
The flame consume my dwelling place.
And when I could no longer look,
I blest His name that gave and took,
That laid my goods now in the dust
Yea so it was, and so 'twas just.[17]

And so, Anne explains that her dwelling in Andover was just a temporary tent, both given by the Lord and then taken by Him. In true Christian hope, again she points to her final home on high, a home that will never perish or burn.

Raise up thy thoughts above the sky
That dunghill mists away may fly.
Thou hast an house on high erect,
Framed by that mighty Architect,
With glory richly furnished,
Stands permanent though this be bled.
It's purchased and paid for too
By Him who hath enough to do.
A price so vast as is unknown
Yet by His gift is made thine own;
There's wealth enough, I need no more,
Farewell, my pelf [money], farewell my store.
The world no longer let me love,
My hope and treasure lies above.[18]

Anne's reflections on this calamity capture in poetic verse the teaching of our Lord Jesus Christ, who exhorts us not to set our hearts on earthly things but to lay up treasures in heaven, treasures that will last forever.

"Do not lay up for yourselves treasures on earth, where moth and rust destroy and
where thieves break in and steal; but lay up for yourselves treasures in heaven,

where neither moth nor rust destroys and where thieves do not break in and steal.
For where your treasure is, there your heart will be also." (Matthew 6:19-21)

Anne's Poetry on History

Many of Anne Bradstreet's poetic works reveal her interest in world history and English history in particular. Her "The Four Monarchies" chronicles the rise and fall of the Assyrian, Persian, Grecian, and Roman empires. Her most popular poem on history is her "A Dialogue between Old England and New." This poem, published in *The Tenth Muse*, was a poem fit for the times. Here Anne creates a fictional dialogue personifying England and New England speaking to one another about the times. Written during the English Civil War, the poem reveals Anne's concern for her mother country of England. Heidi Nichols explains that "personified New England demonstrates true concern for her mother, albeit a desire that Old England's troubles will lead to her purification."[19]

Below are some of the most notable lines from this poem:

New England

Alas, dear Mother, fairest queen and best,
With honour, wealth, and peace, happy and blest;
What ails thee hang thy head and cross thine arms?
And sit i' th' dust, to sigh these sad alarms?
What deluge of new woes thus overwhelm
The glories of thy ever famous realm?
What means this wailing tone, this mournful guise?
Ah, tell thy daughter, she may sympathize.

Old England

Art ignorant indeed of these my woes?
Or must my forced tongue these griefs disclose?
And must myself dissect my tattered state,
Which Amazed Christendom stands wondering at?[20]

Anne goes on to explain that Old England was receiving the chastising judgment of God because of certain common sins.

Old England

Before I tell th' effect, I'll show the cause
Which are my sins, the breach of sacred laws.
Idolatry, supplanter of a nation,
With foolish superstitious adoration,
Are liked and countenanced by men of might,
The Gospel trodden down and hath no right;
Church offices were sold and bought for gain,
That Pope had hope to find Rome here again.
For oaths and blasphemies, did ever ear
From Belzebub himself such language hear?[21]

Thus, Anne used her poetry to diagnose the then-current political situation in England, explaining how the sins of the people had brought God's judgment upon them in the form of a civil war between king and Parliament.

Life Lessons from Anne Bradstreet

Studying the life and writings of Anne Bradstreet opens a window into early American colonial life. Through her writings modern readers gain a better understanding of the blessings and hardships of life in early New England. There are three key lessons that the student would do well to consider.

First, Anne's writings beautifully express the blessings of biblical family life. Truly, Anne realized that marriage and parenting were gifts from God, not a burden to be avoided. Her poems explain family life in a most appealing and winsome way.

He raises the poor out of the dust, and lifts the needy out of the ash heap, that He may seat him with princes—with the princes of His people. He grants the barren woman a home, like a joyful mother of children. Praise the LORD! (Psalm 113:7-9)

Children's children are the crown of old men, and the glory of children is their father. (Proverbs 17:6)

This is a great mystery, but I speak concerning Christ and the church. Nevertheless let each one of you in particular so love his own wife as himself, and let the wife see that she respects her husband. (Ephesians 5:32-33)

Second, through Anne's writings we learn much about suffering and how we might better respond to the trials of life. What is God's role in our suffering? How should we view this present life? Anne's poetry is rich with biblical wisdom. These poems came from the pen of a woman who was intimately familiar with suffering. She knew hard providences but she was also firmly assured of the goodness of God. Her poems gracefully express the teaching contained in the following Scriptures.

These things I have spoken to you, that in Me you may have peace. In the world you will have tribulation; but be of good cheer, I have overcome the world. (John 16:33)

Therefore we do not lose heart. Even though our outward man is perishing, yet the inward man is being renewed day by day. For our light affliction, which is but for a moment, is working for us a far more exceeding and eternal weight of glory, while we do not look at the things which are seen, but at the things which are not seen. For the things which are seen are temporary, but the things which are not seen are eternal. (2 Corinthians 4:16-18)

But may the God of all grace, who called us to His eternal glory by Christ Jesus, after you have suffered a while, perfect, establish, strengthen, and settle you. (1 Peter 5:10)

Finally, Anne Bradstreet's writings serve as a wonderful example for all communicators of how to use the written word for the glory of God. Her poetry is filled with biblical allusions, prayers, confessions, and praise. She was raised under solid biblical preaching and the daily faithful discipleship of her father and mother. She knew the Bible well. But she also walked with God, and her poetry is Christian through and through. Whatever our gifts and calling may be, let us employ them every day as an act of worship to the Lord (Rom. 12:1-2) with praise and thanksgiving (Col. 3:17; 1 Thess. 5:18).

John Eliot (1604-1690)

CHAPTER 4

John Eliot:
America's First Missionary

*How then shall they call on Him in whom they have
not believed? And how shall they believe in Him
of whom they have not heard? And how shall they
hear without a preacher?*

—Romans 10:14

In the 16th and 17th centuries, Protestants lagged behind Roman Catholics in missions. While the Jesuits, the Dominicans, and others were traveling the world bearing the Catholic message, Protestants did little beyond their own borders. The vision for worldwide missions slowly developed, first with the New England Pilgrims and Puritans. William Bradford recorded one of the reasons the Pilgrims came to America:

Last and not least, they cherished a great hope and inward zeal of laying good foundations, or at least of making some way towards it, for the propagation and advance of the gospel of the kingdom of Christ in the remote parts of the world, even though they should be but stepping stones to others in the performance of so great a work.[1]

The original seal of the Puritan Massachusetts Bay Colony included the image of an Indian calling out, "Come over and help us." Despite these good intentions, little was done to evangelize the Indians living in New England until the Lord raised up one man with the heart to carry the Good News to these peoples. It was John Eliot who would become America's first full-time, dedicated missionary for the gospel of the Lord Jesus Christ.

Early Life

John Eliot was born in 1604 in Widford, Hertfordshire, England and grew up in Puritan-rich East Anglia. Little is known about his parents, though we do know they were godly folk who brought up their children in the nurture and admonition of the Lord (Eph. 6:4). John later wrote: "I do see that it was a great favor of God unto me to season my first years with the fear of God, the word, and prayer."[2]

As a young man John Eliot attended Cambridge University, where he showed an aptitude for languages. During the course of his studies John learned

John Eliot's home around 1629

Latin, Greek, and Hebrew. His love for language would later prove to be a great asset in his missionary labors.

After graduating from Cambridge, John became an assistant teacher at a school in Essex. There he came under the influence and discipleship of the school's headmaster, Thomas Hooker. Eliot wrote of the Hooker family: "When I came to this blessed family, I then saw, and never before, the power of godliness in its lively vigor and efficacy."[3]

Through Hooker's influence, John decided to become a pastor. At this time however, England was no friendly place for Puritan ministers, for King Charles I and Bishop William Laud were intent on persecuting the Puritans. Many of the Puritan preachers including Thomas Hooker were forced out of their pulpits. It wasn't long before John Eliot realized that if he wanted to freely preach the gospel, he would have to leave England.

From Old England to New England

In 1631, John Eliot sailed for Boston on board the *Lyon*. Fellow passengers included Governor John Winthrop's wife and children. Upon arriving safely in Boston, John became the pastor of a church in Roxbury. He would shepherd this flock for the next fifty-eight years.

Before he left England, John had become engaged to a young woman named Hannah Mumford. She followed him to Massachusetts in 1632 and they were married there. Hannah was a godly woman, an excellent household manager, and a tremendous help to her husband.

John was generous to a fault. He would freely give away much of his salary to those in need. In fact, on one occasion, the parish treasurer tied John's salary securely into a handkerchief before giving it to him to be sure that he would make it home with all his income in tact. However, John stopped to visit a poor family along the way. Touched by the family's need, John drew forth the handkerchief and tried to untie the knots made secure by the treasurer, in order that he might share a part of his salary with the family. Unable to untie the bundle, John just handed the mother of the family the handkerchief containing the entire sum of money.

Cambridge University

John could also be quite absentminded. On one occasion Hannah teasingly pointed to some cows and asked John who they belonged to, and sure enough, John was unable to identify them as belonging to his family. It was well for him that he had such a devoted, capable wife who managed the household affairs with excellence.

Therefore I desire that the younger widows marry, bear children, manage the house, give no opportunity to the adversary to speak reproachfully. (1 Timothy 5:14)

Despite his absentmindedness, John Eliot proved to be a very good husband and father. John and Hannah had six children, five sons and one daughter, but three of his sons died in their youth. Like Abraham of old, it could be said that John commanded his children and his household after him to keep the way of the Lord (Gen. 18:19). He wrote several catechisms for his own children and those of his local church. With joy he was able to say of his children, "They are all either with Christ, or in Christ."[4]

I have no greater joy than to hear that my children walk in truth. (3 John 1:4)

John was also a man of prayer, often setting aside whole days for fasting and prayer. When he heard any unusual news he would often say, "Brethren, let us turn all this into prayer."[5] He was also a peacemaker, such that Cotton Mather referred to him as "a great enemy to all contention."[6]

On one occasion, John upset one of his hearers by his preaching and the man proceeded to criticize Eliot quite severely. Shortly afterwards the man was wounded, and Hannah Eliot, who happened to be skilled in medicine, treated his wounds. After he had recovered, the man visited Hannah to thank her, and the Eliots invited him for dinner. The man was touched by their kindness, repented of what he had said, and peace was restored.

> Beloved, do not avenge yourselves, but rather give place to wrath; for it is written, "Vengeance is Mine, I will repay," says the Lord. Therefore "If your enemy is hungry, feed him; if he is thirsty, give him a drink; for in so doing you will heap coals of fire on his head." Do not be overcome by evil, but overcome evil with good. (Romans 12:19-21)

Like most English-speaking Christians of the time, the New England Puritans sang metrical psalms (drawn from the Book of Psalms in Scripture). However, many of the metrical versions of the psalms were of poor quality and accuracy. John was appointed to a committee to create a new psalter for New England's churches that would be more faithful to Scripture. Richard Mather, the father of Increase Mather, also served on this committee. The members were chosen for their Hebrew scholarship, to be sure that they understood the original Hebrew idioms used by David to write the psalms. The product of their labors was called *The Bay Psalm Book of 1640*. It was the first book printed in North America.

Missionary to the Indians

> I now send you, to open their eyes, in order to turn them from darkness to light, and from the power of Satan to God, that they may receive forgiveness of sins and an inheritance among those who are sanctified by faith in Me. (Acts 26:17-18)

The Indians of New England were divided into several different tribes. For centuries they had lived in darkness without the light of the gospel. They practiced polygamy and wore very little clothing. The men spent most of their time hunting and fighting their tribal wars, while the women did most of the work, including the farming and cooking. Vengefulness was a way of life for them. If one killed another, a ferocious blood feud would usually break out. Each of the tribes had their priests (or witch doctors) whom they called "powwows." These powwows could work various demonic cures and curses, and the Indians lived in servile fear of these men and the evil spirits who gave them power.

Sometime in the early 1600s a French vessel was shipwrecked off the coast of Massachusetts. Reports were heard of a French preacher who was on board, who preached to the Indians for a while, until they rejected his message and killed him. Just before he died, the preacher told them that "God was angry at them for their wickedness, and would not only destroy them all, but would also people their country with men who would not live after their brutish manners."[7] The Indians replied that God could not kill them, but not long afterwards God sent a plague that decimated the Indian population. By the time the Pilgrims landed in 1620, there were far fewer Indians left in New England.

It was in the early 1640s that the Lord laid it on John Eliot's heart to reach the remaining Indians with the gospel of Christ. He began to study the Algonquin language in 1643. It was a daunting task, as the language could only be learned orally—there was no written language. John would attempt conversations with an Indian and try to pick up enough of the language to decipher its grammar. He discovered that the words were formed by stringing verbs, nouns, adjectives, and other parts of speech together, which produced words of extraordinary lengths. For example, *noowoomantammoorkanunornash* was the word for the English term, "our loves" and *kummogkodonnattootummooetiteaongannunnarash* would be interpreted as "our question."

Compelled by the love of Christ (2 Cor. 5:14), John persevered in this daunting task of learning the native language. He eventually acquired enough Algonquin to translate the Ten Commandments and the Lord's Prayer using Latin characters. Upon finishing his Indian grammar years later, he explained how he did it: "Prayer and pains through faith in Christ Jesus will do any thing."[8]

By 1646, John was able to preach in Algonquin. That year he visited the Indian village of Nonantum to preach and he began with prayer and then preached the gospel to the natives, taking as his text Ezekiel 37:9-10:

> *Then said he unto me, "Prophesy unto the wind, prophesy, son of man, and say to the wind, Thus saith the Lord GOD; Come from the four winds, O breath, and breathe upon these slain, that they may live. So I prophesied as he commanded me, and the breath came into them, and they lived, and stood up upon their feet, an exceeding great army." (Ezekiel 37:9-10 KJV)*

John didn't know there was an Indian chief named Waban listening to his message. That was the Algonquin word for wind. Thus, when John preached "Prophesy to the wind," the Indians heard his words as "Say to Waban." The Lord used these words to reach Waban's heart and draw him to Himself. He then used this chief to proclaim the gospel to others in the tribe, which resulted in more conversions.

On his second visit to Nonantum, John preached to a receptive audience, and went on to teach the young Indian children a simple catechism. During a question and answer time, one of the natives asked, "Can God hear prayers in the Indian language or only those prayed in English?" John assured them that most certainly God does hear prayers in any language. An old Indian asked if it were too late for an old man like him to repent and seek God. This question touched John deeply. He assured the man that it was not too late and told him the parable of the workers hired at the eleventh hour (Matt. 20:1-16). The Indians asked many other questions, clearly demonstrating that their hearts had been touched by the word ōf the Lord. After these first two meetings, John observed:

> *If Englishmen despise the preaching of faith and repentance and humiliation for sin, the poor heathens will be glad of it, and it shall do good to them . . . The deepest estrangement of man from God is no hindrance to his grace, nor to his Spirit of grace. What nation or people ever so deeply degenerated since Adam's fall, as these Indians, and yet the Spirit of God is working upon them.[9]*

Praying Indians

For we ourselves were also once foolish, disobedient, deceived, serving various lusts and pleasures, living in malice and envy, hateful and hating one another. But when the kindness and the love of God our Savior toward man appeared, not by works of righteousness which we have done, but according to His mercy He saved us, through the washing of regeneration and renewing of the Holy Spirit, whom He poured out on us abundantly through Jesus Christ our Savior, that having been justified by His grace we should become heirs according to the hope of eternal life. (Titus 3:3-7)

Before they knew God, the Indians were proud and self-satisfied, not unlike most people today. However, as the Word of God was delivered to them, many came to be broken over their sin. John continued to return to the tribe, sowing more seeds with each visit. Some of the seeds fell on good soil and many Indians were converted. These first Christians in North America came to be known as the "Praying Indians."

Yet there were other Indians who hardened their hearts and opposed the gospel. The opposition came primarily from the powwows and some of the chiefs, and they persecuted the Praying Indians. Sometimes they would drive John Eliot out of their villages, even threatening his life. But John was not to be intimidated. He would tell them:

I am engaged in the work of God, and he is with me. I fear not all the sachems [chiefs] in the country. I shall go on in my work, and do you touch me if you dare.[10]

Despite the opposition, the gospel continued to grow and prevail among the Indians. Particularly noteworthy were the deeply insightful questions the Praying Indians would ask. Their questions concerned the nature of God, man, sin, Satan, and many other topics. One question many would ask was, "If we leave off Powwowing and pray to God, what shall we do when we are sick?"[11] John explained to them that God, the Creator of heaven and earth, was the great physician and He was more powerful than Satan and all the powwows. He also encouraged his fellow Englishmen to teach the Indians about medicine.

Another very thoughtful question posed by the young Indian converts was put this way: "How is it that, when an Indian whom we never saw before, comes among us, and we find that he prays to God, we love him exceedingly; but when our own brother, dwelling at a distance, visits us, if he does not pray to God, though we love him, yet it is not with such a love as we have for the other man?"[12] These Praying Indians were beginning to experience the blessing of being part of the family of God.

And He came and preached peace to you who were afar off and to those who were near. For through Him we both have access by one Spirit to the Father. Now, therefore, you are no longer strangers and foreigners, but fellow citizens with the saints and members of the household of God, having been built on the foundation of the apostles and prophets, Jesus Christ Himself being the chief corner stone. (Ephesians 2:17-20)

Praying Towns

For years, John Eliot traveled throughout the Massachusetts and Plymouth colonies, preaching to many different groups of Indians. His labors inspired other Puritans to take on the missionary work with the native peoples. In 1649 the Society for the Propagation of the Gospel in New England was formed. Also, the Mayhew Family of Martha's Vineyard, a small island off the Massachusetts coast, had a remarkable multi-generational missionary ministry. Four generations of Mayhews (Thomas Sr., Thomas Jr., John, and Experience) preached the gospel to the Indians, continuing their missionary labors on Martha's Vineyard into the 1750s.

As time went by, the Praying Indians requested land where they could build for themselves a permanent settlement. John Eliot made the official request to the Massachusetts General Court and obtained a land grant for the Indians of Nonatum. Often he would intercede for the Indians with the colonial government. He established a good reputation with the tribes, always treating them justly. Without question or qualification, John Eliot loved the Indians, and they loved him.

Martha's Vineyard

John wanted the Praying Indians to establish their own independent communities where they could till their own land and govern themselves. As men and women made in the image of God and renewed in Christ, he knew they could govern themselves according to God's laws. He also believed that civil governments should be organized in a decentralized form, according to the pattern laid out in Exodus 18 and Deuteronomy 1 with rulers of tens, fifties, hundreds, and thousands. And so, he helped the Indians organize praying towns with this approach to government. In 1651, the praying town of Natick was formed, and the people adopted the following covenant:

> *We are the sons of Adam. We and our fathers have a long time been lost in our sins; but now the mercy of the Lord beginneth to find us out again. Therefore, the grace of Christ helping us, we do give ourselves and our children to God, to be his people. He shall rule us in all our affairs, not only in our religion and affairs of the church, but also in all our works and affairs in this world. God shall rule over us. The Lord is our judge; the Lord is our lawgiver; the Lord is our king: he will save us. The*

wisdom which God hath taught us in his book, that shall guide us, and direct us in the way.[13]

John rejoiced to watch as these Christian tribes would "lay down the imperfect starlight of their laws for the perfect sunlight of the Scriptures."[14] Evidence of their joyful embrace of the gospel soon became visible within their communities: The Praying Indians began wearing clothes. Men as well as women began to plant crops and grow food. They asked for and acquired tools for their agricultural work. The women also learned to spin. Some of the Praying Indians became so skilled and industrious that they built a bridge at Natick that survived even longer than some bridges built by the English about the same time.

The Praying Indians' attitude toward death also changed. Before hearing the gospel they had feared death. Their funerals had been characterized by loud lamentation and horrible howling and shrieking. As Christ entered in with His gospel, all of this changed. The Praying Indians died in peace and joy, knowing Jesus, the resurrection and the life (John 11:25). When one of the Praying Indian children died, they gathered together, made a coffin, and solemnly buried the child. An Indian named Totherswamp prayed "with such zeal and variety of gracious expressions, and abundance of tears, both of himself and most of the company, that the woods rang again with their sighs and prayers."[15] It was with joy that John Eliot witnessed these Indians take the initiative to provide a Christian burial; no Englishman had told them to do so.

The Indians were also growing in discernment. In 1650, a heretic named Samuel Gorton came to Rhode Island. Gorton denied the existence of heaven and hell. He also believed there should be no civil magistrates or church officers. Some of the Praying Indians went to Rhode Island to hear Gorton speak and talked with him afterwards. He attempted to convince them of his heretical views, but the Indians defended the truth and refuted Gorton's arguments. This also was a great delight to Pastor John Eliot, as he could see that these brothers could discern the false teachers warned about in Matthew 7.

Beware of false prophets, who come to you in sheep's clothing, but inwardly they are ravenous wolves. You will know them by their fruits. Do men gather grapes from

thornbushes or figs from thistles? Even so, every good tree bears good fruit, but a bad
tree bears bad fruit. A good tree cannot bear bad fruit, nor can a bad tree bear good
fruit. Every tree that does not bear good fruit is cut down and thrown into the fire.
Therefore by their fruits you will know them. (Matthew 7:17-20)

Six years after his first evangelistic outreach to the Indians, John Eliot decided
it was the right time to establish local churches among the native congregations.
In 1652 he held a meeting in the village of Natick to discuss the organization of
churches. Attending the meeting were a number of pastors and elders from the
English churches in the area. The Praying Indians shared their testimonies and
made confessions of their faith in the presence of the elders. A similar meeting
was organized in 1654. Here is the confession of an Indian named, Totherswamp:

You came unto us, and taught us, and said unto us, "Pray unto God"; and after
that . . . I did take up praying to God; yet at first I did not think of God and eternal

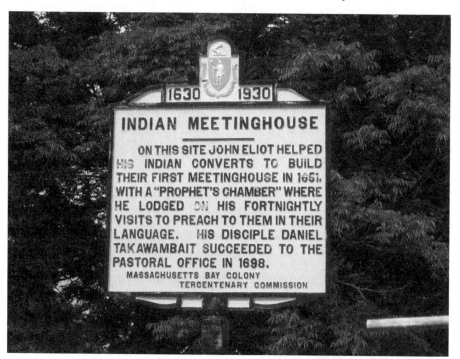

Marker for Indian Meeting House

Life, but only that the English should love me and I loved them. But after I came to learn what sin was, by the Commandments of God, and then I saw all my sins, lust, gaming, etc . . . You taught that Christ knoweth all our hearts, and seeth what is in them, if humility, or anger, or evil thoughts, Christ seeth all that is in the heart; then my heart feared greatly, because God was angry for all my sins . . .

Every day I see sin in my heart . . . I can do no good, for I am like the Devil, nothing but evil thoughts, and words, and works. I have lost all likeness to God, and goodness, and therefore every day I sin against God, and I deserve death and damnation. The first man brought sin first, and I do every day add to that sin, more sins; but Christ hath done for us all righteousness, and died for us because of our sins, and Christ teacheth us, that if we cast away our sins, and trust in Christ, then God will pardon all our sins; this I believe Christ hath done. I can do no righteousness, but Christ hath done it for me; this I believe, and therefore I do hope for pardon.[16]

Despite these moving confessions, an Indian church was not formed for several more years. John Eliot was particularly concerned to ascertain that the Indian conversions were genuine. He held to the popular view among the New England Puritans that, in order to be admitted to communion, one had to testify of a dramatic conversion experience. John also wanted time to test the genuineness of the conversions. Also, he was taking the time to train native pastors who could preach the Word to their own people and shepherd them. Finally, in 1660, the Praying Indians were baptized into the church, they partook of the Lord's Supper, and the first Indian church was planted at Natick.

Three years later, John Eliot finished the translation of the entire Bible into Algonquin. He also wrote an Indian psalter, catechism, primer, and grammar. In addition, he also translated several solid Christian devotionals into Algonquin, including Richard Baxter's *Call to the Unconverted* and *Practice of Piety*.

During the 1650s John Eliot wrote *The Christian Commonwealth*, in which he argued that the form of government established by Moses in Exodus 18 and Deuteronomy 1 should be the model for all civil governments. He made

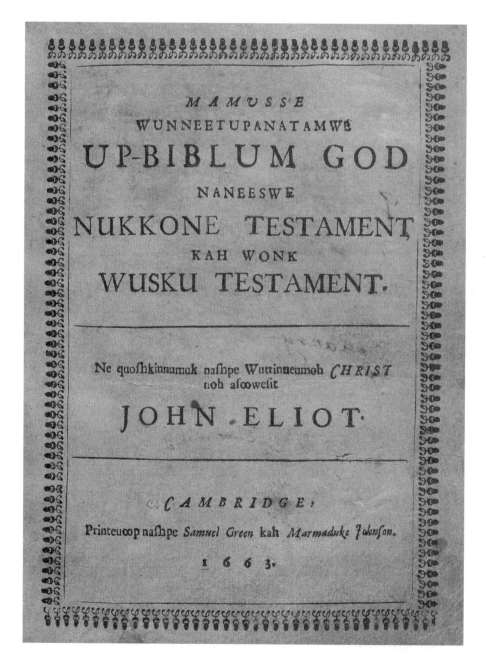

Title page of John Eliot's Algonquin Bible, the first Bible printed in the New World

some remarks which seemed to deny that monarchy was a legitimate form of government. At the time, Oliver Cromwell was in power and England was attempting a republican government. However, Charles II was restored to the English throne in 1660. Subsequently, probably to protect themselves, the government of Massachusetts condemned and suppressed John Eliot's book, and he recanted the material. Who would have known that America would abandon the monarchical form of government a century later? John Eliot's thoughts may have, in some small way, prepared the way for American independence and a republican form of government.

King Philip's War

By 1674, there were fourteen Praying Indian towns, two Indian churches, and about 1,100 Praying Indians in Massachusetts. In God's all-wise providence, however, this was all about to change. In 1675, the Indian chief Metacomet (King Philip) launched an attack on the English settlements. This began a devastating war that lasted three years and ravaged a great part of New England.

During the war years, the Praying Indians were caught between the pagan tribes and the English. Both groups distrusted the Praying Indians. Some of the Praying Indians were falsely accused of murdering English settlers. John Eliot defended them vigorously against these charges. Nevertheless, the English were very suspicious of the Praying Indians and exiled many of them to Deer Island in Boston Harbor. During the war, most of the Praying Indians sided with the English, while a few fought with King Philip. The English eventually won the bloody war, and the Praying Indians were allowed to return to their towns. But many of them had perished in the war, and their towns had been reduced from fourteen to four.

Despite the devastation, John Eliot continued to labor faithfully among the remaining Christian Indians for the rest of his life. Throughout all this time he continued as pastor of the church in Roxbury. Amazingly, he was both a full-time pastor and a full-time missionary. The Roxbury church provided his only salary; he never received financial support for his missionary work.

In 1687, Hannah Eliot died. John dearly loved his wife of fifty-five years and he mourned her loss deeply. At her funeral John testified, "Here lies my dear, faithful, pious, prudent, prayerful wife. I shall go to her but she shall not return to me."[17] In his remaining years, John continued to preach. On one occasion, as the old man was walking slowly up the hill to the meetinghouse in Roxbury, he said to those helping him, "This is very like the way to heaven, 'tis up hill; the Lord by his grace fetch us up."[18] Seeing a nearby thorn bush, he added, "And truly there are thorns and briars in the way too!"[19]

In the last years of his life, John was not done with helping those of other tribes and nations. He taught several African slaves in Roxbury to read. He also helped a blind boy with memorizing large portions of Scripture. As he drew near to death, someone asked him about his health. He replied, "Alas! I have lost every thing; my understanding leaves me; my memory fails me; my utterance fails me; but, I thank God, my charity holds out still; I find that rather grows than fails."[20] John went to be with the Lord on May 20, 1690. His last words were "Welcome Joy!"[21]

Legacy

John Eliot was a remarkable man who stands out among 17th century Protestants. At a time when Protestants lagged behind Roman Catholics in world missions, John stood out as a remarkable exception. He was America's first major missionary. His friend Richard Baxter provides the highest commendation for this remarkable man in a personal letter written to him:

> There is no man on earth whose work I think more honorable and comfortable than yours. The industry of the Jesuits and friars, and their successes in Congo, Japan, China, etc., shame us all, save you.[22]

His humility, service, love, and peacemaking stand out. There is no doubt that John Eliot loved the Indians whom he served. It was his love for them that drove him to spend countless hours learning their language. It drove him to translate the Bible and other books into Algonquin. And it drove him to preach, disciple, and intercede for the Indians for so many years. His love for his local congregation in Roxbury and for his family was also evident. Here was an American of great faith, sacrificial love, and personal piety. He was a man of fervent prayer, and his prayers availed much with God (Jas. 5:16).

John's labors bore real and lasting fruit. The Praying Indians that he evangelized and discipled were weakened by King Philip's War, but they remained steadfast in the faith for generations. Nearly a century after John Eliot's death, many of them fought alongside their fellow Massachusetts patriots in the American War for Independence. Moreover, the pioneering missionary work of John Eliot inspired William Carey and other missionaries to take the world for Jesus by carrying the gospel to the ends of the earth.

And Jesus came and spoke to them, saying, "All authority has been given to Me in heaven and on earth. Go therefore and make disciples of all the nations, baptizing them in the name of the Father and of the Son and of the Holy Spirit, teaching them to observe all things that I have commanded you; and lo, I am with you always, even to the end of the age." Amen. (Matthew 28:18-20)

Increase Mather (1639-1723)

CHAPTER 5

★ ★ ★

Increase Mather:
Rooting a Nation in Faith

Blessed is the nation whose God is the LORD, the
people He has chosen as His own inheritance.

—Psalm 33:12

During the first century of settlement, America's roots pushed down deep in the soil of the colonies in New England. Throughout the 19th century, this nation was to be the most Christian nation on earth. And for almost two centuries, America would provide more missionaries for the Christian faith than any other country in the world. As late as the 21st century, America would claim the highest number of Christian school and Christian home school students in the world. Despite the terrible decline in faith in America (and throughout Europe), small remnants still remained. The roots of American faith ran deep. Those Christians remaining are still thankful for the rich heritage of faith that has continued through the centuries.

The Virginia Colony formed in 1607 marked the first permanent Protestant settlement in America. Two decades later, in 1626, a Dutch Calvinist named Peter Minuit bought Manhattan Island from the natives for 60 silver coins—

about $600 in today's money. This was the beginning of the colony of New Netherland (later called New York). After Massachusetts Bay Colony formed in 1630, nine more colonies appeared between 1633 and 1682:

Year	Colony	Founder
1633	Maryland - Fourth Colony	George Calvert
1636	Rhode Island - Fifth Colony	Roger Williams
1636	Connecticut - Sixth Colony	Thomas Hooker
1638	New Hampshire - Seventh Colony	John Mason
1638	Delaware - Eighth Colony	Peter Minuit
1653	North Carolina - Ninth Colony	Lords Proprietors
1663	South Carolina - Tenth Colony	Lords Proprietors
1664	New Jersey - Eleventh Colony	Lord Berkeley and George Carteret
1682	Pennsylvania - Twelfth Colony	William Penn

By 1660 Massachusetts, Connecticut, and Plymouth made up 43% of the population of the American colonies, with Virginia accounting for another 33%.[1] For at least one generation, the Puritans in New England truly represented the first foundations of the country.

The early Puritan church and civil leaders in America were very concerned about generational faithfulness to God and to the vision laid down by the founding fathers. They were intensely aware of the possibilities that the youth might abandon the faith. But they also realized the amazing blessings God would bring to a nation which held to Christian roots for several successive generations.

William Bradford, the courageous leader of the little Pilgrim colony in Plymouth, wrote this poem thirty-four years after the *Mayflower* landed on the shores of New England:

> *When I think on what I have often read*
> *How when the Elders and Joshua were dead;*
> *Who had seen those great works and them could tell,*

What God had done and wrought for Israel
Yet they did soon forget and turn aside
And in His truth and ways did not abide.
But in the next age did degenerate
I wish this may not be New England's fate.²

Between the 1650s and 1700s, sermons were published in Boston, and these were the best-sellers of the day. The hottest-selling titles were those collections of sermons that addressed multi-generational faithfulness.

Without the Deuteronomy 6:7-9 mandate interwoven into the social fabric of a Christian culture, the faith always wanes. One of the best blessings that came with the Protestant Reformation was the translation and accessibility of the Bible in English and other common languages. Practically every home was given access to the Scriptures. By the mid-1600s it was common for the Presbyterians, Puritans, and Pilgrims to faithfully read God's Word in their homes daily. In most homes, families would read the Word together twice a day—both morning and evening.

Puritan preachers were especially insistent upon this practice. In fact, Richard Baxter recommended excommunication to those fathers who refused to nurture their children in God's Word. Phillip Doddridge warned his congregation that God would "pour His fury" out upon the families that call not on His name (Jer. 10:25). Doddridge preached with a passion on this topic of family worship:

If after all you will not be persuaded,
but will hearken to the voice of

Peter Minuit

cowardice, and sloth, and irreligion, in defiance of so many awakening and affecting reasons . . . if your children raise profane and profligate families; if they prove the curse of their country, as well as the torment and ruin of those most intimately related to them; the guilt is in part yours and (I repeat it again) you must answer it to God at the great Day![3]

As the son of a Puritan, Matthew Henry wrote the most famous Christian commentary of the last 400 years based on his father's daily sessions of family worship. Henry exhorted his own congregants in these words, "You are unjust to your God, unkind to your children, and unfaithful to your truth, if having by baptism, entered your children in Christ's school, and lifted them under his banner, you do not make conscience of training them up in the learning of Christ's scholars, and under the discipline of his soldiers."[4]

In America, this commitment to family worship and the continuity of faith continued in full force. Massachusetts' first governor, John Winthrop, insisted that children be "brought up in the knowledge and fear of God." As early as 1648, Massachusetts laws required parents to teach their children "some short catechism" and the law of God on penalty of a fine.[5] Many Puritans and Pilgrims, including John Robinson, Cotton Mather, and Richard Baxter, wrote extensively on child discipline and education. Parents were directed by law to teach children to read "at least to be able duely to read the

Richard Baxter

Scriptures," to include "the Capital Laws [the Old Testament civil law] . . . and the Main Ground and Principles of the Christian Religion."[6]

In our own day, family life is quite fragmented and relatively weak. However, parents in early America were deeply involved in both the education of their children and their eventual courtship and betrothal. Speaking of the betrothal of his own daughter, Governor John Winthrop wrote to his son, "As for your sister, her constant professions and resolutions have been to do nothing without our approbation, and so hath been very well contented hitherto to submit to such condition as we should see providence directing us."[7] Family unity and cooperation was the norm in Puritan New England.

> *Hear, O Israel: The LORD our God, the LORD is one! You shall love the LORD your God with all your heart, with all your soul, and with all your strength. And these words which I command you today shall be in your heart. You shall teach them diligently to your children, and shall talk of them when you sit in your house, when you walk by the way, when you lie down, and when you rise up. (Deuteronomy 6:4-7)*

A Civil Government that Feared God

> *The Spirit of the LORD spoke by me, and His word was on my tongue. The God of Israel said, the Rock of Israel spoke to me: "He who rules over men must be just, ruling in the fear of God." (2 Samuel 23:2-3)*

The basic requirement for any civil leader must be that he fears God. Although this disposition is extremely rare among leaders in modern countries today, early America provided many examples of this in the colonial governments. Between 1660 and 1689, the Boston churches called for a total of 258 days of humiliation and fasting. Sometimes the magistrates would call for a "day of repentance," as on September 17, 1675, at the commencement of King Philips' War. Commonly, pastors would preach Election Day sermons, usually with the governor and magistrates attending the service and sitting in the front row.[8]

In response to the moral decline of the day, the New England General Court passed a "Provoking Evils" statute in the 1670s. The Court wanted to address the sins that they believed would bring God's judgment on the colony. Matters addressed in the legislation included the opening of businesses on the Lord's Day (Sunday), public swearing and drunkenness, excessively long hair on men, and "strange new fashions [of women's clothing] with naked breasts."[9]

Not everybody who migrated to New England joined the church, however. By 1650 Boston's church membership stood at 700 while the population soared to 3,000.[10] According to standards set in 1647, anyone over 24 years of age could vote in town elections (even if they were not church members). However, the commonwealth elections (for the whole colony) were restricted to church members and freemen. This requirement was dropped in 1664.

It wasn't easy for an American Puritan to become a church member and thereby become eligible to partake in the Lord's Supper. As early as the 1590s, some of the Puritans began raising the bar for church membership and communion. The New England Puritans baptized their children but still required each child to testify to a personal conversion experience before being permitted to become full church members and receive communion. It wasn't long before the churches were full of baptized young people who did not partake in the Lord's Supper because they could not recount a conversion experience to the satisfaction of the elders. As these young men and women married and had children, the question arose: Should the church baptize the children of parents who are not qualified to take communion?

In 1662, the New England Puritans produced an answer to this question: the "Half-Way Covenant." This church policy allowed parents who were not able to take the Lord's Supper to still present their children for baptism. Both parents and children would then be considered half-way members of the church unless or until they could recount their own conversion experience.

This way of handling church membership revealed two weaknesses in the Puritan colonies. First, the requirement of church membership for voting pressured people to obtain church membership for the wrong reasons. Certainly, the Christian church is looking for more conversions and an increase in church membership. But attaching the right to vote in the state elections to church membership introduced an incentive that is not biblical. This itself could easily introduce unbelievers into the church, who wish to be part of the church only because they seek the vote. But also, requiring a dramatic conversion experience before allowing a person to join the church is not biblical. Such requirements are not found in Scripture, and the standards used for determining a "genuine conversion" are often contrived and highly subjective.

Rather, in the records of the early church in Acts, we find that those who were accepted into the early church had received the preaching of the Word with joy. That was the bare requirement for adults:

> *Then those who gladly received his word were baptized; and that day about three thousand souls were added to them. (Acts 2:41)*

According to Ephesians 6:4, children are to be brought up in the "nurture and the admonition of the Lord." They are to be nurtured as little "olive plants" around the table (Ps. 128:3). The need to identify a single radical conversion experience in the life of a child is not emphasized in the Bible. Instead, we should look for a gradual, ongoing growth in faith and holiness throughout the life of a child raised in a Christian home. While all who enter the Kingdom of God must be born again (John 3:3), the external manifestation of this work of the Spirit may vary considerably from person to person.

The Mather Family Dynasty

> *One generation shall praise Your works to another, and shall declare Your mighty acts. (Psalm 145:4)*

Of all the Puritans, it was the Mather family that best represented the generational vision which formed the foundation of America. Four generations of Mathers preached in Boston area congregational churches from 1634 until 1785—Richard, Increase, Cotton, and Samuel Mather.

Richard Mather served as one of the very first patriarchs of this great movement into the New World. The faith he would bring with him to America came to him while he lived with a Puritan family in Toxteth, England. Beginning in 1611, fifteen-year-old Richard boarded with this family who faithfully practiced family worship. They would meet together twice a day for Scripture reading, prayers, and the singing of psalms. As part of the routine, the older children were given responsibility in reading, leading the prayers, and catechizing the younger children. This regular family discipleship in the home brought about a profound change in Richard's life. While still in England, he became a Puritan pastor. However, he soon found it difficult to submit to the regulations imposed on him by King James I and the Church of England. He especially resisted wearing a surplice (a white linen garment) over his robe in the church. So, in 1635 he packed up his wife and three sons, Samuel, Timothy, and Nathaniel, loaded their worldly possessions onto pack horses, and made the 100-mile trip from the Severn Valley to Bristol Bay. From there the family boarded a ship for New England where they joined John Winthrop, Pastor John Cotton, and the other Puritan colonists in Massachusetts Bay.

The family settled in Dorchester, south of Boston (and a little north of Plymouth). After their arrival, Richard threw away the certificate of ordination he had received from the bishops in England and proceeded to organize a Congregational church where he served as pastor until his death. In the Congregational form of church government, pastors, elders, and deacons are elected by the members of the local congregation. No longer would church leaders be appointed by government officials in these Puritan congregations (as they were in England). During the formative years of the church, Richard Mather helped to write a basic church organization position statement which came to be known as the "Cambridge Platform." This essentially governed New England Congregationalism for many years.

America's Last Puritan: Increase Mather

By faith Moses, when he became of age, refused to be called the son of Pharaoh's daughter, choosing rather to suffer affliction with the people of God than to enjoy the passing pleasures of sin, esteeming the reproach of Christ greater riches than the treasures in Egypt; for he looked to the reward. (Hebrews 11:24-26)

Eleazar was born to Richard and Katherine Mather in 1637, and his brother Increase was born in 1639. In their early years the boys were homeschooled by their mother. As they entered their teenage years, their father would assume the responsibility for their education.

Richard's elder sons Samuel and Nathaniel attended Harvard College in the 1640s and afterward returned to England to serve as pastors back in the homeland. Almost one-third of Harvard graduates lost the vision for the "City on a Hill" and returned to England. Honor and influence were more easily obtainable back in the mother country. In 1651 Increase entered Harvard at only 12 years of age (he was one of the youngest to ever attend the college). The coursework was largely rooted in pagan Greek and Roman literature and history. William Shakespeare's plays were beginning to infect the young men during these early years as well. Realizing the dangerous influence the college had on its students, Richard Mather quickly removed Increase from this environment and placed him in the home of a pastor for better discipleship in the things of the Lord. Between his 13th and 16th years, Increase Mather lived with Pastor John Norton, who assumed the pastorate of the largest congregation in Boston after Pastor John Cotton died in 1651. Increase lived with Pastor Norton in John Winthrop's old house several blocks from the church.

It was after his mother's death in 1655 that Increase experienced a spiritual awakening. He wrote, "I was in extremity of anguish and horror in my soul." The fifteen-year-old poured out his heart to God, recording the experience in his diaries: "I gave myself up to Jesus Christ, declaring that I was now resolved to be his Servant, and his only, and his forever, and humbly professed to him, that if I did perish, I would perish at his feet. Upon this I had ease and inward peace in my perplexed soul."[11]

At 16 years of age then, Increase Mather returned to Britain and he attended seminary at Trinity College in Dublin (Ireland). These were the years that the Puritans were expecting political support from Oliver Cromwell, who ruled England until his death in 1658. After graduating from Trinity, Increase found his way into several pulpits in England. He was however, eventually forced to return back to America as persecution broke out against the Puritans at the reinstatement of the monarchy under Charles II.

Upon his return to America, Increase took the pulpit of the North Church in Boston, newly formed in 1653. His father had married John Cotton's widow, Sarah Story Cotton. About the same time, Increase married John and Sarah Cotton's daughter, Maria, which meant that his children would have only a single set of grandparents. The young couple moved into the Cotton house, not far from Boston's First Church. Maria would bear ten children, the eldest of which became the most famous Puritan in America: Cotton Mather.

Struggling to Maintain the Faith from Generation to Generation

A posterity shall serve Him. It will be recounted of the Lord to the next generation, they will come and declare His righteousness to a people who will be born, that He has done this. (Psalm 22:30-31)

In the years that Increase Mather served as the spiritual leader of Massachusetts, he was above all else, a fighter. He fought hard for the faith. He battled strenuously to maintain the generational vision his own father and the fathers of the nation had laid out. Because of the inborn sin nature, retrograde and decline may happen. The tendency for the younger generation is to just let the faith vision of their fathers slip away. Rarely do children of faithful men carry on the vision of their fathers with the same focus and zeal as the previous generation. By the grace of God, the Mather family carried on the faith for four successive generations. Increase Mather fought for faith, for family, and for freedom every inch of the way.

Richard Mather died in 1669, and the next year Increase penned a biography of his father's life, entitled *The Life and Death of that Man of God Mr. Richard Mather*. In it, Increase paid much honor to his father and to his father's vision. In the biography, he included the twenty-four reasons that his father had laid out for coming to America. He explained how Richard had honored his own father and how those sons alive in his day should honor their fathers. Such honor for fathers and mothers is essential for earthly blessing as promised by the fifth commandment.

Honor your father and your mother, that your days may be long upon the land which the LORD your God is giving you. (Exodus 20:12)

Increase would frequently record prayers for his children in his diary:

After I had prayed, as I was in my garden, and had this soliloquy "God has heard my prayer for this child, God will answer me, and the child shall live to do service for the Lord his God and God of his father," . . . My heart was melted before the Lord, and therefore I am not altogether without hope that this child shall be blessed and made a blessing in his generation. Amen, O God in Christ Jesus, Amen . . . Tears gushed from me before the Lord. I trust prayer and Faith shall not be in vain. Oh! I have prevailed and obtained mercy for my poor children. Amen! Lord Jesus![12]

The heart of a father's vision and a pastor's passion for the next generation came out loud and clear in the messages he preached:

If you die and be not first new Creatures, better you had never been born; you will be left without excuse before the Lord, terrible witnesses shall rise up against you at the last day. Your Godly parents will testify against you before the Son of God in that day . . . All you disobedient children that are here before the Lord this day, hearken to the Word of the Lord. There is a Scripture which methinks should strike terror and trembling into your souls. Prov. 30:17 - "The eye that mocketh his father and despiseth to obey his mother, let the ravens of the valley pluck it out, and the young eagles shall eat it." . . . I am not only willing to preach, and to write, but I am willing to die for the conversions of the next generation.[13]

Without question, the biblical faith of Puritanism possessed staying power. It was honor for fathers and mothers, love of their own children, love for God and His kingdom, and a burning commitment to pass on the faith to the next generation which kept the fires of faith burning.

At fifteen years of age Increase's son Cotton began copying down his father's sermons and preparing them for publication. At sixteen years old Cotton preached his first sermon at his father's church and was ordained as assistant pastor at twenty. Cotton would go on to father fourteen children, and thus the Mather legacy continued. By 1697 Cotton Mather was preaching the afternoon sermon at the North Church and his son Samuel Mather (Increase's grandson) preached the morning sermon.[14]

The faith that founded this nation still retained a strong commitment to building generational faithfulness. The following is a short excerpt from Cotton Mather's "A Father's Resolutions." These words reveal the passion and the heart that formed the faith of this nation.

RESOLVED—

1. At the birth of my children, I will resolve to do all I can that they may be the Lord's. I will now actually give them up by faith to God; entreating that each child may be a child of God the Father, a subject of God the Son, a temple of God the Spirit—and be rescued from the condition of a child of wrath, and be possessed and employed by the Lord as an everlasting instrument of His glory.

2. As soon as my children are capable of minding my admonitions, I will often, often admonish them, saying, "Child, God has sent His son to die, to save sinners from death and hell. You must not sin against Him. You must every day cry to God that He would be your Father, and your Saviour, and your Leader. You must renounce the service of Satan, you must not follow the vanities of this world, you must lead a life of serious religion."

3. Let me daily pray for my children with constancy, with fervency, with agony. Yea, by name let me mention each one of them every day before the Lord. I will importunately beg for all suitable blessings to be

bestowed upon them: that God would give them grace, and give them glory, and withhold no good thing from them; that God would smile on their education, and give His good angels the charge over them, and keep them from evil, that it may not grieve them; that when their father and mother shall forsake them, the Lord may take them up. With importunity I will plead that promise on their behalf: "The Heavenly Father will give the Holy Spirit unto them that ask Him." Oh! happy children, if by asking I may obtain the Holy Spirit for them!

4. I will early entertain the children with delightful stories out of the Bible. In the talk of the table, I will go through the Bible, when the olive-plants about my table are capable of being so watered. But I will always conclude the stories with some lessons of piety to be inferred from them.

5. I will single out some Scriptural sentences of the greatest importance; and some also that have special antidotes in them against the common errors and vices of children. They shall quickly get those golden sayings by heart, and be rewarded with silver or gold, or some good thing, when they do it. Such as,

    - Psalm 111:10 - "The fear of the Lord is the beginning of wisdom."

    - Matthew 16:26 - "What is a man profited, if he shall gain the whole world, and lose his own soul?"

    - 1 Timothy 1:15 - "Christ Jesus came into the world to save sinners; of whom I am chief."

    - Matthew 6:6 - "When thou prayest, enter into thy closet, and when thou hast shut thy door, pray to thy Father which is in secret."

    - Ephesians 4:25 - "Putting away lying, speak every man truth with his neighbour."

    - Romans 12:17, 19 - "Recompense to no man evil for evil . . . Dearly beloved, avenge not yourselves."

6. [A] Jewish treatise tells us that among the Jews, when a child began to speak, the father was bound to teach him Deuteronomy 33:4—"Moses

commanded us a law, even the inheritance of the congregation of Jacob." Oh! let me early make my children acquainted with the Law which our blessed Jesus has commanded us! 'Tis the best inheritance I can give them.

7. I will cause my children to learn the Catechism. In catechizing them, I will break the answers into many lesser and proper questions; and by their answer to them, observe and quicken their understandings. I will bring every truth into some duty and practice, and expect them to confess it, and consent unto it, and resolve upon it. As we go on in our catechizing, they shall, when they are able, turn to the proofs and read them, and say to me what they prove and how. Then, I will take my times, to put nicer and harder questions to them; and improve the times of conversation with my family (which every man ordinarily has or may have) for conferences on matters of religion.

8. Restless will I be till I may be able to say of my children, "Behold, they pray!" I will therefore teach them to pray. But after they have learnt a form of prayer, I will press them to proceed unto points that are not in their form. I will charge them with all possible cogency to pray in secret; and often call upon them, "Child, I hope, you don't forget my charge to you, about secret prayer: your crime is very great if you do!"

The Jeremiad — Warnings

Fifty years after the first colonists arrived at Massachusetts Bay, the New England pastors became very concerned as they watched the morals of the colony slipping. The faith of the fathers had been drifting. It was feared that God's judgment was imminent especially as the drumbeats of war with the Indians could be heard sounding in the colonial villages. Increase Mather responded with a message of warning to all of Massachusetts. It was a type of sermon which came to be known as a "Jeremiad," named after the prophet. The title of Increase's sermon in February 1674 was "The Day of Trouble is Near." In the sermon he pointed out the sins of his day, some of which included the "foolish pride" which he thought was obvious in apparel and fashions showing up on the streets of Boston. He also pointed out the abandonment of family prayers and family worship throughout the colony. Many fathers were too busy making money to disciple their own children, he said. It seemed that the judgment of God was hanging over all of Boston. Yet, he still comforted his congregation with the reminder that the colony was in covenant with God and therefore God would not completely destroy them.

Increase Mather's warnings were well-timed. A full 1,000 New Englanders died in King Philips' War between 1675 and 1677. Then in the summer of 1678, more than 300 Bostonians (or 10% of the population) died as a result of a plague of smallpox.

Later in 1680 Increase preached another powerful sermon called "Returning Unto God the Great Concern of a Covenant People." These were the years of covenant renewal for the North Church. Increase hoped that powerful sermons would bring about national repentance and true conversions. However, many of the younger generation did not want to confess Christ publicly. They did not partake of the communion table, and Increase felt an obligation to support the Half-Way Covenant.

Fighting Against the Secularization of the American College

Beware lest anyone cheat you through philosophy and empty deceit, according to the tradition of men, according to the basic principles of the world, and not according to Christ. (Colossians 2:8)

Increase Mather entered the most serious battle for the Christian faith when he went to war against the rise of a man-centered secularism in the college classrooms. Harvard College was founded in 1636. Its 1650 charter set down the mission of the school as "the education of the English and Indian youth of this country, in knowledge and godliness."[15] Harvard's rules and precepts (codified in 1646) included this objective for its students: "Let every Student be plainly instructed, and earnestly pressed to consider well, the main end of his life and studies is, to know God and Jesus Christ which is eternal life (John 17:3) and therefore to lay Christ in the bottom, as the only foundation of all sound knowledge and Learning. And seeing the Lord only giveth wisdom, let every one seriously set himself by prayer in secret to seek it of him (Prov. 2:3)."[16] However, Harvard College soon wandered from its biblical foundations.

Increase assumed the presidency of Harvard in 1685. The first thing he did was to give up his first year's salary to clear the college debts. What this reforming Puritan wanted most was to bring Christian discipleship into the college. He ended the study of pagan Aristotelian ethics at the college, with the goal of reintroducing biblical law as the basis for human ethics. It was plain to Increase Mather that this seminary was undermining the faith in America. He wrote in 1689, "It is much to be lamented, that many Preachers in these days have hardly any other discourses in their Pulpits than what we may find in Seneca, Epictetus, Plutarch, or some such Heathen Moralist. Christ, the Holy Spirit, and (in a word), the Gospel is not in their Sermons."[17]

Not surprisingly, as the coursework turned back towards the Greeks, drunkenness on campus was also on the rise. Increase preached evangelical sermons at the college and cautioned the students against secular books that would "poison their young minds."[18] Increase also took an interest in the spiritual needs of the students practicing one-on-one discipleship. Cotton wrote that his father would "send for the Scholars one by one into the Library, and there consider with them about their [spiritual] state, and quicken their flight unto their Saviour . . . and lay solemn charges of God upon them to turn their life unto Him . . . thus did Dr. Mather continually!"[19] This discipleship approach was much closer to the teaching method Jesus employed with His disciples. It represented a fundamental break with the typical humanist university approach of merely offering knowledge for the mind.

Increase Mather also tried to oppose the humanist thinking of the Greek philosophers. He criticized the Roman Catholic schools for defending "their Pagan Master Aristotle [and] his Principles."[20] In an attempt to maintain a more secular, political control of the college, professors from England were sent to inspect Harvard's classes. When these "overseers" were barred from visiting the college, the Privy Council in England revoked Harvard's charter. It was a power struggle over who would control American churches and American life, and spiritual forces were at work. Increase Mather suggested to Harvard's board that the college forfeit official accreditation from England, and continued to disciple the students in the Scriptures on a one-on-one basis.[21]

Latitudinarianism: Latitudinarians would not call specific doctrinal views dangerous or heretical (especially doctrines that denied the Trinity). The Latitudinarians rejected what they thought were the narrow views of the Puritans. They were especially hesitant to defend doctrines like the Trinity that didn't make sense to human reason.

Unitarianism: Unitarianism is the belief that there is one God and that God is one person. Unitarianism denies that the Father, the Son, and Holy Spirit are distinct persons and equally God.

Trinitarianism: Trinitarianism is the belief that God is one, and He is three persons, and each of the three persons are the same in substance and equal in power and glory.

While Increase Mather was attempting reform, two of his instructors, William Brattle and John Leverett were quietly opposing him. Both were humanists in the sense that they favored the sovereignty of man over the sovereignty of God. They wanted to bring Greek ethics back into the college's curriculum and they wanted Plato's philosophy raised to the same level as the enscripturated revelation of God's law.[22] Eventually these "latitudinarians" would win the battle and humanism would seize control of American schools, colleges, and churches. In 1701, Harvard College's board voted Increase out. Shortly thereafter the old Puritan preached his most important message: "Ichabod—The Glory of the Lord Departing New England." The sermon was one long lament. Chief among Increase's concerns was that Harvard College would "become a Seminary for Degenerate Plants, who will with their Foolish hands pull down those Houses which their Fathers have been building for the Name of the Lord in this wilderness. A Learned man who has written the History of the Bohemian Brethren, observes that the Ruin of those Churches proceeded out of their College."[23]

In 1707, the Massachusetts government chose the teacher most committed to the humanist approach to education, John Leverett, to lead Harvard College as president. Within the next century Harvard would embrace Unitarianism and reject the biblical Trinitarian faith.

The failure of American faith grew largely out of the apostasy within the large colleges which were designed to prepare pastors for the churches. It was a fatal mistake, and the attacks upon the faith would continue in the universities for the next three centuries.

Now when they [the Jews] saw the boldness of Peter and John, and perceived that they were uneducated and untrained men, they marveled. And they realized that they had been with Jesus. (Acts 4:13)

The Battle for Liberty

During the 17th and 18th centuries the English monarchy and parliament continued to increase their power and control over an expanding empire. As with all sinful men, those in positions of authority will work hard to centralize power for themselves. So often this becomes the overriding concern for humanist man and the major objective for civil governments.

As the American colonies were growing into an economic powerhouse, the powers of England recognized more opportunities for control. They saw in America more economic benefits to enrich the mother country. Eventually, this would lead to war in the 1770s. In the meantime, the colonies needed a man who would take a stand for liberty to safeguard some measure of independence from tyrannical English governance. In God's providence one man stepped in to engage the struggle—Increase Mather.

After Oliver Cromwell died in 1656, King Charles II was crowned and the English monarchy was restored. For the next twenty years, the king allowed the colonies to govern themselves, and America continued as a collection of self-governing colonies. But, around 1676, the king created a committee to oversee the colonies called "The Committee for Trade and Plantations." The committee sent Edward Randolph to spy on the Massachusetts colony.

Here was a true "evil genius" as described by historian, Michael Hall. It was this man who quickly brought an end to the Puritan commonwealth in America.[24] In his investigations Randolph discovered that the colonies throughout Massachusetts did not require their leaders to take an oath to the king. And also, the colonial governments were coining their own money instead of using the king's coin. It was clear to Randolph that these Americans were acting as though they were free and independent— much too free. Upon hearing

James II of England

these reports, Charles II was not happy and he asked the colonies to resign their charter. At Increase Mather's urging, they refused the king's request. Clearly, another charter would constitute a disaster for American freedoms. Randolph accused Increase Mather of "Sedition and Treason." Somehow Randolph's spies were able to intercept several of Increase's letters which Randolph considered treasonous. At this point Increase was quickly turning into the most wanted man in America, by the English authorities.

Finally, in August of 1685, James II (successor and brother of Charles II) removed New England's democratically elected government and sent Edward

Randolph to America to set up a "provisional government." The Massachusetts colonists lost control of their civil government. The English proceeded to take away the free press in Boston, another precious liberty Americans held dear. This marked the end of Puritan self-government. On May 21, 1686 the colonial government met for the last time and offered a prayer of thanks "that they had been able to govern in God's name for fifty-six years."[25] They sang a hymn based on the words of Habakkuk 3:17-18:

> *Though the fig tree may not blossom, nor fruit be on the vines; though the labor of the olive may fail, and the fields yield no food; though the flock may be cut off from the fold, and there be no herd in the stalls—Yet I will rejoice in the Lord, I will joy in the God of my salvation.*

One man in the assembly, however, still resisted the king's unjust dealings. In December 1687, Increase secretly requested permission of his church elders to journey to England. During his absence his son Cotton, at only 25 years of age, would take the pulpit at the North Church. However, escaping the watchful eye of the English spies was not an easy task. Edward Randolph tried to interrupt Increase's plans by suing him in court for 500 pounds. Randolph lost the suit. Finally, with his thirteen-year-old son Samuel in tow, Increase snuck out the back door of his house in disguise. Somehow, Randolph's agents discovered the flight and followed in hot pursuit. Father and son took a fishing boat out to Plymouth Harbor. The ship bound to England had already left port, so the small sailboat bearing the two men set out to catch up. Meanwhile Randolph's men began chasing Increase and Sam in another boat. By God's good providence, the father and son outdistanced Randolph's agents and caught up with the *President*, bound for England. From where he was watching on Beacon Hill, Cotton Mather could see his father and brother climb aboard the *President*, and thanked God for His mercies upon his kin and country.

Increase Mather's first meeting with the king took place on May 30, 1688. For three years this man of faith prayed, lobbied, and negotiated for every inch of liberty he could obtain for America. In the history of the country no one fought harder for American liberties than Increase Mather. In God's good providence, his cause was helped by the deposition of James II and the accession of William III in the Glorious Revolution of 1688. During this time Increase was able to secure the land grants and property rights laid down by the original charter in spite of the serious threats to remove these rights. Although the colonial governors would be chosen by the king, the appointment would still be subject to a council elected by the House of Representatives (which was elected by the people). And, the governor could not appoint sheriffs or militia officers without the consent of the council. At the end of all the negotiations and agreements formed, Increase recorded his heart-felt thanksgivings to God in these words:

> *God has been so gracious to me, as to make me instrumental in obtaining for my country a MAGNA CHARTA, whereby religion and English liberties, with some peculiar Privileges, Liberties, and all Men's Properties, are Confirmed and Secured to Them and their Posterity forevermore.*[26]

Historians have pointed out that Massachusetts enjoyed more self-rule and liberty "than any other royal or proprietary colony in America."[27] It was in New England where the battle for independence began. Not surprisingly, the battle for liberty later in the 1770s would initiate once again in New England with men like Samuel Adams, Paul Revere, and others. Before these men, there was America's first father of liberties and he will never be forgotten. Increase Mather had his new hard-won charter, sealed by the king on October 7, 1691.

Spiritual Battles

> *For we do not wrestle against flesh and blood, but against principalities, against powers, against the rulers of the darkness of this age, against spiritual hosts of wickedness in the heavenly places. (Ephesians 6:12)*

The 1680s and early 1690s will be remembered as a period of spiritual decline for the New England colonies. In his *Magnalia Christi Americana*, Cotton Mather points out that "wretched books" on fortune-telling had "stolen into the land."[28] When the provisional government entered in 1686, the English leaders actually encouraged the publishing of an almanac containing astrology.[29] In 1688, a pagan Maypole was erected in Charlestown, Massachusetts. The battle for the soul of America was in full engagement. For the most part the devil had free course, and young people especially were drawn into playing with "little sorceries."[30] These were the conditions under which the infamous witch trials came about.

The Salem Village Church was a seedbed of quarrels and divisions. This too provided opportunity for Satan to take advantage of the congregation. Two previous pastors had quit when the church refused to pay them. When Samuel Parris arrived from Barbados to assume the pastorate in 1689, matters did not improve. The church quit paying Parris his salary. This contention led to more evil gossip and slander within the assembly. Such was the spiritual condition in this church that the pastor himself suggested in a sermon that there were "many devils" among them.[31] Parris was greatly responsible for heightening the hysteria and fear in his own congregation. He told his people, "If ever there were witches, Men and Women in covenant with the Devil, here are multitudes in New-England."[32] During the witch trials that followed, Parris would himself testify against nine people in his own church.

> *Be sober, be vigilant; because your adversary the devil walks about like a roaring lion, seeking whom he may devour. (1 Peter 5:8)*

In more ways than one, Satan and his spiritual forces were active in New England in the early 1690s. The devil's strategies are always deceitful. On the one hand, the devil is thrilled to have men and women playing with incantations, magic, séances, and the like. These people become enamored with demons and, sadly, they even dedicate their lives to conjuring malevolent spirits. At the same time, the devil also loves to create fear and hysteria concerning the demonic realm among those who reject witchcraft. When Satan comes upon a church that is terribly divisive, he will use these conditions to gain an advantage over the congregation as well. In turn, this produces more fear, confusion, and the destruction of innocent lives and communities. Satan was working great confusion in the colonies during the witch trials.

Wild accusations relating to witchcraft flew around Suffolk, England around the year 1645, where eighteen witches were hanged. Thousands were put to death in France around the same timeframe. By the end of the Salem Witch Trials in Massachusetts in May 1693, twenty people had been executed on charges of witchcraft.

The Salem Witch Trials were well underway before Increase Mather returned from England. Almost immediately after his arrival, Increase wrote a seventy-page paper called "Cases of Conscience Concerning Evil Spirits." He obtained signatures on the document from fourteen other pastors and, by the grace of God, this document was instrumental in ending the trials and the killing of innocent people in Salem. Increase believed that witches really did exist and that the civil rulers should keep them out of their communities, but he considered the Salem trials unjust and wrong.

The basic problem with the Salem trials was this: certain young people claimed to be victims of evil spells placed on them by witches. They claimed that the ghosts of certain people in the Salem community had attacked them. The Salem court accepted as evidence the testimony of these young persons

Fanciful representation of the Salem Witch Trials

and used it against those people they accused of involvement with witchcraft. Increase pointed out that Satan could easily deceive the victims by presenting these "ghosts" to the minds of the victims. Therefore, he said this ghost-type of evidence should never have been accepted in a court of law. Towards the turn of the 18th century, another insidious force threatened the Christian church and Western society. It was the modern naturalistic worldview which teaches that Satan does *not* exist. These ideas were just forming during the lifetime of Increase Mather. Of course, the modern world mocks Christians who believe in the spiritual element. During the early years of the Enlightenment, certain scientists were already suggesting that the invisible, spiritual world was not real. Some were questioning God's existence as well as that of the demonic world. This teaching is yet another demonic deception.

Increase Mather and his son Cotton Mather went on to write several books attempting to prove to the scientific mind the existence of the demonic world. Yet, in the attempt to prove the existence of demons, Christians can often give the demons too much credit. This probably happened with some who were weaker in the faith during the spiritual decline of New England.

In the end, Increase Mather concluded that witches really did exist in the land, but he believed that this witchcraft had crept into the country as God's judgment on a people in moral decline.[33] The original source of the problem in Salem may be traced to Barbados (an island in the West Indies governed by the British). Barbados was known for its practice of Obeah Magic, exported from Africa by witch doctors in the 17th and 18th centuries.[34] However, the church in Salem did not have the spiritual strength to resist the forces of the Evil One. They were not sufficiently equipped to stand "in the evil day" (Eph. 6:10-15).

As Christians we must believe and testify that the Lord Jesus Christ conquered Satan at the cross. The devil is a defeated foe. The Christian church, therefore, must declare in true faith that the Lord Jesus sits on the right hand of the Father, far above all principalities and powers and that He is ruling until all His enemies are under His feet. It is only when the church gives in to a spirit of division that it will separate itself from Christ. The church at Salem represented this type of apostasy, and Satan sifted the church like wheat.

[God the Father] has delivered us from the power of darkness and conveyed us into the kingdom of the Son of His love, in whom we have redemption through His blood, the forgiveness of sins. He is the image of the invisible God, the firstborn over all creation. For by Him all things were created that are in heaven and that are on earth, visible and invisible, whether thrones or dominions or principalities or powers. All things were created through Him and for Him. And He is before all things, and in Him all things consist. And He is the head of the body, the church, who is the beginning, the firstborn from the dead, that in all things He may have the preeminence. (Colossians 1:13-18)

Lessons to Learn

As his life came to a close, Increase Mather was concerned for the state of morality in New England. Preaching to his congregation in 1719, he catalogued Boston's sins to include sexual immorality ("the sins of Sodom"), pride, gluttony, and idleness. In his last sermon published in June 1722, Mather declared the glories of the risen Christ, and testified to the "great honor to be a Servant of Jesus Christ." It was August 23, 1723 that Increase Mather died in his son's arms. Continuing on his father's legacy of honoring the generations that went before him, Cotton Mather published a biography of his father, entitled *Memories of Remarkables in the Life and Death of the Ever-Memorable Dr. Increase Mather, Who Expired, August 23, 1723*.

Certainly, these Puritan forefathers were not perfect. They fell short, as all men do. Even the best of men will tend to sow the seeds of their own destruction. Without the constant outpouring of the Holy Spirit upon each generation and without God's grace upholding the churches and the nation, every spiritual work will quickly fall into decline.

Increase Mather's sermons were passionate and urgent almost to the point of appearing foreboding at times. The more he detected moral and spiritual decline among the rising generation, the more urgently he would preach. Did he rely more upon the arm of flesh than the work of the Holy Spirit in bringing about conversions? Were his prayers as importunate as his preaching? These are the challenges that face pastors during times of spiritual decline.

After 1691 Increase Mather's preaching began to reveal a greater focus on end-time events. His sermons suggested that the millennium or some great judgment on the wicked was coming in the near future. This type of emphasis in preaching indicated a weakening of the faith for the Puritans and for the evangelicals (during the 1800s and 1900s). An undue focus on end-time events can easily become a means of shirking responsibility for Christian labor and ministry. This is a pitfall that pastors often stumble into when they become discouraged with the present state of affairs. As they begin hoping for an apocalyptic interference from God Himself, they allow this to distract them from the hard work of discipling the nations, which must always be the business of the church.

The Puritans could have been more suspect of the universities. They should have listened to the old Scottish Reformer John Knox. As he was preparing to die, Knox told his followers, "Beware of the Universities." It was the secular universities that would destroy faith in America, generation by generation. It was Increase Mather who realized the core battle and fought hard to preserve America's biblical foundations.

Increase Mather is considered the last Puritan and the first to engage the fight for freedom in the American colonies. He was the last conservative holdout at Harvard College in a time when humanism was rolling in like a flood. He was the greatest preacher of his generation. He was a man of great faith, strong conviction, courage, and passion for God and His Word. His love for his own children fills the pages of his diary, and his generational vision of a Christian faith continued in the lives of his son Cotton and grandson Samuel.

In the providence of God, a handful of men will direct the flow of history. It is a rare breed of leaders who pursue a vision which will sustain for generations. It is especially rare to find a commitment to the kingdom of God, and a faith to stand for fifty years against the constant pressures of tyranny, spiritual compromise, and Satanic attacks that threaten to destroy the vision. But this is precisely what it takes to establish a nation that will enjoy the manifold blessings of God for three hundred years. This is the legacy of Increase Mather.

David Brainerd (1718-1747)

CHAPTER 6

David Brainerd:
A Life on the Altar

And He said to them, "Go into all the world and
preach the gospel to every creature. He who believes
and is baptized will be saved; but he who does not
believe will be condemned."

—Mark 16:15-16

From the first The Massachusetts Bay Charter of 1630 had envisioned a Great Commission objective for the colony. The charter committed to "win and incite the natives of the Country to the Knowledge and obedience of the only true God and Savior of Mankind, and the Christian faith."[1] The official seal for the colony included the image of an Indian crying out, "Come over and help us!" Throughout the 1600s and early 1700s, only John Eliot and Thomas Mayhew Sr. (and his progeny) had seriously engaged the work of evangelizing the Indians. Pioneering missionary work is long and hard, slow and frustrating. Above all, it is often carried out under thankless and highly strenuous conditions, with almost no financial reward. Such work can only be done by a people of steadfast faith and self-denying love. Missionary endeavors picked up after the Great Awakening of the 1730s and 1740s. Such extraordinary ministry is the product of Holy Spirit revivals that have come to various places and times throughout the history of the Kingdom of Christ.

Spiritual Decline

O LORD, I have heard thy speech, and was afraid: O LORD, revive thy work in the midst of the years, in the midst of the years make known; in wrath remember mercy. (Habakkuk 3:2 KJV)

The early 18th century marked a period of spiritual decline for America. Good preaching was harder and harder to find in the pulpits because the majority of pastors were being trained in secular colleges that had been corrupted by humanist thinking and a spiritual malaise.

The spiritual condition of New England was so degraded during these years that Cotton Mather would lament, "It is confessed by all who know anything of the matter . . . that there is a general and an horrible decay of Christianity, among the professors of it . . . The modern Christianity is . . . scarce a shadow of the ancient. Ah! sinful nation!"[2] In 1727 Charles Chauncy had taken the pastorate at the First Church in Boston, becoming America's first Unitarian preacher. Chauncy rejected the doctrine of the deity of Christ, and he believed that everybody would be saved, no matter what. The influence of Puritanism had clearly waned.

Seal of the Massachusetts Bay Colony

An Inspiration to the Christian World

For to me, to live is Christ, and to die is gain. But if I live on in the flesh, this will mean fruit from my labor; yet what I shall choose I cannot tell. For I am hard-pressed between the two, having a desire to depart and be with Christ, which is far better. (Philippians 1:21-23)

Protestant missions work in the 18th century was moving along at a snail's pace. The Moravian Brethren were just initiating their mission work and a few Lutheran missionaries had reached India's west coast. Besides this, there was precious little missionary spirit among the Christian Protestant churches. It was during this time that the Lord sought out a man to light the fire.

Looking back some three hundred years later, it seems that no other person contributed more to lighting the fire for worldwide missions than David Brainerd. As he lay dying of Tuberculosis at 29 years of age, he didn't realize the impact his contribution would make upon the world. It was the spirit of David Brainerd, as picked up from his diary entries, that God used to stir up missions work in the 18th and 19th centuries.

William Carey (1761-1834), the father of modern missions and the pioneering missionary to India, required his mission team to read Brainerd's diary three times a year. Henry Martyn (1781-1812) became the first missionary to the Muslims in Persia (modern-day Iran), a feat of unfathomable courage and devotion. He died trekking through the land of the Armenians, but not before he had translated the Bible into the Persian language. Martyn wrote of David Brainerd as his exemplar: "I long to be like him. Let me forget the world and be swallowed up in desire to glorify God."[3] It was Martyn who wrote the famous words: "Let me burn out for God!"[4] His passionate cry sounds remarkably similar to Brainerd's testimony: "Oh, with what reluctancy did I feel myself obligated to consume time in sleep. I long to be a flame of fire, continually glowing in the divine service in building Christ's Kingdom to my last and dying moment."[5] John Wesley, Francis Asbury, Robert Murray McCheyne, Samuel Marsden, Robert Morrison, David Livingstone, Andrew Murray, and Sheldon Jackson were also deeply impacted by David Brainerd's life and testimony.

Early Life

But You, O GOD the Lord, deal with me for Your name's sake; because Your mercy is good, deliver me. For I am poor and needy, and my heart is wounded within me. I am gone like a shadow when it lengthens; I am shaken off like a locust. My knees are weak through fasting, and my flesh is feeble from lack of fatness. I also have become a reproach to them; when they look at me, they shake their heads. Help me, O LORD my God! Oh, save me according to Your mercy . . . (Psalm 109:21-26)

David Brainerd was born on April 20, 1718 to Hezekiah and Dorothy Brainerd. Both father and mother came from strong Puritan roots. Dorothy was a pastor's daughter. Hezekiah was speaker of the Connecticut House of Representatives and a member of the colonial senate. As a young boy, David attended a Congregational church where the people sang the psalms (without instrumental accompaniment) and listened to two hour-long sermons every Sunday, one in the morning and another in the afternoon.

At twenty years of age Brainerd developed an interest in the ministry. For a year he was mentored by an old pastor in Haddam, Connecticut, and then by his older brother Nehemiah who also pastored a local church.

Early in 1739 David woke up to his own real spiritual condition. He realized that he had been trusting in his own works for salvation. As a young man who had been raised in a Christian family and who had always attended church, he had become blinded to his own sinfulness. But, by God's grace, David came under a strong sense of his own vileness and sinfulness before God. For several months he vacillated between apathy and heavy conviction of sin. Then, on July 12, 1739, David received a vision of the glory of God. He came to understand who God really was, as God over all and as Savior. And he found that God's way of salvation through Jesus Christ was the "most lovely, blessed, and excellent way."[6]

David entered Yale College in September 1739. By this time, Yale College had forty-five young men enrolled in the student body. The freshman class was made up of mostly younger men (ages 13 through 17), with Brainerd as the oldest member at 21.

At Yale David Brainerd quickly became something of an irritation to the college leadership for his outspoken support for Great Awakening preachers like Gilbert Tennent and George Whitefield. When he was overheard making a critical statement regarding the spiritual lifelessness of a certain teacher, young Brainerd was expelled from Yale College. His hopes were crushed, for this was the accepted path to ministry at the time. Yet, in God's perfect plans, David would be trained for the ministry in a discipleship context. It turns out that discipleship is a

George Whitefield

better approach than the typical classroom approach to transferring knowledge, especially for pastors and evangelists. The Lord Jesus spent a great deal of time in an informal discipleship context with His twelve disciples, and this same method was used for this man of God who would be used so uniquely in the story of world missions—David Brainerd. After his expulsion from Yale, David sat under the mentorship of Jedidiah Mills, a humble pastor serving in a church at Ripton, Connecticut.

From the testimony of his own letters and diary entries we know that David continued to experience humiliation and confusion over his rejection by Yale for many years afterwards. His only crime had been his support for God's work in the Great Awakening and his desire to see a spiritual renewal among the professors at Yale. Now, at only twenty-three years of age, David found himself an outcast of New England society. On April 6, 1742, David was considering the purpose of these providential dealings. The entry in his diary read:

I could think of undergoing the greatest sufferings in the cause of Christ, with
pleasure; and found myself willing (if God should so order it) to suffer banishment
from my native land, among the heathen [Indians] that I might do something for
their souls' salvation.[7]

In the weeks that followed this diary entry, it is clear that the burden for ministering to the Indians was only intensifying. Brainerd confessed to a "special enlargement in pleading for the enlightenment and conversion of the poor heathen."[8] He testified at one point that his whole body was soaking in sweat as he agonized in prayer for the Indians.

Pioneering Mission Work Among the Native Americans

Yea, so have I strived to preach the gospel, not where Christ was named, lest I should
build upon another man's foundation . . . (Romans 15:20 KJV)

On July 29, 1742, David Brainerd was ordained to the ministry by an ad-hoc group of pastors who sympathized with the revivals (and disagreed with Yale's treatment of David). Later that summer he joined a young pastor named Joseph Bellamy at Bethlehem, Connecticut. Twenty-four-year-old Bellamy was ordained to the ministry at eighteen years of age and pastored a church that met in a large barn. On August 12 the two young men headed out to an Indian village called Scaticock up the Housatonic River. For the twenty-four hours before he began preaching, David was full of inward conflicts. Spiritual oppression seemed to overwhelm him. These intense struggles would characterize most of his ministry life. He recorded his thoughts: "I wondered that God would let me live and wondered that people did not stone me, much more, that they would ever hear me preach!"[9] Nevertheless the Holy Spirit entered the young preacher strongly, and the result was a powerful convicting force on the hearers. In his later report, he writes, "Indians cried out in great distress, and all appeared greatly concerned."[10] Earlier that year the Moravian missionary Henry Rauch had planted seeds with this tribe and had baptized three natives.

It was about this time that David Brainerd came under risk of arrest. The Connecticut General Assembly had instituted a law forbidding anyone besides properly licensed clergymen to preach. For a while David went into hiding.

But then, in November 1742, the Scottish Society for Propagating Christian Knowledge commissioned Brainerd to missionary service with the Indians. The year before, Azariah Horton had been assigned to the Indians on Long Island. Horton worked with 400 Indians and baptized thirty-five adults and forty-four children in his nine-year ministry. Yet, despite these numbers, many of his converts were overcome by an addiction to alcohol, and only twenty of these natives remained firm in the faith.

Between March 1742 and March 1743, Brainerd preached at least sixty sermons in thirty-six towns throughout Connecticut, New York, New Jersey, and Massachusetts. The experience he gained from this year was his major training for mission work with the Indians. On March 31, 1743, he began ministering to the Stockbridge or Mohican Indians in Massachusetts. Before his arrival John Sergeant, another missionary for the Scottish Society, had spent eight years working with the Indians in Western Massachusetts. John spent a total of fifteen years as a missionary to the natives and some 129 were baptized into the faith under his ministry. Regrettably, covetous European settlers confiscated these Indian lands after John's death and the Christian Indians were forced to move out towards Oneida Lake.

Not wanting to work where the Gospel had already been preached, David Brainerd moved further west into unreached Indian territory. While there he received threats from the Dutch settlers, who were generally on unfriendly terms with the Indians. David wrote that "[The Dutch] hate me because I preach to 'em." [the Indians][11] Some time in June 1743 he moved into an Indian wigwam and began a daily ministry with the natives, teaching both day and night. During these months young Brainerd survived on very little food. Sometimes he went for days without eating. At other times he had only a little moldy bread to keep starvation at bay. Every day, David brought the same basic message to the natives who gathered:

First, the sinfulness and misery of the estate they were naturally in: the evil of their hearts, the pollution of their natures, the heavy guilt they were under, and their exposedness to everlasting punishment . . . And secondly the fullness, all-sufficiency, and freeness of that redemption which the Son of God has wrought out by His obedience, and suffering for perishing sinners.[12]

Hard Soil

Those who sat in darkness and in the shadow of death, bound in affliction and irons—because they rebelled against the words of God, and despised the counsel of the Most High, therefore He brought down their heart with labor; they fell down, and there was none to help. Then they cried out to the LORD in their trouble, and He saved them out of their distresses. He brought them out of darkness and the shadow of death, and broke their chains in pieces. (Psalm 107:10-14)

David Brainerd faced a major challenge in his labors with the Indians. Frequently the local European settlers provided a bad example for the native tribes. Brainerd spent a great deal of time explaining why the ungodly Europeans engaged in the slave trade, the stealing of lands, and drunkenness. This bad behavior was ruinous to the Indians. One tribal leader told David: "Why do you desire the Indians to become Christians, seeing the Christians are so much worse than the Indians? 'Twas they who first taught the Indians to be drunk. And they stole from one another to the degree that their rulers were obliged to hang them for it . . . None of the Indians have ever been hanged for stealing, and yet they do not steal half so much as the Christians do. I suppose that if the Indians should become Christians they would then be as bad as these."[13] While the Indians were guilty of their own sinful habits including stealing and killing, the hypocrisy and sinful examples of the European immigrants would sometimes get in the way of missionary work. Missionaries serving around the world in the 18th and 19th centuries faced this same hindrance to their mission work wherever they labored. Sometimes the natives would go so far as to kill the European and American missionaries because they associated these men and women of God with the wicked slave traders.

Housatonic River

For a full year David Brainerd ministered to the Kaunaumeek Indians in Western Massachusetts. On May 1, 1744, he headed down the Delaware River to evangelize Indian tribes in Eastern Pennsylvania (near modern-day Allentown). It was on this trip that he began coughing up blood—signs of an onset of tuberculosis. "Rode several hours in the rain through the howling wilderness," he wrote, "although I was so disordered in body that little or nothing but blood came from me."[14]

For entire weeks at a time David lay in bed sick. When he felt a little strength returning to his body, he arose and preached some more to the Indians. Towards the end of the summer of 1744 his health improved slightly and he was able to minister daily to the Delaware Indians. However, David encountered more reluctance among these natives to turn from their idols to serve the true and living God. Afraid of demons and of their local witchdoctors who threatened them with poison and enchantment, the Indians preferred to remain in the darkness (John 3:19-20). To counter their fear and to prove the power of God over idols, David challenged them by asking why their witchdoctors were unable to hurt him. After all, he explained, he was a preacher defying the powers of darkness to which they were enslaved. "I asked them why the powwows did not bewitch and poison me."[15] Obviously the witchdoctors could have worked their worst on David, but God's hand of protection was most certainly upon him.

> *Surely He shall deliver you from the snare of the fowler and from the perilous pestilence. He shall cover you with His feathers, and under His wings you shall take refuge; His truth shall be your shield and buckler. You shall not be afraid of the terror by night, nor of the arrow that flies by day, nor of the pestilence that walks in darkness, nor of the destruction that lays waste at noonday. A thousand may fall at your side, and ten thousand at your right hand; but it shall not come near you.* (Psalm 91:3-7)

On October 1, 1744, David Brainerd organized a team of one other minister and three of his native disciples for a trip into the "hideous and howling wilderness," some twenty-five miles west of the Delaware Forks. The way was marked by treacherous cliffs, and at some point on the journey David's horse tripped, fell, and broke its leg. To David's dismay, they were forced to shoot the horse—this faithful animal friend who had carried him over 5,000 miles in his Christian missionary work.

Finally arriving at the Susquehanna River (north of modern day Berwick, Pennsylvania), David obtained permission from the chief to preach to the local men four times on Saturday and Sunday. The chief invited the team back for ministry, but it was here that David realized the difficulties of reaching these peoples. The Indians had no desire to forsake their idolatries and the memory of certain miracles that their ancestors had witnessed (evidently provided by Satan and his demons). They were also "awed" by their own witchdoctors who apparently had some capability of poisoning people. Culturally the tribes were committed to hunting, which did not leave much time for the men to attend a regular meeting (and receive regular discipleship).

Brainerd soon realized that he must spend days upon days in fasting and prayer to break through these spiritual strongholds. Despite his weakness of body, he still fasted, and then he would experience breakthroughs. He would cry out to God for his own spiritual weakness. In anguish he would ask God for more compassion for the lost souls of men. He struggled for the gift of preaching to these natives with sincerity, compassion, and true concern for their souls.

In May 1745, Brainerd led a small team (himself, another pastor, and his interpreter, Moses Tattamy), back into the Susquehanna territory in an attempt to reach more Indian tribes. The Susquehanna Chief, Shikellamy, rejected his request to preach the gospel at that time. While traveling through the wilds, he became terribly ill and lay for a week in a little hut. Jonathan Edwards wrote:

> As he was riding in the wilderness being seized with an ague followed with a burning fever and extreme pain in his head and bowels, attended with a great evacuation of blood; so that he thought he must have perished in the wilderness. But at last coming to an Indian trader's hut, he got leave to stay there; and though without physic [medicine] or food proper for him it pleased God, after about a week's distress, to relieve him so far that he was able to ride.[16]

It was a discouraging trip for this struggling missionary, for almost no interest was generated in the Christian Gospel message among the natives for whom he risked his life so many times. After two years of ministry, David Brainerd had come to the point where he was about to resign from the Scottish Society's service. Only his interpreter Moses and the man's wife had received the gospel and were demonstrating true fruits of repentance. The walls of brass and the gates of iron do not give way easily in this business.

In God's good providence, however, the hearts of the white settlers had been softened to the gospel. The Holy Spirit of God began moving in the settlements around the Forks. During this time of spiritual awakening, David found himself preaching as much to the settlers as he did to the native tribes. On the weekend of June 7, David preached in Neshaminy to 3,000 or 4,000 gathered for a communion service. Hundreds were "much affected, so that there was a very 'great mourning,' like the mourning of Hadradrimmon (Zech. 12:11)."[17] However, this was not to be the essential fruit of David Brainerd's ministry.

Crossweeksung Revival

Oh, that men would give thanks to the LORD for His goodness, and for His wonderful works to the children of men! For He has broken the gates of bronze, and cut the bars of iron in two. (Psalm 107:15-16)

Since the time of the first Pentecost there have been at least ten, perhaps more, pentecostal outpourings recorded by Christian historians. These Holy Spirit visitations usually result in long-term effects that impact later centuries. More missionary work is spawned during these spiritual awakenings. The Holy Spirit's outpourings visit different tribes and nations at different times. Tremendous revivals were seen with the Korean Presbyterians in Pyongyang in 1907 and then with the Chinese church in the 1990s. In the summer of 1745 the Native Americans received a similar visitation under the ministry of David Brainerd.

The story began on June 18, 1745. On that day a very discouraged missionary made his way south into Crossweeksung, south of Trenton, New Jersey for another visit to the tribe. There he preached to a congregation of four Indian women. The next day he returned to the same spot and discovered a larger crowd awaiting him. The women had traveled ten to fifteen miles to gather their friends from the surrounding area. David preached again the following day, this time to a crowd of about thirty. A tremendous change was coming about. This time, these natives seemed greatly affected by the message, weeping many tears while he spoke. They were beginning to realize "their perishing state, and appeared concerned for a deliverance from it."[18] The response came as a refreshing wave over the poor missionary. "This was indeed a very sweet afternoon for me,"[19] he wrote in his diary. The Indians asked him to continue his preaching routine twice daily. Despite his physical weakness, Brainerd agreed, and at this point the crowd had expanded to 40-50 persons. One of the native women told him, "I wish God would change my heart." For the following days and weeks, the native men and women continued mourning over the condition of their souls.

Upon his return to the Forks on July 14, the Holy Spirit's presence seemed to follow his ministry. He baptized Moses Tattamy and his entire household—the first baptism in David's ministry among the Native Americans.

Then the Holy Spirit came in pentecostal power on August 8, 1745. David was preaching from Luke 14:16-23 on the parable of the banquet feast to about sixty-five Indians in Crossweeksung. David writes of the moment:

> *The power of God seemed to descend upon the assembly "like a rushing mighty wind," and with an astonishing energy bore down all before it. I stood amazed at the influence that seized the audience almost universally, and could compare it to nothing more aptly than the irresistible force of a mighty torrent or swelling deluge, that with its insupportable weight and pressure bears down and sweeps before it whatever is in its way. Almost all persons of all ages were bowed down with concern together, and scarce one was able to withstand the shock of this surprising operation. Old men and women who had been drunken wretches for many years, and some little children not more than six or seven years of age, appeared in distress for their souls, as well as persons of middle age . . . The most stubborn hearts were now obliged to bow . . . They were almost universally praying and crying for mercy in every part of the house, and many out of doors, and numbers could neither go nor stand. Their concern was so great, each one for himself, that none seemed to take notice of those about them, but each prayed freely for himself.[20]*

David was awestruck as he witnessed the work of God upon the hearts of the men, women, and children gathered. A witchdoctor in attendance, who had been found guilty of murder, was there weeping, wailing, and calling out for God's mercy. A woman who had earlier in the day mocked Brainerd now lay prostrate on the ground praying. She continued in this position for hours.

The revival continued the next day as David preached from Matthew 12 on the Parable of the Sower to a larger crowd. Again, many of the men and women in attendance were struck with anguished concern for their souls. He wrote, "I spoke not a word of terror, but on the contrary, set before them the fullness and all sufficiency of Christ's merits, and His willingness to save all that came to Him."[21] The cry went up, one after another, "Guttummaukalummeh!! guttummaukalummeh!! [Have mercy on me! Have mercy on me!]" Instantly the missionary could see a change of heart and life with the Indians. In his diary he testifies that no human cause was employed to bring this about. He had not changed his delivery style. No emotional manipulation was used at the meetings. Rather, Brainerd writes, "God's manner of working upon them appeared so entirely supernatural, and above means, that I could scarce believe He used me as an instrument . . . for it seemed, as I thought, to have no connection with nor dependence upon means in any respect."[22]

The awakening among the Native Americans did not seem to have much of an influence on the white settlers in the area. Brainerd noted that they behaved themselves "more indecently than any Indians I ever addressed." Yet the revival continued among the Crossweeksung Indians. Even the tribes up at the Forks of the Delaware were affected by the revivals.

Brainerd took the 120-mile journey on horseback back down to the Susquehanna in early September 1745. The gospel message was once again soundly rejected by these tribes. Returning to the Crossweeksung tribes in the Trenton, New Jersey area, David resumed his preaching. It was plain that the Holy Spirit was working a very tremendous work of grace there. On Sunday, October 6, 1745, David preached three times and the natives continued in prayer for an additional two hours that evening. Then, on November 3, Brainerd baptized fourteen natives—six adults and eight children. Two of the men baptized had been "singular and remarkable, even among the Indians, for their wickedness."[23] This brought the total number of baptisms to forty-seven. All were exhibiting fruits of repentance—at least three marriages were restored. [24] Family prayers or family devotions were now common among the Indians, an indication that the Gospel had really penetrated. This was indeed the work of the mighty Spirit of God. Several of these young converts became evangelists, traveling back up to the Forks with David to bring the good news of salvation to others. Real spiritual fruit was evident in their lives, as David wrote:

I know of no assembly of Christians where there seems to be so much of the presence of God, where brotherly love so much prevails and where I should take so much delight in the public worship of God, in general, as in my own congregation;

although not more than nine months ago they were worshipping devils and dumb
idols under the power of darkness and superstition! Amazing change this! Effected
by nothing less than divine power and grace![25]

After the services the native people would crowd into his little cottage, where they continued to sing and speak of spiritual matters for hours on end.

It is estimated that 120 converts came from Brainerd's ministry during the year of the Holy Spirit's outpouring (1745-1746)—the same number that gathered in the Upper Room in Jerusalem some 1,700 years earlier. The new congregation of the body of Christ received their first communion on April 27, 1746. Before taking the Lord's Supper, the new believers gathered to hear sermons on Friday and Saturday. During these services, both men and women renewed their commitment to God, renounced their previous idolatries and superstitions, and committed to walking together in love. Later that year, they formed a new Christian community near Cranbury, New Jersey, away from the pagan influences of their previous associations.

Last Days

On August 12, 1746, David Brainerd set out on a journey into the hinterlands of Pennsylvania. It would be his last excursion into Indian country. First the team traveled into the Susquehanna valley to preach the Gospel. Then David insisted that they should press into Shawnee territory in central Pennsylvania. It was a 200-mile journey, in which David continued coughing up blood along the way. His tuberculosis was advancing into its final stages. Although meeting with a few white settlers and traders along the way, David found more fellowship with his Christian Indian family. They sang psalms, prayed together, and shared God's Word throughout the thirty-nine day journey. Although the tribes they met with were resistant to the Gospel, sufficient seeds were planted for future harvest.

Upon returning, David's health had deteriorated to such an extent that he was constrained to preach to his Indians at Crossweeksung while sitting down. On March 20, 1747, he left his little church for the last time and made his way up to Jonathan Edwards' home in Northampton, Massachusetts. Hoping to recover his health by medical means, he proceeded to Boston in the company of Edwards' seventeen-year-old daughter, Jerusha. Upon reaching Boston, David's health collapsed completely, and he was "brought to the very gates of death" (Ps. 107:18).

Experienced doctors attended to his health while Jerusha cared for him at the home of Edward Bromfield, a member of the Old South Church. Jerusha wrote home that, "Doctor Pynchon says he has no hopes of his life; nor does he think it likely he will ever come out of the chamber."[26] However, David did recover temporarily and returned to Jonathan Edwards' home in Northampton. While Edwards was off on a ministry trip, David Brainerd led family worship on August 20, 1747. But that was the last time he was able to leave his bed. Three days later his brother John Brainerd came to visit and reported on the spiritual growth of the church in Crossweeksung. Thirty new members had been added, producing a total of 160 members in the work since the first outpouring of the Holy Spirit exactly two years earlier.

For several more months, David suffered greatly from tuberculosis. On October 2 he made a final entry in his diary: "My soul was this day, at turns, sweetly set on God: I longed to be with Him that I might 'behold His glory' (John 17:24); I felt sweetly disposed to commit all to Him, even my dearest friends, my dearest flock, and my absent brother, and all my concerns for time and eternity . . . Oh, 'come, Lord Jesus, come quickly! Amen' (Rev. 22:20)."[27] After one last conversation with his brother about his Indian congregation in New Jersey, David slipped into eternity at six o'clock in the morning on October 9, 1747. He was buried in the Northampton Church graveyard.

Jonathan Edward's daughter Jerusha had faithfully cared for David through his final months. Edwards commended his daughter as one who had "much the same spirit with Mr. Brainerd. She had constantly taken care of, and tended him in his sickness, for nineteen weeks before his death; devoting herself to it with great delight, because she looked on him as an eminent servant of Jesus Christ. In this time he had much conversation with her on things of religion; and in his dying state, often expressed to us, her parents, his great satisfaction concerning her true piety, and his confidence that he would meet her in heaven."[28]

Jerusha and David were truly kindred spirits. Shortly after his death she contracted tuberculosis and died just four months later. She was buried in the Northampton Church graveyard, next to the man she had loved and cared for.

Lessons and Legacy

Thus, after only five years of ministry, David Brainerd died at the young age of twenty-nine. Yet, despite his young age and the few short years he gave to preaching, he still had a vast impact on generations of future missionaries. This came mainly through the publication of his diary and journal by Jonathan Edwards who dedicated himself to preserving the legacy of his young missionary friend.

Undoubtedly, Brainerd's greatest contribution to Christian history was his diary. Because he never expected it to be printed or read, his diary entries were penned with unbridled passion and brutal honesty. More than anything, it was David's humility that enabled him to have such great inroads in his ministry to the Indians. Throughout his entire ministry David was regularly overwhelmed by a sense of his own sinfulness. He would even become reluctant to preach. At one point he wrote, "I was so pressed with the blackness of my nature that I thought it was not fit for me to speak so much as to Indians."[29] Here indeed is a man qualified to preach to sinners—a sinner sensitive to his own sin and his own need for grace!

Throughout the diary, we find David Brainerd expressing his heart-passion for souls, "I care not where I go, or how I live, or what I endure so that I may save souls. When I sleep, I dream of them; when I awake, they are the first on my thoughts."[30] Perhaps the greatest miracle of all, David's compassion and love for the men and women of these tribes grew throughout his ministry. One of his first converts among the Delaware Indians later told her grandchildren of her impressions of this missionary, calling him the "first white man she could ever love." The grandchild testified, "She loved David Brainerd very much because he loved his heavenly Father so much that he was willing to endure hardships, traveling over mountains, suffering hunger, and lying on the ground that he might do her people good."[31]

Above all, David Brainerd will be known for his generosity and sacrificial living throughout. Clearly, he was willing to give everything up for the ministry. As long as he wasn't coughing up blood or lying sick in bed, he was at work preaching. Every minute of his life seemed to be dedicated to sacrifice, prayer, confession, or preaching. He gave up his inheritance to help a friend pay for his education at Yale College, despite the fact that David himself had been expelled from the same school. To support John Sergeant's ministry with the Indians in Stockbridge, Brainerd contributed out of his own pitiful resources. In a letter to Sergeant, David wrote, "I sold my tea kettle to Mr. Jo. Woodbridge, and an iron kettle to Mr. Timothy Woodbridge, both amounted to something more than four pounds, which I ordered them to pay to you for the school."[32] Some lay up a little treasure for heaven and some put virtually all of it upon the heavenly investment. The latter approach was what David Brainerd took.

> *Do not lay up for yourselves treasures on earth, where moth and rust destroy and where thieves break in and steal; but lay up for yourselves treasures in heaven, where neither moth nor rust destroys and where thieves do not break in and steal. For where your treasure is, there your heart will be also. (Matthew 6:19-21)*

In more ways than one, David Brainerd lived a dangerous life. He sensitized himself to the deepest and most convicting truths of God's Word. He threw himself wholeheartedly into difficult ministry, life-threatening journeys, and pioneering mission work with the Indians. Often he operated alone. He addressed the spiritual conflict alone—only dependent on the presence of the Savior in his courageous exploits. Well could he say at the end:

> *I have fought the good fight, I have finished the race, I have kept the faith. Finally, there is laid up for me the crown of righteousness, which the Lord, the righteous Judge, will give to me on that Day, and not to me only but also to all who have loved His appearing. (2 Timothy 4:7-8)*

Jonathan Edwards (1703-1758)

CHAPTER 7

Jonathan Edwards:
A Passion for God's Glory

*I am the LORD, that is My name; and My glory I
will not give to another, nor My praise to carved
images.*

—Isaiah 42:8

Today, Jonathan Edwards is best known for his famous sermon "Sinners in the Hands of an Angry God," still widely studied as an American classic in high school and college literature classes. In most cases, it is considered more of a historical oddity, an anachronism from a bygone era that could have no possible relevance to the present. However, this sermon was truly a passionate call to sinners to repent and find mercy in the Lord Jesus Christ. Though Jonathan Edwards is still much respected as an American theologian, the message he proclaimed to his generation is hardly taken seriously today. Yet, Pastor Edwards' sermon from 1741 still offers a sober and relevant message to those left in America who fear God and realize His judgment is more imminent today than it was 250 years ago. Jonathan Edwards is remembered as one of the most influential preachers in American history, but there is much more to his life than just a single sermon. Edwards' copious writings help us to know the Scriptures better, to know God, and to serve Him with reverence and godly fear.

In the early 1900s, a study was conducted to trace the various descendants of Jonathan Edwards in America. Jonathan and Sarah Edwards' descendants included "three hundred clergymen, missionaries, and theological professors; 120 college professors; 110 lawyers; more than sixty physicians; more than sixty authors of good books; thirty judges; fourteen presidents of universities; numerous giants in American industry; eighty holders of major public office; three mayors of large cities; three governors of states; three US senators; one chaplain of the US Senate . . . and one vice president of the United States."[1] Edwards' life clearly played an important part in the providentially directed history of America and the world. Though he could claim many influential descendants by physical descent, he also has many more spiritual children that profited greatly by his writings and faith. Christians today continue to find his writings to be uniquely edifying. Jonathan's life-passion for the glory of God is a fire that must be rekindled in today's generation of Christ's followers.

Early Years and Education in New Haven

But you must continue in the things which you have learned and been assured of, knowing from whom you have learned them, and that from childhood you have known the Holy Scriptures, which are able to make you wise for salvation through faith which is in Christ Jesus. (2 Timothy 3:14-15)

Jonathan was born into a family of pastors on October 5, 1703. His father, Timothy Edwards, was pastor of the church in East Windsor, Connecticut. Jonathan's mother, Esther Stoddard, was the daughter of Solomon Stoddard, an influential pastor in the Connecticut River Valley, serving the Northampton Congregational church for almost sixty years. Young Jonathan grew up surrounded by Christian ministry still bearing remnants of the old Puritan heritage in New England. He drank deeply from the well of Scripture as he was raised in a Christian home. From an early age, his father catechized him in

View of the Connecticut River, which travels through Northampton, Massachusetts

the Westminster Shorter Catechism and provided him with robust theological foundations. As was customary for the New England Puritans, Jonathan recorded a date for his conversion at seventeen years of age.

Jonathan Edwards recorded details concerning his spiritual awakening. As he meditated deeply upon 1 Timothy 1:17, it was then that he saw the glory of God as real.

> *Now to the King eternal, immortal, invisible, to God who alone is wise, be honor and glory forever and ever. Amen. (1 Timothy 1:17)*

Jonathan writes of the experience: "there came into my soul, and was as it were diffused through it, a sense of the glory of the Divine Being; a new sense, quite different from any thing I ever experienced before . . . From about that time, I began to have a new kind of apprehensions and ideas of Christ, and the work of redemption, and the glorious way of salvation by Him."[2] In these words Jonathan testified that the glory of God captured his heart and that he believed the truths of the gospel to the saving of his soul. It was this sense of God's glory that captured Jonathan's imagination throughout his life, and became the bedrock of his preaching and writing.

At age thirteen Jonathan entered the Collegiate School of Connecticut (later renamed Yale University). This new school in New Haven, Connecticut was formed as an alternative institution to Harvard, which had already begun to drift from orthodox theology towards liberalism. The founders of the Collegiate School set forth the original vision of the institution in these words: "Everyone shall consider the main end of his life and studies to know God in Jesus Christ."[3] Each student received a copy of the "Orders and Appointments" when they entered the college. This document served as a general code of conduct for the students. Requirements for the students included the following:

> *Every student shall exercise himself in reading Holy Scriptures by himself every day that the word of Christ may dwell in him richly . . . All students shall avoid the profanation of God's holy name, attributes, Word and ordinances and the Holy Sabbath, and shall carefully attend all public assemblies for divine worship . . . All undergraduates shall publicly repeat sermons in the hall in their course, and also bachelors, and be constantly examined on Sabbaths at evening prayer.[4]*

While at college Jonathan Edwards received an education in a large variety of subjects including grammar, history, arithmetic, astronomy, ethics, literature, Greek, Hebrew, and more. He graduated with a bachelor's degree in 1720 and then began pursuing a master's degree. Although he eventually became a pastor, Jonathan possessed a keen interest in the natural sciences. Within the physical world of creation, Jonathan observed God's glory on display. For him, the study of the natural world was an important way to witness and proclaim the glory of God. One of his earliest writings on record is a report written to the Royal Society of London in 1723. Jonathan hoped that this communication would be published as a scientific paper in the Society's publication, *Philosophical Transactions*.

In the report provided in the form of a letter, Jonathan explained some of his investigations into God's creation, noting, "They are some things that I have happily seen of the wondrous and curious works of the spider."[5] Jonathan explained how the intricate and mysterious movements of the flying spider reveal God's glory and wisdom. He noted a sort of pleasure of movement visible in the spider's motions because it moved so freely and gracefully, writing, "Hence the exuberant goodness of the Creator [is visible], who hath not only provided for all the necessities, but also for the pleasure and recreation of all sorts of creatures, even the insects."[6] Indeed, Jonathan understood that the flying spider was just one of many examples in which "the wisdom of the Creator shines."[7] Even in his later years he retained an interest in the sciences, often recording his observations on the natural world in his journals.

The Resolutions

> *But reject profane and old wives' fables, and exercise yourself toward godliness. For bodily exercise profits a little, but godliness is profitable for all things, having promise of the life that now is and of that which is to come. (1 Timothy 4:7-8)*

Upon completion of his master's program in college, Jonathan Edwards accepted a request from a Presbyterian church in New York City to serve as an interim pastor. He was only 18 years of age. Between 1722 and 1723, he preached his earliest sermons at the First Presbyterian Church in New York City, located on Wall Street. During this time in New York, the Lord was at work humbling him for his past sins. Jonathan wrote, "While I was there at New York, I sometimes was much affected with reflections on my past life, considering how late it was, before I began to be truly religious; and how wickedly I had lived till then: and once so as to weep abundantly, and for a considerable time together."[8]

Jonathan was grieved by his past sins, and this grief led to real repentance and godly action. He now dedicated himself to the pursuit of holiness. In order to hold himself accountable to this commitment, Jonathan wrote a number of personal resolutions. These resolutions guided him for the rest of his life. Occasionally he added to the list, eventually writing a total of seventy personal resolutions. Jonathan wrote these resolutions to be, "the guidelines, the system of checks and balances he would use to chart out his life—his relationships, his conversations, his desires, his activities."[9] During this time in colonial America, it was customary for people to write personal resolutions which would guide and direct their conduct in life. For example, Benjamin Franklin also wrote a series of personal resolutions.[10] However, Jonathan Edwards' resolutions were quite different from Franklin's, because they were God-centered, concerned first and foremost with the glory of God.

These resolutions, first written in his 18th year, would be commitments he would maintain for the rest of his life. Importantly, Jonathan realized that apart from the grace of God he could not keep his own resolutions, as his preface notes:

> *Being sensible that I am unable to do anything without God's help, I do humbly entreat him by his grace to enable me to keep these Resolutions, so far as they are agreeable to his will, for Christ's sake.*[11]

This thinking reflects the teaching of the Word concerning the basis for all spiritual growth in holiness:

> *I am the vine, you are the branches. He who abides in Me, and I in him, bears much fruit; for without Me you can do nothing. (John 15:5)*

> *Therefore, my beloved, as you have always obeyed, not as in my presence only, but now much more in my absence, work out your own salvation with fear and trembling; **for it is God who works in you both to will and to do for His good pleasure.** (Philippians 2:12-13, emphasis added)*

Following the preface, Jonathan's first resolution addressed the chief end of the Christian life—the glory of God.

> *1. Resolved, that I will do whatsoever I think to be most to God's glory, and my own good, profit and pleasure, in the whole of my duration, without any consideration of the time, whether now, or never so many myriads of ages hence. Resolved to do whatever I think to be my duty, and most for the good and advantage of mankind in general. Resolved to do this, whatever difficulties I meet with, how many and how great soever.*[12]

The resolutions that followed addressed prayer, the study of Scripture, use of time, acts of service, the defeat of sin, regular self-examination, and regulation of thought life. He leaves no rock unturned in his commitments. For Jonathan Edwards the pursuit of holiness must encompass every area of life. The glory of God is *the goal in everything we do*. As the Apostle Paul said:

> *Therefore, whether you eat or drink, or whatever you do, **do all** to the glory of God.* (1 Corinthians 10:31, emphasis added)

A sampling of the additional resolutions follow:

> *5. Resolved, never to lose one moment of time; but improve it the most profitable way I possibly can.*[13]

> *7. Resolved, never to do anything, which I should be afraid to do, if it were the last hour of my life.*[14]

> *13. Resolved, to be endeavoring to find out fit objects of charity and liberality.*[15]

> *17. Resolved, that I will live so as I shall wish I had done when I come to die.*[16]

> *28. Resolved, to study the Scriptures so steadily, constantly and frequently, as that I may find, and plainly perceive myself to grow in the knowledge of the same.*[17]

> *30. Resolved, to strive to my utmost every week to be brought higher in religion, and to a higher exercise of grace, than I was the week before.*[18]

> *56. Resolved, never to give over, nor in the least to slacken my fight with my corruptions [sins], however unsuccessful I may be.*[19]

Young Christian men and women would do well if they would study these resolutions and even adopt some of them or write new ones for themselves. Though Jonathan was not a perfect man, by the grace of God he continued to grow in godliness. The Word of God teaches the Christian to rely on the grace of God for personal growth in Christ-likeness, and at the same time, to diligently pursue holiness, without which no one will see the Lord (Heb. 12:14).

Marriage to Sarah Pierpont

He who finds a wife finds a good thing and obtains favor from the LORD. (Proverbs 18:22)

In 1724 Jonathan Edwards commenced a three-year courtship with Sarah Pierpont, the daughter of a pastor from New Haven, Connecticut. Between 1724 and 1727, he served as a tutor at Yale University. Then, in February 1727 he was called to serve as an associate pastor alongside his grandfather Solomon Stoddard in Northampton, Massachusetts. Since their pastor was aging (at 83 years of age), the congregation had recommended that he train a replacement. Around this time, Jonathan married seventeen-year-old Sarah Pierpont and they settled into a home in Northampton. The Lord would bless the couple with eleven children.

Although some have characterized Jonathan Edwards as a dour, unfriendly, or even an angry man, his marriage relationship with Sarah does not bear this out. Early on, while he was still working at Yale College, Jonathan recorded his reasons for his interest in this young woman.

> They say there is a young lady in [New Haven] who is beloved of that almighty Being, who made and rules the world, and that there are certain seasons in which this great Being, in some way or other invisible, comes to her and fills her mind with exceeding sweet delight, and that she hardly cares for anything, except to meditate on him.[20]

It was her godliness that drew Jonathan to this woman. When evangelist George Whitefield visited the Edwards home in later years, he recorded his impressions of their family life and of Sarah's graceful demeanor in particular.

> [I] felt wonderful satisfaction in being at the house of Mr. Edwards. He is a Son himself, and hath also a Daughter of Abraham for his wife. A sweeter couple I have not yet seen. Their children were dressed not in silks and satins, but plain, as becomes the children of those who, in all things ought to be examples of Christian simplicity. She is a woman adorned with a meek and quiet spirit, talked feelingly and solidly of the Things of God, and seemed to be such a help meet for her husband,

*that she caused me to renew those prayers, which, for many months, I have put up
to God, that he would be pleased to send me a daughter of Abraham to be my wife.*[21]

Whitefield was so affected by the beautiful relationship between Jonathan
and Sarah that he was inspired to seek out a wife for himself!

Pastoral Ministry in Northampton

*I charge you therefore before God and the Lord Jesus Christ, who will judge the
living and the dead at His appearing and His kingdom: Preach the word! Be ready
in season and out of season. Convince, rebuke, exhort, with all longsuffering and
teaching. (2 Timothy 4:1-2)*

In February 1729 Solomon Stoddard died, and Jonathan became the sole
pastor in the Congregational church at Northampton. Through the following
years, Jonathan developed into a gifted preacher of God's Word. The congregation
at Northampton was described as taking "great content in his ministry."[22] It was
during the 1730s that a mighty work of the Holy Spirit of God began to pick
up momentum in America. The awakening reached the town of Northampton
sometime in 1734. Jonathan recorded in his book, *A Faithful Narrative of the
Surprising Work of God*, how the Lord brought about a great change in the people
of the town. He was utterly convinced that such awakenings are only a product
of the sovereign work of the Spirit and they cannot be manufactured through
human methods.

Pastor Edwards wrote:

*There was scarcely a single person in the town, old or young, left unconcerned about
the great things of the eternal world. Those who were wont to be the vainest and
loosest, and those who had been disposed to think and speak lightly of vital and
experimental religion, were now generally subject to great awakenings. And the
work of conversion was carried on in a most astonishing manner, and increased
more and more; souls did as it were come by flocks to Jesus Christ. From day to
day for many months together, might be seen evident instances of sinners brought
out of darkness into marvelous light, and delivered out of an horrible pit, and*

from the miry clay, and set upon a rock, with a new song of praise to God in their mouths . . . In all companies, on other days, on whatever occasions persons met together, Christ was to be heard of, and seen in the midst of them. Our young people, when they met, were wont to spend the time in talking of the excellency and dying love of Jesus Christ.[23]

Jonathan rightly pointed to the glorification of the name of the Lord Jesus Christ as the prime indication of revival. Wherever repentance for sin and faith in the salvation of Jesus Christ proliferated, true spiritual revival was to be found.

The Years of the Great Awakening

Will You not revive us again, that Your people may rejoice in You? Show us Your mercy, LORD, and grant us Your salvation. (Psalm 85:6-7)

The years 1740-1745 were a time of spiritual awakening in the American colonies unlike any other. This period came to be known as the Great Awakening. As evangelists such as George Whitefield and John Wesley preached throughout Great Britain and North America, hundreds of thousands came to faith in Jesus Christ. Though Jonathan Edwards did not travel as far and wide as Whitefield or Wesley, he also participated in the dramatic events of the awakening. Like the bursting open of a dam, the spiritual revival that took hold of Northampton in 1734 and 1735 now returned. It was on Sunday, July 8, 1741, Jonathan made his most recognized contribution to American history when he preached his legendary sermon "Sinners in the Hands of an Angry God." Previously, Jonathan had preached the same sermon in Northampton with little effect upon the congregation. This time, he had been called to preach at Enfield, Connecticut, a town that had experienced little awakening to date. The sermon was based on the words of Deuteronomy 32:35:

Vengeance is Mine, and recompense; their foot shall slip in due time; for the day of their calamity is at hand, and the things to come hasten upon them.

From these words, first addressed to the children of Israel, Jonathan Edwards declared that it is only the power of God which restrains a sinner from falling immediately into the fires of hell. The following is an excerpt from the sermon:

> *[God] is not only able to cast wicked men into hell, but he can most easily do it. Sometimes an earthly prince meets with a great deal of difficulty to subdue a rebel, that has found means to fortify himself, and has made himself strong by the numbers of his followers. But it is not so with God. There is no fortress that is any defense from the power of God. Though hand join in hand, and vast multitudes of God's enemies combine and associate themselves, they are easily broken in pieces: they are as great heaps of light chaff before the whirlwind; or large quantities of dry stubble before devouring flames. We find it easy to tread on and crush a worm that we see crawling on the earth; so 'tis easy for us to cut or singe a slender thread that anything hangs by; thus easy is it for God when he pleases to cast his enemies down to hell. What are we, that we should think to stand before him, at whose rebuke the earth trembles, and before whom the rocks are thrown down?[24]*

The people at Enfield were deeply moved by the message. As Jonathan preached, people cried out audibly for God's mercy. The preacher motioned for the congregation to quiet down so that he could continue to deliver his message. However, the men, women, and children of Enfield were struck by the fear of God and sobered by the reality of divine judgment. Many fled for refuge to Jesus Christ that day as they contemplated the imminent reality of God's judgment.

Jonathan closed the sermon by pointing the people to the only way of escape: the Lord Jesus and His saving work.

> *And let everyone that is yet out of Christ, and hanging over the pit of hell, whether they be old men and women, or middle aged, or young people, or little children, now hearken to the loud calls of God's Word and providence. This acceptable year of the Lord, that is a day of such great favor to some, will doubtless be a day of as remarkable vengeance to others . . . Therefore let everyone that is out of Christ, now awake and fly from the wrath to come. The wrath of almighty God is now undoubtedly hanging over a great part of this congregation: let everyone fly out of Sodom. Haste and escape for your lives, look not behind you, escape to the mountain, lest you be consumed.[25]*

Not many Americans have a balanced view of Jonathan Edwards' preaching and ministry. While he would preach a strong message of warning concerning God's judgment on occasion, Edwards' preaching covered many other topics. His messages are full of the love of God, the beauty of Christ, the glories of heaven, and the joys of the Christian life.

Jonathan Edward's preaching was used mightily by God for spiritual reviving, but he, himself was also affected by the preaching of the Awakening. As George Whitefield preached to the congregation in Northampton, Jonathan sat with the congregation and wept with the rest of them.

While much spiritual fruit was produced out of the Great Awakening, there were also dangerous teachers active at the same time. In some places, fanaticism and extremism ran rampant. A certain Rev. James Davenport claimed that God revealed Himself directly by giving impressions to the mind. These impressions were interpreted by Davenport as infallible guidance from the Spirit, holding a greater authority than the Bible. When other ministers warned Davenport about his errors, he denounced them as unconverted men. While preaching in New London, Connecticut in March 1743, Davenport called the people to turn away from worldly things; this they must do by burning their possessions. These "worldly possessions" turned out to include decent Christian books, rings, necklaces, and cloaks.

Iain Murray writes:

> *Accordingly, it is alleged, he listed a number of items to be given up and committed to flames; they included cloaks, breeches, hoods, gowns, rings, jewels, and necklaces. This done, more subtle 'evils' were to be destroyed, namely, a number of religious books. On March 6 his followers carried a quantity of books – some of John Flavel's Works and other Puritan books among them – to a wharf where they were burned amidst songs of praise!*[26]

These fake revivals usually include man-made regulations, forbidding the use of certain things, as Paul speaks of in Colossians 2:20-23. They have an "appearance of wisdom in self-imposed religion." But in the end, they hold no real spiritual value.

Such examples of unbiblical and undiscerning extremism led Jonathan Edwards to think more deeply upon the Holy Spirit's real work. Amid such spiritual confusion Jonathan wanted his congregation to rightly distinguish between true Holy Spirit activity and counterfeits. To assist them, he wrote two major works that provided guidance: *The Distinguishing Marks of a Work of the Spirit of God* (1741) and *The Religious Affections* (1746). In *The Religious Affections* Jonathan used Scripture to define the true signs of spiritual life and to distinguish between true and false fruits of spiritual life. He recognized that not all emotions or affections are truly spiritual in nature, but he also insisted that true spiritual life will change our affections and mold them in such a way that we will truly love God. He wrote:

> *That religion which God requires, and will accept, does not consist in weak, dull and lifeless wouldings [wishes], raising us but a little above a state of indifference. God, in his word, greatly insists upon it, that we be in good earnest, fervent in spirit, and our hearts vigorously engaged in religion.*[27]

Edwards did not want dead orthodoxy or Christians that looked like the "frozen chosen." What he wanted was precisely what God's Word calls for in Romans 12:11.

> *Do not be slothful in zeal,* **be fervent in spirit,** *serve the Lord. (Romans 12:11 ESV, emphasis added)*

The Edwards home was a hospitable place, as the pastor would invite a great number of visitors to stay over with his family. In the late 1740s, the young missionary David Brainerd stayed with the Edwards family numerous times as he passed through the area. As Brainerd suffered long and hard with a fatal illness towards the end of his life, he stayed with the Edwards family for months. Jonathan's daughter Jerusha provided daily nursing care for the missionary until he died on October 9, 1747. Shortly thereafter, Jerusha Edwards also contracted the illness and died. Jonathan Edwards took Brainerd's diary, and created a biographical account of his life, entitled, *The Life and Diary of David Brainerd*. This work was published in 1749, and it would become an important inspiration for the Protestant missionary movement of the 19th and 20th centuries.

Dismissal from Northampton and Move to Stockbridge

For of Him and through Him and to Him are all things, to whom be glory forever. Amen. (Romans 11:36)

Jonathan Edward's study habits are well-known—one historian claiming he spent thirteen hours a day in his study.[28] He dedicated himself to the Word and prayer, preparing multiple sermons for his weekly preaching responsibilities. He believed that regular, diligent study of the Bible was an essential part of the minister's life.

Be diligent to present yourself approved to God, a worker who does not need to be ashamed, rightly dividing the word of truth. (2 Timothy 2:15)

Edwards wisely saw the need for times of solitude, study, meditation, and prayer. But these daily study habits eventually contributed to a growing rift between him and the members of the church. Some of the church members saw Jonathan as aloof and uninterested in relationships with others in the town. Biographer Iain Murray writes, "In the eyes of some, he dwelt apart as though he had no time for the common, everyday interests of his people. This certainly lent itself at the time ... to the charge that he was 'stiff and unsociable.'"[29] It was Jonathan's practice not to visit in the homes of families unless he was called for by the sick.[30] At the time, it was not common for New England for pastors to visit with members of the church in their homes on a regular basis. Nonetheless, this neglect eventually contributed to Jonathan Edward's dismissal from the Northampton church. The churches in New England also suffered from a lack of elders, and the church in Northampton was no exception to this.[31] The pastor often labored alone. This made faithful shepherding of the flock very difficult, especially if the pastor was dedicating much of his time to sermon preparation.

A disagreement over church practice also arose in Northampton, not an unusual circumstance in American church life. Jonathan's grandfather, Solomon Stoddard, allowed people to make a profession of faith in order to partake of the Lord's Supper even if their lives did not evidence any change. Stoddard believed that, even if someone was unconverted, the Lord's Supper could serve as a "converting ordinance." He thought perhaps that participants would come to faith through partaking of the Lord's Supper. Jonathan, on the other hand, held that the Scriptures require those partaking not only to make a profession of faith but also to show some evidence of true conversion in their lives. While he pastored the congregation, Jonathan sought to enforce this higher standard to the resistance of a large part of the church. In the end, the congregation called for the pastor's dismissal.

By this time, Edwards was a prominent preacher in the American colonies and he was also well-known in England and Scotland. Although he received invitations to pastorates in Boston and Scotland, Jonathan Edwards decided to become a pastor and missionary in the frontier settlement of Stockbridge, Massachusetts. This small outpost was located about forty miles west of Northampton. The village of Stockbridge was situated near the banks of the Housatonic River. There were only about seventeen homes and a small church building in the little village when Jonathan arrived in 1751.

Stockbridge was considered a frontier town, fairly isolated from much of the colony of Massachusetts. For six years Jonathan preached there to the Mohican and Mohawk Indians and the English settlers. Although Jonathan Edwards had become a leading theologian, here in Stockbridge he humbly served the natives by preaching the simply Gospel. His biographer, Iain Murray writes, "His surviving sermon notes reveal that he worked hard to adapt and simplify sermons for the Indians, dropping illustrations which he had used at Northampton and substituting others which were more familiar to their culture."[32]

Meanwhile, at Stockbridge Jonathan continued writing more books—some of his best. These works include *The Freedom of the Will, The End for Which God Created the World, True Virtue,* and *Original Sin.* In *The End for Which God Created the World,* Jonathan carefully considered a profound question: why did God create the universe? What is the purpose of all things? Jonathan's passion for the glory of God is found in all his writings, but in this book in particular Jonathan meditated with profound depth on his life's passion.

The End for Which God Created the World may be Jonathan Edwards' most difficult book. But the book is important because Edwards' seeks to answer one of the most fundamental questions of life: why did God create the world? In this book the word "end" means the "purpose" or "goal" of something. The answer to "the end" or "purpose" of all things, according to Scripture, is *the glory of God.* Edwards explains:

> *It is manifest that the Scriptures speak on all occasions as though God made himself his end in all his works, and as though the same being, who is the first cause of all things, were the supreme and last end of all things.*[33]

Final Days in Stockbridge and Princeton

The sting of death is sin, and the strength of sin is the law. But thanks be to God, who gives us the victory through our Lord Jesus Christ. (1 Corinthians 15:56-57)

Jonathan Edwards continued writing and preaching in Stockbridge for six years. By this time, he had become a well-respected teacher and theologian in the colonies. He declined an invitation to serve as the president of the College of New Jersey (later renamed Princeton University). Jonathan's son-in-law, Aaron Burr Sr., had been serving as president of the college but he had died unexpectedly on September 24, 1757. As the trustees of the college continued to pressure him to take up the post, Edwards finally accepted and he moved part of his family to Princeton, New Jersey in January 1758.

Jonathan's wife Sarah remained in Stockbridge through the winter. Little did they know that upon Jonathan's departure, they would never see each other again in this life. In March 1758 there was an outbreak of smallpox at Princeton. Jonathan chose to receive an inoculation, although the smallpox vaccine had just been recently developed, and many feared it was not safe. He contracted an infection from the inoculation and died on March 22, 1758. He was only fifty-four years old. At the time of his death, two of Jonathan's daughters were with him at Princeton. He spoke his final words to daughters Esther and Lucy, saying:

Mission house in Stockbridge, Massachusetts, built in 1742

It seems to me to be the will of God, that I must shortly leave you; therefore give my kindest love to my dear wife, and tell her, that the uncommon union, which has so long subsisted between us, has been of such a nature, as I trust is spiritual, and therefore will continue forever; and I hope she will be supported under so great a trial, and submit cheerfully to the will of God.[34]

When Sarah Edwards had received the news of her husband's death, she wrote to daughter Esther:

What shall I say? A holy and good God has covered us with a dark cloud. O that we may kiss the rod, and lay our hands on our mouths! The Lord has done it. He has made me adore his goodness, that we had him so long. But my God lives; and he has my heart. O what a legacy my husband, and your father, has left us! We are all given to God; and there I am, and love to be.[35]

The Legacy of Jonathan Edwards

Even those who reject the faith of Jonathan Edwards still see him as one of the most important figures of colonial American history. Yale University, where Jonathan once studied, has worked for decades to preserve and republish his many writings. There is good reason why Jonathan Edwards is considered so important in American history. He served as a pastor during the momentous years of the Great Awakening. His writings on the revival, both his records and his analysis, have helped future generations understand what happened in the 1740s. His many sermons continue to be read with profit by Christians in the present day. His many theological works on such topics as God's glory, original sin, free will, the nature of love, revival, and the purpose of creation are some of the most important works ever written in the history of Christ's church. Most significantly, it is Jonathan Edward's appreciation for and commitment to the glory of God which constitutes his greatest legacy left for believers here and around the world to this day.

May each of us resolve to pursue the glory of God as our primary purpose in life, following in the footsteps of this great man of God:

> *Resolved, never to do any manner of thing, whether in soul or body, less or more, but what tends to the glory of God; nor be, nor suffer it, if I can avoid it.*[36]

UNIT 2

Foundations of Faith (1760-1800)

In His days the righteous shall flourish and abundance of peace, until the moon is no more. He shall have dominion also from sea to sea, and from the River to the ends of the earth. Those who dwell in the wilderness will bow before Him, and His enemies will lick the dust. The kings of Tarshish and of the isles will bring presents; the kings of Sheba and Seba will offer gifts.

—Psalm 72:7-10

Through the ages some political leaders have bowed to the Lord Jesus Christ, and others have not. In American history, some leaders actually did acknowledge Christ as the Lord. Nevertheless, a ferocious battle of ideas raged hot in the 18th century. Two forces competed for the heart of America between 1760 and 1800—those with a commitment to the living Christ and those who were turning away from Him. Worldly philosophies of the Enlightenment were gaining ground in European and American colleges. America's leaders were turning towards Deism and Unitarianism. Deists did not want a God who was involved in this world, to whom they might be accountable. Unitarians rejected the doctrine of the Trinity and refused to teach the divine nature of Jesus Christ, the Son of God.

The Great Awakening still influenced America in the 1770s, however. Men like George Washington, Patrick Henry, and Samuel Adams were very much affected by a true Christian faith—and, from all indications, they died believing in Jesus Christ as Lord and Savior. Patrick Henry and Samuel Adams were the most influential American leaders from 1760 through 1775, when the War for Independence began. Then George Washington was the most important leader of America between 1775 and 1796. After Washington, with few exceptions, the American presidents through the 1860s did not acknowledge Jesus Christ as their Savior in public or private records. Many American leaders turned from Christ at the turn of the 19th century. They did not want to believe that He died on the cross to pay the price for their sins.

The American War for Independence was a response to Britain's attempt to gain increased centralized control over the colonies. Although the American colonists had been self-governing for 100-150 years prior to the war, the British Parliament gave way to the lure of power. They wanted America to share in the financing of European wars. Britain was jockeying with France in power struggles to control the world, and the conflict spread into America with the French and Indian War (1754-1763). Seeking to raise funds for war debts from the American colonies, the British Parliament introduced the Stamp Act, passed on March 22, 1765. It was a minor tax, only amounting to 60-70 cents. However, beginning with Patrick Henry's Stamp Act Resolutions in the Virginia House of Burgesses, the American colonies reacted with vehemence against these perceived injustices. This set the ball rolling for the issuance of the American Declaration of Independence in 1776 and the war that followed.

Between 1776 and 1789, America remained a Christian country. The governing Continental Congress issued official calls for days of repentance and fasting. In these official proclamations the Congress recognized biblical law as well as Christ's Lordship and kingdom. State constitutions also recognized the Christian God as Almighty (North Carolina, Delaware, Pennsylvania, Vermont,

New Jersey), the Supreme Being (Massachusetts), the Creator (Massachusetts), the Great Legislator of the Universe (Massachusetts), the Governor of the Universe (Pennsylvania, Vermont), and the inspirer of the Scriptures of the Old and New Testaments (South Carolina, Pennsylvania). The Connecticut constitution recognized Christ as Savior and Lord. In order to serve as a public official in Delaware, by the State Constitution of 1776, all public officials were required to take this oath: "I, A B, do profess faith in God the Father, and in Jesus Christ His only Son, and in the Holy Ghost, one God, blessed for evermore; and I do acknowledge the Holy Scriptures of the Old and New Testaments to be given by divine inspiration."

This would change in 1789 after the ratification of the United States Constitution. America turned away from its commitment to Christ as Lord over the nation. Every nation recognizes an ultimate authority over its laws and people. This ultimate authority reveals a nation's faith and worldview. After 1789, America would turn from the Christian faith and the rule of God's law to embrace secularism. Less and less, America's leaders acknowledged the God of the Bible as the ultimate authority over the country. Instead of acknowledging God from the outset, the US Constitution began with "We the people." Over the centuries that followed, America fell prey to the false religion of *vox populi vox dei*, "the voice of the people is the voice of God." The nation and its government were established "for the people" and no longer for the glory of Jesus Christ and for service to the only true and living God.

> *Thus says the LORD: "Cursed is the man who trusts in man*
> *And makes flesh his strength,*
> *Whose heart departs from the LORD.*
> *For he shall be like a shrub in the desert,*
> *And shall not see when good comes,*
> *But shall inhabit the parched places in the wilderness,*
> *In a salt land which is not inhabited.*
> *Blessed is the man who trusts in the LORD,*
> *And whose hope is the LORD.*
> *(Jeremiah 17:5-7)*

Timeline of Important Events

1754-1763	The French and Indian War is fought in North America.
March 22, 1765	The British Parliament passes the Stamp Act.
March 5, 1770	British troops fire on an angry crowd in Boston ("The Boston Massacre").
December 16, 1773	The "Boston Tea Party" takes place at Boston Harbor.
July 4, 1776	The United States declares its Independence from Britain (by approving the Declaration of Independence).
September 19, 1777	American forces win the 1st Battle of Saratoga.
November 5, 1781	John Hanson is elected the first President of the Confederation Congress under the Articles of Confederation.
September 3, 1783	The Treaty of Paris is signed by Britain and the United States, officially ending the War for Independence.
September 28, 1787	Confederation Congress sends the new Constitution to the states for ratification.
April 30, 1789	George Washington is sworn in as the first US President under the Constitution.
September 25, 1789	The United States Congress adopts the Bill of Rights and refers it to the states for ratification.
December 5, 1792	George Washington is re-elected president of the United States.
November 3, 1796	John Adams is elected the second US President under the Constitution.
December 12, 1800	Washington, DC becomes the official capital of the US.

Patrick Henry (1736-1799)

CHAPTER 8

Patrick Henry:
Lighting the Flame for Liberty

The wicked flee when no one pursues, but the righteous are bold as a lion. Because of the transgression of a land, many are its princes; but by a man of understanding and knowledge right will be prolonged.

—Proverbs 28:1-2

For over a hundred years, the respective governments of each of the thirteen British colonies in America were duly elected legislatures. They had been self-governing from the beginning, according to charters provided by the English king. In fact, the first legislative assembly in America met in Jamestown, Virginia in 1619.

However, as America's colonies were governing themselves, Britain was giving in to empire-building fever. Threats to American self-rule dated back to the 1690s when Increase Mather crossed the ocean in hopes of securing a new and better charter from King William for Massachusetts. The quest for power and the centralization of power are what drive the formation of empires. Inevitably, this results in wars between powerful nations competing for that power. These wars cost money and are generally financed by taxes. During the 18th century, the French Empire had reached its zenith, and the British Empire was just developing. These European power struggles spilled over into the colonies. The argument between the French Canadians and the English was over control of the Ohio River Valley and the associated trade routes. As the contention escalated, the French, allied with certain Indian tribes, fought the English, allied with the American colonists and other Indian allies. The French and Indian War turned out to be an especially costly, lengthy affair, lasting from 1754 to 1763.

In order to help pay the bills for the war, the British Parliament tried several legislative initiatives to levy direct taxation on the American colonists. These taxes were imposed without approval from the colonial legislatures (which were made up of leaders elected by the settlers). Parliament also chose to enact legislation that would further restrict the colonies' economic and political well-being. These measures were viewed as tyrannical impositions by the colonists. They regarded the actions taken by Parliament as a violation of their charters, and the colonial governments felt bound to protect the liberties of their people.

The Early Years of Patrick Henry

I thank God . . . when I call to remembrance the genuine faith that is in you, which dwelt first in your grandmother Lois and your mother Eunice, and I am persuaded is in you also. (2 Timothy 1:3,5)

Patrick Henry was born in Hanover County, Virginia on May 29, 1736. He attended a local school for a few months until his father pulled him out to homeschool him. His father John, an Anglican by church affiliation, was not much of a spiritual example for Patrick. However, his mother Sarah was a Presbyterian and strongly committed to passing on the faith to her son. In his twelfth year, Patrick's mother began taking him to hear Samuel Davies preach at the Fork Church in the town of Ashland. For the next twelve years, Patrick would hear this powerful Presbyterian preacher deliver the Word of God. As the family traveled back home on Sunday afternoons, young Patrick would recite portions of the message for his mother and sisters. Due largely to Pastor Davies' ministry, Hanover County became the epicenter of the Great Awakening in Virginia. Later in life Patrick Henry referred to Davies as "the greatest speaker" he ever heard.[1]

John Henry ended his rather slipshod homeschool program in Patrick's fifteenth year, and then financed a country store for Patrick and his elder brother William.

Samuel Davies

Within a few years the brothers managed to run the store into the ground by allowing too many of the patrons to purchase goods on loan. While working the store, Patrick married fifteen-year-old Sarah Shelton (in October 1754). He also tried his hand at farming, but his home burned down and the crops yielded a poor harvest that year. Then in 1758 he again tried running a country store, and once more the business failed.

At twenty-four years of age (in 1760), Patrick borrowed three law texts from a friend, and within six weeks he was ready for the bar exam. He traveled fifty miles to Williamsburg, where he was examined by three members of the Virginia House of Burgesses. Two of the men signed off on his exam, but the third, John Randolph, was turned off by Patrick's country clothing and rough appearance. After examining the candidate, however, Randolph was forced to admit, "You defend your opinions well, sir. I will never trust to appearances again. Mr. Henry, if your industry be only half equal to your genius, I augur that you will do well and become an ornament and an honor to your profession."[2] Henry passed the bar and opened a law practice in Hanover County.

Patrick Henry loved to hunt and fish, typically alone. When working as a country lawyer, he often showed up at the courthouse with "a brace of ducks across his saddle and his blood-stained leather hunting jacket still upon his back."[3]

The Parson's Cause

A bishop then must be blameless . . . not given to wine, not violent, not greedy for money, but gentle, not quarrelsome, not covetous. (1 Timothy 3:2-3)

It was December 1, 1763 when Patrick Henry took on his most celebrated legal case. At that time the Anglican Church of Virginia was supported by taxes as the official state church. In Virginia the farmers were assessed in tobacco, 16,000 pounds for each Anglican minister. However, the Virginia House of Burgesses extended mercy to the farmers during the years 1755 to 1758 because the crop yields were low, and the parsons therefore only received about one third of their normal income. The parsons sued the farmers and won on the grounds that the King of England had never approved the exemption made by the Virginia government. After this victory, a further trial was convened so that a jury could determine the amount of damages due the parsons.

Patrick Henry took up the cause of the farmers. As he walked into the Hanover County Courthouse, the man sitting on the bench to adjudicate the case was his own father, John Henry. As the young lawyer rose to defend his clients, his rhetoric "made their blood to run cold, and their hair to rise on end."[4] His father was said to have wept through his son's impassioned speech. Patrick's basic argument was that all English citizens, according to English constitutional law, should have the right to taxation with their own representation. That is, no taxation may come to a people through a governmental body not elected by the same people. To violate this principle was akin to tyranny. As he spoke these words, some in the courtroom cried out, "Treason! Treason!" Patrick Henry ignored the interruption and continued presenting his case.

Instead of complying with the previous court's decision to require the farmers to pay the back taxes, Henry went on the offensive. He told the jury it was the pastors who ought to have been punished.

> Do [these reverend clergy] manifest their zeal in the cause of religion and humanity by practicing the mild and benevolent precepts of Jesus? Do they feed the hungry and clothe the naked? Oh no, gentlemen! Instead of feeding the hungry and clothing the naked, these rapacious harpies would, were their powers equal to their will, snatch from the hearth of their honest parishioner his last hoe-cake, from the widow and her orphan children, their last milch cow.[5]

In this well-placed rebuke, Patrick Henry rightly pointed out that these bishops should never have sued for their money. They were too given to covetousness, in direct violation of the requirements for pastors found in 1 Timothy 3.

The young lawyer encouraged the jury to respect the previous court's ruling, but only to award damages of one penny for the clergy. In the end, the jury was persuaded by Henry's arguments. This was the case that established Patrick Henry's reputation, and it wasn't long before he had become a household name in Virginia.

The Struggle for Independence

> Like a roaring lion and a charging bear is a wicked ruler over poor people. A ruler who lacks understanding is a great oppressor, but he who hates covetousness will prolong his days. (Proverbs 28:15-16)

It was May 1765 and all eyes were on Virginia, the oldest, most populated and most prosperous of all the American colonies. Just months earlier the British Parliament had passed the Stamp Act, which levied a tax on official documents printed in the colonies. The Virginia House of Burgesses held a legislative session to consider the Act.

The young lawyer rode into Williamsburg to serve as a representative in the

House of Burgesses. He had already made a name for himself at the Hanover County Courthouse two years earlier when he had successfully argued against the Parson's Cause. It was still the principle of taxation without representation that concerned Patrick Henry. The noose of tyranny was tightening, and this freedom-lover of Scotch-Irish heritage did not like it. For much of his youth he had taken to heart the fiery preaching of the famed Presbyterian preacher Samuel Davies. His veins ran with a passion for truth, freedom, and justice as defined by God, not man.

Young Patrick waited until the end of the session, and then moved his resolutions on May 30, 1765. These would become known around the world as the "Stamp Act Resolutions." Henry proceeded in his characteristic manner to defend the resolutions with impassioned zeal and fiery rhetoric. He never kept notes of his speeches, and the only fragment left of this speech was stored in the memory of those who heard it. Patrick ended with these final words: "Caesar had his Brutus, Charles the First his Cromwell, and George the Third—" Henry was here interrupted by shouts of "Treason! Treason!" He finished calmly "—may profit by their example. If this be treason, make the most of it."[6]

It was a moment that shifted the direction of human history—a true David and Goliath moment. One young man was inquiring into the right of the uncircumcised Philistine to defy the law of liberty that God had declared. He was challenging an empire, as he had done with the Parson's Cause. But this time it was in the presence of the most influential leaders in the colony. The passionate rhetoric by which Patrick defended his resolutions persuaded the men in the room to commit themselves to the cause of liberty. Eyewitness Paul Carrington described Henry's eloquence as "beyond my powers of description."[7] At the end of the day, five of the resolutions passed the house.

The next day he mounted his horse and returned to his family and his fields, not bothering to stay around to witness the effects of his resolutions. However, historians still look upon this event as one of the definitive moments in the history of America. Historian Cabell Rives comments:

By his ever memorable resolutions in opposition to the Stamp Act, and the lofty eloquence with which he sustained them, he struck a timely blow which resounded throughout America and the whole world, and roused a spirit that never slumbered till its great work was accomplished. The moment was opportune and critical, and he seized it with a bold and felicitous energy that belonged to his ardent and impassioned nature.[8]

Like Samuel Adams in New England, not another person in Virginia had quite the courage or the foresight to issue such resolutions. Other important leaders were waiting in the wings but lacked the boldness and the vision for liberty of Samuel Adams and Patrick Henry. Over the course of subsequent months, the governments of the other colonies followed suit and produced similar resolutions. Unbeknownst to him, Patrick Henry had managed to topple the first major domino in a sequence of events that would lead to America's independence. In the providence of our sovereign God, He used one man at one moment in time to change the course of history.

But this was not the end of Patrick Henry's contributions to the cause of liberty. The second pivotal event in Virginia's (and America's) road to independence occurred in 1775. The Second Virginia Convention of the Virginia House of Burgesses assembled secretly at St. John's Church in Richmond, to avoid immediate retaliation from royal Governor Dunmore in Williamsburg. The Governor had already confiscated the colonial munitions from the city armory. Tensions were high. Representatives from each of Virginia's counties crowded into the church (the largest building in Richmond at that time). The question before the assembly was whether or not to create a militia. Once again, it was Patrick Henry who moved the resolution, seconded by Richard Henry Lee. After the chairman, Peyton Randolph, entertained several arguments contrary to it from several commissioners, Patrick Henry took the stand and delivered a speech in defense of his resolution. He ended with the words:

If we wish to be free, if we mean to preserve inviolate those inestimable privileges for which we have been so long contending, if we mean not basely to abandon the noble struggle in which we have been so long engaged, and which we have pledged ourselves never to abandon until the glorious object of our contest shall be obtained, we must fight! I repeat it, sir, we must fight! An appeal to arms and to the God of Hosts is all that is left us!

They tell us, sir, that we are weak—unable to cope with so formidable an adversary. But when shall we be stronger? Will it be the next week, or the next year? Will it be when we are totally disarmed, and when a British guard shall be stationed in every house? Shall we gather strength by irresolution and inaction? Shall we acquire the means of effectual resistance, by lying supinely on our backs, and hugging the delusive phantom of hope, until our enemies shall have bound us hand and foot? Sir, we are not weak if we make a proper use of those means which the God of nature hath placed in our power. Three millions of people, armed in the holy cause of liberty, and in such a country as that which we possess, are invincible by any force which our enemy can send against us.

Besides, sir, we shall not fight our battles alone. There is a just God who presides over the destinies of nations; and who will raise up friends to fight our battles for us. The battle, sir, is not to the strong alone; it is to the vigilant, the active, the brave. Besides, sir, we have no [choice]. If we were base enough to desire it, it is now too late to retire from the contest. There is no retreat but in submission and slavery! Our chains are forged! Their clanking may be heard on the plains of Boston! The war is inevitable and let it come! I repeat it, sir, let it come.

It is in vain, sir, to extenuate the matter. Gentlemen may cry, "Peace, Peace" but there is no peace. The war is actually begun! The next gale that sweeps from the north will bring to our ears the clash of resounding arms! Our brethren are already in the field! Why stand we here idle? What is it that gentlemen wish? What would they have? Is life so dear, or peace so sweet, as to be purchased at the price of chains and slavery? Forbid it, Almighty God! I know not what course others may take; but as for me, give me liberty or give me death![9]

The colonial leaders gathered were stunned by these passionate, persuasive, and determined words issued by this man who loved liberty so much. No further speech was offered or solicited on the floor. The motion to form a militia was put

St. John's Church, Richmond, Virginia

to a vote and narrowly passed. A committee was organized with Patrick Henry as its chair. With that, Virginia committed itself to the fight for independence. Henry's famous words also inspired a nation. Words carry more force than bullets, and his words fired the American Patriots to engage the struggle for independence.

Patrick Henry took his position as head of the committee to organize a state militia seriously. When Governor Dunmore confiscated the gunpowder stored in a public magazine in Williamsburg, Patrick Henry collected 5,000 men and marched towards the town. The Governor finally backed down and offered to provide 330 pounds in compensation for the gunpowder he had stolen.

Patrick Henry was later appointed a delegate to the First and Second Continental Congress. With Samuel Adams, he played the most influential role in pressing the nation towards independence. He was elected to serve as Virginia's first independent governor and took office on July 5, 1776. For the next three years he was the key political leader in the state of Virginia. He returned to office between 1784 and 1786, serving a total of five years in the state's top office.

The Governor's Palace, Williamsburg, Virginia

The Christian Legacy of Liberty

If there were two critical moments in Virginia's history that paved the way for the American War for Independence, they were the Virginia Stamp Act Resolutions of 1765 and the Second Virginia Convention of 1775. Without question, Patrick Henry was the major player in both instances. But why this man? How do Patrick Henry and other Founding Fathers differ from the humanist revolutionaries such as Robespierre, Lenin, or Mao Zedong? Why did Americans enjoy great liberty after their War for Independence while the French, Russians, and Chinese suffered terrible tyranny after their revolutions? The difference may attributed to several factors.

1. Patrick Henry loved liberty, and he thoroughly despised big-government tyranny. He did not see government as the solution to problems. Rather, it was governments which refused to restrict themselves to the bounds of God's law that were the problem. It is hard to find any Founding Father who was as excited about liberty and defended it with as much ardor as Henry. He would rather

have died than be enslaved by the rising tyranny of the British Parliament. He knew that civil governments were necessary but believed they should be small and their power should be limited. Some have questioned whether the American War for Independence was a just war. Much has been written on the matter, but a few arguments will suffice for the purposes of this treatment.

First, the colonies were governed by their own elected civil magistrates. They understood the biblical doctrine of interposition defended by John Calvin and Samuel Rutherford, in which lower magistrates are responsible for defending the liberties of the people when those liberties are threatened by a higher magistrate. This doctrine would teach that all are subject to God's law and the laws of the land, including the higher magistrate. When any magistrate rejects the laws, that government has become revolutionary and unlawful, and lower magistrates would then have the duty to resist that tyranny and restore lawful government. The British government was deemed guilty of such tyranny by the colonials. By its parliamentary actions such as taxing without representation, the British government had acted in violation of the constitutional rights of British citizens as guaranteed by constitutional documents such as the Magna Carta and the colonial charters. The colonial magistrates therefore felt justified in resisting the tyranny, and going to war for liberty and independence.

Second, Patrick Henry also realized that given the united support of the colonial legislatures, victory was achievable. In the words of Christ, a king must count the cost before taking on an invading force (Luke 14:31). Henry really believed that the American colonies were able, with their three million colonials "armed in the holy cause of liberty," to confront the armies of Great Britain.

2. Throughout his political career, Patrick Henry successfully resisted the lure of power. Although he reluctantly served as governor of Virginia for three terms (between 1776 and 1778), his real interest was his farm at Red Hill. Though he occasionally spent a few days in Williamsburg changing the world, he always promptly returned home to care for his invalid wife, homeschool his children, read his Bible, and plow his fields. This was the love of his life. Unlike John Adams, Patrick Henry would not allow politics to interrupt his household affairs. He truly lived out his profession. He repeatedly turned down powerful political

positions. In 1796 he was arguably the second most popular man in America. Richard Henry Lee and John Marshall approached him to accept the nomination for President of the United States. On November 3, 1796, the *Virginia Gazette* published a public letter from Henry in which he once for all refused the office. Humbly he turned down the office "on account of my own insufficiency." He wrote that, "within the United States, a large number of citizens may be found, whose talents and exemplary virtues deserve public confidence, much more than anything I can boast of."[10]

Here is the clear distinction between the tyrant and the Christian who stands for law and liberty. The tyrant is willing to sacrifice the liberties of others to gain power and reputation for himself. The Christian freedom-fighter is willing to risk everything he owns for the liberties of others, and he cares little for power or reputation. Few Americans know anything about Patrick Henry. Few monuments have been erected in his honor. He receives one tiny bust in the Virginia State Capitol in Richmond. The Washington Mall contains nothing for him. Patrick Henry leaves the fame to Thomas Jefferson, Abraham Lincoln, Franklin Delano Roosevelt, and others like them who consolidated power and influence in the federal government by their political endeavors.

3. Patrick Henry was willing to lead the way in America's bid for Independence. He was one of the first to raise his voice against the tyrants and the first to pledge his life. It is extremely difficult to break a silence like this when nobody else will. It takes tremendous faith to be the first one to step in front of Goliath and ask the question, "Who is this uncircumcised Philistine that should defy the armies of the living God!?" (1 Sam. 17:26). It takes an extraordinary combination of wisdom, courage, and faith to lead like this. Patrick Henry spoke passionately, plainly, resolutely, and loudly the thing that others feared to say. Eventually, men like George Washington and Thomas Jefferson joined him in support of liberty. But someone had to strike the first blow for freedom, and this was the unique privilege of this very courageous man.

The Battle for the Bill of Rights

And when it was day, the magistrates sent the officers, saying, "Let those men go."
So the keeper of the prison reported these words to Paul, saying, "The magistrates
have sent to let you go. Now therefore depart, and go in peace." But Paul said to
them, "They have beaten us openly, uncondemned Romans, and have thrown
us into prison. And now do they put us out secretly? No indeed! Let them come
themselves and get us out." And the officers told these words to the magistrates,
and they were afraid when they heard that they were Romans. Then they came and
pleaded with them and brought them out, and asked them to depart from the city. So
they went out of the prison and entered the house of Lydia; and when they had seen
the brethren, they encouraged them and departed. (Acts 16:35-40)

It is appropriate for Christians to seek liberty from tyranny, to insist on their lawful rights, as the Apostle Paul did when he was arrested and beaten at Philippi. Patrick Henry continued this legacy not only for his own benefit, but for all American citizens in future generations.

Sensing the strong inclination among key American leaders towards creating a powerful central government, Patrick Henry at first opposed the ratification of the United States Constitution. The critical statement of rights which would protect freedoms for Americans had been rejected by the Constitutional Convention on September 12, 1787. Returning to Richmond in 1788 (after a retirement from politics), Patrick served as the most dominant and influential member of the Virginia Ratifying Convention which debated whether to ratify the Constitution. During the debate on the floor, Henry spoke more than any other delegate. He rose to speak as many as 5-8 times per day, over 18 days of the proceedings. His influence upon Virginia and thus on America was indisputable. In a letter George Washington wrote to James Madison, he noted, "The edicts of Mr. H[enry] are enregistered with less opposition by the members of that body, than those of the Grand Monarch are in the Parliament of France. He has only to say, let this be Law, and it is Law."[11] What follows is a portion of Patrick Henry's plea for a Bill of Rights to be attached to the US Constitution:

If you give up these powers [to the states], without a bill of rights, you will exhibit the most absurd thing to mankind that ever the world saw—government that has abandoned all its powers—the powers of direct taxation, the sword, and the purse. You have disposed of them to Congress, without a bill of rights—without check, limitation, or control. And still you have checks and guards; still you keep barriers—pointed where? Pointed against your weakened, prostrated, enervated state government! You have a bill of rights to defend you against the state government, which is bereaved of all power, and yet you have none against Congress, though in full and exclusive possession of all power! You arm yourself against the weak and defenseless, and expose yourselves naked to the armed and powerful. Is not this a conduct of unexampled absurdity? What barriers have you to oppose to this most strong, energetic government? To that government you have nothing to oppose. All your defense is given up. This is a real, actual defect. It must strike the mind of every gentleman.[12]

Against James Madison's protests, George Mason, the author of Virginia's Bill of Rights, rose to support a fundamental statement of rights for all Americans.

The Constitutional Convention

Patrick Henry's substitute motion on the floor, requiring a bill of rights prior to ratifying the Constitution in the Virginia General Assembly, failed by a vote of 80-88. Following this, Edmund Randolph offered a slightly modified motion which used softer language but still underscored the need for stated rights, and the motion passed. Subsequently, the ratifying convention formed a committee to suggest a list of amendments of rights for the first meeting of the US Congress. Just before the convention convened, Patrick Henry had drafted his own list, most of which the committee incorporated into its final proposal.

The fight was not over yet, however. On October 20, 1788, Patrick returned to the state legislature to complete the job in securing the Bill of Rights as amendments to the US Constitution. As the legislature convened to choose Virginia's first US Senators, once again Patrick Henry acted as the most dominant leader in the assembly. He nominated Richard Henry Lee and William Grayson to represent the state in the US Senate for the sole reason that these men were most likely to fight hard for the Bill of Rights. He would not support James Madison because of his tendency to support big government and his reluctance to include the Bill of Rights in the US Constitution at first. Patrick Henry supported James Monroe for Congress, but James Madison secured the Congressional seat when he finally agreed to propose a Bill of Rights to the first meeting of Congress in 1789.

In the end, the United States Congress complied with Virginia's request for a Bill of Rights. Massachusetts also brought forward a similar request, thanks to motions set forward by none other than Samuel Adams and John Hancock.

Most of the US Constitution has not proved as useful in holding back the ever-expanding grasp of the federal government as its founders hoped it would. But the one-page document appended to the end of the Constitution called "the Bill of Rights" has proven invaluable for freedom. It has protected liberty in many court battles in the last two centuries. It has protected many an innocent person, journalist, pastor, and evangelist who wished to preach the gospel. It has provided a restraint to many a tyrant who would have persecuted innocent citizens and created a police state in the United States.

There were larger concerns at stake for Patrick Henry at the Virginia Ratifying Convention, some of which proved to be prophetic. He feared that America would give in to the "empire impulse." He preferred that the Constitution begin with "We the States" instead of "We the People." He foresaw that America would turn into a democratic tyranny in the years to come and warned of this on the floor of the convention. He argued strongly against "[convert]ing this country into a powerful and mighty empire."[13] Thomas Jefferson, on the other hand, began using the term "Empire" for this country during his presidency only a few short years later.

During the constitutional debates, Henry was concerned that the citizens of the United States would be "transformed from respectable, independent citizens, to abject dependent subjects or slaves."[14] He warned that the Constitution should not give the federal government the power to tax, because then he predicted, "rich, snug, fine, fat Federal officers—the collectors of taxes and excises—will out-number anything from the States."[15] He complained that this direct taxation of the citizens would provide "unlimited powers of harassing the community," and called them, "the visionary projects of modern politicians."[16]

Patrick Henry would have been horrified by the rise of the modern socialist state and the massive increase in the size of the federal government in the United States. He would have denounced the federal income tax, public schools, the 120,000 pages of the Federal Register, compulsory school attendance laws, the child protection services, the gun registration requirements, the regular exercise of eminent domain, the zoning laws, the wetlands enforcement, and the 60% of the GNI (Gross National Income) consumed in government spending as massive incursions on the liberties of a free nation. That is why so few people in our day appreciate the man responsible for spearheading this nation's independence. In 1992 Walter Williams, professor of Economics for George Mason University, pointed out:

> In 1787, federal spending was about $3 million a year, or about $1 per citizen. By 1910, the Fed spent a little more than $600 million, about $6.75 per person. By 1929, the Fed spent $3 billion per year, $29 per person. Today, the Federal Government

spends over $4 billion per day! That comes to more than $6000 per year per person, or controlling for inflation, a 9,000% increase in federal spending between 1929 and today. The Colonists, who were paying about 67 cents a year in taxes, went to war with Great Britain.[17]

The Faith of Patrick Henry

Beloved, while I was very diligent to write to you concerning our common salvation, I found it necessary to write to you exhorting you to contend earnestly for the faith which was once for all delivered to the saints. (Jude 3)

To the end, Patrick Henry maintained a strong faith in God and operated from a Christian worldview. He clearly recognized the sovereign hand of God over the nations of men. During this period of the rise of Deism and humanism, it is truly remarkable that most of the influential leaders in America maintained such a commitment to God's providential direction over all things. In Henry's famous "Give me Liberty" speech, he reminded the delegates that "There is a just God who presides over the destinies of nations; and who will raise up friends to fight our battles for us."[18]

Patrick Henry considered his cause righteous and just, not on the basis of humanist manifestos or by the standards of humanist philosophers like Jean-Jacques Rousseau. A just cause, as defined by Henry, could only be judged by a just God—not by the will of the people. This is significant. Patrick Henry was willing to throw himself and the nation at the feet of the Judge of Nations to beg His mercy. This position would also be supported by the Continental Congress.

Although Patrick Henry did not join the Presbyterian church with his mother, the evangelical sermons of Samuel Davies continued to work on his soul throughout his entire life. While Deism, Unitarianism, and skepticism were wooing the hearts and minds of many colonial leaders away from Christ, Patrick Henry's theological journey went the other direction. He returned to the Lord Jesus Christ. He chose for his Christian mentors the men who were fighting hard for the faith against the skepticism of the day—men like Bishop Joseph Butler and Bishop Thomas Sherlock.

In a letter to his daughter Elizabeth, Patrick complained of the "general prevalence of deism" in the Democratic-Republican Party founded by Jefferson and Madison.[19] In this letter he strongly criticizes Thomas Paine and other skeptics:

> *The religion of Christ has, from its first appearance in the world, been attacked in vain by all the wits, philosophers, and wise ones aided by every power of man, and its triumph has been complete. What is there in the wit or wisdom of the present deistical writers or professors, that can compare them with Hume, Shaftsbury, Bolingbroke, and others? And yet, these have been confuted and their fame decaying; insomuch that the puny efforts of [Thomas] Paine are thrown in to prop their tottering fabric, whose foundations cannot stand the test of time.[20]*

In the same letter Patrick went on to lament that some people accused him of being a deist. "I find much cause to reproach myself that I have lived so long and have given no decided proofs of my being a Christian."[21]

Family worship was a regular daily event in the Henry home throughout the 1780s. Patrick read sermons from Bishop Sherlock aloud to his children, and then they would sing psalms and hymns together, accompanied by the governor playing his violin.

However, it was later in the 1780s that a spiritual revival came to life in the old governor's soul. Earlier in 1775, Patrick Henry had helped start a Presbyterian school not far from his home called Hampden Sydney College. Around 1787 a revival swept through the college. It came about when four students began gathering on Saturdays for prayer. The president of the college, a close friend of Patrick Henry, allowed the students to gather in his own kitchen. Others joined the prayer meeting, wandering in from miles around the college. It was this spiritual revival that made a great impact on Patrick Henry. He began reading the Scriptures regularly, quoting the Bible, and witnessing the gospel everywhere he went.[22] On the bottom of an affidavit for a court case he argued in 1789, we find Patrick Henry's own handwriting, "I will arise and go to my father, and will say Father, Father, I have sinned before God and in thy sight, and am no more worthy to be called a son."[23] It is a personalized testimony of a quotation from the Prodigal Son story in Luke 15:18. Each morning, his children would find him reading his Bible in the dining room.[24] For his remaining years, he would "quote the Bible often and spread the Gospel to those who would listen."[25]

There is some reasonable debate over the faith of many of America's Founding Fathers. However, there is really no question concerning Patrick Henry's Christian faith. Unlike the deists of his day, he was unabashed in his profession of faith in Christ. Writing to his sister Anne upon the loss of her husband, Henry wrote, "O may we meet in heaven, to which the merits of Jesus will carry those who love and serve him."[26]

In the final portion of his will, Patrick Henry included this highly significant message to his children: "I have now disposed of all my property to my family. There is one thing more I wish I could give them, and that is the Christian religion."[27] Henry's dying words included a testimony of his faith in Christ to his bedside doctor, the deist Dr. Cabell. An eyewitness reported:

He prayed in clear words, a simple child-like prayer for his family, for his country, and for his own soul in the presence of death . . . [S]peaking great words of love to his family, he told them that he was thankful for the goodness of God . . . Finally, fixing his eyes with much tenderness on his dear friend, Dr. Cabell, with whom he had formerly held many arguments respecting the Christian religion, he asked the doctor to observe how great a reality and benefit that religion was to a man about to die . . . after which they who were looking upon him, saw that his life had departed.[28]

Conclusion

Patrick Henry's love for liberty is hardly shared by many today. For he was one of the last of a dying breed, and the strongest of those who still held to the Christian faith during the spiritual decline of the latter 18th century. Most modern Americans generally do not resonate with Patrick Henry's moving words anymore because they do not appreciate freedom. They do not seek a liberty as defined by God's law. They prefer slavery to sin and the security offered by their tyrannical leaders. Election after election, they vote tyrants into office of their own free will.

Yet, there is still a faint heartbeat for freedom that resounds in a small minority of Americans today. There are still a few who will make the pilgrimage to the old Virginia Capitol in Colonial Williamsburg. They will pay their respects at St. John's Church in Richmond and recite the words of the famous speech once again. Then they will visit Patrick Henry's old homesteads at Scotchtown and Red Hill to visit the markers and the gravestone of an old freedom fighter and to register their commitment to the age-old, noble cause of liberty once more.

The embers of liberty have pretty well died down now, but they are not entirely extinguished. There is still hope for true freedom somewhere in the world as long as there are still men and women of faith left who follow the One who died to set us free from the bondage of sin.

Stand fast therefore in the liberty by which Christ has made us free, and do not be entangled again with a yoke of bondage. (Galatians 5:1)

Therefore if the Son makes you free, you shall be free indeed. (John 8:36)

Samuel Adams (1722-1803)

CHAPTER 9

— ★ ★ ★ —

Samuel Adams:
Founding Father of American
Independence

*Were you called while a slave? Do not be concerned
about it; but if you can be made free, rather use it.
For he who is called in the Lord while a slave is the
Lord's freedman. Likewise he who is called while
free is Christ's slave. You were bought at a price; do
not become slaves of men.*

—1 Corinthians 7:21-23

B y 1760 the population of the American colonies had exceeded 1.6 million. Virginia boasted the largest population with 340,000 persons, and Massachusetts came in second place with 200,000.

Four years after the birth of Christian missionary David Brainerd, another key figure in American history was born to Samuel and Mary Adams in Boston, Massachusetts. The child would become one of the most important political leaders in the formation of this nation called the United States of America.

Samuel Adams (Jr.) was born at noon on September 22, 1722, and baptized by Rev. Samuel Checkley, pastor of the newly formed New South Church in Boston. Checkley had married Elizabeth, the daughter of Rev. Benjamin Rolfe of Haverhill. Thirteen years earlier she had miraculously escaped from an Indian raid, at which time her father and mother were both killed. Pastor Checkley was known for the steadfast faith and courage he displayed when preaching in the presence of local government leaders. In 1755, he preached a sermon before the Massachusetts government. Looking Governor William Shirley squarely in the eye, Checkley told him:

> So also [in order that you might] approve yourself to him, who is King of kings, and Lord of lords, who standeth in the congregation of the mighty, and who judgeth among the gods, to your royal master also, one of the best of kings, to your own conscience, to the people under your government, and to Christ the judge of all, to whom you, Sir, as well as we, must one day give an account . . . in the name and fear of God, [I] beseech you, to have your eyes upon the faithful in the land; choose men, who, you have reason to think fear God, honor the king, are true friends to the province, and will stand up for the privileges of it, religious as well as civil.[1]

In the same sermon Checkley called the heads of families to a "family reformation" and a revival of "family religion." Young Samuel Adams would grow up and marry his pastor's daughter. Samuel Checkley is generally considered by historians as an orthodox, reformed, Puritan, Christian pastor. His counsel to other pastors was sound: "All souls are precious to Christ. Let them be so to you also, and be ready to spend and to be spent for them. Deal tenderly with distressed and quickened souls, leading them to Christ also for rest."[2] He wanted New England pastors to "assert and explain the great doctrines of the Gospel, such as the Trinity of Persons, the divinity of Christ, and also of the blessed Spirit, the imputation of Adam's sin to his posterity, regeneration, and justification by faith alone."[3]

This was the pastor who discipled Samuel Adams for 47 years. Based on the consistency of his testimony, his church background, and his final will and testament, there is every reason to believe that Samuel Adams was a Christian, a true believer in the Lord Jesus Christ. Though there may be room for serious doubt concerning many of the other founders of the nation, there is little reason to doubt Adams' profession. This is important because Samuel Adams was probably the most prominent leader in the fight for American independence from Britain in the early stages. Why God uses some Christians more than others to oppose tyranny is a mystery, but ultimately those who are set free from their sins are usually the most qualified to oppose other forms of slavery. Our Lord said, "If the Son makes you free, you shall be free indeed" (John 8:36). The Apostle Paul also encouraged the Corinthian Christians to avoid the unnecessary servitude of men. "You were bought at a price; do not become slaves of men" (1 Cor. 7:23). It was men like Samuel Adams who took this charge seriously.

Young Samuel's father was a deacon in the New South Church in Boston and was generally referred to as Deacon Adams. Both his father and mother were devout, faithful Christians in the church. In fact, it was Samuel Adams Sr. who led the effort to build the New South Church in 1715. Sam's older sister Mary was five years his senior. A woman of deep Christian faith herself, she kept a notebook with sermons transcribed from George Whitefield, Jonathan Edwards, Cotton Mather, and Samuel Checkley (all evangelical, Puritan men of God). Church services in Boston were four hours long. Instruction in the Christian faith began early with young Samuel. At six years of age he learned to read using the *New England Primer*, which begins with the words: "In Adam's fall, we sinned all."

Throughout Samuel's childhood his father was active in politics as well as in the church. The young boy often heard his father speak against the efforts on the part of the king to unlawfully increase the powers he held over the colonies. Samuel listened as the older man argued vehemently in favor of holding true to the Charter of 1691 which was established by the hard-fought efforts of Increase Mather.

In an attempt to obtain a firmer hold over the internal government of Massachusetts, the king moved to pay the governor's salary. Sam's father strongly opposed this political maneuver and argued for a fixed salary for the governor provided by the colony. This way the governor would be more accountable to the law and to the people than to the king. So as to raise awareness of the crown's encroachments and to unite the colonists against tyranny, Samuel Adams Sr. formed political clubs comprised of laborers and ship caulkers. These groups began supporting political leaders in the Massachusetts Legislature. These "caulkers" would later come to be called "caucuses." Samuel Jr. would later employ his father's organizational skills to build a larger network of political organizations at an even more crucial time in this nation's founding.

Although young Samuel Adams studied the Greek philosophers during his years at Harvard College, he continued to attend the New South Church, where he sat under the preaching of Samuel Checkley. While in his mid-20s, Samuel began courting the pastor's daughter, Elizabeth. The pair particularly enjoyed discussing theology together. Samuel found himself drawn to Elizabeth largely because his own mother and sister were godly women who delighted in speaking of God's Word in the home.

Hoping that his son would learn to make a good living, Samuel Sr. provided the young man with 1000 pounds (approximately $100,000 in today's money). Regrettably, Sam Jr. proceeded to squander all the money away. Afterwards his father sent him into the family's malt business, an initiatory process used in beer production. Samuel Sr. died in March 1748, and on October 17, 1749, Samuel Adams married Elizabeth Checkley.

By 1756 Samuel Adams had run the brewery out of business. He was afterward elected tax collector but failed to collect sufficient taxes. In 1761, due to Samuel's mismanagement, the town of Boston found itself short 5,000 pounds in tax income.

During the first six years of their marriage Elizabeth bore five children, only two of which survived infancy. Childbirth proved hard on Elizabeth, and she passed away on July 6, 1757. Upon her death Samuel wrote in the family Bible:

To her husband she was as sincere a friend as she was a faithful wife. Her exact economy in all her relative capacities, her kindred on his side as well as her own admire. She ran her Christian race with remarkable steadiness, and finished in triumph! She left two small children. God grant they may inherit her graces.[4]

Adams remarried in 1764 to Elizabeth Wells ("Betsy"), with whom he had three more children. Upon their marriage Betsy brought a slave woman named "Surry" into the family. Samuel utterly repudiated the idea of any form of slavery and insisted, "A slave cannot live in my house. If she comes, she must be free." [5] True to his word, he quickly filed papers that officially emancipated Surry, and she continued to live with the family for the next fifty years.

The Puritan

Some historians refer to Samuel Adams as "the last of the Puritans." He advocated family worship and Bible reading in the home. To his son he once wrote, "Religion in a Family is at once its brightest Ornament and its best security." [6]

A printer in Boston by the name of John Mein called Samuel Adams "The Psalm Singer, with the gifted face." [7] Mein explained that Adams was "noted for Psalm singing, and leader of the Band at Checkleys Meeting," referring to Samuel Checkley's congregation at the New South Meeting House. [8] John Fleming, also called Samuel Adams "the psalm singer" in a letter written in 1775. [9]

Expanding Tyranny and Mounting Tensions with Britain

This will be the behavior of the king who will reign over you: He will take your sons and appoint them for his own chariots and to be his horsemen, and some will run before his chariots. He will appoint captains over his thousands and captains over his fifties, will set some to plow his ground and reap his harvest, and some to make his weapons of war and equipment for his chariots. He will take your daughters to be perfumers, cooks, and bakers. And he will take the best of your fields, your vineyards, and your olive groves, and give them to his servants. He will take a tenth of your grain and your vintage, and give it to his officers and servants . . . And you will cry out in that day because of your king whom you have chosen for yourselves, and the LORD will not hear you in that day. (1 Samuel 8:11-18)

Beginning in 1764, the British began cinching up the government tyranny on the American colonies. The British Parliament first passed the Sugar Act, legislation which added large taxes on imports entering the American colonies. Samuel Adams opposed it strongly. At first he was stunned to find himself the only voice speaking against the act in local town hall meetings and political clubs. Although his friend James Otis had already spoken out against what he called "taxation without representation" in a court case in 1761, it was Samuel Adams who lit the fire under the colony in opposition to the rising tyranny from the mother country.

Long before Patrick Henry opposed the Stamp Act in the Virginia House of Burgesses, Samuel Adams was arguing passionately for liberty at the Boston town meeting. He called the people to refuse any support for all political candidates who opposed self-governance and representative taxation, and he chastised the Massachusetts Legislature for failing to attend to their duties and responsibilities: "We cannot help expressing our surprise that when so early notice was given by the agent of the intentions of the ministry to burden us with new taxes [sugar taxes, etc.], so little regard was had to this most interesting matter."[10]

Samuel Adams then proceeded to draft "instructions" for those who wished to be elected to the legislature. In this way he framed the issues of the 1764 elections. Calling the colonies to unite against unjust British policies, he suggested the formation of a "continental congress" and afterward recommended a boycott against British goods. If nobody bought the goods imported into America, nobody would need to pay the import taxes on the goods, he reasoned. Thus, as witnessed by Governor Thomas Hutchinson in a communication with King George III, it was Samuel Adams who became "the first who asserted the independence of the colonies."[11]

In the spring of 1765, the British Parliament passed the Stamp Act, which levied a tax for every official document filed with local colonial governments. Once again Samuel Adams renewed his call for an official meeting of representatives from all of the colonial governments, but Governor Bernard scoffed at the idea, as did the rest of the governors in the colonies. However, Adams begged his friend James Otis (who was a member of the Massachusetts

Legislature) to press the matter further in the legislature. Otis sponsored the resolution, and the measure calling for the colonial congress passed, but the governor responded by dissolving the Massachusetts Assembly.

Other colonial governments were at first hesitant to join the "congress" because they deemed it "illegal." However, South Carolina jumped on the bandwagon with Massachusetts on August 2, after their assembly heard several impassioned speeches from legislators John Rutledge and Christopher Gadsden. Nine other colonies quickly followed suit.

During these tumultuous days, Samuel Adams probably began privately suggesting independence from Britain. In a backroom conversation with his cousin John Adams, it was likely mentioned. John wrote, "[Samuel] felt an ambition, which was very apt to mislead a man, that of doing something extraordinary."[12] Independence was a radical concept in these early days.

In September 1765, Samuel Adams ran for a seat in the Massachusetts Legislature and won. The first colonial congress made up of representatives from nine states met in October and produced a united petition encouraging the king to revoke the Stamp Act. The representatives noted that only colonial governments (as elected by the people) should levy taxes. This was the first step taken by a unified coalition of the colonies towards American independence.

As an elected representative, nobody worked harder than Samuel Adams. Eighteen hours a day, six days a week, he campaigned against the Stamp Act. In early November 1765, Adams submitted fourteen Stamp Act Resolutions to the Massachusetts House, all of which were adopted. Lieutenant Governor Thomas Hutchinson called them the "Colonial Magna Carta." In March 1767, the British parliament voted to repeal the hated tax.

Following in the footsteps of his father, a political organizer in his own right, Samuel Adams now began recruiting and organizing political resistance to English tyranny. He included his cousin, thirty-year-old John Adams (thirteen years his junior), in the discussions on liberty. He also enlisted John Hancock, the wealthiest man in the colony, in the cause. His abilities to organize and to provide vision did not go unnoticed, as British Governor Francis Bernard would refer to him as, "the most dangerous man in Massachusetts."[13]

Throughout the 1760s and early 1770s, Samuel Adams went to work writing thousands of articles, petitions, and letters to newspapers under a hundred different pen names (by John Adams' estimate). How he obtained income to keep his family fed is anybody's guess, though some have speculated that John Hancock might have slipped the family a bag of wheat here and there.

Sam wrote three letters for the Boston Gazette, each signed simply "A Puritan." In these letters, he intimated that Americans might become "worshipers of the beast," a term he used to refer to Roman Catholicism or what he called "popery."[14]

In a letter written to a pastor in 1765, Adams wrote this concerning the early founders of New England:

> *Here they resolved to set up the Worship of God, according to their best Judgment, upon the Plan of the New Testament; to maintain it among themselves, and transmit it to their Posterity; and to spread the knowledge of Jesus Christ among the ignorant and barbarous Natives. As they were prospered, in their Settlement by Him, whose is the Earth and the Fullness thereof, beyond all human Expectation, they soon became a considerable Object of National Attention, and a Charter was granted them by King Charles the first.[15]*

He closed the letter by encouraging the pastor that, "our hearty Prayer is that you may be succeeded in all your Endeavors to promote the spiritual kingdom of Jesus Christ."[16]

In an oration given in 1765, Samuel Adams presented his concerns in their clearest form. The tyranny of popery had been rooted out by freeing the church from the pope. But now the problem was the growing power of the State—another attempt to curtail liberty. Speaking of the Protestant Reformers, he said,

> *They lopped off, indeed, some of the branches of Popery, but they left the root and stock when they left us under the domination of human systems and decisions, usurping the infallibility which can be attributed to revelation alone. They dethroned one usurper, only to raise up another; they refused allegiance to the Pope, only to place the civil magistrate in the throne of Christ, vested with authority to*

enact laws and inflict penalties in his kingdom. And if we now cast our eyes over the nations of the earth, we shall find that instead of possessing the pure religion of the Gospel, they may be divided either into infidels, who deny the truth, or politicians, who make religion a stalking-horse for their ambition, or professors, who walk in the trammels of orthodoxy, and are more attentive to traditions and ordinances of men than to the oracles of truth.[17]

Clearly, Samuel Adams did not want the political power centers to hijack the church and the pure gospel. Whether he realized it or not, Adams would have had the support of European reformers like John Calvin, Samuel Rutherford, and Pierre Viret in his opposition to this rising tyranny. In a letter written in 1772, Adams actually attributed tyranny to the work of the devil:

To live a life of rational beings, is to live free; to live a life of slaves is to die by inches. Ten thousand deaths by the halter, or the axe, are infinitely preferable to a miserable life of slavery in chains, under a puck of worse than Egyptian tyrants, whose avarice nothing less than your whole substance and income, will satisfy; and who, if they can't extort that, will glory in making a sacrifice of you and your posterity, to gratify their master the devil, who is a tyrant, and the father of tyrants and of liars.[18]

And of course, his most famous quote lambasted those who refused to join the contest for liberty:

"If ye love wealth better than liberty, the tranquility of servitude better than the animating contest of freedom, go home from us in peace. We ask not your counsels or arms. Crouch down and lick the hands which feed you. May your chains set lightly upon you, and may posterity forget that ye were our countrymen." [19]

Liberty and rights, Adams believed, were blessings from God and could only be defined by the laws of God: "The right to freedom being the gift of God Almighty, it is not in the power of man to alienate this gift and voluntarily become a slave . . . [The rights of the colonists] may be best understood by reading and carefully studying the institutes of the great Law Giver and Head of the Christian Church, which are to be found clearly written and promulgated in the New Testament."[20]

The All-Out Battle for Liberty

It was September 1768 when the British began quartering troops in Boston. This increased tensions with the citizens in the town. Independence was becoming a favorite topic of conversation in the churches, the pubs, and the private homes of Boston. On March 5, 1770, five colonials were killed by the "Redcoats" stationed in Boston after a group of men and boys began lobbing snowballs and bricks at the British troops. Once again Samuel Adams took advantage of what he not-so-accurately referred to as "the Boston Massacre." Marching into the governor's council chambers in the company of a committee of colonials, he informed Governor Hutchinson that it was time to withdraw the troops from Boston—all of them. The governor told him that this was not possible, and Adams marched back to the Old South Meeting House and delivered the news to the 3,000 people gathered there. The town council refused to accept the answer, and Adams and his men walked right back into the Old State House for another meeting with Hutchinson. The governor then explained that he had no power to remove the troops. But Samuel pressed the point: "You have power to remove both [regiments]. It is at your peril if you refuse."[21] The governor finally relented and ordered both regiments out of town.

At this time Britain was imposing a dictatorial economic policy on the colonies called mercantilism. Although some businessmen would attempt to smuggle Dutch tea into the colonies at much lower prices, the British wanted

> **Quartering Troops:** The British began quartering troops in New York in 1766. This meant that the army would require housing and food for their troops. Eventually this would involve soldiers living in people's private homes.

Americans buying their own tea via the British East India Company. This kept American money flowing into Britain. In May 1773 Parliament passed the Tea Act, which increased taxes on British tea while cutting its price. Once again Samuel Adams stood up against this "taxation without representation" and campaigned hard for the ensuing months. Three ships laden with tea showed up in Boston Harbor in the fall of 1773. After the governor refused several requests from the townspeople to return the ships and the tea to Britain, a meeting was held at the Old South Meeting House. About 7,000 colonists gathered. Standing before the assembly, Samuel Adams ended the meeting with these famous last words: "This meeting can do nothing more to save the country!"[22] After the colonists dispersed, forty to fifty men dressed in Indian garb entered the ships and dumped the tea overboard into Boston Harbor. This event came to be known as the Boston Tea Party. Furious at this high-handed rejection of its authority, Parliament responded by issuing the "Intolerable Acts" which shut down all trade in Boston until the Bostonians had paid for the tea.

On March 5, 1774, a crowd gathered at the Old South Meeting House to hear John Hancock's fiery speech in which he called for the colonists to free themselves from the tyranny of Great Britain and to form a new country called "the United States of America." A year earlier Samuel Adams had suggested that a congress be formed out of all thirteen colonies, and the First Continental Congress

British ships arriving in Boston in 1768

was scheduled to meet in Philadelphia in September 1774. In preparation for this historic meeting, the Massachusetts Legislature met secretly (while the governor's spies were lurking outside) and elected John Adams, Samuel Adams, and three other local men to represent Massachusetts at the upcoming congress.

However, as he prepared to represent his state at this first meeting of Congress, Samuel Adams found himself faced with a problem beyond his means to address: he had no appropriate clothing to wear to the congress. For over a decade he had worn the same ragged suit and faded red coat. However, one evening that summer a tailor knocked at his door and asked to take his measurements. Hardly a week later, someone delivered a large trunk filled with a new suit, two pairs of hose, a wig, a cocked hat, a gold-handled cane, and a new red cloak.

Samuel Adams traveled with his cousin John and two of the other delegates 300 miles to Philadelphia, a nineteen-day journey by coach. This was Samuel's first trip outside of Massachusetts. Fifty-six representatives from twelve colonies

The Boston Tea Party

> **Mercantilism:** Mercantilism was a economic position taken by the Mother Country overseeing colonies. The government of the Mother Country would not allow the colonials to buy from any country but the Mother Country. This would increase the prices of imports for the colonies. The Mother Country wanted to bring in cheap raw materials and export finished materials at higher prices (without having to compete with other countries). It was a form of a monopoly.

met, including George Washington, Richard Henry Lee, and Patrick Henry from Virginia and Christopher Gadsden from South Carolina.

At Philadelphia, Samuel Adams and his fellow Massachusetts delegates were considered radicals and looked upon with a bit of a jaundiced eye. Nonetheless Samuel Adams proceeded to do what he had always done best. He made friends—lots of them. He met with other delegates in cafes and dining halls, in the foyers of the buildings and on the streets. From the beginning, it was Samuel Adams who insisted that each day begin with prayer. This was resisted at first because of denominational differences. Adams, a Puritan Congregationalist, suggested that Jacob Duche, an Anglican, lead the prayers. This compromise seemed to calm the opposition and at last everyone agreed.

While the Congress was in session, British General Gage seized a large cache of gunpowder that belonged to the town of Charlestown, Massachusetts in Suffolk County. Immediately after the seizure the county prepared a list of resolves (already pre-written by Samuel Adams). The news and the resolves came by horseback via Samuel Adams' good friend, Paul Revere, who made the 300-mile journey in just six days. The Continental Congress unanimously endorsed the Suffolk Resolves, which further steeled their commitment toward armed resistance. A plan initiated by a Philadelphia delegate named Joseph Galloway to attempt a reconciliation with the Mother Country failed by one vote. Congress further instructed all thirteen colonies to arm their militias and prepare for action.

During the meetings of the First Continental Congress, it was Samuel Adams who set the agenda and it was Patrick Henry from Virginia who employed his fiery rhetoric to press it forward. Henry admitted later, "the good that was to

Independence Hall, Philadelphia, Pennsylvania

come from these congresses was owing to the work of [Samuel] Adams."[23] In the struggle for liberty and right there often appears to be a single leader who tips the first domino in the battle. Almost everyone opposes him at first, and then slowly some begin to realize the worthiness of the cause.

Drums of War

Not surprisingly, Britain rejected the demands of the First Continental Congress. Another meeting of the Congress was scheduled for May 1775. In preparation for this event, the Massachusetts Provincial Government met and elected the same four men who had attended the first meeting along with John Hancock as representatives.

Towards the end of March, military Governor Thomas Gage issued an arrest warrant for Samuel Adams and John Hancock. Both men traveled together to Lexington, where they stayed with John Adams' cousin, Pastor Jonas Clarke, his wife, and ten children. Adams and Hancock, two of the most important leaders in the American cause, bunked in one of the children's rooms. Governor Gage, determined to capture the two men, prepared 700 troops to march from Boston to Lexington to make the arrest and to destroy the military supplies at Lexington and Concord. A young boy in charge of the soldiers' horses overheard the plan and sent a warning to Dr. Paul Warren, who then informed Paul Revere. The troops were traveling across the channel "by sea" instead of by land, so Paul Revere had a friend place two lanterns in the high steeple window of the Old North Church to instantly warn the patriots on the other side that the British were coming by sea. Meanwhile it was Paul Revere's job to reach Lexington to warn Samuel Adams and John Hancock that the British were on their way to arrest them.

Taking a boat across the channel, Paul Revere then rode hard to beat the "Redcoats" to the Clarke home. He reached Lexington at midnight and began beating on the door. Someone told him to be quiet because he was making too much noise.

"Noise!" Revere responded, "You'll have noise enough before long! The Regulars are coming out!"[24]

When Adams and Hancock heard the news they immediately sent a guard to assemble the militiamen on the village green. A total of 170 men gathered at 1:00 a.m.—grandfathers, fathers, and sons. John Hancock preferred to stay and fight the British, but over the next three hours Samuel Adams convinced his friend to move out into the woods. From this vantage point they watched the first battle in America's War for Independence.

As dawn approached, several hundred British soldiers arrived at the Lexington Green. Realizing they were outnumbered, the Americans turned to leave. Two men stayed—a grandfather named Jonas Parker and the only African-American soldier, Prince Estabrook. Then, someone fired the first shot and immediately the British released a volley on the Colonials. Eight colonists lay dead; only one British soldier was wounded. It was April 19, 1775, and it was at that moment that Samuel Adams told John Hancock, "Oh! What a glorious morning is this!"[25]

The British moved on to Concord, where they burned the town hall and confiscated weapons and gunpowder. At this point, the colonial volunteers responded with a deliberate and ready force. They approached the British who were guarding Concord's North Bridge. A colonial officer called out, "Fire! Fire! Fire!" Colonial bullets began flying, and the British received thirteen casualties, three dead. The Redcoats immediately began a retreat and the colonists followed hard, firing all the way. Over the twenty-mile flight back to Boston, the British lost about 300 soldiers, while the colonials sustained about 100 casualties. Thus ended the first major battle in America's War for Independence.

Meanwhile, Samuel Adams and John Hancock made their escape to Worcester, Massachusetts, and then finally arrived safe in Philadelphia on April 27, 1775. In June, Massachusetts Military Governor Thomas Gage announced that he would pardon everyone involved in the skirmish except for Samuel Adams and John Hancock, for whom he put out a death warrant—specifically a punishment of death by hanging.

Massachusetts observed a day of fasting and humiliation in May, and Samuel Adams enthusiastically endorsed it, stating, "It is upon the Blessing of God alone that we must depend for the happy Issue to our virtuous Struggle."[26]

At the Second Continental Congress, Samuel and John Adams secured the election of John Hancock as president. In a private conversation both Samuel and his cousin concluded that George Washington should be made commander-in-chief of the Continental Army. When back in session, John made the motion, Samuel seconded it, and George Washington was elected on June 15, 1775 to lead the army. In God's providence these leaders were now well on their way towards establishing the United States of America.

The Congress took a recess in August 1775 and reconvened in September. Samuel was now well aware of the critical nature of the situation. Writing to his wife Betsy, he explained that "the Affairs of our country are at the moment in the most critical situation." He told her that "Mortals cannot command success." Above all, he was completely convinced that the entire outcome was in the hand of God. Continuing his letter to Betsy, he wrote: "I can confidently as well as devoutly pray, that the righteous disposer of all things would succeed our enterprises. If He suffers us to be defeated in any or all of them I shall believe

Paul Revere's Ride

it to be for the most wise and gracious purposes and shall heartily acquiesce in the divine disposal."[27]   Samuel humbly submitted to the will of God and was completely confident of the truth of Romans 8:28:

And we know that all things work together for good to those who love God, to those who are the called according to His purpose. (Romans 8:28)

Throughout these months, Samuel Adams employed all of his persuasive powers in an attempt to build his coalition for independence, drawing most heavily from his father's legacy and gifts. Thomas Jefferson had to admit: "If there was any Palinurus [helmsman] to the revolution, Samuel Adams was the man. Indeed, in the Eastern States, for a year or two after it began, he was truly *the man* of the revolution. He was constantly holding caucuses of distinguished men (among whom was R.H. Lee), at which the generality of the measures pursued were previously determined on, and at which the parts were assigned to the different actors who afterwards appeared in them."[28]

By July 1, 1776, only six colonies were in favor of independence, but Samuel Adams continued lobbying hard for a break with the Mother Country. He convinced one delegate from Pennsylvania to abstain from voting so that the colony's vote would be given in favor of independence and would move the support for independence by a ratio of 7 to 6.

In a speech given on August 1, 1776, Samuel Adams acknowledged the Lordship of Jesus Christ over the nations, something not often seen within the British leadership during that time:

We have this day restored the Sovereign to Whom all men ought to be obedient. He reigns in heaven and from the rising to the setting of the sun, let His kingdom come.[29]

Later Contributions

Because of the transgression of a land, many are its princes; but by a man of understanding and knowledge right will be prolonged. (Proverbs 28:2)

After achieving his life's goal of obtaining independence for the American colonies, Samuel Adams' health declined greatly. Nonetheless, he continued to serve in the Continental Congress until 1781. He then served as governor of Massachusetts from 1793 to 1797. During his time as governor his main concern was the promotion of virtue in his state. In his view, this was essential for the maintenance of a free country. "Liberty will not long survive the total extinction of morals,"[30] he would say. And, "neither the wisest constitution nor the wisest laws will secure the liberty and happiness of a people whose manners are universally corrupt."[31]

As he aged, Governor Adams became even more concerned with the fear of God, especially as he contemplated the final judgment day.[32] Almost every year in office he produced a proclamation for a day of prayer and fasting or a day of thanksgiving, the last of which is attached to the end of this chapter. To the end of his life, Samuel Adams acknowledged God's sovereignty and His glory. "Let the glory be given to Him, who alone governs all events, while we express the just feelings of respect and gratitude due to all those, whom He honours as instruments to carry into effect his gracious designs."[33]

Such writings may be considered radical in a proud day in which scarcely a single magistrate exists who fears God and who gives Him glory in speeches and letters. Indeed, Scripture places reverence and fear of God as the primary requirement for anyone who exercises a role of leadership in human governments:

> *The Spirit of the LORD spoke by me, and His word was on my tongue. The God of Israel said, the Rock of Israel spoke to me: "He who rules over men must be just, ruling in the fear of God." (2 Samuel 23:2-3)*

The two cousins, John Adams and Samuel Adams, exchanged several letters in the 1780s which suggested that the world might be entering into the millennium. Samuel concluded that some great improvement in the world might arise through education. It was a mistake that would be made again and again by future leaders of the country. Yet Samuel did recommend the "study and practice of the exalted virtues of the Christian system" for all schools. One wishes he had pointed to the Gospel of Christ and the regenerating work of God in the heart as the fundamental basis for improvement in the world. Still, Samuel recommended an education that was rooted solidly in the fear of God (Prov. 1:7)

> *Let the divines and philosophers, statesmen and patriots, unite their endeavors to renovate the age, by impressing the minds of men with the importance of educating their little boys and girls; of inculcating in the minds of youth the fear and love of the Deity and universal philanthropy, and, in subordination to these great principles, the love of their country; instructing them in the art of self-government, without which they never can act a wise part in the government of societies, great or small; in short, of leading them in the study and practice of the exalted virtues of the Christian system, which will happily tend to subdue the turbulent passions of men, and introduce that golden age.³⁴*

Samuel envisioned an "education, which lead[ing] the youth beyond mere outside show, will impress their minds with a profound reverence of the Deity."³⁵

A Dying Man's Testimony

> *So they said, "Believe on the Lord Jesus Christ, and you will be saved, you and your household." (Acts 16:31)*

Samuel Adams died on October 2, 1803. For the Christian who is interested in the Christian foundations of the country, the question remains, "Was Adams a genuine Christian?" In an age of spiritual decline, the rise of Deism, and the humanist Enlightenment, the question is significant. The final test of a man's salvation is his faith in Jesus Christ and His merits for salvation. This Samuel Adams provided in his last will and testament:

> *In the name of God, Amen. I, Samuel Adams of Boston, in the County of Suffolk, and Commonwealth of Massachusetts, Esquire, being, through Divine goodness, of sound and disposing mind and memory, and considering the uncertainty of human life, do make and ordain this to be my last will and testament, in manner and form following, viz.: Principally and first of all, I recommend my soul to that Almighty*

Being who gave it, and my body I commit to the dust, relying on the merits of Jesus Christ for a pardon of all my sins.[36]

Such words are not to be found in the last will and testament of the other founders of the nation, such as George Washington, James Madison, and John Adams. Above anything else he ever said or wrote, this dying testimony constitutes his most important words. Yet, it is the compendium of his words, acknowledging Christ as Lord and Savior throughout his life that solidifies for us his true heart commitment.

Samuel Adams and Patrick Henry were two of the most important leaders in the formation of the United States. In a day of mass apostasy and the incursion of humanist rationalism and Deism, both appear as dedicated Christians, strong in faith and well rooted in a solid biblical orthodoxy. However, there are no memorials of any importance for these two men in Washington DC today. This is because the poor wise men who save the nation and salvage liberties are often forgotten, especially if they were the most committed Christians of all.

There was a little city with few men in it; and a great king came against it, besieged it, and built great snares around it. Now there was found in it a poor wise man, and he by his wisdom delivered the city. Yet no one remembered that same poor man. (Ecclesiastes 9:14-15)

Yet we know that "the memory of the righteous is blessed" (Prov. 10:7). May future generations of American Christians remember Samuel Adams with a special gratitude to God.

—— ★ ★ ★ ——

Samuel Adams was one of the few Founding Fathers who acknowledged the Lordship of Jesus Christ and His Kingdom in public statements. As Governor of Massachusetts, he announced a day of fasting for March 20, 1797, with these words:

PROCLAMATION BY HIS EXCELLENCY GOVERNOR ADAMS.

It having been the invariable practice, derived from the days of our renowned ancestors, at this season of the year to set apart a day of public fasting and prayer, and the practice appearing to be in itself productive, if well improved, of happy effects on the public mind,—

I have therefore thought fit, by and with the advice and consent of the Council, to appoint Thursday, the fourth day of May next ensuing, to be observed and improved throughout this Commonwealth for the purpose of public fasting and prayer, earnestly recommending to the ministers of the Gospel, with their respective congregations, then to assemble together and seriously to consider, and with one united voice to confess, our past sins and transgressions, with holy resolutions, by the grace of God, to turn our feet into the path of his law, humbly beseeching him to endue us with all the Christian spirit of piety, benevolence, and the love of our country; and that in all our public deliberations we may be possessed of a sacred regard to the fundamental principles of our free, elective, civil Constitutions; that we may be preserved from consuming fires and all other desolating judgments.

And as at this season the general business of the year commences, it seems highly proper humbly to implore the Divine blessing on our husbandry, trade, and fishery, and all the labor of our hands; on our University and schools of education; on the administration of the government of the United States; and in a particular manner that all misunderstanding between them and a sister republic may be happily so adjusted as to prevent an open rupture and establish permanent peace.

And as it is our duty to extend our wishes to the happiness of the great family of man, I conceive we cannot better express ourselves than by humbly supplicating the Supreme Ruler of the world that the rod of tyrants may be broken into pieces, and the oppressed made free; that wars may cease in all the earth, and that the confusions that are and have been among the nations may be overruled by the promoting and speedily bringing on that holy and happy period when the kingdom of our Lord and Saviour Jesus Christ may be everywhere established, and all the people willingly bow to the sceptre of Him who is the Prince of Peace.

And I do hereby recommend that all unnecessary labor and recreation may be suspended on the said day.[37]

Phillis Wheatley (1753-1784)

CHAPTER 10

Phillis Wheatley: First African-American Writer

For you see your calling, brethren, that not many wise according to the flesh, not many mighty, not many noble, are called. But God has chosen the foolish things of the world to put to shame the wise, and God has chosen the weak things of the world to put to shame the things which are mighty . . .
—1 Corinthians 1:26-27

All of God's works in history are wondrous and praiseworthy. And that should include the work of God in the life of Phillis Wheatley. It comes as an intriguing fact in American history that God chose a teenage slave girl to become the first published African-American writer.

Phillis Wheatley arrived in the port of Boston at only seven years old. She would be sold for as little as ten pounds sterling,[1] but within ten years her name would be known throughout the world. The life of Phillis Wheatley is a testimony to the truth that all human beings are made in the image of God. It matters not one's skin color, or economic and cultural background, or religious heritage—all are equally made in the image of God. All have value because every person born into this world is an image-bearer of the Creator. And, all are redeemable by the atoning work of the Son of God at the cross.

Journey from Africa to America

I was sought by those who did not ask for Me;
I was found by those who did not seek Me.
I said, "Here I am, here I am,"
To a nation that was not called by My name. (Isaiah 65:1)

Phillis Wheatley was abducted somewhere on the shores of West Africa and then brought on a slave ship to the port of Boston in 1761. As a young girl from the continent of Africa, Phillis would have been considered a "refuse slave." Such young girls were seen as having little market value. Whenever human beings are viewed as property, some become more valuable than others. Such was the case when Phillis arrived in Boston, for she was not a desirable purchase in the slave market. But not so with God. The value He placed on this little girl was far more than silver and gold, in that He redeemed her by the "precious blood" of His only begotten Son (1 Pet. 1:18-19).

It is estimated that some twelve million Africans were forcibly taken from the African continent and transported to the Americas between 1492 and 1870.[2] Phillis Wheatley was just one of many millions who underwent the inhumane suffering of the African slave trade. On the journey from the shores of Africa to Boston, about one in four of the slaves died. Phillis was mercifully spared an early death in the transport to America.

Phillis arrived in Boston aboard the slave ship *Phillis*. It was from this ship that Phillis took her name. It would be a constant reminder of her early history. The young girl was purchased by John and Susanna Wheatley. Mr. Wheatley was a successful Boston merchant who made his wealth primarily as a tailor. This Christian family began right away to educate young Phillis in the truths of the faith. Though Phillis assisted the family in various household tasks, the Wheatleys also gave her ample time to study and to write. She received an education that familiarized her with the Bible and certain historical writings. When Phillis embraced the Christian faith, she found a motive for her writing. She wanted to communicate God's truth with her pen and her faith in God would serve as the foundation for all of her writings.

The time of Phillis Wheatley's arrival in America could not have been better - she came shortly after the Great Awakening. English preachers such as George Whitefield, John and Charles Wesley, and American pastors

George Whitefield

like Jonathan Edwards, and William and Gilbert Tennent were witness to the powerful working of the Holy Spirit of God across the English colonies. The Wheatley family and Phillis as well were influenced by this spiritual awakening. Ten years after arriving in Boston, Phillis was baptized in the Name of the Father, Son, and Holy Spirit at the Old South Congregational Church in Boston where the Wheatley family attended.

Early Poetry

A word fitly spoken is like apples of gold in settings of silver. (Proverbs 25:11)

Phillis Wheatley's talent for writing poetry was quickly recognized in her pre-teen years. It wasn't long before her reputation had spread throughout the American colonies. She tried her hand as a poet on numerous "elegies" which she would write upon the death of well-known individuals in England and in the American colonies. When George Whitefield died in September 1770, Phillis' elegy to Whitefield brought her instant notoriety on both sides of the Atlantic.

Incredibly, she wrote this tribute to Whitefield's life at only seventeen years of age, having arrived in America just nine years earlier (without having had any previous knowledge of the English language.)

> Hail, happy Saint, on thy immortal throne!
> To thee complaints of grievance are unknown;
> We hear no more the music of thy tongue,
> Thy wonted auditories cease to throng.
> Thy lessons in unequal'd accents flow'd!
> While emulation in each bosom glow'd;
> Thou didst, in strains of eloquence refin'd,
> Inflame the soul, and captivate the mind.
> Unhappy we, the setting Sun deplore!
> Which once was splendid, but it shines no more;
> He leaves this earth for Heav'n's unmeasur'd height,
> And worlds unknown, receive him from our sight;
> There WHITEFIELD wings, with rapid course his way,
> And sails to Zion, through vast seas of day.[3]

In these words Phillis describes George Whitefield's powers of speech and how he influenced countless hearers by "inflaming the soul" and "captivating the mind." She expresses sadness over his departure, but reminds her readers that Whitefield is now "on his immortal throne." It is still one of Phillis Wheatley's most famous poems.

Needless to say, her contemporary readers were astounded at her poetic abilities especially given her young age. As the Wheatley family came to realize Phillis' unique talents, they decided to assist her in getting her work published.

Publication of First and Only Book

> For exaltation comes neither from the east
> Nor from the west nor from the south.

But God is the Judge:

He puts down one,

And exalts another. (Psalm 75:6-7)

Getting published in the colonies was not easy in the mid-1700s. Any author who wanted to publish a work would have to assume most of the financial risk in the printing and distribution. Authors would often advertise the work before publication in order to gain "subscriptions." Subscribers would agree to buy a copy of the work at a discounted price, which would help to capitalize the project. Because there were few copyright protections in the colonies, many authors sought to publish their works in England instead of America in order to protect their work under British law. The Wheatley family secured a publishing agreement with a printer in London for Phillis' collected poems. The book was titled *Poems on Various Subjects, Religious and Moral.*

The preface to the book included a letter written by John Wheatley to the publisher in which Phillis Wheatley's story is told in brief. The original wording follows:

> *PHILLIS was brought from Africa to America, in the Year 1761, between Seven and Eight Years of age. Without any Assistance from School Education, and by only what she was taught in the Family, she, in sixteen Months Time from her arrival, attained the English Language, to which she was an utter Stranger before, to such a Degree, as to read any, the most difficult part of the Sacred Writings, to the great Astonishment of all who heard her . . . This Relation is given by her Master who bought her, and with whom she now lives.*

JOHN WHEATLEY

Boston, Nov. 14, 1772[4]

The book also included a short address to the reading public containing the names of influential men in Boston who attested to the authenticity of Phillis' work. The idea that a young African-American slave could have written these poems was almost unbelievable. Therefore, it was felt necessary to include an

P O É M S

O N

VARIOUS SUBJECTS,

RELIGIOUS AND MORAL.

B Y

PHILLIS WHEATLEY,

NEGRO SERVANT to Mr. JOHN WHEATLEY,
of BOSTON, in NEW ENGLAND.

L O N D O N:

Printed for A. BELL, Bookseller, Aldgate; and sold by
Messrs. COX and BERRY, King-Street, *BOSTON.*

MDCCLXXIII.

Title page of *Poems on Various Subjects, Religious and Moral* attestation by certain credible authorities who would verify that Phillis really had created these poetic works. These men attested:

> WE whose Names are under-written, do assure the World, that the POEMS specified in the following Page, were (as we verily believe) written by PHILLIS, a young Negro girl, who was but a few Years since, brought an uncultivated Barbarian from Africa, and has ever since been, and now is, under the Disadvantage of serving as a Slave in a Family in this Town. She has been examined by some of the best Judges, and is thought qualified to write them.[5]

The signers included Thomas Hutchinson, the governor of Massachusetts, John Hancock, later signer of the Declaration of Independence, and Increase Mather's grandson, the Rev. Samuel Mather, with numerous other men.

On May 8, 1773, Phillis left Boston for London, in the company of Nathaniel Wheatley, John Wheatley's son. They had arranged a tour to publicize the new book. Phillis met with a number of influential men and women, including Benjamin Franklin, who was in England representing the colonies at the time. She also had an opportunity to be presented before King George III but, due to illness, had to forfeit the meeting. Later that year she returned to Boston to await the arrival of the first printed copies of *Poems on Various Subjects*. Phillis made numerous plans to market and sell the work. She demonstrated "extraordinary business acumen" and showed a keen knowledge of the "business of bookselling."[6] The book became the first work ever published in America by someone of African descent, and Phillis had become the first African female writer the world had ever known.

Later Years and Death

> Your eyes saw my substance, being yet unformed.
> And in Your book they all were written,
> The days fashioned for me,
> When as yet there were none of them. (Psalm 139:16)

Shortly after the publication, the Wheatley family freed Phillis from slavery. She continued to live with the family as she set out to provide her own income through her book. When her mistress Susanna Wheatley died on March 3, 1774, Phillis was struck with grief. She described this difficult time in a letter to a friend.

> *I have lately met with a great trial in the death of my mistress; let us imagine the loss of a Parent, Sister or Brother the tenderness of all these were united in her. – I was a poor little outcast & a stranger when she took me in: not only into her house but I presently became a sharer in her most tender affections. I was treated by her more like her child than her Servant.*[7]

Although she had been emancipated, life was still not easy for Phillis. It was difficult for a free African-American woman living in Boston to make money, even with a book in print. She continued to write, hoping to publish a second book. As biographer Vincent Caretta notes, much of Phillis' life "between 1776 and her death in 1784 remains a mystery."[8] When John Wheatley died in 1778, he left Phillis nothing. Later that year Phillis married a free black man named John Peters. However, this man was laden with legal troubles because of his various debts. The American War for Independence brought additional trouble for John and Phillis. Unable to pay his debts, John Peters was eventually imprisoned. Though Phillis Wheatley wanted to publish a second volume of poems, she was never able to find financial backing for the project. She died in 1784, at about thirty-three years of age. Her cause of death is unknown. Some records say that she had given birth to a number of children in previous years and then died in 1784 due to complications from childbirth. Others believe she died of an illness. With so few records, only God knows what happened to Phillis Wheatley in the last years of her life.

Highlights from Phillis Wheatley's Poetry

> *I will praise You, O Lord my God, with all my heart,*
> *And I will glorify Your name forevermore.*
> *For great is Your mercy toward me,*

And You have delivered my soul from the depths of Sheol. (Psalm 86:12-13)

Phillis' most enduring and popular poetic work is titled "On Being Brought from Africa to America." This poem has been often criticized by those who believe she justifies slavery when she refers to God's mercy. That is an unfair accusation. For there is no sense in which Phillis was out to justify the slave trade. The Atlantic slave trade was truly a despicable injustice. Nonetheless, Phillis points out how the evil of the slave trade was used, in the wise purposes of God, to introduce her to the gospel of the Lord Jesus Christ. Phillis is only describing the truth of how God turns the evil endeavors of men to good ends. This is what God did with Joseph, when his brothers intended to get rid of him by selling him to the Ishmaelite slave traders. Joseph says, "You meant evil against me, but God meant it for good" (Gen. 50:20). Of course, ungodly literary critics do not understand this theological explanation, nor do they see the benefit in the salvation Jesus Christ provides.

> *But as for you, you meant evil against me; but God meant it for good, in order to bring it about as it is this day, to save many people alive. (Genesis 50:20)*

Similarly to Joseph's explanation, Phillis tells how she was saved from a life of heathen ignorance by the mercy of God.

> *'Twas mercy brought me from my Pagan land,*
> *Taught my benighted soul to understand*
> *That there's a God, that there's a Saviour too:*
> *Once I redemption neither sought nor knew.*
> *Some view our sable race with scornful eye,*
> *"Their colour is a diabolic die."*
> *Remember, Christians, Negros, black as Cain,*
> *May be refin'd, and join th' angelic train.*[9]

In "Thoughts on the Works of Providence," Phillis praised God for His wisdom and love daily demonstrated in His works of providence.

Arise, my soul, on wings enraptur'd, rise
To praise the monarch of the earth and skies,
Whose goodness and beneficence appear
As round its centre moves the rolling year,
Or when the morning glows with rosy charms,
Or the sun slumbers in the ocean's arms:
Of light divine be a rich portion lent
To guide my soul, and favour my intent.
Celestial muse, my arduous flight sustain,
And raise my mind to a seraphic strain![10]

In the same poem, Phillis describes God as the king over all things, who shows goodness to all through the creation itself.

Infinite Love where'er we turn our eyes
Appears: this ev'ry creature's wants supplies;
This most is heard in Nature's constant voice,
This makes the morn, and this the eve rejoice;
This bids the fost'ring rains and dews descend
To nourish all, to serve one gen'ral end,
The good of man: yet man ungrateful pays
But little homage, and but little praise.
To him, whose works array'd with mercy shine,
What songs should rise, how constant, how divine![11]

Here Phillis describes God's providence serving the good of man even though unredeemed humanity will not praise God for His undeserved mercies. This is usually referred to as "common grace." In the words of our Lord Jesus Christ,

He makes His sun rise on the evil and on the good, and sends rain on the just and on the unjust. (Matthew 5:45)

In her poem "Atheism," written in 1769, Phillis quite convincingly exposes the folly of unbelief.

Where now shall I begin this Spacious field
To tell what curses unbelief doth yield.
Thou that dost daily feel his hand and rod
And dare deny the essence of a God.
If there's no heaven whither will thou go?
Make thy elysium in the shades below.
If there's no God from whence did all things spring?
He made the greatest and minutest thing.[12]

Responses to the Writings of Phillis Wheatley

And He has made from one blood every nation of men to dwell on all the face of the earth, and has determined their preappointed times and the boundaries of their dwellings. (Acts 17:26)

Phillis Wheatley's writings were truly historic. For this reason, she became the center of numerous debates surrounding the equality of all ethnic peoples. How were Africans to be viewed in the colonies and elsewhere in the Western world? Some European and American intellectuals believed the African peoples were "another species of men," fundamentally different in some way from white Europeans.[13] The non-Christian philosopher David Hume wrote in 1753 of the African people, saying:

I am apt to suspect the Negroes, and in general all the other species of men (for there are four or five different kinds) to be naturally inferior to the whites. There never was a civilized nation of any other complexion than white, nor any individual eminent either in action or speculation. No ingenious manufacturers amongst them, no arts, no sciences . . . In Jamaica indeed they talk of one Negro as a man of parts and learning [Francis Williams]; but tis likely he is admired for very slender accomplishment, like a parrot, who speaks a few words plainly.[14]

Here Hume argues that there was no true example of a race other than the "white race" that has produced real art or made real scientific discoveries. Hume even dismisses one known example of a man in Jamaica who was educated, but Hume insists the man only repeats what he has learned "like a parrot." In a few short years, by the amazing providence of God, Phillis Wheatley surfaced as living proof to contradict the wild, evolutionary theories of these worldly philosophers and racists.

The German philosopher Immanuel Kant wrote with a similar opinion:

Mr. Hume challenges anyone to cite a single example in which a Negro has shown talents, and asserts that among the hundreds of thousands of blacks who are transported elsewhere from the countries, although many of them have been set free, still not a single one was ever found who presented anything great in art or science or any other praiseworthy quality . . . So fundamental is the difference between these two races of man, and it appears to be as great in regard to mental capacities as in color.[15]

When Phillis' poetry began to gain popularity, people debated whether she was truly producing art. They questioned whether commonly held opinions about black people were wrong in light of her tremendously gifted work. The influential French thinker of the Enlightenment, Voltaire, had to admit that Phillis' poetry proved that blacks could write poetry—although he continued to uphold racist, evolutionary views. The American Founding Fathers also disagreed over what to do with Phillis' writings. Benjamin Franklin appreciated her work and supported her publishing efforts. When Phillis wrote an ode to George Washington, the General responded with a letter thanking her for the beautiful words she wrote of him. It is possible that Phillis Wheatley had an impact on Washington's more liberalizing views on slavery later in his life.

Despite Phillis' gift for poetry so clearly displayed in her published volume, Thomas Jefferson would not change his mind about blacks. Jefferson wrote in a whiff of arrogance: "the compositions published under her name are below the dignity of criticism."[16]   He went on to say:

Comparing them by their faculties of memory, reason, and imagination, it appears to me that in memory they are equal to whites, in reason much inferior, as I think one could scarcely be found capable of tracing and comprehending investigations of Euclid; and that in imagination they are dull, tasteless, and anomalous.[17]

Though Jefferson would admit that black people possessed human souls, he still considered them intellectually "inferior" to most other races. Such presuppositions about blacks obviously blinded Jefferson from making a fair analysis of Phillis' writings.

Despite the racist theories of Jefferson and others, God has proven them wrong over and over again, by raising up pastors, scientists, thinkers, and literary men and women of African descent who have contributed much to this world, and to the kingdom of Christ. Looking back over the last two hundred years, it should be obvious that the opinions of these humanist philosophers and racists were very foolish indeed.

These arguments are not merely refuted by the facts of history. More significantly, it must be the Word of God that will condemn the opinions of Hume, Kant, and Jefferson. The Scriptures teach that all human beings are made in the image of God (Gen. 1:26-27). We have all descended from our first parents —Adam and Eve (Rom. 5:12). We are all made from "one blood" (Acts 17:26). And, the grand plan of redemption in history will bring about the salvation of people from every tribe, tongue, and nation through the work of the Lord Jesus Christ.

Thomas Jefferson

And they sang a new song, saying:
"You are worthy to take the scroll,
And to open its seals;
For You were slain,
And have redeemed us to God by Your blood
Out of every tribe and tongue and people and nation,
And have made us kings and priests to our God;
And we shall reign on the earth." (Revelation 5:9-10)

The beautiful, inspirational, and profoundly thoughtful content found in Phillis Wheatley's writings may have shocked the worldly thinkers of the 19th and 20th centuries. Yet from a Christian worldview perspective, this sort of genius is to be expected from one who has been made in the image of God and redeemed by the blood of Christ. In Phillis' writings we find a human soul renewed in the image of God, in knowledge, righteousness, and holiness (Eph. 4:24, Col. 3:10), raised up to praise her Creator and Redeemer. We find a woman created in the image of God using her God-given creativity to glorify God. Far from simply acting as a parrot repeating things her masters taught her, Phillis' poems are the product of thoughtful reflection. Although her life on this earth was short, Phillis Wheatley left behind for successive generations an important historical testimony to the truth of what the Declaration of Independence declared: "We hold these truths to be self-evident, that all men are created equal."

You have put off the old man with his deeds, and have put on the new man who is renewed in knowledge according to the image of Him who created him, where there is neither Greek nor Jew, circumcised nor uncircumcised, barbarian, Scythian, slave nor free, but Christ is all and in all. (Colossians 3:9-11)

George Washington (1732-1799)

CHAPTER 11

★ ★ ★

George Washington:
The President Who Feared God

Moreover you shall select from all the people
able men, such as fear God, men of truth, hating
covetousness; and place such over them to be rulers
of thousands, rulers of hundreds, rulers of fifties,
and rulers of tens.

—Exodus 18:21

The American War for Independence began on April 19, 1775 when a shot was fired on Lexington Green while Samuel Adams and John Hancock watched from a nearby wood. At the Battle of Bunker Hill (just outside Boston) on June 17, the colonials put up a good fight against the better equipped British. While the Americans lost ground, the British sustained twice as many casualties. These initial skirmishes signaled to the Empire that this would not be an easy fight.

On June 19, 1775, upon the encouragement of Samuel Adams and John Adams, the Continental Congress chose George Washington to command the Continental Army. In March 1776, General George Washington fortified

Dorchester Heights, an eminence overlooking the City of Boston. Sensing their vulnerability to attack, the British troops withdrew to Canada. Following this Washington moved his troops to Long Island, New York, in anticipation of a British attack there.

In late summer of 1776, the British Parliament sent an army of 32,000 men to America (including some German "Hessian" mercenaries). It was the largest force ever sent by Britain to fight in a foreign nation to date. There was no question by this time—the American colonies were facing the most powerful empire on earth.

British General William Howe moved his troops into New York in July 1776. The Americans stationed on Long Island were unable to hold their ground against the advancing British forces. Under cover of night and accommodated by a providential fog, Washington was able to withdraw his troops to New York City, after which Howe forced him to evacuate the city. Washington then retreated to Pennsylvania, losing control of much of New Jersey to the British.

On Christmas Day 1776, George Washington and his troops stealthily

Washington crossing the Delaware river

crossed the Delaware River and attacked a Hessian garrison at Trenton. The maneuver was a complete victory for the Americans and helped boost morale for the country. In early January, British General Cornwallis attempted to attack Washington's position in New Jersey but failed on three separate attempts.

Meanwhile, the British recaptured Fort Ticonderoga (earlier taken by Ethan Allen and the Green Mountain Men). Then British General John Burgoyne marched his troops down the Hudson River Valley, attempting to cut New England off from the rest of the colonies. His troops battled American General Horatio Gates' army at Saratoga, New York between September 19 and October 7, 1777. Saratoga marked the first great victory for the American colonies. The British suffered 1,100 casualties and 7,000 captured, while the Americans counted only 90 killed and 240 wounded. The victory at Saratoga was a shock to the British and an encouragement for the French to enter the war on the side of the colonials.

It wasn't all going to be easy for the Patriots, however. On September 11, 1777, General Howe seized control of Philadelphia, and General Washington lost another battle at Germantown on October 4, 1777.

During the winter months of 1777-1778, George Washington chose to bivouac his troops at Valley Forge, about 20 miles northwest of Philadelphia. Because the colonial legislatures failed to provide provisions for their soldiers, disease and starvation resulted in the loss of about 2,000 men during these terrible months.

In June 1778 the British armies pulled out of Philadelphia to return northwards to New York City. Washington attacked them from the rear at Monmouth Courthouse. The battle was a tactical draw but boosted American morale.

Between 1778 and 1780, British and American troops held a virtual standoff in the North. Meanwhile, between the fall of 1779 and the summer of 1780, the Americans were facing the very worst of conditions in the South. The French Navy, allied to the colonial cause, had miserably failed in its attacks on Newport, Rhode Island and Savannah, Georgia. In the most devastating setback of the war, British General Clinton captured Charleston, South Carolina on December

26, 1779. In May 1780 the colonials suffered a tremendous defeat at Waxhaws, resulting in a massacre of Virginians. Then, to make matters worse, General Gates' troops were routed by British General Tarleton, a man known for his cruelty, on August 16, 1780 at Camden. In the North, George Washington was confronting the problem of mutiny among his troops. Some of his regiments were going days without food, reminiscent of the Valley Forge experience. He had also just received news of Benedict Arnold's treason. Circumstances could hardly have been worse.

Washington at Valley Forge

The decisive event which turned the tide came about on October 7, 1780. In the early fall of 1780, the British and Loyalist armies in the South were feeling confident the war was well in hand. British Major Patrick Ferguson had warned the Carolina Patriots that he was coming to "hang your leaders, and waste your country with fire and sword."[1] The threat of scorched-earth warfare (as condemned in Deut. 20:19-20) became a real concern for the local citizens in the Carolinas. As Ferguson and his troops approached a place called Kings Mountain near the border of North Carolina, the major vowed that he would be "'King of that mountain,' and . . . even God almighty could not remove him."[2] This arrogant proclamation turned out to be a dire mistake. To deny the sovereignty of God while claiming sovereignty to oneself is a hazardous business.

Meanwhile, out on the western frontier, in a town called Sycamore Shoals, Tennessee, the settlers had organized a militia to defend hearth and home from the invading force. They called themselves the "Over-Mountain Men," largely consisting of Scots-Irish Presbyterians. As the men prepared for battle, they solicited the aid of their Presbyterian pastor to preach a parting sermon. The little-known Reverend Samuel Doak preached what may have been the most powerful sermon in the history of this country. He ended his final prayer with these passionate words from the Old Testament Scriptures: "The sword of the Lord and of Gideon!" (Judges 7:20).[3]

With that pastoral encouragement, the men marched off to the battle of Kings Mountain on the South Carolina border. It would prove to be the shortest and most decisive battle in the history of American warfare. In a single hour the men shattered Ferguson's army and Ferguson himself was killed. It was a total rout. The British lost 1,100 men by death or capture, and the Over-Mountain Men lost only twenty-eight. But, in the most significant sense, this would be the turning point for the colonials in the war. It was a decisive moment in American history.

One historian summarizes the effects of the battle: "The Victory at Kings Mountain was the first in a series of remarkable events that would change the direction of the war in America's favor."[4] British General Henry Clinton himself admitted this concerning Kings Mountain in his report to King George III: "Though in itself confessedly trifling, [this defeat] overset in a moment all the happy effects of his Lordship's glorious victory at Camden, and so encouraged the spirit of rebellion in both Carolinas that it never could be afterward humbled."[5]

General Clinton's assessment was entirely accurate. War is all about morale. The delicate balance of powers bearing such historical import will shift in wartime when the morale of the armies shifts. Ultimately, there is nothing human leadership can do to maintain a certain morale. Such critical elements lie in the hand of God, and certain obscure battles really do shift morale in one direction or another.

The next momentous battle occurred on January 17, 1781, also on the Southern front. British General Tarleton pursued Brigadier General Daniel Morgan with 1,100 British troops through the South Carolina backcountry for weeks. Finally, Morgan elected to take a stand at a broad meadowland called Cowpens on January 17. The Americans were outnumbered again, but it was a complete rout in favor of the colonials. Almost the entire British force was either dead or captured by the end, and Tarleton fled the battlefield alone. This concluded a series of victories secured by disparaged, motley bands of mostly Presbyterians. General Daniel Morgan was also a devout Presbyterian layman of Welsh background.

Reports have it that General Morgan rode across the field praising God for the victory. Later he recorded these words concerning the Battle of Cowpens: "Such was the inferiority of our numbers, that our success must be attributed under God . . . to the justice of our cause and the bravery of our troops!"[6] An Irish Presbyterian soldier from the Carolina backcountry described the battle more plainly in his prayer: "Good Lord, our God that art in heaven, we have great reason to thank Thee for the many battles we have won . . . the great and glorious battle of King's Mountain, and the iver glorious and memorable battle of the Cowpens, where we made the Proud Gineral Teartleton run doon the road helter-skelter!"[7]

General George Washington also recognized the importance of these battles and the providential hand of God over these events. He wrote shortly after Cowpens: "The remarkable interpositions of the divine government in the hours of our deepest distress and darkness have been too luminous to suffer me to doubt the happy issue of the present contest."[8]

Following several minor setbacks for the colonials, the war was over. The Battle of Yorktown was fought just ten months after Cowpens, upon Washington's troops moving to the Southern front, where the British army had been badly weakened.

George Washington's Raising

George Washington was born February 11, 1732 on the family farm in Westmoreland County, Virginia about a mile from the Potomac River. His father Augustine was a hard-driving businessman and farmer. His mother, Mary Ball Washington was his second wife, a godly, hardworking woman who had been orphaned as a child. She named her son George for the family friend who had raised her (after she been orphaned on her parents' death).

George's mother was particularly careful about her son's Christian education. She would read to him daily from a book called *Contemplations Moral and Divine* written by the Puritan jurist Sir Matthew Hale. The biblical gospel message was clearly found in this instruction:

Who it was that thus suffered?

It was Christ Jesus the Eternal Son of God clothed in our Flesh, God and Man united in one Person, his Manhood giving him a Capacity of suffering and his Godhead giving a Value to that suffering, and each Nature united in one Person to make a complete Redeemer, the Heir of all things (Heb. 1:2), The Prince of Life. The Light that lighteneth every Man that cometh into the World (John 1:9), as touching his Divine Nature, God over all Blessed for ever (Rom. 9:5), and as touching his Human Nature, full of Grace and Truth, (John 1:14) . . . But could no other Person be found that might suffer for the Sins of Man but the Son of God? Or if the business of our Salvation must be transacted by him alone could it not be without suffering and such suffering as this? No. As there was no other Name given under Heaven by which we might be saved nor was there any found besides in the compass of the whole World that could expiate for one sin of Man, but it must be the Arm of the Almighty that must bring Salvation (Isa. 63:5). So if the blessed Son of God will undertake the Business and become Captain of our Salvation he must be made perfect by suffering (Heb. 2:1, 5:9). And if he will stand instead of Man he must bear the wrath of his Father if he will become sin for Man.[9]

Throughout his teachings Hale, the old Puritan, faithfully adhered to the reformation doctrines of the sovereignty of God, justification by faith alone, and the holy law of God. George kept copies of the books he received in his Christian education, some signed by his own hand at 13, 14, or 15 years old. These included:

1. A handbook explaining the *Book of Common Prayer* to children.

2. A book called *The Sufficiency of a Standing Revelation*, encouraging a high view of the Scriptures in a day of skepticism.

3. A science textbook called *The Wisdom of God Manifested in the Works of Creation*.

4. *The Young Man's Companion*, which was written by a W. Mather with the goal that his readers would "build upon no other foundation besides the Rock Christ Jesus."

As a twelve-year-old boy George wrote a sample will, stating that "I recommend my Soul to God who gave it hoping for salvation in and through the merits and mediation of Jesus Christ."[10] These words are perhaps the closest thing to a public profession of faith in Christ to be found in any of Washington's letters and personal records.

Young George seemed cut out for battle from his earliest years. While at play he often formed his friends into little battalions and ran them through military drills. George was a born leader. He was always organized, known for taking copious notes and keeping them for future reference. Recognized early on for his athletic abilities, he was without rival when it came to horseback riding, wrestling, and running. To the delight of his friends, he once threw a rock to the top of Natural Bridge, a height of 215 feet.[11]

George's father died when he was eleven years old, and his tutoring and education came under the oversight of his mother and brother Lawrence, who was fourteen years his senior. Lawrence inherited the family estate in Fairfax County and called it "Mount Vernon." Previously Lawrence had joined the British Navy. But, when George was offered the opportunity to do likewise, his mother objected. He had already sent his clothes ahead to the ship, but upon his mother's strong admonitions, George relented. At thirteen years of age he

Mt. Vernon

began studying surveying, and in his sixteenth year traveled to western Virginia to help survey a large tract of land for Lord Thomas Fairfax. In 1751 George accompanied his brother Lawrence on a trip to the West Indies in hopes that the weather would help Lawrence's worsening lung problems. The voyage didn't help, and in the providence of God Lawrence died on July 26, 1752. In his will Lawrence left Mount Vernon to twenty-year-old George.

Called to the Battle

A thousand shall fall at your side, and ten thousand at your right hand, but it shall not come near you. Only with your eyes shall you look and see the reward of the wicked, because you have made the LORD, who is my refuge, even the Most High your dwelling place. (Psalm 91:7-9)

From the outset of his military career, it was plain that God's hand was upon George Washington in an extraordinary way. In February 1753 George was assigned to train a militia by the Governor of Virginia, Robert Dinwiddie. In the fall of the same year he was sent on a dangerous mission up the Ohio River, at the outbreak of the French and Indian War. The French were building forts on American/British territory, and Washington was carrying a letter from Governor Dinwiddie requesting that they cease and desist. An Indian attempted a shot at Washington at fifteen yards' distance and missed. George's assistant wanted to retaliate and kill the Indian, but Washington insisted that the man be allowed to go on his way.

They later crossed an icy river on a raft and nearly drowned. The eleven-week excursion was, in Washington's words, "as fatiguing a journey as it is possible to conceive."[12]

As the war intensified, a British general named Edward Braddock took command of the Virginia troops. In early July 1755 Braddock moved his army into western Pennsylvania to the Monongahela River outside of modern-day Pittsburgh. With George Washington as his personal assistant, Braddock's orders were to launch attacks on the French who were attempting to control the Ohio territories. In God's providence, Washington became sick on the march and was forced to ride in a covered wagon at the rear of the army. Braddock, disregarding the counsel of his Virginian volunteers, rode his troops directly into an ambush, and the French and Indian warriors proceeded to slaughter the American and English soldiers—almost 1,000 men lay dead and wounded at the end of the engagement.

But not confounded by his superior officer's mistakes, George Washington grabbed a horse and rallied what few troops remained to provide a resistance in the rear guard. In the fighting that ensued, Washington had two horses shot from under him. His coat was shot through in four places, and his hat came through the battle sporting two musket-ball-shaped holes. One officer noted that Washington handled himself with "the greatest courage and resolution."[13] Quite a number of times in the skirmish the enemy fired on him from point-blank range. God's providential hand of protection on the man was astounding even to the Native Americans who were present during the battle. Fifteen years later, an old chief visited Washington and explained to him how he had tried to take a direct shot at him during the Battle of Monongahela:

Our rifles were leveled, rifles which, but for him, knew not how to miss—It was all in vain, a power mightier than we, shielded him from harm. He cannot die in battle. I am old, and soon shall be gathered to the great council fire of my fathers, in the land of shades, but ere I go, there is something, bids me speak . . . The Great Spirit protects that man, and guides his destinies.[14]

George explained to his brother in a letter written a week after the battle, "I now exist and appear in the land of the living by the miraculous care of Providence, that protected me beyond all human expectations."[15] The Presbyterian pastor Samuel Davies made almost a prophetic call on the life of Washington in a sermon he gave on August 17, 1755. In reference to the Battle of Monongahela fought a month earlier, he included mention of that "heroic youth, Colonel Washington, whom I cannot but hope Providence has hitherto preserved in so signal a manner for some important service to his country." [16] There were two other important Americans who survived the Monongahela massacre—Daniel Boone and Daniel Morgan, the future victor at the critical Battle of Cowpens.

The American War for Independence—God's Hand Still on the Man

Blessed be the LORD God of our fathers, who . . . has extended mercy to me before the king and his counselors, and before all the king's mighty princes. So I was encouraged, as the hand of the LORD my God was upon me; and I gathered leading men of Israel to go up with me. (Ezra 7:27-28)

Facing off with the greatest empire on earth was not an easy challenge for George Washington. America had no trained army, and the colonial militias had very little experience in battle. The many successes met with in the War for Independence, Washington believed, were provided him by God alone. He wrote to a friend, "I shall most religiously believe, that the finger of Providence is in it, to blind the eyes of our enemies."[17]

The fortification of Dorchester Heights was accomplished in a single night. While the Americans were building the fortified wall, the British general considered sending men across the channel to stop the work, but the Lord sent a storm that evening which prevented the interruption. As he watched 8,900 British troops evacuate Boston in 78 ships, Washington noted: "[This] must be ascribed to the interposition of that Providence, which has manifestly appeared in our behalf through the whole of this important struggle . . . May that being, who is powerful to save, and in whose hands is the fate of nations, look down with an eye of tender pity and compassion upon the whole of the United Colonies."[18]

God's hand of protection continued to follow the General through the war. In one exchange with the enemy in New York, a cannonball landed just six feet from Washington, but he sustained no injury whatsoever. An officer poisoned a dish of peas set before the General, but a young woman intervened and saved his life.

The British General Howe's 32,000 men were poised to wipe out the last of Washington's 8,000 men in Brooklyn Heights, New York. But, again, weather prevented the attacks. Washington took the opportunity to evacuate his men on August 29, 1776. A storm had raged for three full days, but on the third night at 11:00 p.m. the storm abated and was followed by a deathly quiet. The Continental soldiers began their evacuation during this lull, but as the morning dawned a large percentage of the men were still waiting for boats to convey them across the river to safety. Just in time, however, the Lord commanded a fog to descend upon the bay. Major Benjamin Tallmadge described the scene:

> As the dawn of the next day approached, those of us who remained in the trenches became very anxious for our own safety, and when the dawn appeared there were several regiments still on duty. At this time a very dense fog began to rise (out of the ground and off the river), and it seemed to settle in a peculiar manner over both encampments. I recall this peculiar providential occurrence perfectly well, and so very dense was the atmosphere that I could scarcely discern a man at six yards' distance. [19]

The fog remained over the British camps until all the American boats had left Long Island. Throughout the war the weather often seemed to favor the Americans, including Trenton, Cowpens, and Yorktown.

Yet, the most astounding act of Providence, at least in the mind of George Washington, was the discovery of Benedict Arnold's treason. British Major John Andre in civilian clothes happened to be identified and captured by three American soldiers. These men discovered incriminating evidence on Andre that revealed Benedict Arnold's intention of surrendering West Point into British hands. Had this plot succeeded, it would have been a "fatal stab" into the heart of the American armies. General Washington wrote to a friend, "Happily the treason has been discovered to prevent the fatal misfortune. The providential train of circumstances which led to it affords the most convincing proof that the Liberties of America are the object of Divine Protection."[20]

After securing the victory at Yorktown, George Washington wrote to a pastor that, "in the midst of our Joys, I hope we shall not forget that, to divine Providence is to be ascribed the Glory and the Praise."[21]

Writing to Henry Knox after a full victory over Britain had finally been achieved, Washington voiced his heartfelt conviction that nothing but the mercy and lovingkindness of God had safely carried the Colonies through their long war with Britain:

> I feel now, however, as I conceive a wearied traveller must do, who, after treading many a painful step with a heavy burden on his shoulders, is eased of the latter, having reached the haven to which all the former were directed; and from his house-top is looking back, and tracing with an eager eye the meanders by which he escaped the quicksands and mires which lay in his way; and into which none but the all-powerful Guide and Dispenser of human events could have prevented his falling.[22]

The Presidency

When a land transgresses, it has many rulers, but with a man of understanding and knowledge, its stability will long continue. (Proverbs 28:2 ESV)

For the eight and a half years of full-time service provided for his country's defense during the War for Independence, Washington had foregone all financial compensation. Both the Pennsylvania and Virginia state governments offered him some remuneration after the war, but he refused it all. In 1780 he wrote, "If sacrificing my entire estate would effect any valuable purpose, I would not hesitate one moment in doing it."[23] George Washington's generosity was only outdone by his humility. When the Continental Congress announced his appointment as commander-in-chief of the American armies, he quickly exited the room and hid in the library. He told his wife that he had "used every endeavor in my power to avoid it."[24] His adopted daughter Nelly Custis reported that she "never heard him relate a single act of his during the war."[25]

When elected to the presidency in April 1789, Washington made this inauspicious note in his own diary: "About 10:00 I bade adieu to Mount Vernon, to private life, and to domestic felicity; and, with a mind oppressed with more anxious and painful sensations than I have words to express, set out for New York . . . with the best disposition to render service to my country in obedience to its call, but with less hope of answering its expectations."[26]

The greatest contribution left by George Washington in his service as president was his commitment to keep America out of European squabbles. His cabinet did not agree with him on this issue and, when war broke out between France and Britain, Thomas Jefferson aligned himself with France while Alexander Hamilton sided with Britain. However, Washington wanted complete neutrality for America in these wars. He wrote, "War having actually commenced between France and Great Britain, it behooves the government of this country to use every means in its power to prevent the citizens thereof from embroiling us with either of those powers by endeavoring to maintain a strict neutrality."[27]

Both France and Britain persecuted the United States for the next twenty years because the country refused to take sides in their disagreement. The French went so far as to send an agent to America to stir up trouble. Edmund Charles Genet formed Jacobin clubs around the United States and tried to initiate a revolution against Washington in 1793. Ten thousand people were threatening "to drag Washington out of his house and effect a revolution in the government, or compel it to declare war in favor of the French Revolution and against England,"[28] as John Adams put it. Thankfully, Genet fell out of favor with the Revolution and the French sought to kill him. Fearing execution if he returned to France, Genet requested permission of President Washington to remain in America. Even though Genet had recently been plotting Washington's overthrow, the president mercifully granted Genet's request and thus saved the life of his enemy. Washington's handling of the Genet affair is a beautiful illustration of Christ's command: "Love your enemies, do good to those who hate you, bless those who curse you, and pray for those who spitefully use you" (Luke 6:27-28). Genet retired to Upstate New York and, thanks to Washington's prudent international policies, the radical and dangerous influence of the French Revolution did not destroy the newly-formed United States during these early years.

The young United States toyed with anarchy and revolution during these years. It is far too easy for a nation to move from tyranny to anarchy and vice versa. Both conditions are miserable, and only a wise leader can navigate between these two curses. George Washington faced the chaos of the French Revolution bleeding into America, the Whiskey Rebellion, and other signs of unrest. In the providence of God, he was probably the only man who could have held the nation together during these years. Washington served two terms as President from 1789 to 1797.

> *My son, fear the LORD and the king; do not associate with those given to change;*
> *for their calamity will rise suddenly, and who knows the ruin those two can bring?*
> *(Proverbs 24:21-22)*

Slavery

> *I am sending him [the slave Onesimus] back. You therefore receive him, that is, my*
> *own heart, whom I wished to keep with me, that on your behalf he might minister*
> *to me in my chains for the gospel. But without your consent I wanted to do nothing,*
> *that your good deed might not be by compulsion, as it were, but voluntary. For*
> *perhaps he departed for a while for this purpose, that you might receive him forever,*

no longer as a slave but more than a slave—a beloved brother, especially to me but how much more to you, both in the flesh and in the Lord. (Philemon 12-16)

In his letter to Philemon, Paul did not coerce the slave master to emancipate his slave. Paul does not recommend slave revolts or civil wars, but instead pushes for a voluntary release of the slave. The Christian is always looking for a work of love in the heart of the slave master. He seeks social change by regeneration, a change of heart in both the slave and the slave master. Apparently this change of heart really did come upon George Washington in his life.

Although born into a slave economy and inheriting slaves himself, few of America's founders came to hate slavery as intensely as did George Washington. While acting as president of the United States, he signed the first anti-slavery legislation, The Northwest Ordinance. Some 75 years later, the Fourteenth Amendment which finally abolished slavery in the United States would be patterned after this legislation. In 1786 Washington wrote, "There is not a man living, who wishes more sincerely than I do, to see a plan adopted for the abolition of [slavery]."[29]

George Washington certainly represented a repentant attitude towards slavery, first attempting to shut down the slave trade by the Fairfax Resolves he penned with George Mason in 1774. In his last will and testament, Washington ordered the emancipation of all of his slaves. "Upon the decease [of] my wife, it is my will and desire that all the slaves which I hold in [my] own right shall receive their freedom."[30] He also made sure that all of them "shall be comfortably clothed and fed by my heirs while they live."[31] In addition, Washington provided a means of education for the young slaves who were to be freed.

Whereas men like Thomas Jefferson (and later, Abraham Lincoln) would seek to banish the African Americans to a separate colony, George Washington would have nothing of the sort. He wanted a racially mixed community and an end of slavery in America.

The Character of George Washington

Was George Washington a Christian? Hardly any question in all of American history is more hotly debated than this one. Washington was not a pastor and he was not a theologian, but his writings are replete with references to God.

It is important to consider that although not a pastor, George Washington still had his own spiritual struggles and as a Christian would have had to live out a life of repentance and faith himself. In his younger years George was somewhat interested in gambling. In May 1772 his personal records indicate that he gambled twelve times in a single month. Yet, as he grew older, he realized these to be moral failings. Writing to his nephew Bushrod in 1783, he warned of this vice of gambling: "It is the child of avarice, the brother of inequity, the father of mischief. It has been the ruin of many worthy families, the loss of many a man's honor, and the cause of suicide."[32]

Washington certainly expressed a reverence and fear of God throughout his entire life of leadership. On February 15, 1763, George Washington took an oath in agreement with the "Doctrine and Discipline of the Church of England." The oath included the Thirty-Nine Articles of Religion, in which it is stated: "We are accounted before God only for the merit of our Lord and Saviour Jesus Christ, by faith, and not for our own works or deservings." Since Washington espoused these beliefs, it would be difficult to disprove his faith unless he quit the church or personally disavowed his previous commitment. The records give no indication that this ever occurred. Moreover, George Washington called himself a Christian on many occasions. He also encouraged the Delaware Indian chiefs in May 1779: "You do well to learn our arts and ways of life, and above all, the religion of Jesus Christ." [33]

Perhaps the clearest witness to a simple faith we can find in Washington's writings comes in a letter he sent to the Marquis de Lafayette, his military friend from France who served under Washington during the War for Independence. Washington was asking forgiveness of his friend, and put it this way:

I stand before you as a Culprit: but to repent and be forgiven are the precepts of

Heaven: I do the former, do you practice the latter, and it will be participation of a divine attribute.[34]

He also encouraged the entire nation to "confess their Sins before God . . . to implore the Lord, and Giver of all victory, to pardon our manifold sins and wickednesses."[35]

The true measure of faith is ultimately known by a man's fruits and the character of his life. With Washington, it is difficult to find a clear verbal profession of his faith in Jesus Christ. This may have been due in part to his reluctance to use the name of Christ in what some historians see as a respect for His Name. Nonetheless, George Washington's maxim was "deeds not words." He resented any kind of a pretense of religion.

> *And let us consider one another in order to stir up love and good works, not forsaking the assembling of ourselves together, as is the manner of some, but exhorting one another, and so much the more as you see the Day approaching. (Hebrews 10:24-25)*

Throughout his life, George Washington was relentlessly faithful in attending church. He served as a vestryman (lay-elder) in several Anglican churches before the war, missing only eight Sabbaths over more than ten years. When not attending his home church, he favored Presbyterian churches. He was concerned with the "errors" in the Roman Catholic Church, but also warned against "insulting them."[36] In 1762 George went so far as to rebuke his brother-in-law Burwell Bassett for missing church on Sunday:

> *I was favoured with your Epistle written on a certain 25th of July when you ought to have been in Church, praying as becomes every good Christian Man who has as much to answer for as you have; strange it is that you will be so blind to truth that the enlightening sounds of the Gospel cannot reach your Ear . . . could you but behold with what religious zeal I hye me to Church on every Lords day, it would do your heart good, and fill it I hope with equal fervency.*[37]

During the war there were times at which there was no chaplain available on Sundays. In such cases the General would perform the service himself, "reading the scriptures and praying with [his men]."[38]

While Washington served as president, his private secretary found him on his knees with the Bible opened before him, "and he believed such to have been his daily practice."[39] During his presidency, the Washingtons attended church on Sunday mornings, and in the evenings George would read a sermon to his wife.[40]

Washington's Death

Although facing death many times on the battlefield, Washington never once appeared afraid to die. At the Battle of Monmouth he rallied General Lee's retreating troops. His horse was killed under him, but he never faltered; he merely mounted another horse and continued shouting orders. A cannon ball exploded yards away, bespattering him with dirt. A colonel was killed only a few yards from him. One of his officers wrote: "Our army loves their general very much, but they have one thing against him, which is the little care he takes of himself in any action. His personal bravery, and the desire he has of animating his troops by example, make him fearless of danger. This occasions us much uneasiness. But Heaven, which hitherto has been his shield, I hope will still continue to guard so valuable a life."[41]

While serving as president, George Washington became very ill. It was then he turned to his doctor and said, "I am not afraid to die . . . I know I am in the hands of a good Providence."[42]

On December 12, 1799, George Washington contracted a cold while riding his horse around his farms surrounding Mount Vernon. Two days later his condition worsened. At 5:00 p.m. he told his doctors, "I am not afraid to go. I believed from my first attack, that I should not survive it."[43] As Martha read from the Scriptures at the foot of his bed, George Washington passed on to his Maker around 11:00 p.m.

Thus a great man died, and the nation mourned. At least 700 sermons and orations were given in churches, colleges, and legislatures around the country. The chief justice of the US Supreme Court, John Marshall, put it well when he said: "More than any other individual, and as much as to one individual was possible, has he contributed to found this our wide-spreading empire, and to give to the western world, independence and freedom."[44]

Between 1776 and 1800, George Washington was clearly the prime leader in the founding of the United States of America. No single person was more important in unifying the nation or leading the nation in the battle for independence. Patrick Henry and Samuel Adams, both Christians, planted the first seeds of liberty, but George Washington became the figure around which the nation would unify during its formative years. Of the founders of this nation, these three were the most committed Christians. Other Founding Fathers like John Adams, James Madison, James Monroe, Alexander Hamilton, Thomas Jefferson, and Benjamin Franklin moved away from orthodox Christianity. Yet, at this critical time in the history of America, God chose three key Christians—Patrick Henry, Samuel Adams, and George Washington—to plant the seeds for an independent, free, and prosperous nation.

Blessed is the nation whose God is the LORD; and the people whom He has chosen for his own inheritance. (Psalm 33:12)

Noah Webster (1758-1843)

CHAPTER 12

Noah Webster: Christian Educator and American Patriot

The fear of the LORD is the beginning of wisdom,
And the knowledge of the Holy One is understanding.
—Proverbs 9:10

The name "Webster" is one of the most well-known surnames in America. There is good reason for this. For almost 200 years, the dictionary of choice for the American household has been the Merriam-Webster English dictionary. To this day, Webster's classic dictionary (in one of its modern forms) sits on the shelf of many homes in America (or appears as an app on many smartphones). Noah Webster's contributions to the English language are enormous.

However, Noah Webster's contributions to American History go far beyond his dictionary. He remains one of the most important educators in early America. He is still recognized as a true American intellectual who wrote on numerous topics of public interest and contributed to the establishment of Christian education during the developmental years of the nation.

Early Life and Upbringing

Noah Webster was born in West Hartford, Connecticut in 1758 to Noah and Mercy Webster. He was a descendant of the Pilgrim Separatists and Puritans who came to New England in the early 1600s. William Bradford, the first governor of Plymouth Colony, was Noah's great-great-grandfather on his mother's side. As with most boys growing up in New England in the mid-1700s, Noah was raised in the Congregationalist church. This was the main form of Christianity in New England, particularly in Connecticut.

In the decades before Noah's birth, the Great Awakening had already deeply impacted the English colonies in America. But still, many parts of the church continued to experience nominalism and spiritual apathy. The Reverend Nathan

West Hartford, Connecticut

Perkins, who served as the pastor of the Fourth Church of Hartford, where the Webster family attended, complained that he could see few signs of spiritual life, and conversions were very rare (in the 1770s).[1]

Despite the shallow church conditions in which Noah was raised, he did receive Christian instruction from his parents. He was dutifully taught the Bible from his earliest years. Even after he left home as an adult, his parents continued to exhort him to walk in the truth. In a letter dated 1782, Noah Webster Sr. and Mercy Webster wrote to their son:

> *I wish to have you serve your generation and do good in the world and be useful and may so behave as to gain the esteem of all virtuous people that are acquainted with you and gain a comfortable subsistence, but especially that you may so live as to obtain favor of Almighty God and his grace in this world and a saving interest in the merits of Jesus Christ, without which no man can be happy.[2]*

During his growing up years, Noah worked alongside his father, mother, and brothers on the family farm while attending the local grammar school. There he received a basic education which included reading, writing, arithmetic, spelling, and learning a catechism. The three primary school books that Noah used were a speller, the Bible, and a psalter. According to biographer Alan Snyder, Noah was the only member of his family who had a strong interest in book learning and who wanted to expand his education beyond grammar school.[3] At fourteen years of age, the young man sought out a college education at Yale, despite his father's limited financial means.

In those days, preparation for college usually entailed additional tutoring. For two years, Noah received a tutorial from his pastor, Nathan Perkins in Latin and the ancient classics. After receiving a certificate from Pastor Perkins testifying to his fitness to enter Yale, Noah began his formal studies. In order to cover his academic expenses, the Websters mortgaged their farm.

Attending college in the middle of a war is never an easy prospect. The first battles of America's War for Independence occurred at the end of Noah's first year in college. During his second year, he helped organize a college militia. The school faced a number of hardships during the war years, including the cancellation of classes due to a serious shortage of food.[4] At that point the college was forced to send the students home until the situation improved.

Seeking a Profession: Schoolmaster and Lawyer

Noah Webster graduated from Yale with a Bachelor's degree in 1778. Employment opportunities were scarce, so he went back home to work his family's farm for a time. He began to seek out a career in law, but this time his father could not help him with the additional education required. Finally, the day came when his father sent him out into the world to make his own way. Noah Sr. "put into his hand an eight dollar bill of continental currency, then worth three or four dollars; saying to him, 'Take this; you must now seek your living; I can do no more for you.'"[5]

With that, Noah Webster spent the next few years teaching school children in Connecticut. It was these early years of teaching that convinced him of the need for school reforms. He found the schools overcrowded, often with seventy to eighty boys and girls of all ages in a single classroom, and with too few well-trained teachers.[6] Noah persevered in teaching children while he studied for law.

In the spring of 1781 young Webster completed the bar examination and began practicing law in Hartford, Connecticut. As the war was still ongoing, he found little opportunity for employing his skills. So he continued as a schoolmaster in several small towns throughout New England. Unmarried, without employment, and mostly broke, Noah was discouraged. He recounted this season of life in his memoir, writing in the third person about himself:

> *In addition to these circumstances, his health was impaired by close application, & a sedentary life. He was without money & without friends to afford him any particular aid. In this situation of things, his spirits failed, & for some months, he suffered extreme depression & gloomy forebodings.*[7]

These were difficult and lonely years for Noah, but they were important years that would set the stage for much of his future labors. Here he began to conceive of various curriculum ideas that could be developed for use in American schools. He little knew the immense impact his curriculum publications would have on America and on the whole world for centuries to come.

Early Publications

These words which I command you today shall be in your heart. You shall teach them diligently to your children, and shall talk of them when you sit in your house, when you walk by the way, when you lie down, and when you rise up. You shall bind them as a sign on your hand, and they shall be as frontlets between your eyes. (Deuteronomy 6:6-8)

In the late 1700s, most American schoolhouses used textbooks imported from England. It seemed inappropriate to this young schoolmaster that this new and independent nation should continue to use books published for English children in England. A nation must have its own culture and language, and therefore it should develop its own spellers and grammars, he thought. Historian Alan Snyder explains, "Since the most basic element of education is the ability to read and spell, Webster concluded that a spelling book with a distinctive American perspective was a pressing need."[8]

After a few years of work on it, Noah Webster had his first speller ready for publication. Twenty-five years of age and practically penniless, he covered the initial printing costs for a run of 5,000 copies produced in October 1783.

The first edition of Noah's speller was entitled *A Grammatical Institute of the English Language*, a rather unwieldy moniker suggested by Noah's friend and president of Yale College, Ezra Stiles. The speller was later given the more accessible title, *The American Spelling Book*. It became familiarly known as the *Blue-Back Speller* because later editions were bound in a blue hardcover. Noah's publication replaced the English speller written by Thomas Dilworth, called *A New Guide to the English Tongue*.

Webster had concluded that Dilworth's speller was not suitable for American school children for a number of reasons. First, references were often made in Dilworth's speller to locations and villages in England.[9] Secondly,

Noah believed a speller should do more than simply teach how to read. He also thought it should teach how to spell and how to write.[10] Thirdly, Noah wanted a speller that would not be dependent on Latin and Greek grammar so much to explain English grammar. Noah's speller was much easier to understand because it avoided complex discussions of grammar that Noah thought irrelevant. Fourthly, Noah wanted a speller that provided a uniform approach to pronunciation.[11] Not only would a single approach to pronunciation make the learning of English easier, it would also provide a basis for national unity and a common form of English for the new nation.

Unlike the secular educational systems that control the minds of children today, there was still a strong Christian influence in almost every school of Noah Webster's day. Biblical references and reverence for God made up the most basic element in the education of children. That is why one of Webster's alterations to Dilworth's speller was quite controversial. Dilworth's speller was filled with references to God and to biblical teachings, and Noah set out to reduce these references. He explained his reasoning behind this:

> Nothing has a greater tendency to lessen the reverence which mankind ought to have for the Supreme Being, than a careless repetition of his name upon every trifling occasion. Frequent thoughtless repetition renders the name as familiar to children as the name of their book, and they mention it with the same indifference.[12]

In his speller therefore, Noah chose to use passages of Scripture that taught principles of morality but did not mention the divine name. Although his intention was to deepen reverence for the name of God by avoiding reference to God, this was not a solution to the hypocrisy and the irreverence of the day. The problem with a hypocritical faith is people want to "honor God with their lips, but their hearts are far from Him" (Matt. 15:8).

The fear of God is basic and foundational to all education. Moreover, Deuteronomy 6:7 requires that the Word of God be as a sign before children's eyes in their schooling and life. This change from Dilworth's speller and other American textbooks was not a helpful modification. Also, Webster's emphasis on Scriptures that dealt only with outward morality caused his original speller to promote a moralistic view of the Christian faith. For example, in his original speller Noah gives this advice to young people:

> Play not with bad boys; use no ill words at play; spend your time well; live in peace, and shun all strife. **This is the way to make God love you, and to save your soul from the pains of hell.** (emphasis added)[13]

This suggests that God loves us because of our own good behavior and that we will be saved from hell by our own works. The Scriptures rather teach that we are all sinners who do not deserve the grace of God. Our good works cannot earn our place in heaven. Indeed, God demonstrated his love for us in that "while we were yet sinners, Christ died for us" (Rom. 5:8). And we are saved by grace through faith, apart from works (Eph. 2:8).

Noah Webster's defective views of the Christian faith came out strongly in his first speller. But his view of God, faith, and morality would undergo a dramatic change after 1808.

Webster's speller became one of the most published books of all time. As many as 70 million copies were printed in various editions. With the exception of the Bible, it was the most influential book in America for a hundred years. It would be no exaggeration to say that America's children were raised on the speller for at least five generations. Well into the 20th century schools continued to use later editions of the *Blue-Back Speller*.

When Noah Webster first published his original speller, the book title included the phrase "Part I." It was his intention to produce two more volumes of his *Grammatical Institute*. The following year Noah completed the second part of his work on English grammar. This work was different from previous English grammars in that it did not rely so heavily on Latin constructions. Noah also made an economical change from previous grammars by publishing his grammar as a separate volume. Historian Harlow Unger explains:

> Previous spellers and grammars had been published in a single volume, with the grammar filling the rear pages, to be studied after the child mastered the spelling materials in the first half of the book. As a caring schoolmaster, Webster had noticed

that, by the time the child advanced to the grammar section, constant handling by tiny hands had usually torn the book to shreds, leaving the grammar section indecipherable. Parents invariably had to buy a second, identical book to allow their children to proceed with their studies of grammar. Webster cleverly offered the two books for the price of one.[14]

The next year (1785) Webster released the final and third volume of his *Grammatical Institute*. It was a reader containing a variety of literature which would aid the student in reading. The reader contained various types of American literature and was designed to inculcate a love of country and patriotism. Examples of the literature contained in the reader included the Declaration of Independence, addresses of Congress, orations on the Boston Massacre, brief histories of America and the American Revolution, and studies in American geography.[15]

About this time, Noah Webster made an important contribution to American government with his *Sketches of American Policy*. This short 48-page booklet was published a few years before the ratification of the United States Constitution. Unger notes "the framers of the Constitution incorporated almost all its principles in the framework they created for the new American government."[16] George Washington was said to have been heavily influenced by Noah's *Sketches of American Policy*.[17]

In 1789, the same year the new Constitution was ratified, Noah Webster was happily united in marriage to Rebecca Greenleaf. Noah recorded his thoughts in his diary on his wedding day:

This day I became a husband. I have lived a long time a bachelor, something more than thirty one years. But I had no person to form a plan for me in early life & direct me to a profession. I had an enterprising turn of mind, was bold, vain, inexperienced. I have made some unsuccessful attempts, but on the whole have done as well as most men of my years. I begin a profession, at a late period of life but have some advantages of traveling and observation. I am united to an amiable woman, & if I am not happy, shall be much disappointed.[18]

Noah's marriage with Rebecca produced eight children, six daughters and two sons—Emily, Frances Juliana, Harriet, Mary, Eliza, Louisa, William, and Henry. In God's wise providence, most of his children survived childhood. However, Noah's second son Henry died shortly after he was born.

In the years that followed, Noah Webster dedicated most of his time to law although this business proved to be a meager source of income. Nevertheless, Noah continued to receive a steady income from the sales

Noah Webster's wife, Rebecca Greenleaf Webster

of his speller and other books. Copyright law in the young nation had still yet to be developed, and it was largely through the work of Noah Webster that copyright protections were established and expanded in the late 1700s and early 1800s. These copyright protections ensured that authors like Webster could reap some income from their arduous labors. Throughout his life Noah tried his hand at journalism, contributing essays on various topics including government, education, foreign policy, social conditions, health, and morality.

Noah's Conversion in 1808

For it is God who commanded light to shine out of darkness, who has shone in our hearts to give the light of the knowledge of the glory of God in the face of Jesus Christ. (2 Corinthians 4:6)

The year 1808 marks an important turning point in Noah Webster's life.

Between 1760 and 1800, following the Great Awakening, the nation had gone into a spiritual slump. Although Noah had grown up in a home where the Bible was read and revered, he had distanced himself from certain essential doctrines of the faith. Increasingly, he had taken on a humanistic religion, testing biblical doctrines by the fallible standard of human reason. His college training and intellectual pursuits had seriously undermined his early training in the Christian faith. But in 1808, with a little encouragement from his wife and children, Noah went to hear a local preacher.[19]

It was as he heard Moses Stuart's preaching that Noah Webster experienced a dramatic change of mind concerning the things of God. He records the significance of this life-change in these words:

> In the year 1808, the religious views of NW [Noah Webster] were materially changed. Information of this fact coming to the knowledge of his brother in law, Judge Dawes of Boston, the judge sent him a letter with a pamphlet containing sentiments not in accordance with those which NW [Noah Webster] had embraced. This called forth a reply from NW [Noah Webster], in which he gave a succinct relation of the manner in which his views had been changed.[20]

Noah proceeds to describe how this change came about:

> These impressions I attempted to remove by reasoning with myself, and endeavoring to quiet my mind, by a persuasion, that my opposition to my family, and the awakening was not a real opposition to a rational religion, but to enthusiasm or false religion. I continued some weeks in this situation, utterly unable to quiet my own mind, and without resorting to the only source of peace and consolation. The impressions however grew stronger till at length I could not pursue my studies without frequent interruptions. My mind was suddenly arrested . . . I closed my books, yielded to the influence, which could not be resisted or mistaken and was led by a spontaneous impulse to repentance, prayer, and entire submission and surrender of myself to my maker and redeemer. My submission appeared to be cheerful and was soon followed by that peace of mind which the world can neither give nor take away.[21]

Noah Webster had finally found peace with God through the blood of Jesus Christ. This peace, brought about by the work of the Holy Spirit, also brought a new humility to the man. Doctrines that he once rejected for their mysterious nature were now embraced by him as having scriptural authority behind them. Noah explained:

> *You will readily suppose that after such evidence of the direct operation of the divine spirit upon the human heart, I could no longer question or have a doubt respecting the Calvinistic and Christian doctrines of regeneration, of free grace and of the sovereignty of God. I now began to understand and relish many parts of the scriptures, which before appeared mysterious and unintelligible, or repugnant to my natural pride.*[22]

Noah was deeply convicted of his lack of gratitude to his Creator. He saw now that he had "so long neglected the duties of piety," and this caused the "deepest contrition and remorse."[23] He now rested upon the merits of Jesus Christ, the righteous one. His eyes had been opened to the truth and he experienced something of the pentecostal power of conviction related in Acts 2:

> *Now when they heard this, they were cut to the heart, and said to Peter and the rest of the apostles, "Men and brethren, what shall we do?" Then Peter said to them, "Repent, and let every one of you be baptized in the name of Jesus Christ for the remission of sins; and you shall receive the gift of the Holy Spirit." (Acts 2:37-38)*

Noah's new faith in the true and living God, the God of the Bible now permeated his thinking. His longstanding interest in government, education, and language would continue, but now his thinking on those subjects would be informed by the inspired and infallible Word of God.

Views of Education

Your word is a lamp to my feet and a light to my path. (Psalm 119:105)

This conversion produced a ripple effect in all of Noah's future work.

Whereas he had neglected Scripture in his earlier speller, grammar, and reader, now he was completely committed to the fear of God as the foundation of all true education. Noah confessed now that: "the first principle to be established in the human mind, is reverence for the character and laws of God. The fear of God is the beginning of wisdom."[24] In Noah's 1828 Dictionary he provided this definition of "educate":

> To bring up, as a child; to instruct; to inform and enlighten the understanding; to instill into the mind principles of arts, science, morals, religion and behavior. To educate children well is one of the most important duties of parents and guardians.[25]

He argued that life's most important questions could not be properly answered without the aid of divine revelation found in the Scriptures. For this reason, he said the Bible is the most important book to be studied.

> The first questions a rational being should ask himself are "Who made me?" "Why was I made?" "What is my duty?" [metaphysics, teleology, ethics] **Reason, unaided by revelation, cannot answer these questions.** The experience of the Pagan world has long since determined this point. **Revelation alone furnishes satisfactory information on these subjects.** Let it then be the first study that occupies your mind, to learn from the scriptures the character and will of your maker; the end or purpose for which he gave you being and intellectual powers, and the duties he requires you to perform. In all that regards faith and practice, **the scriptures furnish the principles, precepts and rules, by which you are to be guided.** (emphasis added)[26]

In his instructional materials, Noah would urge young people to choose their companions wisely. He warned them never to "maintain a familiar intercourse with the profane, the lewd, the intemperate, the gamester, or the scoffer at religion."[27]

> He who walks with wise men will be wise, But the companion of fools will be destroyed. (Proverbs 13:20)

Prior to his conversion in 1808, Noah held an optimistic view of the nature of man. He believed that the general diffusion of knowledge through education would solve many social problems—a theory of education that dominates the modern secular world. However, following his conversion, he was far less optimistic concerning the effectiveness of a secular education. He could see that the problem with man was to be found in the heart. Man has a depraved heart and a sin problem that runs deep. Noah Webster came to realize that increasing knowledge through education could never solve the world's problems. The power of true reform comes only through the grace of God and the inward working of His Spirit. It is this power which is essential for the recovery of fallen man. For this reason Noah called for the teaching of the Christian faith as essential for true education.[28]

Contributions to the English Language

For the weapons of our warfare are not carnal but mighty in God for pulling down strongholds, casting down arguments and every high thing that exalts itself above the knowledge of God, bringing every thought into captivity to the obedience of Christ. (2 Corinthians 10:4-5)

With the publication of his famous *Blue-Back Speller*, Noah Webster was already working towards developing a national language, which he hoped would encourage national unity among the American people. In 1806 he followed up with a dictionary titled *A Compendious Dictionary of the English Language*. It was a first attempt with limited effect, but actually Webster had a much more ambitious project in mind.

Noah's most well-known contribution to American literature appeared in 1828 under the title *An American Dictionary of the English Language*. It was a gigantic work, offering the most comprehensive dictionary published to date.

In the battle of ideas and worldviews, some have said, "He who defines the terms, wins." If this is the case, Noah Webster could have been the most influential Christian in American history. His Christian worldview is clearly evident in the 1828 Dictionary, reflecting his matured views of faith, morality,

Webster's home in New Haven where he produced his famous
dictionary, now relocated to Dearborn, Michigan

government, and education. With this work, Noah demonstrated the fact that language is a gift of God, the Bible is the source of all truth, and all definitions of words must be taken captive to the Word of God.

Unlike most modern English dictionaries that attempt to present words in a "neutral" manner, Noah's dictionary was thoroughly Christian. He often quoted Scripture to illustrate the meaning of words. Sometimes he included short exhortations within his definitions. For example, his definition of a Christian is "a real disciple of Christ; one who believes in the truth of the Christian religion, and studies to follow the example, and obey the precepts, of Christ; a believer in Christ who is characterized by real piety."[29]

For his definition of "love," Noah includes a beautiful description of God's love:

The Christian loves his Bible. In short, we love whatever gives us pleasure and delight, whether animal or intellectual; and if our hearts are right, we love God above all things, as the sum of all excellence and all the attributes which can communicate happiness to intelligent beings. In other words, the Christian loves God with the love of complacency in his attributes, the love of benevolence towards the interest of his kingdom, and the love of gratitude for favors received.[30]

For the word "meritorious," Noah speaks of the work of Jesus Christ for sinners: "We rely for salvation on the *meritorious* obedience and sufferings of Christ."[31] Noah realized that words must mean something, and the meaning is important. How words are used and what they mean reflect the beliefs and values of a people. He described his objective in presenting the definitions this way:

I am convinced that words or names often have more influence on the mass of men than things, and that the abuse and misapplication of terms may counteract the best, and promote the worst, political measures.[32]

The Scriptures likewise teach that words are highly important. Their definitions are important, but even more so how they are used.

For we all stumble in many things. If anyone does not stumble in word, he is a perfect man, able also to bridle the whole body. Indeed, we put bits in horses' mouths that they may obey us, and we turn their whole body. Look also at ships: although they are so large and are driven by fierce winds, they are turned by a very small rudder wherever the pilot desires. Even so the tongue is a little member and boasts great things. (James 3:2-5)

No doubt Noah possessed a natural gift for language, but his extensive knowledge of English and other languages came by much strenuous labor. When he began to work on his magnum opus, the 1828 Dictionary, he found himself in need of a much more extensive knowledge of other languages in order to trace the meaning of words and their development in English. Noah sought to re-learn Greek, Latin, and Hebrew and to further his studies of French. He also studied Danish, Anglo-Saxon, Welsh, Persian, and several other languages.

This researcher and linguist was unceasing in his labors. His granddaughter later described his intensive study and labors each day as he researched and wrote the dictionary one word at a time:

> He would take the word under investigation and standing at the right end of the lexicographer's table, look it up in the first dictionary which lay at that end. He made a note, examined a grammar, considered some kindred word, and then passed to the next dictionary of some other tongue. He took each word through the twenty or thirty dictionaries, making notes of his discoveries, and passing around his table many times in the course of a day's labor of minute and careful study.[33]

It was this unceasing labor for some twenty years that produced one of the most significant contributions to American literature ever produced. In the preface to the dictionary, Noah includes this significant dedication:

> To that great and benevolent Being, who, during the preparation of this work, has sustained a feeble constitution, amidst obstacles and toils, disappointments, infirmities and depression; who has twice borne me and my manuscripts in safety across the Atlantic, and given me strength and resolution to bring the work to a close, I would present the tribute of my most grateful acknowledgments.[34]

The first printing of Noah Webster's dictionary was made available to the American public in 1828. It contained a total of 70,000 words, every definition of which was written by Noah himself. He would be the last lexicographer to write a dictionary entirely on his own. All future dictionaries would be assembled by a team of scholars.

Lessons from the Life of Noah Webster

The most important thing to remember about Noah Webster is that his life was changed by the grace of God. Noah used the many natural gifts he received from God for many important ends. It would hardly be an exaggeration to say that the majority of 19th century American children learned how to read and write using Noah Webster's schoolbooks until McGuffey's readers came out in 1836. From 1783 until his death in 1843, America grew up on Noah Webster's primers. Webster's writings on American government influenced the Founding Fathers as they worked on the nation's founding documents. And, his journalistic essays influenced public opinion on many controversial matters of the day. It wasn't until 1808 that Noah Webster came to a true understanding of Christianity and a saving knowledge of Jesus Christ. God was merciful to Noah, and He saved Noah's most important work until the point at which he had committed himself to serving the Lord. The *American Dictionary* would be his best contribution to the nation and to preserving the Christian heritage of America for at least a century.

Noah Webster's many writings published before and after his conversion demonstrate the influence of worldviews upon every area of life. In his early writings, he did not rely on the Scriptures but was instead more influenced by secular thinkers such as Plato and Rousseau. He had an optimistic view of human nature and the ability of education to change men for the better. By the gracious work of the Holy Spirit, Noah began to see the world through biblical lenses. He came to understand the necessity of God's grace. He realized the utter necessity of God's revelation to light our path in a dark world where the minds of men have been clouded by sin. He called for an education rooted in the fear of God, an education formed upon the Word of God as its very foundation.

Blessed is the man who walks not in the counsel of the ungodly, nor stands in the path of sinners, nor sits in the seat of the scornful. But his delight is in the law of the LORD, and in His law he meditates day and night. (Psalm 1:1-2)

Daniel Boone (1734-1820)

CHAPTER 13

Daniel Boone: American Pioneer

Then God blessed them, and God said to them, "Be fruitful and multiply; fill the earth and subdue it; have dominion over the fish of the sea, over the birds of the air, and over every living thing that moves on the earth."

—Genesis 1:28

Daniel Boone was a prominent pioneer in the 18th and early 19th centuries, known particularly for taking a leading role in the settlement of Kentucky. Even during his lifetime he was seen as a symbol of the American frontier in the minds of Americans and Europeans. Not only did he experience lively adventures that captured the imagination of generations of Americans, but he also played an important role in a westward movement that would shape the American identity for years to come. While laboring for the preservation and wellbeing of his own family and friends, Boone was also driven by a vision for generations yet to be born. He wanted to pioneer a path though the wilderness to prepare a land for his grandchildren and great-grandchildren. Unlike some in the present day who live for self-gratification and immediate pleasures, Daniel Boone chose a hard life. He willingly set aside the luxuries of everyday living to devote himself to the arduous task of opening up a new land and preparing it for settlement by millions of people still to come. By God's good providence, Daniel Boone's life and labors would be blessed far beyond his own expectations.

America During the Life of Daniel Boone

Daniel Boone's life spanned almost eighty-six years. It was a time at which the country developed from a group of British colonies along the Eastern Seaboard into a federal union stretching as far west as the Rocky Mountains. Westward expansion came first from the British Isles to North America and then continued into the interior of the new world.

Daniel Boone's life was impacted by various European conflicts which drew Native American tribes into the fighting. This included the French and Indian War (1754-1763), the American War for Independence (1775-1783), and the War of 1812. These European-originated conflicts incited the Indian tribes to war against the settlers, breeding mistrust and ongoing skirmishes long after the wars ended.

Childhood in Pennsylvania

Daniel Boone was born to Squire and Sarah Boone on October 22, 1734 out on the Pennsylvania frontier, forty-five miles northwest of Philadelphia. Squire Boone had emigrated to Pennsylvania around 1714 from Bradninch, Devonshire in southern England. Sarah came from a Welsh family who had also settled in Pennsylvania. Having become Quakers about ten years earlier, the Boones joined the Quaker migrations, most likely seeking religious liberty and economic opportunity in the new land.

Daniel was the sixth of eleven children. It was a busy family economy for the burgeoning household. They kept five or six looms in operation, weaving wool into fabric, and the family farmed 250 acres. Squire was a blacksmith, and one of Daniel's childhood friends, Henry Miller, was employed in Squire's blacksmith shop where he taught Daniel the trade. In his tenth year, Daniel began to accompany his mother during "grass season" as she would seek better pasture for the cows several miles from their home. Sarah attended to the milk and Daniel herded the cows and hunted, first with a club and then with a rifle. It was hunting that especially appealed to Daniel. He took every opportunity to head off into the woods in search of wild animals, even to the neglect of his other chores and duties. When Daniel's uncle complained about his lack of success with tutoring Daniel in reading and writing, Squire Boone told him, "Let the girls do the spelling and Dan will do the shooting."[1] Daniel's sister-in-law Sarah Day Boone finally succeeded in providing him with the basics of reading and writing in his teen years. Although he would take up a little more education along the way, Daniel Boone would always be much better suited for exploring the wild and mastering the use of the rifle.

Quakers: Quakers believed that the inner light from God in each person, rather than Scripture or the teachings of the church, was the true source of truth and authority. The Quakers originated with the teachings of George Fox around 1652 in London. Quakerism became popular quickly, attracting some 60,000 followers in England and Wales by 1680. Also known as the Society of Friends, the Quakers wore plain clothes and avoided terms that showed respect to rank or privilege. They refused to take oaths and were pacifists. These beliefs alienated them from society and led to persecution through the 1680s. Pennsylvania was founded by a charter of the king issued to the Quaker, William Penn in 1681. It became a haven for those seeking religious liberty and protection from persecution.

The Boones were faithful members at the local Quaker meetinghouse, and Daniel's father became a trustee there in 1736 and an overseer in 1739. After Daniel's sister Sarah got into trouble for marrying a non-Quaker and for falling into sexual sin outside of the bounds of marriage, trouble began with the church. When she confessed her sin, and her father confessed his fault in allowing it to happen, they were restored to the community. However, five years later, Daniel's brother Israel also married a non-Quaker. This time Daniel's father did not believe the young man had done anything wrong. Evidently, Squire was not convinced of the sinfulness of marrying outside of the Quaker sect, perhaps thinking that his children were "at liberty to be married to whom [he or she] wishes, only in the Lord" (1 Cor. 7:39). Upon his refusal to admit to wrongdoing in his son's marriage, Squire Boone was expelled from membership with the Quakers' "Society of Friends" in 1748. It is possible that the Boones had already initiated plans to move, but the disruption with the Quaker group likely proved to be the last straw. In Daniel's fifteenth year (in 1750), Squire moved his family southwest, into the sparsely-populated frontier of North Carolina's Yadkin Valley.

> *Therefore let us pursue the things which make for peace and the things by which one may edify another. Do not destroy the work of God for the sake of food. All things indeed are pure, but it is evil for the man who eats with offense . . . Do you have faith? Have it to yourself before God. Happy is he who does not condemn himself in what he approves. But he who doubts is condemned if he eats, because he does not eat from faith; for whatever is not from faith is sin. (Romans 14:19-23)*

Young Man in North Carolina

> *Houses and riches are an inheritance from fathers, but a prudent wife is from the LORD. (Proverbs 19:14)*

In North Carolina (near present-day Mocksville), Squire Boone acquired 1,280 acres of land. Daniel continued to help with farming, blacksmithing, and driving farm goods and animal furs to market in the town of Salisbury. Throughout the fall and winter months, Daniel spent more of his time hunting and trapping. As he hunted for deer, bear, and even buffalo, and trapped beaver and otter, he began carving out a living for himself. He would sell the meat, oil, and especially the skins or furs, which were considered quite valuable at the time.

Sometimes he would be absent from the home for months at a time, usually trekking out with one or two other hunters.

The Boones came to play a significant role in the local community. Squire Boone became a justice of the peace and a member of the county court. The family operated a public house, serving food and drink and providing a place for travelers to stay. In a move that would characterize Americans in the years to come, the family switched church denominations, attending Boone's Ford Church, led by Baptist Pastor John Gano.

French and Indian War: The French and Indian War was fought between Great Britain and France over disputed territory in North America. It pitted Great Britain and its colonies and native allies against France and its less populated colonies and more numerous native allies.

In 1755 General Braddock led a force of British regulars and colonial troops against the French at Fort Duquesne (near present-day Pittsburgh). Among the colonial troops were George Washington and twenty-year-old Daniel Boone, who served as a teamster driving a supply wagon for the army. His first experience with frontier warfare left him with a harsh lesson. The British/American troops were caught off-guard as they approached the fort and suffered a humiliating defeat, losing 900 out of 1,400 troops. The wagoners were the first to pull out of the carnage, and Daniel would live to fight another day. It was during this campaign that Daniel met a trader named John Finley who told him tales of Kentucky from his experiences trading with various Indian tribes.

Upon his return to the Yadkin Valley, young Daniel Boone became interested in a young woman named Rebecca Bryan. They had first met in 1753 when his sister married Rebecca's uncle. The story is told how Daniel found out something of her character on a day they were picking cherries with a group of young people. As the story goes, Daniel cut a corner of her apron with his knife as they were sitting together, either by accident or on purpose. In either case, Daniel witnessed an even temper with the young lady. Instead of reacting in anger, Rebecca didn't say anything about it. Daniel figured that a woman like this with such self-control and who didn't care so much for fine clothing would make a good companion on the frontier. Rebecca turned out to be all he hoped for and more—patient, resilient, and practical. They were married on August 14, 1756. Daniel was twenty-one years old and Rebecca was seventeen. Not long after the wedding, they found themselves caring for the two orphaned children of Daniel's brother Israel. Their son James was born the following May, the first of ten children.

In 1758 the Cherokee tribe joined up with the French and they pushed the English settlers out of the western frontier of the Carolinas. The situation became so dangerous that the Boones were pressed to move to safer regions in northern Virginia. Daniel enlisted under Captain Hugh Waddell and went to the front lines of the war. After the English made peace with the Cherokees in the fall of 1761, Daniel moved his family back to North Carolina.

Daniel settled back into farming and hunting, but he was growing restless. While off on his long hunts, he would travel far afield across western North Carolina and eastern Tennessee. He explored as far south as Florida with a group of friends in 1765, considering a possible settlement there. On some of his shorter hunts he would take his eight-year-old son James along with him. Although he had acquired half of his father's land in 1759, Daniel decided to sell out in 1764 and the family moved further up the Yadkin River to the foot of the Appalachian Mountains. As more settlers moved into the area, the wild animal population dropped significantly. And, as the population grew, more of the unscrupulous crowded in to profit from extortion and corruption. Daniel also was feeling the pressure of his own debts incurred by some of his more risky investments. Above all of this however, it was his own love for God's beautiful wilderness and the freedom of the hunt which led him to explore further into the mountainous regions of the American frontier.

Exploring Kentucky

So God blessed Noah and his sons, and said to them: "Be fruitful and multiply, and fill the earth . . . Every moving thing that lives shall be food for you. I have given you all things, even as the green herbs." (Genesis 9:1, 3)

An attorney whom Daniel Boone had relied on for legal matters, Richard Henderson, had formed the Transylvania Company for the purpose of investigating the possibility of settling Kentucky. At this point "Kentucky" was simply an Indian word describing the region claimed as a hunting ground by various tribes, most notably the Shawnee and Cherokee. British law restricted settlers from going west beyond the mountains. However Henderson believed he would have the legal right to the land if he bought it directly from the Indians. He employed Daniel Boone to scout out the land, the people who lived there, and the best routes for travel.

Daniel took his brother Squire and friend William Hill into the lands of eastern Kentucky for the first time in 1762. They hunted buffalo and traveled down the Big Sandy River. It was rugged country and at one point they were caught in a snowstorm and were forced to stay in camp. It was an exciting time for the young explorers, coming into this region with forbidding hills and mountains.

Upon his return from this first foray into Kentucky, Daniel received a visit from John Finley, a man who had taken part with him in Braddock's campaign. Together the two men began to strategize a better route into Kentucky. On May 1, 1769 Daniel and John with four others set out "to wander through the wilderness of America in quest of the country of Kentucke."[2] It was on this trip they discovered the Cumberland Gap, an important mountain pass into Kentucky. Although the pass had been discovered first by Dr. Thomas Walker in 1750, the way had been largely forgotten by this time. They crested a hill at Cumberland Gap on June 7 and came upon the fertile region on the other side of the mountains. Here the Kentucky River flowed along a valley containing rich soil covered by patches of bamboo-like cane and vast forests. Hundreds of buffalo could be seen carving large trails through the woods to natural saltwater springs. Daniel later described the place in glowing terms: "Nature was here a series of wonders, and a fund of delight."[3]

It was on this exploratory hunt that Daniel and his brother-in-law, John Stewart, were twice taken captive by a group of Shawnee hunters. Though they escaped with their lives, the group lost all their furs and most of their equipment to the Indian thieves. Stewart failed to return to camp on a day in 1770 and turned up dead after an Indian attack. The rest of the team made it back safely despite the harrowing experiences encountered along the way. Daniel continued trapping with his brother Squire, and only twice that year did Squire return to the settlements with their furs to pay their debts and pick up new supplies. Daniel continued exploring Kentucky throughout the hunts, covering hundreds of miles through uncharted wilderness. He was almost continually exposed to dangers from competing Shawnee hunters as well as wolves and bears, yet he was still at home in the wilderness of God's amazing creation. In his words:

> *I was happy in the midst of dangers and inconveniences. In such a diversity it was impossible I should be disposed to melancholy [depression]. No populous city, with all the varieties of commerce and stately structures, could afford so much pleasure to my mind, as the beauties of nature I found here.*[4]

As they returned to the settlement in 1771, Daniel and his brother were robbed by a band of Cherokee and fled for their lives. When they arrived safely home after the two year expedition, Daniel's financial situation was not much better than when he had set out. He was not discouraged however. At this point, he wrote that he had "returned home to my family with a determination to bring them as soon as possible to live in Kentucke, which I esteemed a second paradise, at the risk of my life and fortune."[5]

A Commitment to God

> *So they said, "Believe on the Lord Jesus Christ, and you will be saved, you and your household." Then they spoke the word of the Lord to him and to all who were in his*

house. And he took them the same hour of the night and washed their stripes. And immediately he and all his family were baptized. (Acts 16:31-33)

Before moving to Kentucky, the Boones lived a year in eastern Tennessee nearby their family friend, James Robertson. As Daniel prepared to lead a group of settlers in the settlement of Kentucky, he took an important step in his relationship with God. Later towards the end of his life, he would testify, "I always loved God ever since I could recollect."[6] In 1772, at 38 years of age Daniel was baptized into the church—"he and all his household" (Acts 16:33). A traveling Anglican clergyman did the service for Daniel, his wife Rebecca, their seven children, and three of the Robertson children at the Robertson's house.[7] The Quakers did not practice baptism, and Daniel had never joined the Baptist church his family attended in the Carolinas. So it was here in Tennessee that Daniel Boone officially moved away from the Quaker religion toward a public profession of faith in Christ. Records of this household baptism coordinate with Daniel's son Nathan Boone's later description of his father's faith:

[He] fully believed in the great truths of Christianity . . . [and] seemed most partial towards the Presbyterians . . . [and] had all his children, when he could, regularly christened.[8]

Daniel and his family returned to North Carolina in 1773 to assemble a group of settlers for a move into Kentucky. After saying an affectionate farewell to his mother, Boone set out with the settlers towards the Cumberland Gap. However, bitter tragedy struck the party while they were still traveling across western Virginia. Several young men, including Daniel's sixteen-year-old son James, had been sent for supplies. On their return, they were overtaken by a band of Shawnee and brutally tortured and killed. The tragedy so discouraged and saddened the group that they gave up the attempt to reach Kentucky. Daniel moved his family to Moore's Fort in Virginia temporarily. Meanwhile, hostilities were breaking out with the Shawnee, culminating in Lord Dunmore's War and the battle of Point Pleasant, in which the Shawnee were defeated and made to relinquish their claims to Kentucky. During this war, Daniel Boone and Michael

Daniel Boone passing through the Cumberland Gap

Stoner were sent into Kentucky to warn a group of surveyors of the conflict. They successfully completed the assignment—"a tour of eight hundred miles, through many difficulties, in sixty-two days."[9]

The Move to Kentucky

The year 1775 began with new hope. Peace had returned with the Shawnee, and Daniel was now working for Richard Henderson to bring the Cherokee tribe to a council to determine the sale of Kentucky to the Transylvania Company. The contract was settled on March 17, 1775 for £10,000 in goods. As the final negotiations were wrapping up, Daniel set out with a band of axmen to clear the Wilderness Road through the Cumberland Gap all the way to the Kentucky River. Daniel's fourteen-year-old daughter Susannah had married William Hays a month before, and the two of them joined the party. Susannah and another

> **Transylvania:** Transylvania, organized by the Transylvania Company, sought to become the fourteenth colony and sought recognition from the Continental Congress. It was soon decided that Kentucky belonged to Virginia, and it remained part of Virginia until it became a state in 1792.

woman were the only two women in the group, providing the food for the twenty axmen. Once this road had been constructed deep into the American frontier, the team began working on Fort Boonesborough along the Kentucky River.

As it turned out, the signed treaties were not all that effective at providing peaceful relations for the Kentucky settlements. Some of the natives were not so easily persuaded to give up on their hunting grounds. New settlers were greeted by Indian raids, causing some families to abandon the project. Nevertheless, Daniel Boone persevered, and it wasn't long before Richard Henderson and other settlers joined up in Fort Boonesborough. It was about this time that Daniel was elected as a representative from the fort to the first legislative assembly of Transylvania.

In the summer of 1775, Daniel returned to Virginia to bring the rest of his family to the fort in Kentucky. His dream had finally come true. Now he faced the challenge of holding on to the land on which they had settled.

Securing the Kentucky Settlement

Do not be afraid of them. Remember the Lord, great and awesome, and fight for your brethren, your sons, your daughters, your wives, and your houses. (Nehemiah 4:14)

While Fort Boonesborough was under construction, the American War for Independence had begun in Lexington, Massachusetts. As would be expected, the war fired up hostilities among the native tribes, some of them allying with the British. By offering the Indian tribes land west of the Appalachians, the British figured they could gain their support. In the series of complaints contained in the Declaration of Independence, the last noted that the king "has . . . endeavoured to bring on the inhabitants of our frontiers, the merciless Indian Savages, whose known rule of warfare, is an undistinguished destruction of all ages, sexes and conditions."

Just ten days after the declaration was signed, Daniel Boone's thirteen-year-old daughter, Jemima, and two of her friends, Betsy and Fanny Callaway, were captured by a small band of Cherokee and Shawnee warriors. The girls were taken by surprise while canoeing on the Kentucky River just outside the fort. Daniel and the men in the fort heard the girls' screams and started off in hot pursuit. As they were dragged away by their captors, the girls broke branches and tore off bits of clothing along the way, leaving a trail of clues behind them. They did their best to slow down the band of warriors by coming up with excuses and moving as slowly as they could. It was on the third day that Daniel and his men finally caught up with the band of Indians as they were cooking a meal. The frontiersmen crept up on the warriors and, with a volley of shots fired, routed the captors and rescued the girls. They were brought back safely to the fort, and within the year all three of the young women were married to young men who had formed part of the rescue party.

Throughout the war with Britain, the settlers dwelling at Fort Boonesborough and the other Kentucky forts were periodically attacked by Indian war parties. Fort Boonesborough was attacked twice in 1777 by major war parties of one to two hundred warriors. During one of these battles, Daniel Boone was wounded in the ankle outside the fort and saved by a young twenty-two-year-old Simon Kenton. Simon shot three warriors coming upon Daniel Boone to kill him. He dispatched a fourth with his clubbed rifle, and then carried Daniel into the fort.

In January 1778 Daniel Boone led a group of men from the fort to a saltwater spring called Blue Lick to make salt. As he was hunting alone for food for the men, he was surprised by a band of one hundred Shawnee warriors and taken captive. Apparently, the Indians were headed for Fort Boonesborough and immediately Daniel realized that the salt-makers and the fort were both extremely vulnerable to capture. Strategizing for the best of circumstances, he told his captors that he would convince the men at the salt springs to surrender as long as they would not be ill-treated. He also suggested this was not a good time to take the women and children of Boonesborough into captivity as it was winter. In the providence of God, the Shawnee chief Blackfish was persuaded to agree to the plan.

Although this plan saved the lives of many women and children, the men were not happy when Daniel showed up with the Indians convincing them to surrender. They were fairly treated, however. Daniel on the other hand, had received no promise concerning his own treatment. And when the Indians made camp that evening, he was forced to run the gauntlet. The Indians lined up in two parallel lines, each man equipped with a stick, club, or even a tomahawk. The captive was then forced to run the length of the path created between the two lines while the warriors would attempt to strike him down. Captives were often seriously wounded or killed by running the gauntlet, but Daniel managed to escape unhurt by using a surprising technique. Instead of running headlong down the line, he dexterously zigzagged from side to side, avoiding their blows and even running over one last warrior towards the end who blocked his path.

Upon returning to their towns, the Shawnee "adopted" Daniel and a number of his men into their tribe. Daniel was formally adopted as the son of Blackfish. In the ensuing months, he continued to build trust with the Shawnee by hunting for their meat, making salt for them, and caring for his little adopted sisters. His friendliness even convinced some of the other captives that he had betrayed the Kentucky settlers. As he established friendships with the Shawnee, he also secretly stored away lead, powder, and dried venison and awaited an opportune moment to make his escape.

In June of 1778 Daniel discovered that the Shawnee were assembling four hundred warriors to attack Fort Boonesborough and the other Kentucky settlements. Daniel knew that he must find a way to warn the settlers of the intended attack. His chance arrived on June 16, when the Indian men of the village had organized a hunting expedition. As soon as the men were gone, he mounted his horse and rode as hard and long as the beast could take him. By the next morning the horse gave out and Daniel took to his heels, covering the remaining distance to the fort on foot. In an astonishing act of intrepid determination and physical endurance, Daniel reached the fort in four days, having covered a total distance of 160 miles.

When he arrived at Fort Boonesborough, Daniel found that most of his family had returned to the safety of North Carolina to stay with relatives. Only his daughter Jemima and her husband Flanders Callaway, along with the family cat, had remained. Once he had recovered from his strenuous journey, Daniel set down to prepare the fort's defenses in anticipation of the coming attack. His escape had delayed the Shawnee expedition, but the war party finally arrived in early September. Over four hundred Shawnee warriors as well as a dozen French-Canadians were gathered to assault the fort made up of 135 settlers, with only fifty men and boys. As the siege commenced, the frontiersmen sought to make themselves look strong and to delay the attack. A peace agreement was attempted, but it turned out to be a ruse and Daniel and the other men barely made it back to the fort alive. Over the next nine days, the frontiersmen received flaming arrows, sniper fire, sudden attacks, false retreats, and attempts on the part of the enemy to build underground tunnels. In God's good providence, frequent rain showers discouraged the enemy, preventing the fire arrows from

Daniel Boone National Forest, Kentucky

doing any damage to the fort, and causing the tunnels to collapse on themselves. Finally, the Shawnees were forced to retreat to the other side of the Ohio River.

After the siege was over, Daniel Boone returned to North Carolina to retrieve his family. They returned in 1779, bringing a new group of settlers with them. The Boones moved a few miles away from Fort Boonesborough to establish Boone's Station. Daniel continued his rise to prominence as a noted leader. He was promoted to lieutenant-colonel of the militia in 1780. A year later, he served as the county coroner and in 1782 he became the county sheriff. He also represented the county in the Virginia Legislature beginning in 1781 serving alongside fellow representative Patrick Henry and Governor Thomas Jefferson.

Disaster struck in 1782 however, when the militia was pursuing a large war party across the Licking River at Blue Licks. Against Colonel Boone's better judgment, a lower-ranking officer called for the men to follow him in an attack on the Indians, accusing those who held back of cowardice. As the militia crossed the river, they found themselves outnumbered two to one by the enemy. When the battle was done, over one-third of the 176 Kentuckians were killed, including Daniel's twenty-two-year-old son, Israel. The enemy lost about sixty out of their 400 warriors but secured the victory.

In two more battles conducted between 1782 and 1786, the first commanded by George Rogers Clark and another under Colonel Logan, the settlers were able to push the violence out of the main settlements in Kentucky.

Growing Restless in Kentucky and (West) Virginia

Daniel recounted his adventures in his expeditions and battles for John Filson, who edited them into an autobiography called *The Adventures of Col. Daniel Boon, containing a Narrative of the Wars of Kentucke* (1784). Though some of the vocabulary and rhetorical flourish in the book might have originated with Filson, Daniel Boone still embraced the account as his own and enjoyed it. The autobiography quickly became popular in America and Europe, as it was translated and printed in French in 1785 and German in 1790.

Meanwhile, Daniel tried to adapt to the ways of civilization by engaging in several business projects with only limited success. He became a deputy surveyor of two counties and mapped out properties for newcomers. He moved to Limestone, Kentucky along the Ohio River where he operated a tavern and managed a warehouse. He also tried his hand at buying and selling land. In 1788 he grew a crop of ginseng and brought it to market in Hagerstown, Maryland. It was on this trip he made the decision to move out of Kentucky. Clearly, Daniel Boone's passion for hunting and love of exploration exceeded his business savvy.

This time Daniel journeyed to western Virginia (present-day West Virginia) where there were fewer settlers, more wild animals, and more danger from hostile natives. Daniel first settled in Point Pleasant along the Ohio River where he ran a trading post, and served once more as a representative in the Virginia Legislature (in 1791). His hunting expeditions conducted in the company of his sons extended as far out as present-day Ohio, where the men found plentiful deer, beaver, bear, and buffalo. They experienced several close encounters with native warriors on their hunts, but this time Daniel Boone avoided capture and theft.

Continuing threats from Indians made life difficult, and Daniel was growing restless once more. In 1795 the Boones moved back to Kentucky, cleared more land, built a cabin and continued farming and hunting. But now his son, Daniel Morgan Boone, was scouting out other opportunities in the footsteps of his father. The young man traveled down into present-day Alabama and Mississippi in 1795, and in 1797 reached the Spanish colony of Upper Louisiana (present-day Missouri). Having spied out the land, he returned with a good report and Daniel Boone now well into his sixties was eager to move on into this final frontier.

Westward to Missouri

Children's children are the crown of old men, and the glory of children is their father. (Proverbs 17:6)

Hoping to attract new settlers for the development of their colony, the

Upper Louisiana: Upper Louisiana covered what is now the north-central part of
the US, from Missouri to Montana. It contained several small French settlements,
mostly along the Mississippi River, but had been governed by the Spanish since
1763. Upper and Lower Louisiana would be purchased by the United States in 1803
and explored by expeditions led by Meriwether Lewis and William Clark (1804-
1806) and Zebulon Pike (1805-1807).

Spanish offered grants of free land and unofficial religious toleration to any who
would settle within their boundaries. No property tax would be levied, and
the plan developed for Daniel Boone to serve as the local commandant, militia
leader, and judge for a new district laid out for the American settlers. Beaver and
other animals were abundant, and the rich soil of the area was promising.

An aging Daniel Boone arrived with his wife, children, grandchildren,
relatives, and friends. At this point, he was seen more as a patriarchal leader
than a government official. Daniel had acquired 850 acres along the Missouri
River, but he and his wife chose to live with their son Nathan on his 680 acres
located twenty-five miles southwest of the French town of St. Charles. In 1803,
the United States made the Louisiana Purchase, adding 827,000 square miles,
including Missouri, to its territory.

Despite his age, an irrepressible Daniel Boone continued attending long
hunts three to six months in length. He traveled across the (present) state of
Missouri and a little beyond into Kansas, trapping beaver and hunting deer. On
one particularly successful hunt, he and a friend acquired 900 pounds of beaver
pelts. On another occasion, he fell through the ice while walking across the
Missouri River and the 71 year old frontiersman was helped back to a fire on
shore by his sons. He was usually able to negotiate with the Osage natives on his
hunts, although once he was forced to hide in a cave for three weeks to avoid a
confrontation.

When the War of 1812 began and some of the Indian tribes allied themselves
with the British, 78-year-old Daniel volunteered for service but was turned down
due to his age. This time it would be his sons and grandsons who would lead

the troops into battle. Still in 1816 he was off on another multi-month hunt at 81 years of age with a man known as Indian Philips—a hunt which took him off to Missouri's western border.

The next year the old man came close to death after falling ill on a hunt with his grandson James. When he was finally able to return home, he found that his son Nathan had hastily prepared a coffin for him. Daniel was disappointed, however, with the quality of the coffin and had one made that would fit him better. After this last hunt he stayed closer to home, read his Bible more, and spent more time with his family. Around this time he wrote these words in a letter to his sister-in-law Sarah Day Boone:

> All the Relegan [religion] I have [is] to Love and fear god beleve in Jesus Christ Dow all the good to my Nighbor and my Self that I Can and Do as Little harm as I Can help and trust in gods marcy for the Rest.[10]

By the mercy of God, Daniel Boone did not die on a hunting trip or in battle. He passed away to glory in Nathan's large stone house surrounded by his loving family on September 26, 1820 at almost 86 years of age. His family concluded that he had died from eating too many of the sweet potatoes, cakes, nuts, and buttermilk that his grandchildren served him.

Life Lessons from Daniel Boone

Daniel Boone seems to have had a relentless desire to explore the wilderness, to delight in God's creation and develop its resources, and to lead pioneer families to new lands for the purpose of creating new communities. His ruling passions were in accordance with God's ancient mandate to humanity found in Genesis 1:28. Although he would grow restless once a land became settled, Filson records that Daniel delighted to behold "a howling wilderness . . . become a fruitful field; this region, so favourably distinguished by nature, now become the habitation of civilization."[11] Though Daniel was often away from home for part of the year, his life centered around his family. From his youth to old age, he depended on his family and worked for their good. They were very industrious, providing for their own needs, engaging in many kinds of businesses, and seeking new opportunities. In the end, Daniel and Rebecca had ten children, seventy grandchildren, and at least 364 great-grandchildren. Many of them became leading citizens in their communities and quite a number of them continued moving further west.

> Blessed is the man who fears the LORD, who delights greatly in His commandments. His descendants will be mighty on earth; the generation of the upright will be blessed. (Psalm 112:1-2)

While it was popular in his day to despise and even degrade the Native American Indians, Daniel Boone treated them with respect. He did not find any joy in fighting them and usually preferred to negotiate. Some of the Shawnee he had lived with in Ohio continued to be his friends after his family moved to Missouri. His relations with Indians could be rather complex and treacherous at times. When his son James was brutally killed and his daughter Jemima was taken captive, the war parties were led by men who had been entertained by the Boones in their home. As he rejoiced to see Kentucky settled by his fellow Americans, Daniel was also careful to see that lands claimed by Indian tribes were first lawfully purchased before the settlers moved in. Throughout his life he sought justice for both American and Indian alike.

> If it is possible, as much as depends on you, live peaceably with all men. (Romans 12:18)

Daniel's true interest was to improve the lot of these native tribes. While a captive of the Shawnees, he "took great pains to enlighten Black Fish in the principles of civilization and what great comforts would accrue to his people if they would more nearly conform to the mode of living among the whites, cultivating the soil more extensively, raising cattle and sheep, manufacturing cloth, and constructing more commodious and comfortable houses."[12]   He wanted to see the Shawnee men engage more in tending the crops, rather than perpetually passing the household economy over to the squaws.

> A man's heart plans his way, but the LORD directs his steps (Proverbs 16:9).

Daniel Boone was also a humble man who trusted in God and His providential guidance. He never went out of his way to seek fame, although it did follow him at times. He mainly intended to provide for his family and to pursue the calling he loved. In his older years he told a visitor, "With me the world has taken great liberties, and yet I have been but a common man."[13] He realized that his success and fame had come from the fact that God had used his efforts in a bigger plan. Another visitor reported that during his final years Daniel "spoke feelingly, and with solemnity, of being a creature of Providence, ordained by Heaven as a pioneer in the wilderness, to advance the civilization and the extension of his country," despite having "entered into the wilderness with no comprehensive views or extensive plans of future improvement."[14]

Daniel Boone simply strove to be faithful to his calling and to work hard for his family and friends, trusting that God would take care of the rest. He was blessed to see the fruit of his labors with a country, peaceful and free, stretching from his native Pennsylvania to the far west he had only just begun to explore.

> *Blessed be the LORD my Rock,*
> *Who trains my hands for war,*
> *And my fingers for battle—*
>
> *My lovingkindness and my fortress,*
> *My high tower and my deliverer,*
> *My shield and the One in whom I take refuge,*
> *Who subdues my people under me.*
>
> *LORD, what is man, that You take knowledge of him?*
> *Or the son of man, that You are mindful of him?*
> *Man is like a breath;*
> *His days are like a passing shadow . . .*
>
> *Rescue me and deliver me from the hand of foreigners,*
> *Whose mouth speaks lying words,*
> *And whose right hand is a right hand of falsehood—*

That our sons may be as plants grown up in their youth;
That our daughters may be as pillars,
Sculptured in palace style;

That our barns may be full,
Supplying all kinds of produce;
That our sheep may bring forth thousands
And ten thousands in our fields;

That our oxen may be well laden;
That there be no breaking in or going out;
That there be no outcry in our streets.

Happy are the people who are in such a state;
Happy are the people whose God is the LORD!
(Psalm 144:1-4, 11-15)

UNIT 3

Prideful Expansion and Internal Turmoil (1800-1865)

Stand now with your enchantments and the multitude of your sorceries, in which you have labored from your youth—perhaps you will be able to profit, perhaps you will prevail. You are wearied in the multitude of your counsels; let now the astrologers, the stargazers, and the monthly prognosticators stand up and save you from what shall come upon you. Behold, they shall be as stubble, the fire shall burn them; they shall not deliver themselves from the power of the flame; it shall not be a coal to be warmed by, nor a fire to sit before! Thus shall they be to you with whom you have labored, your merchants from your youth; they shall wander each one to his quarter. No one shall save you.

—Isaiah 47:12-15

T hus comes God's warnings to Babylon, as well as to any nation that turns away from Him. America turned away from God during the first half of the 19th century. This was especially evident in the lives of the presidents and most of the nation's leadership. There was a reticence to acknowledge Jesus Christ as Lord and Savior. Unitarianism controlled the ruling class in the North. The literary elite, including men like Henry David Thoreau, Ralph Waldo Emerson, and Nathaniel Hawthorne, turned to a bad worldview called "Transcendentalism." It was a pantheistic view of the world similar to what the pagan Hindu religion taught. Witchcraft became increasingly popular with feminists and others of the literary group. Séances (the calling up of the spirits of dead people) were popularly known to have been held in the White House under Presidents Franklin Pierce and Abraham Lincoln. These were dark days for America.

Church attendance dropped off from 40-50% (following the Great Awakening) to 5-10% around the turn of the 19th century.[1] The influence of the humanist Enlightenment on this country was devastating. Little progress was made to recover lost ground through the Second Great Awakening. The Christian Church broke into more factions, and wayward cults developed. The Methodists, Baptists, and Presbyterians also split between North and South, paving the way for the war that would follow.

Greed more and more came to dominate the hearts of Americans. President Thomas Jefferson began to speak of "empire." President Andrew Jackson refused to abide by treaties made with the Cherokee and Creek Indian Tribes. This resulted in the Trail of Tears, in which thousands of Indians were forced to migrate to the Oklahoma Territory, many of whom died on the way. A slave-based economy developed in the Southern states throughout the 18th and well into the 19th century.

Yet, there were bright spots along the way. God used a slave boy named Lemuel Haynes to preach the true gospel during these years of decline. Large numbers of African immigrants and Native Americans came to profess faith in Christ over the years, and many would became Christian pastors. Adoniram Judson became one of America's first foreign missionaries who would serve as an inspiration to thousands more faithful men and women who were willing to lay down their lives for Christ on the field in the 19th century. Faithful missionaries like Samuel Worcester gave their lives for the Cherokee and Creek tribes. Although this period was spotted with fake revival and the rise of wayward cults, men like Asahel Nettleton did witness authentic conversions and real revival here and there throughout America.

Historically, Christians like Augustine (of North Africa) and Patrick (of Ireland) fought hard against the slave trade. Christians never support slave-based systems, even if the system is set up as a pretended means of reaching a certain class of persons with the gospel.

Eventually, God's righteous judgment fell upon the United States of America in the form of a terrible civil war which took place between 1861 and 1865. We cannot point out the specific reasons for these judgments. However, it is enough to review the sins of the North and the South which came to define the nation at this time and to be forewarned that God will most certainly call the nations of the world to account.

> *There were present at that season some who told Him about the Galileans whose blood Pilate had mingled with their sacrifices. And Jesus answered and said to them, "Do you suppose that these Galileans were worse sinners than all other Galileans, because they suffered such things? I tell you, no, but unless you repent, you will all likewise perish." (Luke 13:1-3)*

Timeline of Important Events

1803	The Louisiana Purchase
1804	Meriwether Lewis and William Clark explore the West to the Pacific.
1805	The US battles the Barbary Pirates
1807	Congress prohibits the importation of slaves.
1812	The War of 1812 begins.
1819	Adams-Onis Treaty results in the purchase of Florida from Spain.
1825	Charles Finney begins preaching as a revivalist in New York State.
1830	Passage of the Indian Removal Act.
1837	The Battle of the Alamo occurs between Texans and Mexicans (in San Antonio).
1838	The Trail of Tears begins as the Cherokees and Creeks are driven out of Georgia.
1846	The Mexican-American War begins, ending in 1848.
1848	Gold is discovered in California, beginning the gold rush.
1851	California is admitted to the union.
1856	John Brown conducts his massacre in Kansas.
1860	The Pony Express begins and Abraham Lincoln is elected President.
1863	The Battle of Gettysburg is fought in Pennsylvania.
1865	The Civil War ends and Abraham Lincoln is assassinated.

John Quincy Adams (1767-1848)

CHAPTER 14

John Quincy Adams: Keeping Faith During the Decline of American Faith

> *But you, beloved, remember the words which were spoken before by the apostles of our Lord Jesus Christ: how they told you that there would be mockers in the last time who would walk according to their own ungodly lusts. These are sensual persons, who cause divisions, not having the Spirit. But you, beloved, building yourselves up on your most holy faith, praying in the Holy Spirit, keep yourselves in the love of God, looking for the mercy of our Lord Jesus Christ unto eternal life.*
>
> —Jude 1:17-21

It was an age when civilized man in the Western world felt he had achieved the heights of virtue, dignity, honor, and moral rectitude. The budding pride of modern man was about to come into full bloom and religious

John Quincy's father John Adams

skepticism was on the rise. The proud humanist Enlightenment of the 1700s had fully matured by the turn of the 19th century. New England Unitarians were throwing out every Bible doctrine that did not make sense to the minds of arrogant men. Almost every key Christian teaching defended during the Protestant Reformation was discarded between 1760 and 1820. This occurred in large part because of humanist Enlightenment philosophies. According to the thinking of modern man, if a particular doctrine of Scripture doesn't make sense or cannot be explained to the satisfaction of human reason, it must be rejected out of hand. Thus, to President John Adams, for example, the doctrines of the Trinity, the divinity of Christ, the atonement of Christ, miracles recorded in Scripture, and the immaculate conception of Jesus appeared to stand against reason. These doctrines just didn't make sense to the "very intelligent" and "virtuous" men of the 19th century. There is only one word to describe European man and American man in 1800—"proud."

Before destruction the heart of man is haughty, and before honor is humility.
(Proverbs 18:12)

When asked about the atonement of Christ, John Adams responded: "An incarnate God! An eternal, self-existent, omnipotent author of this stupendous universe suffering on a cross! Absurdity!"[1] He rather insisted that man's salvation depended on his "upright conduct and good works."[2] Such departures from a biblical doctrine were devastating to this generation, and no doubt resulted in many abandoning the Christian faith altogether. Rejecting the Lord Jesus Christ and His work on the cross out of human pride and self-righteousness is a horrible thing for anyone to do and could only result in terrifying eternal consequences.

Yet, John Adams' son John Quincy *did not* entirely reject the miracles recorded in the New Testament or the divine nature of Jesus Christ. In spite of his confusion and ignorance at many points, John Quincy Adams still clung tenaciously to the mercy of God to the end of his life.

John Quincy's father and mother John and Abigail Adams turned away from the orthodox Christian faith in which they were raised. The consequences

John Quincy's mother Abigail Adams

of a broken faith were almost immediately obvious among the young men in their families. Abigail's brother William became an alcoholic and died at forty years of age. John and Abigail's son Charles died at thirty years of age, completely overcome by the sin of drunkenness. Their third son Thomas faced problems with drunkenness throughout his life as well. In God's mercy, their eldest son John Quincy was salvaged from these terrible life choices. Nonetheless, John Quincy's eldest son George Washington Adams committed suicide at twenty-eight years of age, and his second son John II died of the same alcoholic problem that afflicted his two uncles. Very obviously, the fruits of the apostasy rampant in New England in the early 19th century yielded terrible fruits.

An Extraordinary Education

John Quincy Adams was born to John and Abigail Adams on July 11, 1767 in Braintree, Massachusetts. At seven years of age, John Quincy heard the cannon blasts on Bunker Hill as the colonials attempted to prevent control of Boston Harbor from falling into the hands of the British. On February 12, 1778 John Adams embarked on a journey with his eldest son, an experience that would set the direction for John Quincy's life. Together father and son set out to cross the Atlantic in the dead of winter. The objective of the journey was to win the favor of the French in America's War for Independence. In some respects, it was a tremendous benefit for young John to spend five of his most formative years in the near presence of his father. Yet in other respects, the European trip proved harmful in that the young man was exposed to the influence of the worst of Europe's cultural revolutions, the French Enlightenment.

John Adams homeschooled his son on the ship over to France, as well as at his home, at court, and just about everywhere else. As the ship sailed across the Atlantic, John Quincy was well into his French studies. Attacks from enemy ships, harrowing storms in which several men were killed, and sickness attended the voyage. Although the trip turned out to be the worst that either of them would ever experience, John Quincy held up very well, all things considered. His father commented in a letter, "My Johnny's behavior gave me a satisfaction that I cannot express—fully sensible of the danger, he was constantly endeavoring to bear it with a manly patience."[3]

Upon reaching Paris, John Adams enrolled his son in a boarding school and permitted him to attend the Parisian theater. Such plays would have been forbidden in Boston. Yet John Quincy wrote home to his mother that he would "rather be amongst the rugged rocks of my own native town than in the gay city of Paris."[4]

Father and son came home to Boston in the summer of 1779, only to return again to Paris the following November. John Adams would have preferred to leave his son at home but decided against it for two reasons. First, the French ambassador had encouraged him to take "the young gentleman, your son" back with him. And, secondly, John felt that his son would receive a better home education with him than anything he could obtain in war-torn America.

The second voyage to Paris did not go well. The ship sprang a leak and the captain chose to harbor in Spain. Father and sons (both John Quincy and Charles) traveled across Spain under the roughest of conditions. They slept in barns next to animals and there were no baths to be had. John Quincy reported back home that the poverty across Europe was stifling, and only the Catholic priests appeared well-fed. They arrived in Paris in February 1780. Not long after arriving in France, the three Adamses moved to the Netherlands where John Adams continued his efforts to seek financial support for the American cause. Just for fun, John Quincy began attending lectures at the University of Leiden and immersed himself in Greek and Latin studies with a tutor by the name of Benjamin Waterhouse.

Just before he turned fourteen years of age, the United States government appointed John Quincy Adams as secretary to Charles Dana, recently assigned as minister to Russia. Because the penny poor US Congress had no money for the office, Charles Dana settled for this precocious young man who was most eager to volunteer for the position. It was a fifty-five-day, 2,500 mile journey across Germany, Poland, and Russia to reach their destination in St. Petersburg. Arriving in September 1781, John Quincy Adams and Charles Dana hung around the Russian court for two years, finally returning to Holland via Finland and Sweden in the spring of 1783.

John Quincy's mother and sister joined them in Paris during the summer of 1785. John Adams took his family to the French theater during their visit, a horrifying experience for his wife. John Quincy summarized the Parisian plays as "almost universally . . . very indecent." The public taste, he also noted "seems to be entirely corrupted."[5] Given the moral degradation of Paris during these years, it was unsurprising that the nightmarish revolution commenced just four years later.

Upon returning to the United States in May 1785, John Quincy entered Harvard College at eighteen years of age. He graduated second in his class in 1788 and immediately apprenticed for law with Theophilus Parsons, a lawyer in Newburyport.

At this point John Quincy was attending church mainly as a form of entertainment. He would evaluate the sermons on the basis of the intellectual and rhetorical ability of the preacher. During these years, this proud young intellectual was far more interested in Shakespeare, Milton, Pope, Voltaire, Hume, and Samuel Johnson than he was in the Bible.

However, somewhere around 1791, John Quincy began waking up to the radical atheism and revolutionary humanism coming out of France. Thomas Paine had endorsed the French Revolution with his book *The Rights of Man*, and he was openly advocating the abandonment of any and all divine law. Thomas Jefferson and James Monroe likewise approved of Paine's views of the revolution. In response to these radical ideas, John Quincy wrote eleven letters to a Boston newspaper arguing against humanist autonomy. "That a nation has a right to do whatever it pleases, cannot in any sense whatever be admitted as true," he wrote. If the democratic majority are "bound by no law human or divine, and have no other rule but their sovereign will and pleasure to direct them, what possible security can any citizen of the nation have for the protection of his unalienable rights?"[6] Adams asked. During these years, both John Adams and his son stood in opposition to the wild revolutionary sentiments seeping into America from France.

Between 1793 and 1800, John Quincy reentered the world of foreign diplomacy, acting as "America's most valuable official abroad."[7] That's the term George Washington used to describe the 26-year-old diplomat who was strongly relied upon to assert this infant nation's place among the nations of the world. Adams served in the Netherlands, Portugal, and Prussia, negotiating treaties and pushing for America's neutrality in European conflicts. In 1797 he married Louisa Catherine Johnson, the daughter of a Maryland businessman who was residing in London at the time. The couple came back to the United States in 1800, and then returned to the foreign service in 1809. For the next five years during James Madison's administration, Adams served as foreign ambassador to Russia. In 1814 he negotiated the Treaty of Ghent with Britain, officially ending the War of 1812, after which he was appointed as the United States foreign minister to Britain.

An Internal Battle for Faith

By the turn of the 19th century, the Christian faith was under all-out assault in the colleges and among the mainline churches and leaders in America. In the mercies of God however, He would not leave John Quincy Adams to himself. Louisa Catherine's health turned fragile. She experienced two miscarriages in 1798, and in 1799 another pregnancy was not going well. She fainted during a party with the Prussian king and queen in Berlin. In the early weeks of 1800 she miscarried a third time. John

John Quincy Adams at age 29

Quincy wrote in his diary at this time, "I can only pray to God."[8] For a while he was unable to sleep at night. His brother Charles died in November 1800 after living for years in a state of almost constant compulsive drunkenness—another shock to the family. Yet again, in God's providential dealings, a further traumatic event transpired in John Quincy's life on December 31, 1800. A young army officer dropped dead at a New Year's party at which he was in attendance. In his diary John noted the "vanity and frailty of earthly enjoyments."[9] He wrote it was that very night when he bowed "in prostration to the Being who directs the universe with thanksgivings for His numerous blessings in past times, and with prayer for a mind to bear whatsoever the future dispositions of His providence may be, in such a manner as may be most conformable to His will."[10]

It was during this time that John Quincy Adams was becoming increasingly sensitive to the apostasy of the day. He noted that men like the German philosopher Johann Fichte were no different than atheists. These liberals were denying the divinity of Jesus and attempting to present a form of Christianity which discounted miracles. Finally, on April 12, 1801, the Lord graciously provided a healthy son to the young couple. John Quincy confided in his diary, "I have this day to offer my humble and devout thanks to almighty God for the birth of a son." [11]

A different man—one with holy sobriety and growing humility—was emerging. This appears to be the beginning of a genuine faith for the future president of the United States. Unquestionably, his journey towards faith was taking a decidedly different direction than that taken by his father and other important leaders in the country.

Upon his return to the United States in 1801, John Quincy Adams entered the political arena. Elected to the US Senate, he served from 1803-1808. It was around this time that he began reading through the Bible every year, dedicating a full hour to the exercise each morning. [12]

Secretary of State

In 1817 President James Monroe appointed John Quincy Adams to the third most powerful office in the country—Secretary of State. No one had as much experience as John at the time, and the appointment was thus very sensible. It was his primary objective above everything else to keep America out of all foreign wars. Secretary of State Adams advocated strongly against any further European interference in South America. He laid out the fundamental principles of the Monroe Doctrine in 1823. The policy was named for the president, but the wording and the political philosophy originated more with John Quincy Adams.

Basically, the Monroe Doctrine stated that any further attempt on the part of foreign powers to control any country in North or South America would be taken as a political move against the United States. In turn, the US would recognize and not interfere with existing European colonies in the Americas. Mercifully, the policy kept America out of devastating foreign wars. The nation's government would abide by the Monroe Doctrine until the Spanish-American War of 1898.

In a speech John Quincy Adams gave to the House of Representatives in 1821, he spoke strongly against any further attempt to establish nations by conquest. He displayed the original copy of the Declaration of Independence (fairly tattered at this point, having been stuffed into a drawer at the State Department). He pointed out that this nation had added a special chapter in the historical battle for liberty. He said, "It demolished at a stroke the lawfulness of all governments founded upon conquest. It swept away all the rubbish of accumulated centuries of servitude."[13] His point was that this nation was founded by a voluntary social compact made by duly elected representatives of the people. European empires would continue their quest for domination over other nations for another century. Though not perfectly, America would remain less interested in such quests, thanks to the influence of men like John Quincy Adams.

Another heartbreak visited John Quincy and his wife when they lost their daughter Louisa Catherine just after her first birthday. Shortly after this, John began attending church twice on Sundays, sometimes catching three services a day. He publicly professed faith shortly after his father died in 1826.

The Presidency

In the 1824 election, John Quincy Adams was elected to the presidency of the United States with only 31% of the popular vote to Andrew Jackson's 41%. However, there were four candidates in the race, and Henry Clay threw his support to John Quincy Adams. This resulted in a final win for John Quincy after a vote was taken in the House of Representatives.

With far less than a majority vote, it was plain from the outset that John Quincy Adams would not be a popular president. While he fought for fair dealings with the Creeks and Cherokees in Georgia, the rest of the nation generally opposed him. Regrettably, he was in favor of high tariffs and big government programs. Since the tariffs typically favored the North over the South, this approach to strengthening the federal government also created disunity in the nation. After being defeated by Andrew Jackson in the 1828 presidential election, John Quincy returned to government, serving in the US House of Representatives.

A Battle Against Slavery and the Ill-Treatment of the American Indians

Lying lips are an abomination to the LORD, but those who deal truthfully are His delight. (Proverbs 12:22)

When President Andrew Jackson condoned the forcible removal of the Cherokees from their lands in Georgia, Alabama, Mississippi, and Florida, John Quincy Adams was incensed. It was nothing less than a travesty. For it was clear that the American government had broken treaties with the Indians and had not dealt truthfully with them. About a quarter of the 19,000 natives died on the "Trail of Tears" between Georgia and the Oklahoma Territory. John Quincy took on almost a prophetic role in his famous lament over these national sins: "We have done more harm to the Indians since our Revolution than had ever been done to them by the French and English nations before . . . These are crying sins for which we are answerable before a higher jurisdiction."[14] In 1841 Adams was appointed head of the Congressional Office for Indian Affairs, but he turned down the appointment outright. America's treatment of the Native Americans was unconscionable in his mind. In his diary he recorded a prescient remark which would be realized twenty years hence:

> [America's treatment of the Native Americans] is among the heinous sins of this nation, for which I believe God will one day bring them to judgment—but at His own time and by His own means.[15]

As early as 1804, John Quincy pushed for an amendment to the US Constitution which would have eliminated the three-fifths provision (in which slaves were counted as only 60% of a person for purposes of the census). In 1839 he attempted another constitutional amendment which would have abolished hereditary slavery and ended the selling of slaves in Washington DC. When he brought petitions signed by slaves into the House of Representatives, he was shouted down and subjected to a "gag" rule. The pro-slavery opposition attempted to censor him but the vote failed by a 106-93 count. He continued to fight the "gag" rule for five years, finally winning a vote on December 2, 1844. This was Adams' best attempt to keep the slavery matter on the table before a nation which would eventually resolve the matter by war.

John Quincy Adams was seeking a peaceable way to end slavery. He feared that it would become "the wedge which will ultimately split up this Union."[16] The addition of new slaves states to the Union like Missouri and Texas only added to the tension between North and South.

The Case of the Amistad

"Shall you reign because you enclose yourself in cedar? Did not your father eat and drink, and do justice and righteousness? Then it was well with him. He judged the cause of the poor and needy; then it was well. Was not this knowing Me?" says the LORD. "Yet your eyes and your heart are for nothing but your covetousness, for shedding innocent blood, and practicing oppression and violence." (Jeremiah 22:15-17)

Looking back at the life of John Quincy Adams some 175 years later, more than anything else it was most probably his role in the Amistad Supreme Court case that sealed his legacy in American history.

International treaties had shut down the slave trade by 1820. However, the Spanish were reluctant to comply with the treaties. Spain was the first European country to initiate modern slavery in the late 1400s and early 1500s, and this fading empire was not eager to shut it down. A Spanish ship drifted into Long Island Harbor, New York in August 1839. There were fifty-three Africans aboard—men, women, and children, along with two Spanish slave traders. As the story came out, it became clear that these Africans had been recently traded in Havana, Cuba. While the slave traders were moving their captives by ship to another location on Cuba, the Africans revolted and took command of the ship. They killed the captain and the cook and kept the two Spaniards alive. The mutineers were hoping they would navigate the ship back to their native land. This did not happen. While pretending to head east across the Atlantic, they allowed the ship to drift north to American shores.

The case was a political hot potato for the courts, Congress, and the president. The nation was already divided on the slavery question. Martin Van Buren's administration took a strong stance in favor of sending the Africans back to Cuba, where they would no doubt have been tried and hung.

The lower courts quickly settled the question of whether or not the Africans should be considered slaves by ruling in the negative. At least three of the Africans were teenage girls, and none of them knew any Spanish. They could only speak their own African dialect, a clear indication that they had been forcibly brought to Cuba well after 1820. The courts ruled that they should be sent back to Africa, but then the United States Government intervened and appealed the case to the US Supreme Court.

Advocates for the fifty-three Africans appealed to John Quincy Adams for the defense. As he looked into the case, Adams was appalled to discover that the Martin Van Buren Administration had falsified or mistranslated the Spanish documents. It seemed to him that the administration was doing its best to paint these Africans as Spanish slaves. Moreover, the federal government had also positioned a ship off the coast of Connecticut in readiness to take the Africans back to Cuba. This irritated the seventy-three-year-old lawyer-statesman to no end. Yet, there was one problem for Adams—he had not practiced law for thirty years. Also, the odds seemed to be stacked against the case. Five of the nine Supreme Court justices were slave owners. This included Justice Roger Taney, who would write the Dred-Scott decision sixteen years later. Six of the judges had been appointed by Presidents Jackson and Van Buren, political opponents of John Quincy Adams. Despite these obvious drawbacks, this congressman, retired president, and attorney decided to take up the case.

From his diary, we learn that Adams entered the Supreme Court chambers with much trepidation and "fervent prayer."[17] The arguments were presented in court on February 24, 1841. Adams spoke for four and a half hours, arguing from the Declaration of Independence, the US Constitution, and common law. His major point was that these prisoners had a right to receive American justice because they were arrested on American soil. He appealed to God's laws on the matter.

I know of no other law that reaches the case of my clients, but the law of Nature and of Nature's God on which our fathers placed our own national existence. The circumstances are so peculiar, that no code or treaty has provided for such a case. That law, in its application to my clients, I trust will be the law on which the case will be decided by this Court . . . In the Declaration of Independence the Laws of Nature are announced and appealed to as identical with the laws of nature's God, and as the foundation of all obligatory human laws. But here Sir William Scott proclaims a legal standard of morality, differing from, opposed to, and transcending the standard of nature and of nature's God. This legal standard of morality must, he says, in the administration of law, be held, by a Court, to supersede the laws of God, and justify, before the tribunals of man, the most atrocious of crimes in the eyes of God.[18]

Adams had only made it halfway through his case before the court was dismissed for the day. In the providence of God, that very night one of the Supreme Court justices, Phillip Barbour, died. This delayed the case for five days, but when the court reconvened, Adams took another four and a half hours to complete his case. Here this American political leader certified his absolute commitment to the fear of God as fundamental for leadership in the state. He closed the case with a solemn warning to the justices of the final judgment of Almighty God.

I can only [make] a fervent petition to heaven that every member of [this honorable Court] may go to his final account with as little of earthly frailty to answer for as those illustrious dead [referring to the justice who had just died]. And that you may, every one, at the close of a long and virtuous career in this world, be received at the portals of the next, with the approving sentence, "Well done, thou good and faithful servant; enter thou into the joy of thy Lord."[19]

The justices must have taken this argument into account, for they ruled in favor of the Africans by a vote of 7 to 1. The Amistad Africans had been illegally shipped to Cuba. Adams was elated by the decision. By the grace of God, he had saved the lives of fifty-three African men, women, and children, securing their freedom to return home.

A Leader who Feared God

The Spirit of the LORD spoke by me, and His word was on my tongue. The God of Israel said, the Rock of Israel spoke to me: "He who rules over men must be just, ruling in the fear of God." (2 Samuel 23:2-3)

After his presidency, John Quincy Adams reentered politics and won a seat in the House of Representatives. This indicates something of the humility of this leader. Not many would accept such a "demotion," but Adams wanted to continue serving his country as best as he could. He continued in this service until his death seventeen years later.

John Quincy's 14,000-page personal diary gives historians the best first-hand account of the era which brought us into modernity. From his records, one thing is clear—the man was a consummate peacemaker. Nobody hated war more than John Quincy did. He negotiated the final peace treaty with Britain at Ghent in 1814. As Secretary of State under James Madison, he negotiated the Transcontinental Treaty of 1819 (which ceded Florida to the United States). In 1835 it was Congressman Adams who was able to avert war with France by writing three resolutions. His more diplomatic approach softened the blow which President Andrew Jackson had dealt to the French government by his policy statements. Congress unanimously approved Adams' resolutions. At this stage in American history, nobody understood international politics better than he did.

Down to the last weeks of his life, John Quincy Adams opposed President James K. Polk's commitment to enter into war with Mexico. He insisted on making public certain documents which would have undermined Polk's claim that this was a just war.

Blessed are the peacemakers, for they shall be called sons of God. (Matthew 5:9)

John Quincy Adams was probably the most intelligent and most widely read of all the presidents—a true scholar. He translated ancient books into the English language and continued to improve his knowledge of the English language throughout his life.

Above all, John Quincy Adams was a leader who feared God. He was the only Senator to support a bill in 1806 because he held to principle. He wrote that "the magistrate is the servant not of his own desires, not even of the people, but of his God."[20]

As skepticism and atheism gained ascendance in America, it was John Quincy Adams who stepped up to give lectures on the importance of faith in God and the inspiration of the Bible. He wrote a number of hymns, twenty-two of which were published. No other president in American history is known to have read the Word of God for an hour a day, encouraged others to read it, attended public worship weekly, prayed almost constantly, expressed gratitude to God throughout his journals, and wrote sacred hymns. On one particular Sunday during his presidency, John Quincy stayed late at the service for Christian fellowship. When he arrived back at the White House, he found all the doors locked. Thankfully, a servant heard him banging on the windows and allowed the president back into his residence.

What Mattered Most

Let us hear the conclusion of the whole matter: fear God and keep His commandments, for this is man's all. For God will bring every work into judgment, including every secret thing, whether good or evil. (Ecclesiastes 12:13-14)

John Quincy Adams was far from a perfect man. He had no solid rooting in biblical doctrine. His rejection of the doctrines of the depravity of man and original sin resulted in bad policy decisions. He placed too high a confidence in education. He was too idealistic in his commitment to put an end to the evils of the earth that come as a consequence of sin. In his own words, he had to admit, "I would, by the irresistible power of genius and the irrepressible energy of will and the favor of Almighty God, have banished war and slavery off the face of the earth forever. But the conceptive [creative] power of mind was not conveyed upon me by my Maker.[21] " He still believed that it might be in the power of some other government to solve these problems.

Adams' idealism gave way to permissiveness in the raising of his sons. His firstborn George was sent to boarding school at six years of age and he was largely neglected by both father and mother. John Quincy allowed George to read whatever immoral novels were available at the time. His second son, John Jr. preferred sports over his studies, and his father pretty much gave up on any discipline, leaving his sons to themselves. He believed that a passion for learning should be natural, and considered it "useless to impose it on a youth as a task."[22] By twenty-six years of age, George Washington Adams had been completely overcome with drunkenness, gambling, and a "licentious life." Two years later he was dead—a tragedy that would sadden John Quincy and his wife for the rest of their lives. However, John Quincy's third son Charles Francis Adams would serve as a US Congressman and ambassador to the United Kingdom.

How a man dies is even more important than how he lives. The condition of his soul at the end of his life tells us more about his eternal destiny than how he began. While John Quincy Adams' famous father was moving quickly away from the orthodox Christian faith, John Quincy Adams headed the other direction. Towards the end of his life, John Quincy was discouraged about the condition of the country, but he was much less likely to doubt God. As one biographer put it, "while Adams' confidence in the union sometimes faltered, his faith in God grew stronger in his later years."[23]

Multiple times in his long diary, we find evidences that John Quincy Adams humbled himself before God. After hearing a sermon at the Second Presbyterian Church on a Sunday in 1837, he wrote, "I know that I have been, and am, a sinner—perhaps, by the depravity of the human heart, an unreclaimable sinner; but I continue to believe in God's tender mercies."[24] This is the best thing to be said of this man, whose life was one very long monumental spiritual struggle. Towards the end of his life he wrote, "I have daily and nightly warnings to be prepared for a sudden summons to meet my Maker. My hope is of mercy."[25] He referred to Jesus Christ as "my savior" and "my redeemer" regularly, but he would stop short of taking a definitive position on the deity of Christ and His work of atonement. He was horrified by all the doctrinal divisions and schism which had developed in the Christian church.

The thing John Quincy Adams wanted most of all was the mercy of God. That is the most essential need of the human soul, above and beyond all else. In one of his last hymns, the old statesman penned this beautiful personal testimony:

My last great Want—absorbing all—
Is, when beneath the sod,
And summoned to my final call,
The Mercy of my God.[26]

And the tax collector, standing afar off, would not so much as raise his eyes to heaven, but beat his breast, saying, "God, be merciful to me a sinner!" I tell you, this man went down to his house justified rather than the other; for everyone who exalts himself will be humbled, and he who humbles himself will be exalted. (Luke 18:13-14)

Adoniram Judson (1788-1850)

CHAPTER 15

Adoniram Judson: A Living Sacrifice

I beseech you therefore, brethren, by the mercies of God, that you present your bodies a living sacrifice, holy, acceptable to God, which is your reasonable service.

—Romans 12:1

The sacrifice of Adoniram Judson on the mission field of Burma (modern-day Myanmar) is a story that powerfully displays a true heart love and commitment to Jesus Christ and His kingdom. Few Christians in modern life have experienced the suffering endured by this great missionary of the faith. But his life of constant sacrifice produced fruit that continues to abide and grow to the present day. Adoniram was one of the very first American missionaries sent to a foreign mission field. His example as one of the first pioneering missionaries laid a foundation for gospel work that future American Christians would build upon. Today, by most accounts, America sends more missionaries to foreign lands than any other nation in the world. The costly service of Adoniram Judson may have been a single drop rippling through a vast ocean, but by God's amazing power his contributions have impacted many generations for the kingdom of our Lord and Savior, Jesus Christ.

Early Years

Adoniram Judson was born in Malden, Massachusetts on August 9, 1788 and was named after his father. His mother, Abigail, had married Adoniram Sr. two years earlier. At the time, he was serving as pastor of the Congregational church in Malden, but two weeks after his first son was born, the young father was dismissed from his congregation. In the years that followed, Adoniram Sr. would serve as pastor in Wenham, Massachusetts.

For a good many years the pastor struggled through many difficult ministerial labors in various small towns. These humbling circumstances and apparent lack of success seemed to motivate him to press his son Adoniram Jr. towards accomplishing some great work. Biographer Francis Wayland explained Adoniram Sr.'s ambitions for his young son:

> *His father stimulated his ambition to the utmost. He seems early to have formed the hope that his boy was to become a great man, and he took no pains to hide this expectation; so that even in childhood Adoniram's heart came to be full of worldly ambition, which in subsequent years had to be nailed to the cross.*[1]

In one sense, Adoniram Sr.'s wishes were fulfilled in the life of his son. For Adoniram Jr. would leave a lasting legacy known throughout the Christian world. However, it was not success in terms of how the world defines it. Rather he would leave behind a legacy of costly sacrifice, a life laid down on the altar for the glory of Jesus Christ and the gospel.

As a boy Adoniram was academically gifted. His mother taught him to read when he was three years old, and by age ten, he was proficient in Greek and Latin. His God-given abilities with languages would stand him in good stead with translation work in Burma.

Lapse in Faith and Conversion

For we must all appear before the judgment seat of Christ, that each one may receive the things done in the body, according to what he has done, whether good or bad. Knowing, therefore, the terror of the Lord, we persuade men; but we are well known to God, and I also trust are well known in your consciences. (2 Corinthians 5:10-11)

Adoniram was raised in a Christian home, but as with many young men in the modern age, he was led astray at college. It was his friendship with a certain young man named Jacob Eames that did much damage at Rhode Island College. Adoniram was impressed by Jacob's intelligence and talents, and he came to adopt this friend's system of belief known as Deism.

Deism: Deists believe that a supreme being and creator exists, but they reject the idea that this god would interact with mankind or providentially direct history. Deists reject the Scriptures and they do not accept the Christian gospel. This was the system of belief that Adoniram adopted during his college years.

While Adoniram and Jacob continued their studies at Rhode Island College, they would dream of how they could make a name for themselves in the world. After his graduation Adoniram returned home and disclosed his new beliefs to his father and mother. Of course, the Judsons were astonished and heartbroken to learn of Adoniram's apostasy. In his pride, this young man rebuffed his father's counsels and he left home to seek fulfillment in the world.

Adoniram journeyed westward into New York State, where he hooked up with a group of traveling young actors. They were a loose and profligate crowd, everything the book of Proverbs warns the young man of:

My son, if sinners entice you, do not consent. If they say, 'Come with us, let us lie in wait to shed blood; let us lurk secretly for the innocent without cause; let us swallow them alive like Sheol, and whole, like those who go down to the Pit; We shall find all kinds of precious possessions, we shall fill our houses with spoil; Cast in your lot

among us, Let us all have one purse,' my son, do not walk in the way with them,
keep your foot from their path . . . (Proverbs 1:10-15)

Adoniram later wrote of his experience with this unsavory crowd:

In my early days of wildness I joined a band of strolling players. We lived a reckless,
vagabond life, finding lodgings where we could, and bilking the landlord where we
found opportunity . . . in other words, running up a score, and then decamping
[departing suddenly] without paying the reckoning.[2]

In the midst of his foolish wanderings however, one night the Lord
mercifully sent a startling warning to young Adoniram. He had stopped off at
a country inn to sleep. The owner of the inn apologetically offered the young
rebel a room situated right next to the room in which another young man lay
dying. The owner said to him "[I hope this should] occasion you no uneasiness."[3]
Adoniram assured the landlord that it was alright, but it was not all right. He
couldn't sleep the whole night, as he heard the tossing and turning and groaning
of the sick man in the adjoining room. To himself Adoniram wondered whether
the young man was ready to face eternity. And then, he began to think of himself.
Given all of his newfound Deist beliefs, was he ready to face eternity?

The next morning Adoniram gathered his things, but just before he departed,
he asked the innkeeper how things went with the young man in the next room to
him. The owner replied, "He is dead."[4] Shocked and overcome by the news, he
inquired as to the identity of the man.[5] The owner said, "O, yes. It was a young
man from Providence College, a very fine fellow. His name was Eames, Jacob
Eames."[6]

The realization that the dying man was his friend and Deist mentor both
stunned and terrified Adoniram Judson. Here was the proud young man who
had convinced him to abandon his Christian beliefs, now dead. Immediately,
Adoniram took this as a clear and gracious warning from the Lord concerning
the state of his own soul. He abandoned his travel plans and directly returned
home to his parents who were now residing in Plymouth, Massachusetts. Two
prominent pastors came to visit the home—Dr. Moses Stuart and Dr. Edward

Griffin. They introduced their plans to open a new seminary in Andover, Massachusetts, and they invited Adoniram to apply for admission. In the company of other godly mentors, they assured him he could work through his spiritual struggles and doubts. The timing couldn't have been better. He gladly accepted their invitation and began his studies at Andover.

Preparations for Gospel Missions

All the ends of the world shall remember and turn to the LORD, and all the families of the nations shall worship before You. For the kingdom is the LORD's, and He rules over the nations. (Psalm 22:27-28)

The Holy Spirit of God was at work in Adoniram's life during his seminary years. In December 1808 he dedicated himself to God. The following May he publicly professed his faith in the Lord Jesus Christ at the Third Congregational Church in Plymouth, Massachusetts to his parents' great joy. There was no looking back for Adoniram Judson. From this point on, he would dedicate himself to serving His Lord and Master, Jesus Christ.

During Adoniram's senior year of seminary he read a printed sermon that would profoundly influence his future ministry labors. Entitled "A Star in the East," was preached by Dr. Claudius Buchanan. Drawing from Matthew 2:2, Buchanan outlined how the gospel was making inroads into the eastern parts of Asia.

Now after Jesus was born in Bethlehem of Judea in the days of Herod the king, behold, wise men from the East came to Jerusalem, saying, "Where is He who has been born King of the Jews? For we have seen His star in the East and have come to worship Him." (Matthew 2:1-2)

Adoniram later wrote of how the sermon had made such a strong impression upon him:

Though I do not now consider that sermon as peculiarly excellent, it produced a very powerful effect on my mind. For some days I was unable to attend to the studies of

my class, and spent my time in wondering at my past stupidity, depicting the most
romantic scenes in missionary life, and roving about the college rooms declaiming
[speaking in an impassioned way] on the subject of missions . . . I have always felt
thankful to God for bringing me into that state of excitement, which was perhaps
necessary, in the first instance, to enable me to break the strong attachment I felt to
home and country, and to endure the thought of abandoning all my wonted pursuits
and animating prospects.[7]

Judson went on to read up on eastern lands. After his initial excitement wore off, he could not stop thinking about the possibility of foreign missions. Then the day came when he reached a settled conviction that he must leave America and take the gospel to foreign lands. That day, it was Mark 16:15 that weighed heavily upon him. He received it from Jesus as a personal mandate.

And He [Jesus] said to them, "Go into all the world and preach the gospel to every
creature." (Mark 16:15)

Adoniram Judson would be among the very first American foreign missionaries. His plans were not without opposition. When he notified his family of his intentions to take the Gospel into Asia, his parents were disappointed and distraught. His mother and sister feared that this would be a quick end to his life, and his father was disappointed that Adoniram was forgoing ministerial opportunities in Massachusetts. However, he was not alone in his aspirations for foreign missions in these early years. Missionary fervor was spreading through Andover Seminary. Between 1810 and 1835, sixty-seven Andover men were commissioned to missionary service.[8] The first wave of missionaries to Hawaii, mostly from Andover, sailed in the fall of 1819.

Early in 1810 Judson and his classmates made an appeal to the assembly of the Congregationalist churches meeting in Bradford, Massachusetts for the support of missions. Adoniram read the following for the assembly of ministers:

The undersigned members of the Divinity College, respectfully request the attention
of their reverend fathers, convened in the General Association at Bradford, to the
following statement and inquiries:

They beg leave to state that their minds have been long impressed with the duty and importance of personally attempting a mission to the heathen; that the impressions on their minds have induced a serious, and, as they trust, a prayerful consideration of the subject in its various attitudes, particularly in relation to the probable success and the difficulties attending such an attempt; and that, after examining all the information which they can obtain, they consider themselves as devoted to this work for life,

Ann Hasseltine Judson

whenever God, in his providence, shall open the way . . . The undersigned, feeling their youth and inexperience, look up to their fathers in the church, and respectfully solicit their advice, direction, and prayers.[9]

The men of the assembly were moved by this humble, God-glorifying petition, and they agreed to form the American Board for Foreign Missions under the oversight of the Congregationalist churches. While visiting Bradford, Adoniram also met a young lady named Ann Hasseltine. He was immediately attracted to her and a month later he asked her hand in marriage. Ann graciously accepted Adoniram's proposal but told him that her parents must give their permission. In a remarkably direct letter written to Ann's father, Adoniram provided full disclosure. He asked for permission to marry his daughter and to take her to foreign lands:

I have now to ask, whether you can consent to part with your daughter early next spring, to see her no more in this world; whether you can consent to her departure, and her subjection to the hardships and sufferings of missionary life; whether you can consent to her exposure to the dangers of the ocean, to the fatal influence of the southern climate of India; to every kind of want and distress; to degradation, insult, persecution, and perhaps a violent death. Can you consent to all this, for the sake of him who left his heavenly home, and died for her and for you; for the sake of perishing, immortal souls; for the sake of Zion, and the glory of God? Can you consent to all this, in hope of soon meeting your daughter in the world of glory, with the crown of righteousness brightened with the acclamations of praise which shall redound to her Savior from heathens saved, through her means, from eternal woe and despair?[10]

Here Adoniram was brutally honest concerning the hardships of missionary life. This was hardly an exaggerated description of what they would encounter on the field. In the end, the young woman's father agreed to the proposal, and Ann most willingly submitted herself to the marriage and the dangerous mission to which they were called. She wrote to her friend Lydia, saying:

I feel willing, and expect, if nothing in Providence prevents, to spend my days in this world in heathen lands. Yes, Lydia, I have about come to the determination to give up all my comforts and enjoyments here, sacrifice my affection to relatives and friends, and go where God, in his Providence, shall see fit to place me.[11]

First Years in Burma

Oh, that men would give thanks to the LORD for His goodness, and for His wonderful works to the children of men! For He has broken the gates of bronze, and cut the bars of iron in two. (Psalm 107:15-16)

In February 1812 Adoniram and Ann were married in her parents' home in Bradford. That same month the young couple departed, bound for India aboard the *Caravan*. The couple arrived in Calcutta, India in June 1812, where they met up with the famous English missionary William Carey. Since Judson was interested in Bible translation work, he hoped to learn something of Carey's translation efforts in India. Having studied the doctrine of baptism on the voyage to India, Adoniram became convinced of the Baptist view, and both Adoniram and Ann were baptized by immersion in India.

Almost a year later the Judsons departed for Burma, arriving in the large city of Rangoon (modern-day Yangon) in July 1813. Not long after, Ann gave birth to their first child, who was stillborn. It would be the first of many tragedies for the couple while on the mission field. Soon after arriving in Burma, Adoniram and Ann met Felix Carey, another missionary who had been laboring in the country for some time.

Both Adoniram and Ann began their instruction in the Burmese language using a tutor. The going was slow at first because their teacher did not speak any English. Adoniram started out by pointing to objects around the house, the teacher would say the Burmese words, and Adoniram would repeat them back. It was a slow and arduous process, but the Judsons were committed to the cause of bringing the gospel to the Burmese. They stayed at it until they had gained proficiency in the language. After a year of study, Ann reported in a letter, "Our progress in the language is slow, as it is peculiarly hard of acquisition. We can, however, read, write, and converse with tolerable ease, and frequently spend whole evenings very pleasantly in conversing with our Burman friends."[12]

Sharing the Gospel in Burma

Now while Paul waited for them at Athens, his spirit was provoked within him when he saw that the city was given over to idols. Therefore he reasoned in the synagogue with the Jews and with the Gentile worshipers, and in the marketplace daily with those who happened to be there. (Acts 17:16-17)

Even as the Apostle was provoked when he saw the idols in first-century Athens, the Judsons were shocked and disturbed by the prevailing idolatry of Burma. The majority of Burmese were Buddhist, and the city of Rangoon was filled with Buddhist temples and shrines.

While pursuing his language studies, Adoniram started up his translation work, using some of the first translations completed by Felix Carey. Felix had started a few chapters of the Gospel of Matthew, and had worked on some portions of a small Burmese grammar. As Adoniram gained a better understanding of Burmese, he came to realize that the language did not have words adequate to convey some of the important theological truths of the Bible. Without a common terminology for important biblical truths, it was clear that this task of communicating the gospel would require a long term commitment.

On September 11, 1814, the Judsons' second child was born. They named the boy Roger Williams Judson after the famous Rhode Island leader. Eighteen months later, Roger contracted fever and died in May of 1816. The grief that the young parents experienced after this second bereavement was almost too much to bear. But they continued trusting that "the LORD is righteous in all His ways, gracious in all His works" (Ps. 145:17). In a letter to her parents, Ann reported her grief:

> *Death, regardless of our lonely situation, has entered our dwelling, and made one of the happiest families wretched. Our little Roger Williams, our only darling little boy, was three days ago laid in the silent grave . . . But what shall I say about the improvement we are to make of this heavy affliction? We do not feel a disposition to murmur, or to inquire of our Sovereign why he has done this. We wish rather, to sit down submissively under the rod and bear the smart, till the end for which the affliction was sent, shall be accomplished. Our hearts were bound up in this child; we felt he was our earthly all, our only source of innocent recreation in this heathen land. But God saw it was necessary to remind us of our error, and to strip us of our only little all. O may it not be in vain that he has done it.*[13]

The Judsons continued their missionary labors pressing through the grief of bitter providences. One of the most important religious sites in Buddhism was located in Rangoon. The "Shwe Dagon Pagoda" attracted thousands of visitors throughout the year. Adoniram relocated his missionary residence on a road

> **Pagoda:** A pagoda is a traditional term used for a Hindu or Buddhist Temple. Most pagodas are multi-tiered towers, primarily found in India and East Asia.

Pagodas in Burma (Myanmar)

leading to the pagoda so as to gain more opportunities to share the good news of Jesus with worshipers coming to the site. As people traveled the road towards the temple, Adoniram called out to them and invited them into conversation about religion. However, after nearly six years of missionary labors, the Judsons still had not seen a single convert to the faith. Though they had many opportunities to interact with the Burmese people, they found these native to be stubborn in their traditions and uninterested in the truth.

By God's grace, the light of the gospel finally broke through on May 5, 1819. That was the day a man named Maung Nau confessed his sins and put his trust in Jesus. Adoniram wrote, "he has found no other Savior but Jesus Christ; no where else can he look for salvation; and therefore he proposes to adhere to Christ, and worship him all his life long."[14] This first conversion encouraged the Judsons onwards, and it wasn't long before the Lord opened the eyes of more Burmese to the truth of the gospel.

In 1819, Adoniram Judson adopted a set of rules that would govern his missionary work. These rules reveal a man who was committed to the pursuit of holiness and redeeming the time.

1. Be diligent in secret prayer, every morning and evening.

2. Never spend a moment in mere idleness.

3. Restrain natural appetites within the bounds of temperance and purity. "Keep thyself pure."

4. Suppress every emotion of anger and ill will.

5. Undertake nothing from motives of ambition, or love of fame.

6. Never do that which, at the moment, appears to be displeasing to God.

7. Seek opportunities of making some sacrifice for the good of others, especially of believers, provided the sacrifice is not inconsistent with some duty.

8. Endeavor to rejoice in every loss and suffering incurred for Christ's sake and the gospel's, remembering that though, like death, they are not to be willfully incurred, yet, like death, they are great gain.[15]

Imprisonment during the Anglo-Burmese War

For to this you were called, because Christ also suffered for us, leaving us an example, that you should follow His steps. (1 Peter 2:21)

Although the Judsons had already faced many harrowing trials, their most difficult hardships were still to come in the years 1824 to 1826. War broke out between Burma and the British Empire in March 1824. The Burmese had already been suspicious of foreigners before hostilities began, and the war with Britain only made things worse. Suspecting that all foreigners were acting as spies for the British, the Burmese imprisoned almost all of them regardless of their nationality. Thus, the American missionary Adoniram Judson would endure twenty-one months of torture and suffering in Burmese prisons.

At night, Adoniram was forced to sleep in the prison while hanging upside down with only his shoulders touching the ground. Biographer Christie explains: "As night fell, a long, horizontal bamboo pole suspended from the ceiling was lowered by pulleys. After being passed through the prisoners' fettered legs the pole was again hoisted into the air. The prisoners' feet were raised by the pole until only their shoulders and heads rested on the floor."[16] Almost every day, Judson would witness the execution of fellow prisoners, wondering when his time would come. For almost two years, his faithful wife Ann worked to free Adoniram, or at the very least to get him moved into better, more humane conditions. Every day Ann would walk the two miles from their little home, in hopes she could keep her husband alive with a little food and drink. Eight months after Adoniram's arrest, she gave birth to their third child, Maria. And after the birth, she continued walking the two miles both ways, baby in tow, to minister to her husband in the prison. Later, Ann wrote of these trying times:

> Sometimes for days and days together, I could not go into the prison, till after dark, when I had two miles to walk, in returning to the house. O how many, many times, have I returned from that dreary prison at nine o'clock at night, solitary and worn out with fatigue and anxiety . . . and endeavoured to invent some new scheme for the release of the prisoners . . . But the consolations of religion, in these trying circumstances, were neither 'few nor small.' It taught me to look beyond this world, to that rest, that peaceful happy rest, where Jesus reigns, and oppression never enters.[17]

Eventually, Ann put a makeshift shelter together somewhere near the prison where she stayed in between visits. She feared that she or the baby would die if they were to continue making the journey in the blazing heat. She described the condition in the prison in her memoirs:

> The situation of the prisoners was now distressing beyond description. It was at the commencement of the hot season. There were above a hundred prisoners shut up in one room, without a breath of air excepting from the cracks in the boards. I sometimes obtained permission to go to the door for five minutes, when my heart sickened at the wretchedness exhibited. The white prisoners, from incessant perspiration and loss of appetite, looked more like the dead than the living . . .[18]

While the British troops advanced on Rangoon, the prisoners were taken on a death march to a remote area north of the city. It was rumored that the prisoners were to be burned alive. Still Ann would not leave her husband, but followed the prisoners first by boat and then in a cart. With her came three-month-old Maria and two Burmese children whom she had more or less adopted. During this second period of imprisonment, Ann was able to convince the jailer to allow her and her children to share space in his little hut. Curled up in the corner of the two-room cottage, she became very sick, so much so that she had no milk for her baby. In these pitiful, desperate straits, she bribed the jailer to allow Adoniram out of prison to carry the baby about the village, begging other nursing mothers to let Maria have a little of their milk.

When things could not get any worse, in God's good providence, the war ended. The prisoners were quickly released, and Adoniram Judson was hurried back to the capitol city to help with the peace negotiations, since he could speak Burmese. For two short weeks, Ann and Adoniram enjoyed a wonderful reunion. But while Adoniram was drawn away for further negotiations, Ann's health broke down and she succumbed to cerebral meningitis. She died at thirty-six years of age. She had given up her life for him. She had kept her wedding vows. She had given her life for the cause of Christ in heathen lands and now she had departed to be with Him. Adoniram Judson was now left alone to continue the noble mission they had begun together.

Shortly thereafter, Maria died too. Adoniram recorded the sad details of the death and burial of his child in a letter to his mother-in-law:

> "The next morning we made [Maria's] last bed in the small enclosure that surrounds her mother's lonely grave. Together they rest in hope, under the hope tree, which stands at the head of the graves, and together, I trust, their spirits are rejoicing after a short separation of precisely six months. And I am left alone in the wide world. My own dear family I have buried; one in Rangoon, and two in Amhurst. What remains for me but to hold myself in readiness to follow the dear departed to that blessed world, "Where my best friends, my kindred dwell, Where God my Saviour reigns."[19]

Second Marriage to Sarah Boardman

Though disheartened, Adoniram Judson would not give up the mission to which he had set his hand. He teamed up with a young missionary couple, George Boardman and his wife Sarah. Together they founded a mission work in Tavoy on the southeast coast of Burma. It was at this time that Adoniram ran into a slave of the Karen peoples named Ko Tha Byu. The man had been a bandit and a murderer, professing to have killed at least thirty people in the past. However, Adoniram bought the man's freedom and proceeded to disciple him in the gospel of the Lord Jesus Christ. Ko was radically saved, and the Lord used him to reach his tribe—the animist, primitive Karen tribe that roamed through the jungles of the Salween River.

In 1831 George Boardman died of tuberculosis. Not long afterwards, Adoniram did the one thing a practical missionary would do in such a case—he married the widow Sarah Boardman and the two continued the mission work. Adoniram was forty-six years old and Sarah was thirty-one. Together they had eight children, and Sarah contributed much to the work. She translated *The Pilgrim's Progress* into Burmese, a work that is still used among Christians in that country to this day. She also translated the New Testament into the Peguan language.

Adoniram finally finished a Burmese translation of the complete Bible in 1834. It was a labor of love and sacrifice that took him at least fifteen years to complete, produced in the most careful, scholarly manner. He meticulously translated each verse using the original Greek and Hebrew texts to ensure accuracy and clarity. The first edition of the Burmese Bible totaled 1200 pages. Judson's work would be highly praised by later missionaries over the generations that followed, as one missionary testified:

> *The translation of the Holy Scriptures into the Burman language by the late Dr Judson is admitted to be the best translation in India; that is, the translation has given more satisfaction to his contemporaries and successors than any translation of the Bible into any other Eastern language has done to associate missionaries in any*

other part of India. It is free from all obscurity to the Burmese mind. It is read and understood perfectly. Its style and diction are as choice and elegant as the language itself.[20]

Once Adoniram had completed the Burmese Bible, he turned his attention to an English-Burmese Dictionary. This dictionary would serve as a tool for future missionaries and translators, making the work of translation much quicker. Before his death in 1850, Adoniram finished the majority of the dictionary, leaving the rest to his friend Edward Stevens.

Of the eight children born to Adoniram and Sarah, three died at an early age. Having lost his first wife and six children on the field, the missionary's sufferings were not yet ended. For on his return trip to America in 1845, Sarah became ill at sea and died. Once again Adoniram was bereaved of his wife, one whom he would refer to as "the worthy successor" of his first wife Ann.[21]

Judson finally arrived in America after thirty years of service in the foreign mission field. As one of America's first pioneering missionaries, by this time he was well-known all over the country. Thousands flocked to hear him speak. And his visit did a great deal to inspire more interest in foreign missions among the Protestant churches.

While in America, Adoniram also made the acquaintance of a young woman named Emily Chubbuck, a young author who wrote fictional works to support her aging parents and extended family. Adoniram was on the hunt for a talented author who could write a memoir of his late wife Sarah. Initially the two met to discuss this biographical work, but the connection quickly turned into something more than that. Within a month, Adoniram made a proposal of marriage. She gratefully accepted Adoniram's proposal, and they were married.

Adoniram and Emily returned to Rangoon, but the couple enjoyed only a few short years of marriage together. Having suffered from repeated bouts of illness over the years, Adoniram's voice had weakened, causing him great difficulty preaching and evangelizing. In the early months of 1850 Adoniram contracted an illness from which he could not recover. Upon medical counsel, he set out on a ship to sea in hopes this would afford some healing for his body.

It didn't, and Adoniram Judson died in Jesus on April 12, 1850. Four months later the news reached Emily in Burma, and she decided to return to the United States, taking the remaining Judson children with her. The few short years in Burma took a toll on Emily's health as well, and she died three years later at the age of thirty-six.

Enduring Fruit from the Life of Adoniram Judson

Most assuredly, I say to you, unless a grain of wheat falls into the ground and dies, it remains alone; but if it dies, it produces much grain. (John 12:24)

Truly, it can be said that Adoniram Judson laid down his life for the sake of the gospel. Like the grain of wheat Jesus spoke of in the Gospel of John, Adoniram died and he was buried in the ground. But that seed produced great fruit in the generations that followed. To this day Adoniram's life continues to bear fruit. When the Judsons arrived in Burma in 1813, there was not a single Christian in the country. Now, according to *Operation World*, modern Myanmar claims over 4 million believers in the Lord Jesus Christ.[22] The largest denomination of Christians in Myanmar is the Myanmar Baptist Convention, the church birthed out of Adoniram's first labors. By the time of his death at sixty-one years of age, Adoniram could identify sixty-three churches planted throughout Burma populated by some 100,000 members, mostly of the Karen people. Many of the Karen have held on to the faith through thick and thin despite much persecution which continues into the present day.

Added to this growth of Christianity in Myanmar, Adoniram's life story has also impacted foreign missions everywhere around the world. Hundreds of thousands of missionaries have been inspired to follow in his wake, taking the gospel to the uttermost parts of the earth. One may read the many sufferings of Adoniram, his successive marriages, and the loss of a number of children, and wonder, "was it all worth it?" Our Lord Jesus answers that question:

Judson Memorial Church in Myanmar

And everyone who has left houses or brothers or sisters or father or mother or wife or children or lands, for My name's sake, shall receive a hundredfold, and inherit eternal life. (Matthew 19:29)

What kept Adoniram going through his many trials? His own writings reveal the truths that he rested upon through his many difficult labors. He wrote in his diaries:

O slow of heart to believe and trust in the constant presence and overruling agency of our almighty Saviour![23]

Had it not been for the consolations of religion, and an assured conviction that every additional trial was ordered by infinite love and mercy, I must have sunk under my accumulated sufferings.[24]

Adoniram's birth was later memorialized at his birth-home in Malden, Massachusetts where visitors will read these words etched on a plate:

Rev. Adoniram Judson
America's First Foreign Missionary
1788-1850
Malden, His Birthplace
The Ocean, His Sepulchre
Converted Burmans and the
Burman Bible, His Monument
His Record is On High

Asahel Nettleton (1783-1844)

CHAPTER 16

★ ★ ★

Asahel Nettleton: America's Forgotten Evangelist

I charge you therefore before God and the Lord Jesus
Christ, who will judge the living and the dead at
His appearing and His kingdom: Preach the word!
Be ready in season and out of season. Convince,
rebuke, exhort, with all longsuffering and teaching.
—2 Timothy 4:1-2

Some called him the greatest evangelist since George Whitefield. Historical records indicate that about 30,000 people came to know Christ through his ministry during the Second Great Awakening. While there were many spurious revivals going on in the 1800s, most of this evangelist's converts continued steadfast in the faith and not many fell away. Yet today Asahel Nettleton is almost entirely forgotten. Few Christians have even heard of him. His legacy was washed away in the confusion of the false revivals, burned-over districts, and further-fracturing of the Christian church that visited the nation in the years before the American Civil War.

America During the Life of Asahel Nettleton

As the 19th century dawned in America, the Christian church splintered into more denominations and heretical, false sects arose out of the revivalism. Elements of the Second Great Awakening had created rough conditions in Western New York State. The revivalist, Charles Finney, was most familiar with this area and would call it the "Burned Over District." When man comes to believe that he is in control of who gets saved, terrible things begin to happen. Charismatic leaders try to control their followers. They manipulate the emotions of their audience. They will create a message that focuses on the sensational, and they will present themselves as prophets who understand the message of the end times better than others. This "burned over district" in New York State offered an incubating ground for a number of cults and end-times sects.

Also at this time America had courted a national apostasy toward more Unitarianism, Deism, and Transcendentalism. The country's religious downfall came about primarily through the colleges and seminaries, like Harvard College. Once the Unitarians captured Harvard, the faith of New England began to sink fast. The evil one had gained a foothold.

This was an abandonment of the first legacy of the country. It was the year 1636 when Pastor Thomas Hooker led about one hundred Puritan settlers through the wilderness from Massachusetts into the fertile Connecticut River Valley, where they founded the Connecticut Colony. These Puritans wrote the Fundamental Orders of Connecticut in 1639—possibly the first written constitution in the world. They also adopted the Latin motto *Qui Transtulit Sustinet*, meaning "He Who Transplanted Still Sustains." These hard-working Puritan settlers quickly turned Connecticut into a prosperous, well-ordered society.

Asahel Nettleton was a descendant of these Puritans. Many of the most important events in the early history of the American Republic took place during his lifetime. In 1783, the year Asahel was born, Britain recognized American Independence. Four years later the Constitution was written, and the foundations of the republic were laid. During Nettleton's life America expanded quickly in population, territory, and economic production. Inventive, enterprising Americans produced the telegraph, manufacturing centers, and railroads, and the country began to industrialize. The Louisiana Purchase of 1803 nearly doubled the size of the nation, and by Nettleton's death in 1844 the United States of America stretched to the Pacific Ocean. Important religious changes also took place during this time. The Second Great Awakening made a deep impact on the nation, changing American evangelical Christianity in ways that still affect the church to this day.

Early Years

For it is the God who commanded light to shine out of darkness, who has shone in our hearts to give the light of the knowledge of the glory of God in the face of Jesus Christ. (2 Corinthians 4:6)

Asahel Nettleton was born in Killingworth, Connecticut on April 21, 1783 to Samuel and Amy Nettleton. They were middle class farmers and Samuel had fought in the Continental Army during the War for Independence. Asahel was the eldest son and the second of six children, two of whom died in childhood.

Asahel's parents were half-way church members according to the terms of the Half-Way Covenant adopted by New England's Congregationalist churches. Though both Samuel and Amy had made an honest profession of faith and their lives were free from scandalous sin, they were not allowed to become full church members and take communion because they could not recount a conversion experience. Nevertheless, the Nettletons brought up their children in the nurture

> **Half-Way Covenant:** This New England church policy allowed parents who were *not* able to take the Lord's Supper to still present their children for baptism. Both parents and children would then be considered half-way members of the church unless or until they could recount their own conversion experience. It was a man-made attempt to keep the church membership pure by relying on "conversion experiences."

and admonition of the Lord. They taught their children to work hard on the family farm and trained them in the Westminster Shorter Catechism. Later in life, Asahel would express his gratefulness for such a godly upbringing.

While growing up, Asahel often thought seriously about matters of life, death, and eternity. He was something of a moral and upright youth, but he still doubted whether he had been truly converted. The setting of the sun each day would remind him that his life was a vapor soon to be over and gone. In the fall of 1800, seventeen-year-old Asahel attended a community dance (as was his habit in those days). He hoped that the merrymaking would ease his anguished soul but instead he kept thinking of the futility of a life without Christ.

For several months the young man passed through a period of deep conviction of sin. For a while he tried to be good in his own strength, but then he realized the futility of these efforts and the depths of his own sin. Doubts flooded in and he began to question the truth of the Bible and the existence of God. Then he feared he had committed the unpardonable sin. At last however, the Lord mercifully worked a change in his heart and brought peace to his soul. Asahel's biographer writes of how much he was filled with joy and peace as he came to faith (Rom. 15:13).

> The character of God now appeared lovely. The Saviour was exceedingly precious; and the doctrines of grace, towards which he had felt such bitter opposition, he contemplated with delight. He saw clearly, that if there was any good thing in him towards the Lord God of Israel, it was not the result of any effort of his own, but of the sovereign and distinguishing will of God . . . He now felt a peculiar love for the people of God, and a delight in the duties of religion, to which before he was a total stranger.[1]

In God's providence, Asahel would be able to use what he had learned during this time to counsel and disciple others to faith.

Preparation for Ministry

For if I preach the gospel, I have nothing to boast of, for necessity is laid upon me;
yes, woe is me if I do not preach the gospel! (1 Corinthians 9:16)

After his conversion, the Lord infused in the young man a burning desire to share the gospel with others. A biographer records:

While laboring in the field, he would often say to himself: "If I might be the means
of saving one soul, I should prefer it to all the riches and honours of this world."[2]

First, Asahel considered foreign missionary service, as Americans were just beginning overseas missionary work. Nettleton realized at this point he needed additional education and training to be a missionary, but found obstacles in his way. In 1802 a plague swept through Killingworth, and Asahel's father Samuel and younger brother David both died. As the eldest son, the responsibility of providing for the family fell upon him.

With these added responsibilities, the 19-year-old young man found it even harder to prepare for the mission field, but he continued undeterred. He acquired books and filled what little spare time he had with his studies. After long days of labor in the fields during the summer, Asahel would take up the books in the evenings under the tutelage of his local pastor. During the winter months while there was less farm work to do, he signed up as a school teacher. Finally in 1805, after three years of hard work and study, Nettleton had saved enough money and was adequately prepared to enter Yale College.

America had experienced a great revival in the mid-1700s during the First Great Awakening. But by the 1790s the effects of this spiritual revival had largely worn off. European skepticism and radical Enlightenment ideas from France had infected the new country. Its colleges were rife with atheism and infidelity, and Yale was no exception. Reports have it that "intemperance, profanity, and gambling were common; yea, and also licentiousness."[3] The students would call each other "Voltaire, Rousseau, and D'Alembert" after the radical, atheistic French philosophers.[4] A second great awakening was desperately needed in the churches, the seminaries, and the schools.

In 1795 Jonathan Edwards' grandson Timothy Dwight became president of Yale. A devout Christian, Dwight was horrified at the spiritual condition of the college. In his first address to Yale's senior class, Dwight posed the question, "Are the Scriptures of the Old and New Testament the Word of God?" Not one member of the class answered the question in the affirmative. Dwight went on to challenge the students to consider the question, and he argued for Scriptural inspiration in a series of lectures throughout the school year. The soil was hard at first. However, seven years later in 1802, a revival broke out on campus and at least one third of Yale's 230 students professed faith in Christ. One student wrote of the revival:

> *The whole college was shaken. It seemed for a time as if the whole mass of the students would press into the kingdom. It was the Lord's doing, and marvelous in all eyes. Oh, what a blessed change! It was a glorious reformation.*[5]

By the time Nettleton entered Yale in 1805, the fields were whiter and the spiritual condition of the college had much improved. While open unbelief and immorality were gone, however, most of the students still seemed more focused on academics than wholeheartedly serving the Lord. Asahel found some friends at Yale who shared his passion for Christ. In 1807 an additional revival broke out at the college and this time Asahel played a large part in it. He could often be seen walking arm in arm with a fellow student, sharing the gospel, and counseling. If he sensed a student was not receptive, Asahel would not press him but would commit himself to pray for him.

These were not easy years for Nettleton however. From time to time he would have to leave Yale to help on the family farm. In his off hours he continued his work as a teacher in New Haven to cover the bills. Still he managed to graduate in four years of study. In those days ministerial candidates usually interned with a local pastor for at least a year as part of their training. Asahel received this mentorship or discipleship from Pastor Bezaleel Pinneo, and afterwards he was licensed to preach by the Congregationalist church in 1811.

Asahel was still looking to serve as an overseas missionary. Adoniram and Ann Judson left for Burma the year following his ordination, and the first

Congregationalist missionaries to Hawaii sailed off in 1819. Nevertheless, the Lord had other plans for Asahel Nettleton. He would become a preacher and evangelist in his native land.

Evangelistic Ministry

I now send you, to open their eyes, in order to turn them from darkness to light, and from the power of Satan to God, that they may receive forgiveness of sins and an inheritance among those who are sanctified by faith in Me. (Acts 26:17-18)

Following his licensure, Asahel Nettleton went on to fill the pulpit in the desolate churches of southeastern Connecticut. These churches were small, divided, and spiritually weak. Many of them could not afford a full-time pastor. Regrettably, the congregations had been ravaged by divisive itinerant evangelists coming out of the First Great Awakening.

The worst effects of revivals are seen when the local churches are weakened instead of strengthened. Southeastern Connecticut had felt the brunt of the worst elements of the 1740s Awakening, through an "evangelist" named James Davenport. This man charged into the local parishes to which the local pastors had not invited him, denouncing them as "rabbis," "pharisees," and "unconverted" enemies of God. He gathered his own followers around him and called them "brother" or "sister" while he would refer to the other church members as "Mr." or "Mrs." He urged his converts to forsake their "corrupt" churches and form new "pure" congregations. He also placed great stock in visions, trances, and emotional impressions of the "Spirit." Eventually Davenport repented and acknowledged that he had been the tool of Satan. Nonetheless, the churches he had wounded were still bleeding when Nettleton arrived on the scene some seventy years later.

Young Pastor Nettleton did his best to heal these wounds. He preached brotherly love and peace to divided and antagonistic congregations. Since he was a first hand witness to the ruinous effects of bad revivalism, this equipped him to better identify dangerous excesses with 19th century revivalism soon to come.

> **Itinerant Evangelist:** An itinerant evangelist is a preacher who is not a settled pastor in a local church. Instead, he spends his time traveling to various churches and preaching the gospel in many different locations. George Whitefield, John Wesley, and Billy Graham were all itinerant evangelists.

Throughout his ministry as an itinerant evangelist, Asahel Nettleton was always careful to work with and support local pastors. He came only at their invitation and never sought to undermine them. As a result, pastors throughout America came to love and trust him.

In 1813 Asahel Nettleton met Lyman Beecher, a Congregationalist pastor in Litchfield, Connecticut. Lyman Beecher was the father of liberal preacher Henry Ward Beecher and Harriet Beecher Stowe, author of *Uncle Tom's Cabin*. Upon their first meeting, the two men greeted each other in biblical language.

Lyman Beecher

Encountering Asahel at the door, Lyman exclaimed: "Thou hast well done that thou art come" (Acts 10:33). To which Asahel replied, "I ask for what intent ye have sent for me?" (Acts 10:29). Beecher responded, "To hear all things that are commanded thee of God" (Acts 10:33).[6] This was the beginning of a close friendship between the two men that lasted for many years.

For the next several years, Asahel preached in many towns across Connecticut. In the pulpit he was solemn and serious. He recognized the weightiness of his message. His piercing eyes seemed to gaze into the souls of his hearers. He had a thorough acquaintance with the human heart under conviction of sin, obtained by study of Scripture and his own experience. His biographers describe his preaching this way:"It often seemed to individuals while listening to his preaching, that he must know their thoughts."[7] He was able "to place the naked truth upon the conscience, and to demolish with a few heavy strokes, all the vain excuses and refuges of lies to which sinners resort to screen themselves from the force of truth."[8]

He was not known for his eloquence or dramatic emotional power but for plain, direct, heartfelt, Scriptural speech. Like the Apostle Paul, "[his] speech and [his] preaching were not with persuasive words of human wisdom, but in demonstration of the Spirit and of power, that your faith should not be in the wisdom of men but in the power of God" (1 Cor. 2:4-5). His biographer develops further on the powerful effects of preaching:

> He was able to bring the awesome realities of the eternal world home to the souls of men. When he talked about the heinousness of sin, they felt its sting. When he portrayed the sufferings of Christ, they felt the trauma of Calvary. When he proclaimed the holy character of God, they trembled at the vision. When he thundered forth the judgements of hell, men were moved to escape that place.[9]

From a sample of his sermon, the reader will notice the simplicity and sincerity in his words:

> Christ finds the sinner. He finds him in his sins—careless about his soul—casting off fear and restraining prayer—wandering farther and farther from God, from happiness, and from heaven. He often comes upon him by surprise in the midst of his wickedness, and awakens him to a sense of his guilt. He trembles and is alarmed; but he is unwilling to return, and would fain flee out of the Saviour's hand. No sinner will ever awaken himself. Left to himself, not another sinner in this house will ever begin in earnest to seek the salvation of his soul. "The wicked, through the pride of his countenance, will not seek after God" (Ps. 10:4). "There is none that understandeth, there is none that seeketh after God" (Rom. 3:11). Every Christian knows this to be true in relation to himself. He knows that, after he was awakened,

if the Spirit of God had left him, he should have returned to his sinful courses. All who have found the Saviour will acknowledge that the Saviour first found them.[10]

In addition to preaching, Asahel held regular prayer meetings and visited families in their homes. Sometimes the Word fell on rocky ground, but at other times it fell on good soil, bringing forth a fruitful harvest. This evangelist well understood that revival is a sovereign work of the Holy Spirit, not something that can be scheduled. If he sensed that the Spirit seemed to be moving, Nettleton would hold inquiry meetings for those under conviction of sin. At these meetings he preached first, then counseled each person individually. One of his friends wrote:

I verily believe that no great warrior ever studied military tactics with more enthusiasm, or better understood the art of killing men with the sword of war, than Nettleton did how to wield the sword of the Spirit, to deliver them from captivity to sin and Satan, and save their souls.[11]

Asahel Nettleton was also careful to avoid giving new converts a false assurance. He believed the marks of true conversion were brokenness over sin, humility, fervent devotion to the glory of God, and a changed life of holiness. While he may not have always given weak, struggling believers enough comfort, very few of his converts apostatized. He maintained ongoing relationships with them as best as he could—praying for them, writing them letters, and giving them spiritual counsel. He also connected them with local pastors who could disciple them further. Thirty years after he preached in a town, he would find these men and women still walking in the truth. They could still remember his first Spirit-filled ministries in their lives.

> **Revival:** Revival is an extraordinary outpouring and manifestation of the presence and power of the Holy Spirit. It brings salvation to sinners and renewal to the church. It is a sovereign work of God, not something that can be planned or scheduled. Examples of revival include the Reformation, the First Great Awakening, and parts of the Second Great Awakening.

Whenever Mr. Nettleton was seen to enter a house, almost the whole neighbourhood would immediately assemble to hear from his lips the Word of life. Husbandmen would leave their fields, mechanics their shops, and females their domestic concerns, to inquire the way to eternal life . . . This favoured servant of Christ came with no trumpet sound before him, in the meekness of his master, and the Lord was with him in very deed.[12]

The revivals that occurred under his ministry were characterized by deep conviction of sin, reverential silence and stillness, and power. He discouraged emotional excesses and he had people removed from his meetings if their emotional outbursts were overly disruptive.

In 1816 Asahel was preaching in the town of Bridgewater, Connecticut, and almost the whole town came to hear him at a local school building. There was living in this town a hardened atheist, a certain Mr. C. This man had fought against the gospel tooth and nail and he had refused to attend church for many years. However, the excitement surrounding Nettleton's visit brought him to the building out of curiosity, just to catch a glimpse of the famous "fanatic." He chose not to enter, but to stand at the door just to observe the proceedings from a distance. However, the sovereign God over all had other plans for this man. The powerful preaching of the Word pierced his soul. Right then and there, Mr. C realized that he was a lost sinner headed for hell. The proud rebel was subdued. Nettleton later reported, "To see this bold blasphemer, bewailing his sinfulness and crying for mercy, in distress and anguish too great for human nature to sustain, was a most affecting sight."[13] By the mercies of God, Mr. C received assurance of salvation. And before long, he was telling everyone what great things the Lord had done for his soul and urging others to repent and believe in Christ.

On another occasion, Asahel Nettleton and a local pastor named Heman Humphrey were leading a service in Pittsfield, Massachusetts. It was the Fourth of July. Humphrey began preaching from the text, "If the Son therefore shall make you free, ye shall be free indeed" (John 8:36 KJV). He had scarcely begun to preach when someone shouted "Fire!" and a cannon was fired off just outside the church. Soldiers began to march back and forth in front of the church while drums beat and fifes played in the background. Apparently, a collection of village atheists had decided to "celebrate" the Fourth by disrupting the service.

However, their plan backfired on them. In God's providence, the drums, music, and cannon blasts were each perfectly timed to emphasize the main points of Humphrey's sermon. If the preacher had shared his manuscript with the atheists beforehand, they could not have done a better job of emphasizing his points. Far from being distracted, those inside listened with a heightened attention. Then in the evening, Nettleton preached at a second service to a larger crowd. About 140 persons believed in the Lord Jesus Christ and were added to the church. Many of these were fathers who afterward began discipling their families and leading family worship in their homes. This would become another strong indication of a true work of the Holy Spirit in real spiritual revival.

Such revivals seemed to follow Nettleton everywhere. If however, he sensed that a church was relying on himself to bring about revival, he would leave the place. He was well aware that "the flesh profits nothing" (John 6:63) and that there could be no true revival in a community unless the people depended on the Lord alone. His hearers "felt that if they were ever saved from their dreadful depravity and wretchedness, it must be by sovereign grace."[14]

Opposition and Illness

All who desire to live godly in Christ Jesus will suffer persecution. (2 Timothy 3:12)

By the 1820s Asahel Nettleton had become one of the most well-known preachers and evangelists in New England. He had been the instrument used by the Lord to transfer thousands from the kingdom of darkness to the kingdom of Christ. It is not surprising that Satan resorted to vicious attacks upon this man of God. Asahel was subjected to much slander, even accused of impropriety in his relationships with women. All of these accusations were groundless. The Lord had provided this great evangelist with a true gift of celibacy. Asahel Nettleton never married, as he devoted every ounce of his strength and life to the ministry of the gospel. His life and character were above reproach, and he chose not to respond to any of his critics. Like the Lord Jesus, he "committed Himself to Him who judges righteously" (1 Pet. 2:23). In the end, the Lord vindicated his servant. The slanders were so utterly baseless that only a few atheists were convinced by them.

Asahel's busy preaching schedule eventually took a toll on his health. In October 1822, he was stricken with typhus, a life-threatening disease. For the next few months he lay on the verge of death. Although he did recover, his health would never be the same. For two years he preached only occasionally and took time to assemble a new hymnal. At this time most New England churches sang Isaac Watts' hymns and psalm paraphrases, which had displaced the older metrical psalms of the Puritans. But Asahel and others believed there was a need for a newer hymnal to supplement Watts' work. In 1824 Nettleton published "Village Hymns," a collection that would become quite popular in the American church. Included in the hymnal were hymns themed on revivals and missions. He also wrote music to accompany hymns, including the well-known tune for "Come Thou Fount of Every Blessing." The royalties he received from the hymnbook would help support him financially during these years.

Charles Finney and the New Measures

As many as received Him, to them He gave the right to become children of God, to those who believe in His name: who were born, not of blood, nor of the will of the flesh, nor of the will of man, but of God. (John 1:12-13)

While Asahel Nettleton had been preaching throughout New England, a different kind of revival was breaking out further west in Upstate New York. These revivals were different because the preachers were using what was called the "New Measures," which meant they relied on social and emotional manipulation in the services. Some revivalists would pray for known unbelievers by name in public meetings and they would use overly familiar language with God in prayer. In worship services, women spoke publicly to groups of

Charles Grandison Finney

both men and women. Preachers protracted the length of meetings to pressure people into making decisions, and they would schedule meetings at abnormal times. These evangelists would then call their hearers to come forward to a place designated as the "Anxious Bench," at the front of the church, to make a commitment to Christ. This was the origin of the modern altar call.

One of the most prominent New Measures preachers was Charles Grandison Finney. A lawyer by trade, Finney had been ordained a Presbyterian minister in 1824 without even so much as having read the confession of the church. In his *Memoirs* Finney described his methods when addressing a meeting:

> [*I would say:*] "Now I must know your minds, and I want that you who have made up your minds to become Christians, and will give your pledge to make your peace with God immediately, should rise up; but that, on the contrary, those of you who are resolved that you will not become Christians, and wish me so to understand, and wish Christ so to understand, should sit still." After making this plain, so that I knew that they understood it, I then said: "You who are now willing to pledge to me and to Christ, that you will immediately make your peace with God, please rise up. On the contrary, you that mean that I should understand that you are committed to remain in your present attitude, not to accept Christ—those of you that are of this mind, may sit still."[15]

These New Measures pressured people to "make a decision for Christ." Those who did so were counted as converts, and any such evidence would prove to all that some kind of revival had occurred. Other preachers who did not produce equally "successful" results were despised and criticized. The emphasis on crisis conversions also downplayed the importance of ongoing Christian education and discipleship.

Behind the New Measures lay a new theology. Earlier revival preachers like George Whitefield and Jonathan Edwards understood that men and women are born with a depraved sin nature. They are enemies of God and slaves of sin who will not repent and believe unless the Holy Spirit first regenerates them. For this reason, the preacher's job is to preach the Word faithfully and pray for the Lord to open the hearts of those He has ordained to eternal life (Acts 16:14; 13:48). Revival then comes by the will of God and at the time ordained by God. It is an extraordinary outpouring of the Spirit in awakening sinners. Christians can pray for revival, but they cannot schedule it or make it happen.

Charles Finney and the advocates of the New Measures however, believed that people are not born with a sin nature and they are not slaves of sin. Instead, they taught that the preacher can and should persuade the will of man to accept the truth and believe. In a sermon entitled "Sinners Bound to Change Their Own Hearts," Finney preached:

> *Sinner! Instead of waiting and praying for God to change your heart, you should at once summon up your powers, put forth the effort, and change the governing preference of your mind.*[16]

Finney further explained in his writings:

> *The object of the ministry is to get all the people to feel that the devil has no right to rule this world, but that they ought all to give themselves to God, and vote in the Lord Jesus Christ as the governor of the universe.*[17]

Thus Charles Finney and others made salvation ultimately depend on man's choice, rather than the will of God. They also believed that revivals could be brought about simply by employing the proper means; hence the New Measures. Finney wrote:

> *Revivals are not miracle . . . they are brought about by the use of means like other events. No wonder revivals formerly came so seldom and continued so short a time,*

> **Revivalism:** Revivalism is the belief that revivals are not sovereign works of the Spirit but can instead be brought about by the use of the right techniques. It is based on man-centered theology that denies man's radical depravity. Emotional manipulations are often used to foster an environment in which people are pressured to make a decision for Christ. Signs announcing that a "revival" is scheduled for a particular place and time reflect the influence of Revivalism.

when people generally regarded them as miracles, or like a mere shower of rain, that will come on a place and continue a little while, and then blow over; that is, as something over which we have no control . . . Human agency is just as indispensable to a revival as divine agency.[18]

Historian Iain Murray summarizes this great shift that was coming about in American evangelicalism:

If conversion was the result of the sinner's decision, and if the inducing of that decision was the responsibility of a preacher, assisted by the Holy Spirit, then any measure that would bring the unconverted 'right up to the point of instant and absolute submission' had to be good. For men to be converted, [Finney] argued: 'it is necessary to raise an excitement among them.'[19]

This viewpoint has come to be known as Revivalism.[20]

Contending Earnestly for the Faith

Beloved, while I was very diligent to write to you concerning our common salvation, I found it necessary to write to you exhorting you to contend earnestly for the faith which was once for all delivered to the saints. (Jude 3)

This focus on Revivalism instead of biblical renewal alarmed Asahel. He had already seen the devastation caused by bad revivalists in the First Great Awakening. So, in 1826 he made a trip to Upstate New York to review the state of the churches after the revivals had swept through. He found conditions to be worse than he had feared. Not only had the New Measures produced false pretenses and spurious results, but many of those promoting them were divisive and harshly critical of any who disagreed with them. Nettleton met with Charles Finney on two separate occasions, but sadly, Finney was not humble or teachable and the meetings turned out to be fruitless. After this, Asahel published an open letter warning of the dangers of the New Measures.

In 1827 a meeting took place in New Lebanon, New York between supporters and opponents of the New Measures. Those present at the New Lebanon Conference included Asahel Nettleton, Charles Finney, and Lyman Beecher. Nettleton and Beecher brought a list of concerns to Finney and confronted him with the error of his ways, but to no avail. Charles Finney remained extremely influential and his Revivalism would redirect and redesign American evangelicalism for the next two centuries. And Asahel Nettleton would be largely forgotten.

> *This wisdom I have also seen under the sun, and it seemed great to me: There was a little city with few men in it; and a great king came against it, besieged it, and built great snares around it. Now there was found in it a poor wise man, and he by his wisdom delivered the city. Yet no one remembered that same poor man. (Ecclesiastes 9:13-15)*

The long-term fruit of the Second Great Awakening was mixed. While some were genuinely converted to Christ, a great many of these man-made revivals produced temporary professions and apostasies. Towards the end of his life, Finney himself had to admit that "the glory has been departing and revivals have been becoming less and less frequent—less powerful."[21] He also came to realize that many of those he thought had been converted had become a "disgrace to religion."[22]

Moreover, the Second Great Awakening produced more disunity in the church, new denominations, and a number of cults. These included the Restorationists, the Mormons, and the Millerites, from whom came the Seventh Day Adventists and the Jehovah's Witnesses. These were the fruits that came out of the revivals conducted by a "Burned-Over" theology in the "Burned-Over District" in Upstate New York.

Meanwhile, back in New England, many of the Congregationalist churches were quickly turning Unitarian by the late 1820s. This was another form of apostasy, through the rejection of basic Christian doctrine concerning the nature of Christ and the persons of the Trinity. In 1828 Nathaniel Taylor, a Yale theology professor, began publicly teaching what became known as the New Haven Theology. Taylor rejected the doctrine of man's sinful nature and original sin (that infants are born with a sinful nature). He also believed that man possesses total sovereignty and absolute free will; and God cannot and will not constrain man's free will. Although Taylor was a sophisticated scholar, and Finney was a frontier preacher, the doctrinal errors of both men were very similar.

This man-centered theology soon captured Yale and many of the New England churches that had not succumbed to Unitarianism. American Christianity was collapsing, and the faith was dissipating in the churches. However, Asahel Nettleton continued to contend earnestly for the faith against these trends, although his old friend Lyman Beecher did not. Earlier at the New Lebanon Conference, Beecher had opposed Finney and warned him not to come to New England to spread his views there, but later Beecher capitulated to this new man-centered theology. He went on to support both Taylor and Finney. In 1831 Lyman Beecher invited Charles Finney into the pulpits of New England. His son, Henry Ward Beecher would become one of the most famous, liberal, and wicked pastors in America.

Later Years and Legacy

And the things that you have heard from me among many witnesses, commit these to faithful men who will be able to teach others also. (2 Timothy 2:2)

Asahel Nettleton was deeply wounded by his friend's defection. It was a crushing disappointment, and indicative of the breaking down of the faith in America. Nonetheless, the old evangelist continued to wage the good warfare (1 Tim. 1:18). He helped organize the remaining Congregationalist churches in Connecticut which still held to the old orthodox truths of God's sovereignty and man's depravity. With Yale having fallen to New Haven Theology, Asahel helped organize the Theological Institute of Connecticut in 1833, later renamed Hartford Theological Seminary. He spent many of his remaining years teaching young students the biblical approach to preaching, evangelism, and true revival. He loved the students, took a personal interest in their lives, and discipled them.

Toward the end of his life, as his health declined, Nettleton had more time for reading. His favorite volumes included Merle D'Aubigné's *History of the Reformation*, Joseph Tracy's *History of the Great Awakening*, and the writings of Andrew Fuller and John Bunyan. But the book he loved, treasured, and read most was the Bible, which he studied in its original languages. Often he would say, "There are many good books, but after all, there is nothing like the Bible."[23]

In 1844 Asahel fell seriously ill and the time of his departure from this life drew near. On his deathbed he exhorted his friends, "While ye have the light, walk in the light" (John 12:35-36). As he spoke these words, his face shone with "peculiar lustre."[24] He told his friends he was not afraid to die because he had peace with God through the Lord Jesus Christ. His last words were, "It is sweet to trust in the Lord."[25] And then he went to be with the Lord, on May 16, 1844.

Asahel Nettleton very well could be the greatest evangelist America ever produced. In his day, many called him the greatest evangelist since George Whitefield. He had many similarities with Whitefield but also some differences. Both preached the same truths but they employed different styles. Nettleton's preaching was less dramatic and eloquent, but just as earnest and full of power.

His friend Francis Wayland said of Nettleton: "I suppose no minister of his time was the means of so many conversions . . . [He] would sway an audience as the trees of the forest are moved by a mighty wind."[26]

Asahel was called to labor in very difficult times, as American churches were departing from the truth. Some fell to Unitarianism while others embraced the man-centered theology of Finney and Taylor. His faith and steadfastness is to be commended and copied by those who live in like difficult times. It was Asahel Nettleton's greatest legacy that he faithfully preached the gospel and contended earnestly for the faith in the worst of times. All those who long for the Holy Spirit to return with true revival and reformation in the American church should thank God for the life and legacy of Asahel Nettleton, and pray for more men like him.

Though mostly forgotten, these are the greatest heroes of history—the men who continue to stand and fight when all else abandon the field.

> *And after him was Shammah the son of Agee the Hararite. The Philistines had gathered together into a troop where there was a piece of ground full of lentils. So the people fled from the Philistines. But he stationed himself in the middle of the field, defended it, and killed the Philistines. So the LORD brought about a great victory. (2 Samuel 23:11-12)*

Lemuel Haynes (1753-1833)

CHAPTER 17

Lemuel Haynes:
First African-American Minister

*For you see your calling, brethren, that not many
wise according to the flesh, not many mighty, not
many noble, are called. But God has chosen the
foolish things of the world to put to shame the wise,
and God has chosen the weak things of the world to
put to shame the things which are mighty; and the
base things of the world and the things which are
despised God has chosen, and the things which are
not, to bring to nothing the things that are, that no
flesh should glory in His presence.*

—1 Corinthians 1:26-29

In the perfect wisdom of God, the tapestry of history is filled with men
and women who are insignificant in the world's eyes, yet our God has
seen fit to use them in extraordinary ways. Lemuel Haynes was one such
man. To many, it would seem that Lemuel's background as an orphan with an
African-American lineage would have prevented him from ever playing such an

important role in American history. But the Lord had important plans for this orphaned boy who became a preacher of the everlasting gospel of our Savior Christ. Although Lemuel's story is not very well known by most Americans today, it is an important part of the larger story of God's people in America.

Orphan Upbringing in the Rose Home

Lemuel Haynes was born on July 18, 1753 in West Hartford, Connecticut. Very little is known of his biological father and mother because he was abandoned by his mother at only five months of age. Early on, he was held as an indentured servant to Deacon David Rose, whose family lived in Granville, Massachusetts. Lemuel's placement in this family was no accident. The Rose home was committed to serving the Lord, and hence Lemuel received the truths of God's Word from an early age.

Lemuel Haynes' lineage as an African immigrant living in New England in the mid-1700s played an important role in determining his life opportunities. He did receive unkind racial slurs throughout his life, and he felt that his dark skin was "an obstacle to his being identified in interest and in life with those among whom he dwelt."[1] But God would use what many considered a weakness with cultural assimilation for the glory of Christ's name.

Still, though Lemuel was abandoned, the Lord was merciful to him. He truly experienced the fatherly hand of God in his life as described by David in Psalm 27.

When my father and my mother forsake me, then the LORD will take care of me.
(Psalm 27:10)

Lemuel recounted his early experiences in the Rose family with these words:

When I was five months old I was carried to Granville, Massachusetts, and bound out as a servant to Deacon David Rose till I was twenty-one. He was a man of singular piety [godliness]. I was taught the principles of religion. His wife, my mistress, had peculiar attachment to me: she treated me as though I was her own child. I remember it was a saying among the neighbours, that she loved Lemuel more than her own children.[2]

Lemuel learned to hallow the name of the Lord through daily prayer, regular Bible study, and observance of the Sabbath as a day of worship. He lived in the home of Deacon Rose until he was ordained a pastor in his twenties. Lemuel proved to be a faithful hard worker, and the deacon began to entrust him with additional responsibilities on the family farm as he grew older.[3]

> *Most men will proclaim each his own goodness, but who can find a faithful man?* *(Proverbs 20:6)*

Growing up in the Rose home, Lemuel came to a saving understanding of the gospel, leaning upon Christ alone for his salvation. As an indentured servant, he did not receive a formal education, but he made use of the family's collection of books to educate himself. Here we find an illustration of the truth contained in 2 Timothy 3:14-17:

> *But you must continue in the things which you have learned and been assured of, knowing from whom you have learned them, and that from childhood you have known the Holy Scriptures, which are able to make you wise for salvation through faith which is in Christ Jesus. All Scripture is given by inspiration of God, and is profitable for doctrine, for reproof, for correction, for instruction in righteousness, that the man of God may be complete, thoroughly equipped for every good work. (2 Timothy 3:14-17)*

Lemuel's biographer Timothy Mather Cooley explains Lemuel's study habits:

> *Lemuel Haynes got his education in the chimney corner. This is literally true... Here he studied his spelling-book and psalter till he had literally devoured them. He studied the Bible till he could produce by memory most of the texts which have a bearing upon the essential doctrines of grace; and could also refer, with nearly infallible accuracy, to the book, chapter, and verse where they might be found.[4]*

The young man's memory of Scripture and other important Christian writings was practically unparalleled. Once Lemuel became a pastor, his strength of memory enabled him to preach, often with few or no notes at all. He could easily quote from Scripture by memory to makes his points.

Lemuel faithfully labored as a servant in the Rose home for many years, and he grew in wisdom and knowledge as he studied the Word. Eventually his God-given gifts for the ministry were discovered by the Rose family. It was the custom of the family to spend time in biblical instruction on Saturdays to better prepare for the public worship of God the following day. Usually the family read a printed sermon from faithful preachers such as George Whitefield or Philip Doddridge. Then on one particular evening, Lemuel decided to read a sermon that he had written without telling the family beforehand that it was his own composition. With this first sermon, he chose to explain and apply the words of Jesus to Nicodemus from John 3:3:

> *Jesus answered and said to him, "Most assuredly, I say to you, unless one is born again, he cannot see the kingdom of God." (John 3:3)*

Lemuel skillfully explained the words of our Lord to the Rose family, developing on the doctrine that one must be born again from above by the will of the Father. His sermon well demonstrated that he was a man with a deep understanding of the Word of God, and for the first time the family recognized his gift of preaching. He emphasized especially the sovereign working of God in the salvation of sinners.

> *It is a work too great to attribute to men or angels to accomplish. None but He who, by one word's speaking, spake all nature into existence, can triumph over the opposition of the heart. This is the work of the Holy Spirit, who is represented in Scripture as emanating from the Father and the Son, yet coequal with them both. It is God alone that slays the native enmity of the heart.*[5]

The family was so deeply impressed by his powerful sermon that the deacon had to ask him, "Lemuel, whose work is that which you have been reading? Is it Davies's sermon, or Watt's, or Whitefield's?"[6] When Lemuel confessed he was the author of the sermon, the family realized that this man must have a special calling on his life. Soon others in the community of Granville were becoming aware of his gifts and Lemuel was encouraged to pursue pastoral ministry.

Service in the War and Early Ministry

I charge you therefore before God and the Lord Jesus Christ, who will judge the living and the dead at His appearing and His kingdom: Preach the word! Be ready in season and out of season. Convince, rebuke, exhort, with all longsuffering and teaching. (2 Timothy 4:1-2)

Before Lemuel Haynes could pursue further opportunities in ministry however, he was called to serve in the war effort against the British in 1775. He first served as a minuteman in the local militia in Massachusetts, joining the garrison occupying Fort Ticonderoga in Upstate New York. Having enlisted with the Continental Army in October 1776, Lemuel came down with Typhus and was quickly relieved of duty the next month. Lemuel's love for American liberties was strong, and he would always hold George Washington in high regard for the leadership he exhibited during the early years of the nation.[7]

After his service in the war, Lemuel returned to the Rose home and continued his self-studies for the ministry. His understanding of the Bible and theology was formed mainly through his reading of Jonathan Edwards, George Whitefield, and Philip Doddridge.[8] In 1779 Lemuel began a mentoring relationship with two local pastors, Daniel Farrand and William Bradford. Under these men he pursued further studies in Latin and Greek, eventually gaining the ability to read the New Testament in the original Greek. He was licensed to preach on November 29, 1780.

Lemuel began a public ministry as an itinerant preacher to various towns throughout the region. His biographer, Timothy Mather Cooley summarized this early preaching:

His sermons are the earliest which I now remember to have heard, and, though preached more than half a century ago, are at this time recollected . . . They uniformly left the impression of the majesty of God; the importance of immediate repentance; the awful solemnity of the judgment day; the attractive loveliness of Christ; and the pleasantness of wisdom's ways.[9]

Fort Ticonderoga, New York

In 1783, a friendship developed between Lemuel and a schoolteacher by the name of Elizabeth Babbit. Under Lemuel's teaching, the young woman came to a "deep religious anxiety" about the state of her soul. She would eventually come to profess faith in the Lord Jesus Christ. Shortly thereafter, the two of them began courting and they were married on September 22, 1783. Together they would enjoy the fruitful blessings of ten children.

Lemuel labored in various congregations as a licensed preacher for about five years. He was then ordained as a Congregationalist minister in 1785. He was the first African-American to be ordained by a Christian denomination in this country.

For about three years, Lemuel served in a congregation in Torrington, Connecticut. Then he was called to serve as the pastor of the congregation in Rutland, Vermont where he would serve for thirty continuous years, preaching and shepherding an all-white congregation.

In God's providence, he would discover Vermont to be a dark and difficult place to minister. The light of the gospel was desperately needed in the spiritually barren environment of that state. Cooley summarizes the situation in Vermont during Lemuel's years of ministry:

> *It was a season of great moral darkness through New England when Mr. Haynes commenced his ministry . . . Great apathy was prevalent among professing Christians, and the ruinous vices of profaneness, Sabbath-breaking, and intemperance were affectingly prevalent among all classes. The spark of evangelical piety seemed to be nearly extinct in the churches. Revivals of religion were scarcely known except in the recollections of a former age. Some of the essential doctrines of grace were not received even by many in the churches. Such was the character of the age. Such, too, was the place in which Mr. Haynes commenced his labours. Against the errors and vices of the times he exerted a powerful influence.[10]*

During Lemuel's first years of ministry in Rutland, he shepherded a small group of forty-two church members. Most of them were elderly, although there were few young people in the congregation.[11] By God's mercy, one by one of the townspeople of Rutland came to the faith and humbled themselves before the Lord. In 1803 God blessed the church with a unique spiritual awakening. In a letter to a fellow pastor written on April 5, 1803, Lemuel reported on the great work going on in Rutland:

> *Since I have been in this place, for the most part of the time it has been a time of stupidity. Only about thirty have been added to the church for fifteen years. We have kept up prayer meetings once a week or fortnight during the whole time. The spirits of God's people have been sunk; but very few attended; our harps were hung upon the willows. Matters grew more and more gloomy till some time in November last. I was almost determined in my own mind to ask for a dismission, when it pleased God to arrest the attention of a very thoughtless youth, who on Sabbath evening opened his distress to me.[12]*

This young man's spiritual struggle became the catalyst for a great work of spiritual reviving in Rutland. Lemuel goes on:

We appointed a conference-meeting that week and, to our astonishment, the house was crowded, and a great number appeared to be under deep impressions. The work spread from week to week, till it was difficult to find any dwelling-house that would hold the people . . . The great inquiry among the youth and others was, "What shall we do to be saved?" Children of eleven and twelve years of age seemed to be more engaged about religion than they were about their play . . . Some of the most open enemies have been bowed to sovereign grace, and brought to sit at the feet of Jesus, and in their right mind. We have, I believe, now but few prayerless families among us in comparison to what there were previous to the awakening . . . We ask an interest in your prayers, that those who have named the name of Christ may be enabled to walk worthy of their profession, and that God would continue his work here and through the world. [13]

The Lord continued to bless Lemuel's labors, and in 1808 another awakening occurred in Rutland in which over one hundred people were added to the church in a single year! [14]

Though Lemuel saw much spiritual fruit come through conversions to the faith, he also had to endure the opposition of false teachers and unbiblical doctrines in his ministry. He combated those heresies prevalent in the New England region, including Deism, Universalism, and Arminianism. Universalists claim that all people will be saved and that no one will go to hell, negating the importance of conversion, urgent preaching, and church involvement. Some years later in his public ministry, the pastor engaged in a notable controversy with a universalist named Hosea Ballou. Lemuel attended a meeting where Hosea presented his position, and afterwards he asked Lemuel to say a few words in response. Without prior preparation, the faithful preacher laid out what would become one of his most well-known sermons. He opened with the words of Genesis 3:4:

Then the serpent said to the woman, "You will not surely die." (Genesis 3:4)

Pastor Haynes then proceeded to show how this verse was relevant to the false doctrine of universalism. He explained how the devil was a very old preacher who led Eve astray and had been leading fallen humanity astray ever since that first lie. He noted that the teaching of universalism was really the same old message that Satan delivered to Eve: you will not die, there is no eternal death, and there is no judgment. Lemuel argued, "If [these universalists] preach 'ye shall not surely die,' they only make use of the devil's old notes that he delivered almost six thousand years ago."[15] Here is one example how this man of God proved himself fearless in opposing those teachings not originating in the truths of the Bible.

Views on Government and Slavery

Lemuel Haynes became an influential preacher in the churches of New England and New York. But his influence extended beyond the churches, and many came to know about him through his public addresses and writings on other important matters such as government and slavery. In 1776 Lemuel produced a short work titled *Liberty Further Extended: Or Free Thoughts on the Illegality of Slave-keeping*. In this work the pastor pointed out that American slavery was out of accord with the Bible. He addressed the matter of slavery once more in 1801. On the twenty-fifth anniversary of American Independence, Lemuel delivered an address titled "The Nature and Importance of True Republicanism." Again in this address Lemuel argued that the principles of American government were also inconsistent with the practice of American slavery.[16]

In *Liberty Further Extended*, Pastor Haynes explained how the gospel is the power of God unto salvation for *all* peoples of the earth. When Jesus Christ came, He abolished ethnic barriers between Jew and Gentile.[17] His position was firmly based on Paul's teaching in Ephesians 2:

> *For He Himself [Jesus Christ] is our peace, who has made both one, and has broken down the middle wall of separation, having abolished in His flesh the enmity, that is, the law of commandments contained in ordinances, so as to create in Himself one new man from the two, thus making peace, and that He might reconcile them both to God in one body through the cross, thereby putting to death the enmity. (Ephesians 2:14-16)*

Then using 1 Corinthians 7:21-23, Lemuel pointed out that freedom is a high value in the Christian faith. It is the ideal for those believers who find themselves in various forms of servitude.

> *Were you called while a slave? Do not be concerned about it; **but if you can be made free, rather use it.** For he who is called in the Lord while a slave is the Lord's freedman. Likewise he who is called while free is Christ's slave. **You were bought at a price; do not become slaves of men.** (1 Corinthians 7:21-23, emphasis added)*

Lemuel exposited the text further for his readers this way:

> *So that the apostle seems to recommend freedom if attainable, as if to say, "If it is thy unhappy lot to be a slave, yet if thou art spiritually free, let the former appear so minute [small] a thing when compared with the latter that it is comparatively unworthy of notice; yet since freedom is so excellent a jewel, which none have a right to extirpate, and if there is any hope of attaining it, use all lawful measures for that purpose."[18]*

Lemuel also took on the pro-slavery position which argued that those brought out of Africa were in a better condition because they had more access to the truth of the Christian faith. To this he pointed out that slave traders heading to the African coast did not "aim at the spiritual good" of the Africans they captured.[19] Lemuel quoted from Romans 3:8, noting that Paul interacted with the same argumentation.

> *And why not say, "Let us do evil that good may come"?—as we are slanderously reported and as some affirm that we say. Their condemnation is just. (Romans 3:8)*

So Lemuel rejected the claim that some good "ends" justified the evil "means" of slave trading. The Scriptures plainly condemn the kidnapping of a human being (Ex. 21:16, 1 Tim. 1:10). While many Africans did come to faith in the Lord Jesus Christ after coming to America, this in no way justifies the evil actions of "man-stealing." From the Old Testament, we remember that Joseph's brothers sold him into slavery. It was an evil deed, and yet Joseph points out that what man means for evil, God used to bring about good (Gen. 50:20). But still, the good result does not justify the evil action of Joseph's brothers in selling him into slavery. Lemuel Haynes as well as other Americans in his day knew full well the evil intentions of those who engaged in the slave trade. In his essay, Lemuel put it bluntly and forcefully: "But should we give ourselves to inquire into the grand motive that indulges men to concern themselves in a trade so vile and abandoned, we shall find it to be this: namely, to stimulate the carnal avarice, and to maintain men in pride, luxury, and idleness."[20]

Lemuel also argued that liberty was basic to human existence. He wrote, "Liberty & freedom is an innate principle, which is unmovably placed in the human Species. As a gift from God, liberty is a jewel."[21] These early treatises on American slavery are historically significant because they come from the pen of an African-American pastor in the earliest years of the Republic.

Significantly, Lemuel Haynes wrote on the important connection between civil government and religion as well. While American pastors and civil leaders were drifting from the doctrine of the inspiration and sufficiency of Scripture, this Vermont pastor was holding on to the faith and the commandments of God in Old and New Testaments. Lemuel insisted that a proper foundation for good government could only be established on the principles of Scripture:

> *How absurd to discard the book commonly called the Holy Scriptures and yet be advocates for good civil government! They are so coincident and congenial in their nature and tendency that it is really a doubt whether a man can, upon right principles, be an honest advocate for one, whose heart rises against the other . . . He that is acquainted with the laws of the land will see that they mostly point to this great object and are a sort of comment on or copy of the sacred oracles. A contempt for the Holy Scriptures, domination, anarchy, and immorality are inseparable companions.*[22]

Here Pastor Haynes argues that without biblical law as a guide, the nation will inevitably drift into tyranny on the one hand, lawlessness on the other, and immorality in every case. Lemuel explains that, if Americans hope to have good civil government, they must regulate their behavior by the "written Word of God."[23]

Not unlike the Puritans that came before him, Lemuel Haynes taught that the church has a responsibility before God to bear witness to the truth for those in positions of governmental authority. If a pastor sees a nation heading towards destruction, he has a duty to cry out against the wickedness of the land and call for repentance.

> *But when in their view they [pastors] see a nation going to destruction, is it their duty to be silent? Does such conduct comport with the solemn charge given them by Him to whom they are amenable for all they do, and before whose tribunal they may expect every moment to appear? Let us, my brethren, read with trembling the declaration of the Almighty: "If the watchmen see the sword come, and blow not the trumpet, and the people be not warned; if the sword come, and take any person from among them, he is taken away in his iniquity; but his blood will I require at the watchman's hand" (Ezek. 33:6).[24]*

Lemuel went on to solemnly warn that no ministers were fit for the office if they were not willing to "sacrifice their salaries, their reputation—yea, their lives—for the cause of God and their country."[25]

Final Years of Ministry in Granville, New York

> *For I am already being poured out as a drink offering, and the time of my departure is at hand. I have fought the good fight, I have finished the race, I have kept the faith. Finally, there is laid up for me the crown of righteousness, which the Lord, the righteous Judge, will give to me on that Day, and not to me only but also to all who have loved His appearing. (2 Timothy 4:6-8)*

Lemuel Haynes labored for the flock of God in Rutland for thirty years. Due to doctrinal disagreements with various members of the congregation, he was finally dismissed from the church in 1818. He served a church in Manchester, Vermont for a time, and then he accepted a call to serve as the pastor of a church in Granville, New York from 1822 until his death in 1833.

Many of Lemuel's letters and writings in these final years are filled with meditations on heaven and future glory. As his health declined in old age, his hope for future glory with Jesus grew sweeter year by year. By this time, he was intimately acquainted with the suffering of ministers in this life, "The wearisome and tiresome nights they spend here in running their race and in finishing their course will only prepare them for a more sweet repose and rest at their journey's end, when the morning shall break forth."[26]

In March 1833 Pastor Lemuel Haynes fell ill with a severe gangrene infection in his foot. In the months that followed, he retired to his home and spent his remaining time on earth in prayer, meditation, and conversation with friends and family. Come July of that year physicians were consulted on whether to amputate the limb, and it was decided that there was nothing further to be done to help him. Lemuel contentedly accepted this conclusion and wrote to one of his sons, these final words: "I am in the hands of God, and in a measure

Home of Lemuel Haynes, Granville, New York

reconciled to his will . . . Oh! remember your Creator! Let not all the fashions of the world divert your minds from eternity!"[27]

In his last days the dying man composed his own epitaph for his tombstone. It is a fitting summary for the life of Lemuel Haynes. Above all, this great man of God wanted the world to know Jesus Christ, the King of kings and Lord of lords, the only Mediator between God and man, the only way to eternal life.

> *Here lies the dust of a poor hell-deserving sinner who ventured into eternity trusting wholly on the merits of Christ for salvation. In the full belief of the great doctrines he preached while on earth, he invites his children, and all who read this, to trust their eternal interest in the same foundation.*[28]

For fifty-three years, Lemuel Haynes labored faithfully for the Gospel during a period when American Christianity languished. The Word of God was despised, the law of God abandoned, and the doctrine of God was heavily compromised during these years, especially in New England. Yet God used a slave boy, a man of African descent to "keep the faith" during these dark years. In God's amazing providence, those who are last into the kingdom of God are sometimes given priority over the first.

Truly, Lemuel Haynes took his role seriously as he worked to disciple the nation "to observe whatsoever the Lord had commanded." He dedicated his life not to pursue his own interests, but the glory of God and the kingdom of Christ. His greatest desire was that the name of Jesus Christ would be magnified, not his own name. He wanted his own children to carry on the faith of their father—a faith in Christ and the great truths of the Word of God. May the reader also venture into eternity with this same commitment, trusting only in Jesus Christ for salvation. May each one rest their eternal interest upon that same foundation—the merits and the Person of Christ.

> *There will be weeping and gnashing of teeth, when you see Abraham and Isaac and Jacob and all the prophets in the kingdom of God, and yourselves thrust out. They will come from the east and the west, from the north and the south, and sit down in the kingdom of God. And indeed there are last who will be first, and there are first who will be last. (Luke 13:28-30)*

Jedediah Smith (1799-1831)

CHAPTER 18

Jedediah Smith:
The Best Explorer of the American West

Great is our Lord, and mighty in power; His understanding is infinite. The LORD lifts up the humble; He casts the wicked down to the ground . . . He does not delight in the strength of the horse; He takes no pleasure in the legs of a man. The LORD takes pleasure in those who fear Him, in those who hope in His mercy.

—Psalm 147:5-11

In May 1804 Meriwether Lewis and William Clark left St. Louis, Missouri, to start their famous journey to explore the western part of America. The two explorers had been commissioned by President Thomas Jefferson to find a "direct water communication" from the Atlantic to the Pacific Ocean "for the purposes of commerce." The president hoped that the Missouri waterways would extend deep into western Canada and that America could claim more land to the north. The team of thirty-one men reached the Pacific Ocean at the mouth of the Columbia River on November 20, 1805. The expedition provided contact with twenty-four Indian tribes and opened up friendly trade relations with most of them. The Arikara and Sioux tribes turned out to be the most warlike and unreliable in trade relations. Meriwether Lewis drank heavily, attempted suicide at least once, and finally was said to have committed suicide in 1809. William Clark went on to serve as governor of the Missouri Territory from 1813 to 1820.

Christopher "Kit" Carson was born in Richmond, Kentucky in 1809, the son of a Presbyterian Scotch-Irish settler. When Daniel Boone moved to Missouri, the Carsons followed close behind. Kit's dad purchased land from Daniel Boone's sons, and the Boone and Carson families remained close. These were frontier-minded people, seeking to cultivate land that had yet to be settled by the

Meriwether Lewis and William Clark on the Columbia River

indigenous tribes. As a young teen, Kit Carson worked for a saddler in Franklin, Missouri. Tales told by the trappers who had traversed the Santa Fe Trail down into New Mexico allured the young seventeen-year-old lad with western fever. So in August 1826, he joined a company of fur trappers leaving town, beginning his long and exciting life in the Wild West.

Carson fought a duel for his first wife, an Arapaho Indian woman named Singing Grass. He nearly lost his life in the conflict but won the woman in the end. Singing Grass died in childbirth and Carson married another Native American who divorced him. His third wife was of Mexican roots.

During the 1840s Kit Carson led explorative campaigns and military expeditions over the Oregon Trail into Washington and Oregon and then back down into California and New Mexico. Extreme conditions sometimes attended the expeditions, and on one occasion they fed the horses their own tails and the men consumed the leather saddles to survive. Over the years Kit wandered away from his Presbyterian roots into the Roman Catholic Church, although the remnants of his faith must have been still in his mind as his life winded down. Before his death Carson visited Washington DC with several Ute tribal leaders. During one agonizing night in which he was suffering a great deal of pain, he woke up to find one of the chiefs cradling his head. The chief told him, "You called your Lord Jesus." Carson responded, "It's only Him that can help me where I stand now."[1]

Jim Bridger was born in 1804. When the boy was eight years old, his family packed everything into a covered wagon and headed west to Mississippi, just south of St. Louis, Missouri. Orphaned at fourteen years of age, Jim apprenticed with a blacksmith. Similar to Kit Carson, Jim Bridger was soon bored of the job. When General William Henry Ashley advertised in a St. Louis paper for men to work a trapping expedition, Jim signed up along with another young man by the name of Jedediah Smith. Bridger explored the Rocky Mountains from southern Colorado to the Canadian border and led many expeditions across the Wild West. He also established Fort Bridger as a trading post in southwest Wyoming.

The Ultimate Mountain Man of the West

You are the salt of the earth; but if the salt loses its flavor, how shall it be seasoned?
It is then good for nothing but to be thrown out and trampled underfoot by men.
(Matthew 5:13)

Some of the American Christian salt had lost its flavor by the 19th century. Meriwether Lewis (although raised by a pious Christian mother) was given to alcohol and "had no interest in converting Indians to Christianity."[2] Members of the Lewis and Clark team "frequently" broke the seventh commandment with native women on the expedition.[3] Jim Bridger also married several Native American women without giving much thought to the Christian faith. In far too many cases the unchristian nature of these Western men resulted in bad treatment of the Indians. Kit Carson's Klamath Lake Massacre in 1846 was an instance of vengefulness which resulted in the killing of at least one Indian woman.[4] This was mild in comparison with Colonel John Chivington's massacre of the Sand Creek Indian village in 1864, where 75-500 Indians were massacred (including many women and children).

However, there was one frontiersman of strong Christian character who excelled all of these men in his contributions to the American West. The man's name was Jedediah Smith. Within ten short years of exploration, he would become the first American to discover the South Pass (just south of Lander, Wyoming). He would be the first to cross the Sierra Nevada Mountains. He was the first to reach Oregon by way of California. He was the first to travel the entire body of the Great Basin in Nevada. Miraculously, God protected his life despite his involvement in all three of the greatest disasters encountered during the American fur trade wars of the 1820s. Jedediah Smith's character was unassailable, his courage unflagging, and his faith in Christ constant throughout his outstanding career in the American Wild West.

Jedediah Smith's Raising

Jedediah Smith was born of Puritan stock—his forefathers arriving on the shores of Massachusetts in the early 1630s. His great-great-grandfather Samuel Smith settled in America in 1634. He was known as "The Fellmonger" because he was a tanner by trade and a dealer in skins and furs of animals—a legacy which would carry on 150 years later in the life of Jedediah. Evidently, Samuel Smith was a godly man, as historians have learned that he left one copy of the Bible for each of his grandchildren in his will.

Jedediah Sr. and Sally Smith moved to Bainbridge, New York, where Jedediah Jr. was born on January 6, 1799. The pioneering spirit still strong in the blood, the family moved again to Erie County, Pennsylvania in 1810, and then on into the Ohio country (Ashland County) in 1817. In his teen years, a family friend named Dr. Titus Simons presented young Jed with a copy of the *Narrative of Meriwether Lewis and William Clark*. It was a book that would remain in Jed's possession until the end of his life.

First Expeditions

Then Jesus was led up by the Spirit into the wilderness to be tempted by the devil. And when He had fasted forty days and forty nights, afterward He was hungry. Now when the tempter came to Him, he said, "If You are the Son of God, command that these stones become bread." But He answered and said, "It is written, 'Man shall not live by bread alone, but by every word that proceeds from the mouth of God.'" (Matthew 4:1-4)

In the spring of 1821, Jedediah set off to northern Illinois to join General William Ashley, who was in the process of organizing a fur trading company based in the Missouri territory. Two boats left St. Louis on the expedition in May 1822. Jedediah Smith was on the second boat. One hundred men ascended the Missouri River, including some of the very first of the famous mountain men, such as James Beckwourth, John S. Fitzgerald, David Jackson, William Sublette, Jim Bridger, and Thomas Fitzpatrick.

Jedediah entered the West with his rifle in hand, his only clothes on his back, his Bible in his sack, and very little else. As one historian put it, "he took his religion with him into the wilderness and let nothing corrode it."[5] He is described as "a young man modest and unassuming, quiet and mild of manner, one who never smoked or chewed, never uttered a profane word, and partook of wine or brandy only sparingly on formal occasions."[6] His hunting companions noted his toughness of spirit, his ability to act under pressure, an endurance beyond what most men could handle, and above all, "his troubled sense of unworthiness in the sight of God."[7]

In their first year, General Ashley's group trapped for beaver pelts up the Missouri River into the Marias River in northern Montana. Jedediah's team camped at the mouth of the Musselshell River. Plenty of meat was to be had. For some time their camp at the river was surrounded by literally thousands of buffalo. The river froze to four feet deep, and the team was encamped for the winter, unable to embark again until April 4.

On May 30, 1823, General Ashley and his team of ninety men (including Smith) attempted to trade with several Arikara villages on the Missouri River. The negotiations went badly and the Arikaras attacked Ashley's men on the sandbar. Thirteen of Ashley's men were killed as they tried to escape to the boats. Jedediah Smith was the last to jump into the river as he continued to pump shots into the Arikara assault on the small band.

An eyewitness to the attack wrote a letter to a father of John S. Gardner who was killed in the melee, providing a sense for the role Jedediah played with the men.

> *Dear Sir,*
>
> *My painful duty it is to tell you of the death of your son who befell at the hands of the Indians 2nd June in the early morning. He died a little while after he was shot and asked me to inform you of his sad fate. We brought him to the ship when he soon died. Mr. [Jedediah] Smith, a young man of our company, made a powerful prayer who moved us all greatly and I am persuaded John died in peace. His body we buried with others near this camp and marked the grave with a log. His things we will send to you.*[8]

After the massacre, most of the crew abandoned the expedition and took a boat back downstream to St. Louis. However, a team of seventeen remained, and General Ashley chose the Christian to lead the group on another fur trapping expedition out of Fort Kiowa in South Dakota down the White River. Traveling with Jedediah were Thomas Fitzpatrick, William L. Sublette, and James Clyman, whose records remain important for the details of the adventure.

Somewhere around the Wyoming border on Black Thunder Creek, a grizzly bear attacked Jedediah head-on. The bear grabbed Jed's head in its mouth and threw him to the ground. The intrepid mountain man managed to stick a knife into the bear as it sank its teeth into his ribs. His partners shot the bear dead as Jed lay bleeding. Clyman reports:

> *None of us [had] any surgical knowledge [or knew] what was to be done. One said, 'come take hold,' and he would say why not you? So it went around. I asked the Capt what was best. He said one or two go for water and if you have a needle and thread, git it out and sew up my wounds around my head which was bleeding freely. I got a pair of scissors and cut off his hair and then began my first Job of dressing wounds. Upon examination I found the bear had taken nearly all of his head in his capacious mouth close to his left eye on one side and close to his right ear on the other and laid the skull bare to near the crown of the head . . . One of his ears was torn from his head out to the outer rim. [I stitched] all the other wounds in the best way I was capable and according to the Captain's directions.*[9]

The surgery completed (without anesthesia—and the doctor not entirely trained or literate for that matter), Jed climbed back onto his horse and the group rode back to the camp. Clyman concluded his report, "This gave us a lisson on the character of the grissly Baare which we did not forget."[10] From that point on, Jed wore his hair long to cover the scars on his eyebrow and left ear.

The team wintered in a Crow Indian Village during the winter of 1823-1824. In the spring Jedediah discovered the South Pass over the Rocky Mountains, with an elevation of only 7,412 feet. The discovery would enable many a wagon train to cross over the mountains without having to climb the 9,000 to 11,000-foot passes in Colorado and elsewhere along the Rockies. For the next fifty years, wagon trains would wind their way through this pass into California, Utah, and Oregon.

For the next three years, Jedediah trapped beaver throughout Wyoming, Colorado, Utah, and Idaho. In July 1825 he met with General Ashley and agreed upon a partnership in the fur trade.

The California Expeditions

It is God who arms me with strength, and makes my way perfect. He makes my feet like the feet of deer, and sets me on my high places. He teaches my hands to make war, so that my arms can bend a bow of bronze. You have also given me the shield of Your salvation; Your right hand has held me up, Your gentleness has made me great. You enlarged my path under me, so my feet did not slip. (Psalm 18:32-36)

In October and November of 1826 Jedediah trapped along the Colorado River and its tributaries, following the waterways down through Utah. His group of fifteen men barely survived the journey, and half of their horses were dead by the time they made it to south central Arizona. Jedediah then made the decision to seek refuge in California, hoping to obtain more horses and free passage to San Francisco. It took fifteen days to cross the San Bernardino Mountains. The Spanish were extremely unfriendly to the expedition, suspecting that the Americans might attempt to wrest control of California out of their hands.

Great Salt Lake, Utah

While visiting the Spanish mission, Jedediah walked the vineyards, sampled the wines, and drank chocolate drinks. Finally, the Spanish authorities released him to return to America. However, Jed and the men took their time and explored California's Central Valley and returned to the Great Salt Lake via the Sierra Nevadas—the first white man to ever accomplish the feat. They survived the journey by eating their horses and burying themselves in the sand to cool off in the hot Nevada desert. Jed and two of his men reached Bear Lake on July 2 after six weeks of grueling travel over mountain, river, and barren wilderness.

The mountain man was not yet done with his traveling, however. He wanted to further explore California and break a path into the Oregon Territory from the south. His second expedition set out on July 13, 1827, this time with eighteen men and two women (Indian squaws, probably married to the two Canadians in the group). However, trouble met them at a Mojave village on the Colorado River (at the Arizona/California border). A battle between another party of trappers and the Mojave Indians the previous fall had stirred up bad blood. After trading peacefully with the Indians for three days, Jedediah was quite unaware of what was about to happen. As he took half of his men and some of the supplies to a raft and began crossing the river, the Mojaves attacked those left on the shore. Ten men were killed instantly and the women were captured. The survivors ditched most of the supplies, leaving them on the sand bar, and headed off on foot towards California. Within a few minutes, however, hundreds of Mojave warriors descended on them. The eight men, armed with only five guns, took refuge behind a few cottonwood trees. Jed recorded the scene in his journal:

> It was a fearful time. Eight men with but five guns were awaiting behind a defence made of brush the charge of four or five hundred Indians whose hands were yet stained with the blood of their companions. Some of the men asked me if I thought we would be able to defend ourselves. I told them I thought we would. But that was not my opinion. I directed that not more than three guns should be fired at a time and those only when the shot would be certain of killing. Gradually the enemy was drawing near but kept themselves covered from our fire. Seeing a few Indians who ventured out from their covering within long shot I directed two marksmen

to fire. They did so and two Indians fell and another was wounded. Upon this the Indians ran off like frightened sheep and we were released from the apprehension of immediate death.[11]

Once again, it was Jedediah's clear thinking and forthright leadership that saved the remainder of the expedition from further harm.

The team made its way across the California border and retraced their footsteps from the previous year up the Central Valley towards San Jose. They arrived at Mission San Jose on September 23, 1827. However, this time the Spanish were even less friendly to Jedediah than the last time and less sympathetic to his exploring fever. He was finally released by the Spanish authorities and began his expedition north out of San Jose on January 1, 1828. Now his objective was to find a way into Oregon from the south. The men trapped California rivers through the spring and summer and crossed over into Oregon on June 20. The Northwest Indians were not friendly and the expedition lost twelve horses fording the Rogue River while trying to escape an attack.

Mission San Jose

The men were encamped on the Smith River in the Willamette Valley on the morning of July 14. Jedediah had pushed off in a boat to scout out a route north, warning his men not to allow any natives into the camp. Regrettably, the men failed to obey the instruction and allowed one hundred Indians to wander in. Almost immediately the Indians fell on the Americans, killing sixteen of them. Upon his return to the camp with an Indian guide via the river, Jed could tell something was wrong. None of his men were present on shore to greet him. An Indian spoke to the guide who grabbed Jed's rifle and leaped into the water. The other Indians began firing on his boat. Jed paddled ferociously to the other side, climbed out, and ran for his life. He reached Fort Vancouver (one hundred miles north) by August 10 and was there reunited with just three of his men. Thus, in the merciful providence of God, Jedediah Smith survived the third of the most severe Indian attacks in the history of the mountain men.

The Regrets and the Faith of a Mountain Man

And let us consider one another in order to stir up love and good works, not forsaking the assembling of ourselves together, as is the manner of some, but exhorting one another, and so much the more as you see the Day approaching. (Hebrews 10:24-25)

Jedediah Smith expressed some regrets over his life on the trail. In a letter he wrote to his parents from Wind River (near modern day Thermopolis, Wyoming), Jed noted, "I feel the need of the watch and care of a Christian church—you may suppose that our society is the roughest of kind. Men of good morals seldom enter into business of this kind. I hope you will remember me at the throne of Grace."[12] Out in the Wild West, he had come to realize the necessity of "assembling ourselves together" (Heb. 10:25). True believers will always seek out fellowship with the body of Christ as an essential element of the Christian life.

In a letter to his brother Ralph not two months before he died, Jed encouraged him to be more grateful to God "for the gift of His dear Son." With a note of wonderment, Jed added, "Is it possible that God so loved the world that He gave His only begotten Son that whosoever believed on Him should not perish, but have everlasting life? [John 3:16]."[13]

Jed wrote another letter to Ralph, once more expressing his deep concern over "the perverseness of my wicked heart." Then he testified a faith commitment to "depend entirely upon the Mercy of that Being, who is abundant in goodness, and will not cast off any who call."[14] With this letter, Jed included a little money for his parents, "to smooth the pillow of their age & as much as in us lies, take from them all cause of Trouble."[15] His concern to financially support his parents in their old age is something of an application of Christ's words in Matthew 15:3-6:

> He answered and said to them, "Why do you also transgress the commandment of God because of your tradition? For God commanded, saying, 'Honor your father and your mother'; and, 'He who curses father or mother, let him be put to death.' But you say, 'Whoever says to his father or mother, "Whatever profit you might have received from me is a gift to God"—then he need not honor his father or mother.' Thus you have made the commandment of God of no effect by your tradition."

Although he made a great deal of money in his strenuous endeavors, Jedediah Smith made it a point never to spend it on himself. He also never gave way to sexual sin with the squaws as the other men would. Though he was constantly surrounded by profane and dissolute men of the worst kind, it was said that "no evil communication proceeded out of his mouth."[16]

> Let no corrupt communication proceed out of your mouth, but that which is good to the use of edifying, that it may minister grace unto the hearers. (Ephesians 4:29 KJV)

Upon his return to St. Louis, Jed bought a farm for his brother Ralph at a price of $1,500, and he purchased a house for another brother. Concerned for the spiritual condition of his younger brother Ira, Jed enrolled him in a Presbyterian college in Jacksonville. When he heard that another younger brother was considering a move to St. Louis, a city overflowing with vice, Jed wrote, "My brother! This is the last place to which youngsters should be sent."[17]

A young man named Jonathan Trumbull made his way to St. Louis with the intent of becoming a mountain man himself. Jedediah did his best to dissuade him, pointing out that this was no life for a "Christian man."[18]

The Death of Jedediah Smith

In the early months of 1831, Jedediah Smith made plans for his final expedition—to Santa Fe. He hoped to publish a book and map and thus further open up a trade route into Mexican-controlled Texas and New Mexico. Before leaving, he wrote his will, providing $200 per month annuity for his father for the rest of his life; the rest was divided among his siblings. Eighty-three men joined the team, and they pulled out of St. Louis on April 10th. Indian trouble began near Pawnee Fork, when several hundred Comanches approached the expedition. The men loaded the cannon they had brought with them, the six-pounder barked, and the Indians scattered. However, one of the young men was separated from the others during a hunt and a band of Pawnees killed him. The trail was supremely unsafe for any travelers.

After leaving the Arkansas River and heading south into Oklahoma, the men went three days without water. On May 27 Jed left a few men to dig in a dried-up water hole while he traveled three miles south to explore for more water sources. That was the last they saw of their fearless leader—Jedediah Smith.

Later, Spanish traders learned something of the story of his death. As Jed approached a water hole, 15-20 Comanche warriors approached him. He rode directly towards the chief and attempted to establish terms of peace, but they would have nothing of it. The warriors disturbed his mount. The horse wheeled, and as Jed lost his bearings the Commanches shot him in the back. As he fell to the ground, he shot the chief dead and then reached for his revolvers, but it was too late. The others were on him with lances and knives.

His brother, Austin Smith, conveyed the news in a letter to his father, comforting him with the Word of God: "The Lord giveth, the Lord taketh away. [His nature] was the kind who trusted and confided in the Giver of all Good, and may we not hope that his religion was true, and will be rewarded. 'Come unto me all ye ends of the earth, and be saved' [Isaiah 45:22]."[19]

The eulogy written for Jedediah Smith summarized his short life and death in this way: "Yet, was he modest, never obtrusive, charitable, without guile . . . a man whom none could approach without respect or know without esteem. And though he fell under the spears of savages, and his body has glutted the prairie wolf, and none can tell where his bones are bleaching, he must not be forgotten."[20]

Repay no one evil for evil. Have regard for good things in the sight of all men. If it is possible, as much as depends on you, live peaceably with all men. (Romans 12:17-18)

Thomas "Stonewall" Jackson (1824-1863)

CHAPTER 19

Thomas "Stonewall" Jackson: A Godly Soldier

Come, behold the works of the LORD, Who has
made desolations in the earth. He makes wars cease
to the end of the earth; He breaks the bow and cuts
the spear in two; He burns the chariot in the fire.
Be still, and know that I am God; I will be exalted
among the nations, I will be exalted in the earth!

—Psalm 46:8-10

Modern slavery was introduced into the Americas by the Spanish in the early 1500s. During the next century, this terrible scourge began spreading into the American colonies, especially in the South. At the time of America's War for Independence with Britain, strong opinions had already developed among Americans for and against slavery. For the next few decades after the war, an uneasy unity prevailed. Nonetheless, the disagreement between North and South increased in intensity especially as new states were added to the union between 1830 and 1860.

John Brown's terrorist actions in Kansas and Virginia introduced fear into

JOHN BROWN.

Abolitionist and Terrorist John Brown

the hearts of many Southerners. John Brown and his followers were opposed to slavery for what they thought were religious reasons. However, Brown resorted to murdering innocent people, which only created terror in the hearts of Southerners and stirred up war sentiments. These lawless actions met with approval among Northerners, and this only increased alarm in the South.

A power struggle between North and South continued for about forty years. Northern states pushed for higher tariffs which protected their industry and enriched Northern businessmen at the expense of the South.

When Abraham Lincoln was elected to the presidency in 1860, the die was cast. Lincoln said he "had no purpose . . . to interfere with the institution of slavery in the States where it exists."[1] Nevertheless, he did commit to increase the tariff rates, which everyone knew would hurt the Southern states. The new tariffs would effectively pare down Southern economic power. South Carolina would have none of it and turned out to be the first state to secede from the Union on December 20, 1860. The first shots were fired at Fort Sumter in South Carolina on April 12, 1861. This was the beginning of the horrible nightmare known as the American Civil War.

When the state of Virginia seceded in 1861, the primary reason was that Virginians did not want to join the North in a fight against its neighbor states to the south. Most Virginians saw the massing of federal troops in the North as a military threat, a foreign army preparing to invade their soil.

Orphan T.J. Jackson

The LORD opens the eyes of the blind; the LORD raises those who are bowed down;
the LORD loves the righteous. The LORD watches over the strangers; He relieves
the fatherless and widow; but the way of the wicked He turns upside down. (Psalm
146:8-9)

Thomas J. Jackson was born in Clarksburg, Virginia in 1824 to Jonathan and
Julia Jackson. Not much is known of his father except that he was a compulsive
gambler and he ran the family into bankruptcy before he died. Still only a
small infant at the time, Thomas was left fatherless. His mother remarried,
but her second husband was abusive as well as financially irresponsible. Then
another tragedy struck in Thomas' seventh year when his mother passed away.
Orphaned of both parents, Thomas along with his sister Laura went to live with
some of Jonathan Jackson's bachelor brothers at Jackson's Mill in modern-day
West Virginia. It was a rowdy home of hardworking aunts and uncles. The
homestead was also the biggest and wealthiest in the county. The Jackson clan
owned the most successful sawmill in the area, a grain mill, a blacksmith shop,
and a general store.

The farm where Thomas and Laura grew up was on a river. With a little help
from one of the slaves on the farm, young Tom built a raft. He would often take
his sister across the river on the raft, where they would rest under the maples and
poplar trees on the other side for hours at a time.

There was much to do on the busy farm, however, and young Thomas
hardly had any time to experience loneliness with all the hustle and bustle of
the home. Between the ages of nine and sixteen, he cut down trees and hauled
them into the sawmill for cutting into boards. It was this work that must have
helped him develop that character some would call an "indomitable physical
endurance."[2]

Although his uncle Cummins Jackson was not a Christian, he treated
Thomas with much kindness as if he were his own son. Cummins related to
Thomas more as a companion and shared most of his private business with the

lad in a sort of mentorship. He raised racing horses and trained Thomas to ride them in competitions, something that would come in handy for the young man later on in life. As Thomas improved in riding competence, eventually he turned into the winningest jockey in the county.

Regrettably, few churches existed on the West Virginia frontier at the time. Nevertheless, somehow the "purifying force of a Christian mother's teachings and prayers"[3] continued with young Thomas. His Uncle Cummins' moral influence was not the best, as the older man had gained the reputation of being dishonest in business and generally ungodly in his character. It had to have been the grace of God that saved Thomas from this kind of life.

Quite the opposite of his uncle's example, Thomas became well-known in Lewis County for his dependability and integrity. At only seventeen years of age, he was appointed county constable or sheriff by the justice of the peace. In this position, he served warrants, arrested suspects, and summoned witnesses to court. It was about this time that Thomas Jackson had a conversation with a friend in which he stated that slaves should be freed. Contrary to the perspective of other Southerners around at the time, Thomas also felt they should be taught to read, in his words, "so they could read the Bible."[4]

Seeking Military Glory

> But the LORD said to Samuel, "Do not look at his appearance or at his physical stature, because I have refused him. For the LORD does not see as man sees; for man looks at the outward appearance, but the LORD looks at the heart." (1 Samuel 16:7)

At eighteen years of age, Thomas was received as a cadet at West Point Military Academy. While at West Point, he still did not display any signs of having embraced the Christian faith. However, he produced a list of moral codes for himself, none of which indicated that there was a heart change that only comes by the power of God.

Thomas was not an exceptional student. He was of average intelligence, although he tended to do well in mathematics. Through sheer hard work,

West Point Military Academy

however, he managed to work his way up to the twelfth position in his class. Young T.J. Jackson appeared awkward to his friends and he moved awkwardly, usually with unnaturally lengthy strides. His suit was always a little disheveled and his feet and hands looked to be about 30% too big for his body. His speech was somewhat stilted, and he was generally a man of few words. With those first meeting Jackson, he would come off as shy, unassuming, and rather unimpressive. In his personal life he remained simple, rigorous, and borderline ascetic. During his single years and during the war, his food was typically stale bread and water. At one point he wrote, "I have not to my recollection used any other drink than cold water."[5]

While in the army, Thomas proved himself disciplined and committed to duty. One day, when a superior told him to "remain as you are until further orders,"[6] Thomas continued sitting on a camp stool with his saber across his legs until the following morning. His superintendent was shocked to see him still sitting in the same position.

Without question, the one thing that marked Thomas Jackson above everything else was his bravery. He proved his courage right away in military action in the Mexican-American War of 1846-1848. After graduating from West Point on June 30, 1846, he was quickly transferred to Monterrey in northern Mexico. Soon thereafter, the army sent him to join the Mexico City campaign under the leadership of General Winfield Scott. In battle after battle, Lieutenant Jackson distinguished himself for bravery. At the battle of Vera Cruz he received a promotion for "gallant and meritorious conduct."[7] It was at Contreras that he faced the most harrowing action. For three hours he fought against superior Mexican artillery. His men were falling right and left around him. When other commanders were shot down, he continued to advance through the smoke and fire. Again he was recognized for "his coolness and determination . . . whilst under fire."[8]

In the battle over Mexico City, the Americans found themselves trapped on a causeway leading into Chapultepec Castle. There they were exposed to enemy fire without cover. Thomas later reported to his sister Laura: "[We were] in a road which was swept with grape and canister, and at the same time thousands of muskets from the Castle itself pouring down like hail."[9] All twelve of Thomas' horses were shot in the melee. Immediately Jackson began firing his two cannons against the Mexican's eight. One of his guns was destroyed and the rest of his artillerymen abandoned the field. Left alone, Thomas continued firing on the Mexicans. A Mexican cannon ball was shot between his legs, and he called out to his men, "There is no danger! See? I am not hit!"[10] One of his sergeants crawled back up on the road to help him continue the fight against the Mexican forces.

When General William J. Worth came close enough to see the front lines, he reported seeing a single soldier advancing, firing his only cannon against a significant portion of the entire Mexican Army—Lieutenant Jackson. When told to pull back, Jackson refused. Another soldier dragged a second six-pounder cannon to where Thomas was facing down the Mexican army, and he began working both guns at the same time. Not long afterwards the Americans gained control of the castle.

But the battle was still not over. In the hours that followed, Lieutenant

Jackson continued to pursue Santa Anna's army towards the gate of Mexico City, with his two guns in tow. Instead of waiting for General Scott's cavalry (who were about a mile behind him), he took forty men and for about half a mile continued attacking Santa Anna's cavalry of 1,500 men from the rear with his two cannons. The Mexican Army retreated into the city gates and the city surrendered the next day.

Seeking God and Finding Him

Thomas was not a professing Christian during the Mexican War. While still in Mexico however, he sought out the top cleric in the Roman Catholic Church, the Archbishop of Mexico, to question him about the faith. Although the bishop represented the Catholic faith well, Jackson did not accept it. He could not see how the Roman Catholic faith represented what the Bible taught. Yet, for two more years he continued to seek answers. Where was the true faith, and to which church should he join himself?

After a brief stint with the US Army in New York City, Jackson moved to Lexington, Virginia in 1850 to teach at the Virginia Military Institute (VMI). It was here that he was discipled into the Christian church by a Colonel Taylor. He also received some Christian instruction from an evangelical Episcopal chaplain named Mr. M. Parks. Although Thomas could not commit himself to the Episcopal Church, he agreed to be baptized by Mr. Parks in 1851. He was twenty-six years old at the time. By 1853 he was writing letters to his sister Laura which indicated a strong faith in Christ.

> [I throw] myself on the protection of Him whose law book is the wonderful Bible. My dear sister, I would not part with this book for countless universes. I feel ready to make every sacrifice to carry out the will of Him who so loved us as to give His only begotten Son to die for me.[11]

What strengthened his faith more than anything else, however, was his marriage to Ellie Junkin on August 4, 1853. Ellie's faith was the "conscientious, God-fearing faith of the old Covenanters,"[12] as her sister put it. Increasingly, God was becoming for Thomas Jackson an ever-present reality. As a friend testified of him, "God was in all his thoughts . . . God, God Himself, the living, personal and present God . . . possessed his whole being."[13] Thomas prayed constantly throughout the day, on every possible occasion—when receiving a glass of water, mailing a letter, entering a classroom, or receiving a letter. When a friend asked him if he ever forgot to pray, he answered, "I can hardly say that I do; the habit has become almost as fixed as to breathe."[14] It was around this time that Thomas Jackson came to realize that he was no longer interested in his quest for military glory.

Sadly, Ellie died in childbirth in 1854, only fourteen months into their marriage. Thomas mourned her loss deeply, but trust in God's providence sustained him. In 1857 he married Mary Anna Morrison, also a devout Christian.

Preparations for War

Many people shall come and say, "Come, and let us go up to the mountain of the LORD, to the house of the God of Jacob; He will teach us His ways, and we shall walk in His paths." For out of Zion shall go forth the law, and the word of the LORD from Jerusalem. He shall judge between the nations, and rebuke many people; they shall beat their swords into plowshares, and their spears into pruning hooks; nation shall not lift up sword against nation, neither shall they learn war anymore. (Isaiah 2:3-4)

Although slavery was an important reason for the war in the minds of many in both North and South, Thomas Jackson was not supportive of the institution. He bought three slaves only because he was asked to do so. He had no need for them in his household. When his first slave, Albert, contracted a long-standing illness, Jackson took care of the man for the duration of his suffering. Then an elderly woman named Amy who asked to be taken in by him came down with an illness. Jackson paid for her medical expenses and funeral expenses when she died. Then there was four-year-old Emma, whom he purchased from a local slave owner. He tried to teach her to read, though it turned out she had a serious learning disability.

Against the recommendations of the community, Jackson insisted on starting a Sunday school for African American children in Lexington. Between eighty and one hundred students showed up for his classes. Jackson would open in prayer, lead the children in a rousing rendition of "Amazing Grace," and then teach them from the Bible. Throughout the year he would award a copy of the Bible to students who excelled in the class.

One day three lawyers approached Thomas on the street and informed him that his Sunday school was an "unlawful assembly" by Virginia statute. He responded with, "Sir, if you were, as you should be, a Christian man, you would not think so or say so."[15] One of the lawyers later wrote an apology to Jackson for what he had said. Before he got the letter off, Jackson was at his door apologizing for the harsh tone he had used in the confrontation. The Sunday school continued in operation for thirty years.

On several occasions, Thomas considered becoming a foreign missionary for Christ. Once he wrote to an aunt, "I would not be surprised if I were to die on a foreign field, clad in ministerial armor, fighting under the banner of Jesus."[16]

When it came to politics, Jackson was a Southern Democrat. This party preferred that local government bodies retain power rather than surrendering it to a centralized federal government. Thomas Jackson would advocate a strict limitation on the powers of the federal government, in line with men like Patrick Henry, Samuel Adams, and George Mason.

As passions rose against the Union throughout the South, Thomas Jackson opposed the idea of secession and shuddered at the very thought of war. He wrote against it at every opportunity. No one was more aware of war's horrors than Jackson. "They do not know its horrors. I have seen enough of it to make me look upon it as the sum of all evils,"[17] he wrote to his pastor. His wife Anna wrote, "I have never heard any man express such utter abhorrence of war."[18] Amazing words for a man who would turn out to be the greatest soldier in the war.

In desperation, Thomas Jackson applied all his energies to avert the coming war. He prayed. But, more than that, he petitioned his pastor and wrote letters to church leaders in both the South and North, suggesting a national day of prayer. Sadly, the US federal government had not called days of prayer and fasting since the administration of Thomas Jefferson, over half a century earlier. The nation had become proud and secular with the influence of the humanist Enlightenment. Christian faith was weak in American leadership from 1800 through 1860, with notable exceptions like John Quincy Adams. Yet, Jackson wrote his letters, hoping that some churches would get behind a national day of prayer "to overturn the political idiocies of the past half century."[19] Sadly, his calls went unheeded. There would be little support for a national day of humility and prayer either encouraged by the churches or supported by the national government. Apparently, the nation preferred to suffer the loss of 1,264,000 men in the bloodiest war in America's history rather than humble themselves before God. The US Senate would finally propose a day of humility and prayer in 1863, shortly before Gettysburg, the defining battle of the war.

The cadets at the Virginia Military Institute (VMI) in Lexington were generally supportive of secession. When the young men almost came to arms against a pro-Union crowd in town, VMI's administrator, Colonel Francis H. Smith, and Thomas Jackson intervened. Colonel Smith spoke to the cadets. When it was Jackson's turn to speak, he gave a very short speech. He told the men, "The time for war has not yet come, but it will come, and that soon. And when it does come, my advice is to draw the sword and throw away the scabbard."[20] The men sat in stunned silence at the force of his words. They would never forget that short prophetic statement as long as they lived.

War

Come near, you nations, to hear; and heed, you people! Let the earth hear, and all
that is in it, the world and all things that come forth from it. For the indignation
of the LORD is against all nations, and His fury against all their armies; He has
utterly destroyed them, He has given them over to the slaughter. (Isaiah 34:1-2)

By 1860 America had become a nation in rebellion against God. The sins of witchcraft, religious apostasy, humanist liberalism in the universities, and slave-based economies brought a curse upon the nation—North and South. The sins of the nation had multiplied over the previous seventy years, and the nation was ripe for the judgment of Almighty God.

Hundreds of thousands of American men were dragged into the war to fight for their governments. As T.J. Jackson entered the war, he truly believed he was fighting for his country. After all, every state considered itself a country before the 14th Amendment was ratified in 1868. Fighting on Virginia soil against an invading force was something most Virginians felt obliged to do. Despite his misgivings about secession and his opposition to war in general, Thomas felt an obligation to defend his country.

Jackson's first major battle took place in Manassas, Virginia, about twenty-five miles west of Washington DC. It is commonly referred to as the First Battle of Bull Run. Much to Jackson's disappointment, the battle was fought on Sunday, July 21, 1861. This was a day of rest, a day to remember the resurrection of Jesus Christ from the grave. Nonetheless, Jackson opened the day on his knees. On his mind that morning was Psalm 118.

"The LORD is on my side; I will not fear: what can man do unto me? The LORD taketh my part with them that help me: therefore shall I see my desire upon them that hate me" (Ps. 118:6-7).

As Jackson's troops drew near the battleground, they ran into fellow Virginians panicked and running from the lines. "The battle is lost," they said. Confederate General Bee told Jackson, "General, they are beating us back!" Jackson's only reply was, "Sir, we will give them the bayonet."[21] Jackson set his men on a nearby hill and went to work. He entered the battle with his 2,600 men against a much larger force. His small band became the center of the battle against 20,000 Union soldiers. For hours Jackson held off the much larger force. One objective was strong on his mind—hold the line! He rode across the front lines on "Little Sorrel," his battle horse, repeating again and again, "Steady, men, steady. All's well."[22] When General Bee rounded up some of his frightened men and reentered the battle, he looked over to where Jackson was standing on Henry Hill and told his men, "There stands Jackson like a stone wall! Rally 'round the Virginians!"[23] From this point on, Thomas Jackson would be known as "Stonewall Jackson."

When the much larger Union force noticed a weakening of Jackson's artillery battalion on the hill, they charged. This was the point at which the general came alive. With a thrill in his voice, he told his men to wait until the enemy came within fifty yards, then charge, fire, and give them the bayonet! And one more thing, he told them to "Yell like Furies."[24] That is what the Southern boys did, and this was the beginning of the Rebel Yell that would continue through the war and mark American fighting in years to come.

As Jackson's regiments charged forward, it seemed as if nothing could stop them. For an entire hour they fought at the "white hot center" of the battle, during which time Jackson was wounded in the hand and his coat was pierced by multiple bullets. His men suffered heavy casualties in the melee, but they held out long enough for Confederate reinforcements to arrive. They had held the ground for four hours against a much larger force. As the Federal troops began to withdraw, it became clear this would be a rout. The battle was a critical loss for the Union side and commanding General Irvin McDowell.

After the First Battle of Bull Run, Stonewall Jackson became the hero of Virginia and the most famous name in the South. In the evening after the battle however, Jackson sat down to write a letter to his pastor. As the minister opened the letter weeks later, he was excitedly expecting to read of the great battle fought at Bull Run. Instead, he read these words, "My dear pastor, in my tent last night, after a fatiguing day's service, I remembered that I had failed to send you my contribution for our colored Sunday-school. Enclosed you will find my check for that object, which please acknowledge at your earliest convenience, and oblige yours faithfully, T.J. Jackson."[25] This Christian general had better things on his mind than war, on the evening following the most outstanding battle he ever fought.

In the spring of 1862, General George McClellan sent an army of 62,000 men into the Shenandoah Valley with hopes of controlling this breadbasket of the Confederacy. McClellan was a proud man. He wrote to his wife, "Were I to win some small success now I could become Dictator or anything else that might

Battle of Bull Run

please me."[26] He kept the President of the United States waiting in his home for several hours while he went to bed. He went so far as to refer to the President as "the gorilla." He also told his wife that all his superiors were "my inferiors, socially, intellectually & morally."[27] Rich, pompous, and popular with others, McClellan was the exact opposite of his nemesis T.J. Jackson.

But, with a mere 17,000 men, General Thomas "Stonewall" Jackson held off the larger Federal force from March through June of 1862. His strategy was simple: Jackson merely worked harder than virtually everyone else in the war. His forces moved quickly on the ground, marching incredible distances on foot, earning them the nickname, "foot cavalry." He would march his men sometimes for half the night. Disciplined himself, the General would regularly sleep on the ground or on "the floor of a good room." He found sleeping in the rain, "slightly objectionable," but nothing worse.

Although never angry or emotional, Jackson would never permit a challenge to his authority. And though intensely disciplined with his army, his men were often surprised by Jackson's "almost motherly" concern for them. It was what some called a "mingling of tenderness and strength."[28]

During the Shenandoah Valley Campaign, Thomas marched his men over 646 miles in 48 days, "fighting five major battles, and skirmishing almost daily. He made flashing strikes in unexpected places, falling on the enemy from behind mountain ranges and out of steep passes."[29] His smaller army sustained 5,000 casualties. They seized 9,000 arms along with huge amounts of stores. Nothing on either side of the war came close to the speed and aggression that characterized Jackson's fighting force.

In June 1862 Stonewall Jackson's army joined General Robert E. Lee to defend Richmond in the Seven Days Battles, in which they successfully pushed the Union armies back down the Lower Peninsula toward the Chesapeake Bay.

In August, Stonewall Jackson returned to Bull Run, where he fought another engagement with Union General John Pope's armies, and won. He successfully held off General McClellan's troops in Antietam in September. Not long after this, Abraham Lincoln removed proud General McClellan from the job of commanding the Army of the Potomac.

The Battle of Fredericksburg was fought in December 1862, and once again the Confederates won with help from J.E.B. Stuart's cavalry and Stonewall Jackson's troops. By this time Jackson had become a popular hero in the South. Songs were written to his honor—as, for example, "Stonewall Jackson's Way."

> Come, stack arms, men! Pile on the rails,
> Stir up the campfire bright;
> No matter if the canteen fails,
> We'll make a rousing night!
> Here Shenandoah brawls along,
> And burly Blue Ridge echoes strong,
> To swell our brigade's rousing song
> Of "Stonewall Jackson's way."
>
> Silence! ground arms! kneel all! caps off!
> Old "Blue Lights" going to pray.
> Strangle the fool that dares to scoff!

Attention! it's his way.
Appealing from his native sod,
In forma pauperis to God,
Say "Bare Thine arm; stretch forth Thy rod,
Amen!" "That's Stonewall Jackson's way."

Ah! maiden, wait and watch and yearn
For news of Jackson's band!
Ah! widow, read, with eyes that burn,
That ring upon thy hand;
Ah! wife, sew on, pray on, hope on;
Thy life shall not be all forlorn
The foe had better ne'er been born
That gets in "Stonewall's way."[30]

Jackson viewed his fame with a humble realism. He wrote to his wife Anna: "Don't trouble yourself about representations that are made of your husband. These things are earthy and transitory. There are real and glorious blessings, I trust, in reserve for us beyond this life. It is best for us to keep our eyes fixed upon the throne of God and the realities of a more glorious existence beyond the verge of time. It is gratifying to be beloved and to have our conduct approved by our fellow-men, but this is not worthy to be compared with the glory that is in reservation for us in the presence of our glorified Redeemer."[31]

Of much greater importance to Stonewall Jackson were the revivals occurring in the Confederate camps. He was thrilled by the camp meetings and revival services going on under the preaching of Pastor Joseph Stiles. Excitedly, he wrote to his chief of staff, R.L. Dabney: "It appears to me that we may look for growing piety and many conversions in the army; for it is the subject of prayer."[32]

It was about this time that Thomas testified of his faith to a fellow officer, who later wrote of it: "[He said that] both fear and love actuated his repentance. As his assurance became more clear of the Redeemer's mercy to his soul, his obedience became less servile, and more affectionate; until, in the most favored saints, perfect love cast out fear. He then declared that he had been himself, for a long time, a stranger to fear of wrath; because he knew and was assured of the love of Christ to his soul; that he felt not the faintest dread that he should ever fall under the wrath of God, although a great sinner; because he knew that it was forever reconciled by the righteousness of Christ, and that love for God and Christ was now the practical spring of all his penitence."[33]

When his friend and fellow officer J.E.B. Stuart bought him a fancy military coat complete with gold buttons, Thomas didn't know what to do with it. He told his men to "give Stuart my best thanks . . . The coat is much too handsome for me, but I shall take the best care of it, and shall prize it highly as a souvenir."[34] With that, he folded it up carefully and put it in his chest of drawers. The humility of General Jackson stood in stark contrast to the pride of General George McClellan.

Stonewall Jackson's Final Days

And he showed me a pure river of water of life, clear as crystal, proceeding from the throne of God and of the Lamb. In the middle of its street, and on either side of the river, was the tree of life, which bore twelve fruits, each tree yielding its fruit every month. The leaves of the tree were for the healing of the nations. And there shall be no more curse, but the throne of God and of the Lamb shall be in it, and His servants shall serve Him. (Revelation 22:1-3)

Jackson's final battle took place at Chancellorsville, Virginia. The Virginians fought hard to defend their home state from those whom they saw as invaders. Once again, the Southern armies were massively outnumbered by 60,000 to 130,000.

It was Jackson's brilliant tactics and aggressive attack on the Union right flank that won the battle for the South. His troops positioned themselves in record time and advanced against the enemy, outnumbered by five to one. Chancellorsville was arguably the greatest victory for the Southern armies in the war. Robert E. Lee acknowledged the victory was due to the skill and energy of his greatest general, Stonewall Jackson.

However, in God's providential plan, Jackson was mortally wounded in the battle. It was friendly fire that took him down as he launched a daring evening attack at 9:00 p.m. on May 2, 1863. Three bullets cut through his hand and arm, laying him low.

As he lay wounded, Thomas told his men, "You find me severely wounded, but not unhappy or depressed. I believe that it has been done according to the will of God; and I acquiesce entirely to His holy will. It may appear strange, but you never saw me more perfectly contented than I am today, for I am sure my heavenly Father designs this affliction for my own good."[35] Doctors amputated his left arm, to which Robert E. Lee said, "He [Jackson] has lost his left arm, but I have lost my right arm."[36]

Several days later, Jackson's wife Anna joined him at a home where he was being cared for near Guinea Station. As he began to fade, Thomas told everyone, "I am willing to abide by the will of my heavenly Father."[37] As his death approached on Saturday night, he asked his wife and her brother Joseph to sing hymns for him. They sang to Jesus:

King of glory! Reign forever—
Thine an everlasting Crown.
Nothing from thy love shall sever
Those whom thou hast made thine own;
Happy objects of thy grace,
Destined to behold thy face.
Hallelujah, Hallelujah, Hallelujah!

His wife asked him, "Do you not feel willing to acquiesce in God's allotment, if He wills you to go today?" Weakly, Thomas replied, "I prefer it." Then, even louder, "I prefer it." Anna reminded him, "Before this day closes, you will be with the blessed Savior in His glory." "I will be an infinite gainer to be translated," he replied. Anna brought their only daughter into the room, eighth-month-old Anna. Thomas smiled and said, "Little darling! Sweet one!" Then he closed his eyes to pray for the little one.[38]

Stonewall Jackson's final words would call to mind his experience under the poplar trees and maples across the river from the farm at Jackson's Mill. It was his best conception of heaven. As a "smile of ineffable sweetness" came over his face, he said, "Let us cross over the river and rest under the shade of the trees."[39] And he did.

Conclusion

And David behaved wisely in all his ways, and the LORD was with him. Therefore, when Saul saw that he behaved very wisely, he was afraid of him. But all Israel and Judah loved David, because he went out and came in before them. (1 Samuel 18:14-16)

As God would have it, practically every battle with which this godly military captain engaged during the Civil War was a victory for the Southern Confederates. As long as ol' "Blue Light" was on his knees, the outcome of the battle seemed to turn in his direction. Each morning he would fall on his knees and pray to his God for His mercy and favor. Hardly anyone could doubt that God was hearing the General's prayers.

The Southern armies' success in battle pretty much ended with the death of General "Stonewall" Jackson. In Jackson's own words, this was undoubtedly done "according to the will of God." Union General Gouverneur K. Warren wrote that he was rejoiced "at Stonewall Jackson's death as a gain to our cause," but added, "I cannot but see him as the best soldier of all this war and grieve at his untimely end."[40] A Northern newspaper, the *Washington Chronicle*, noted:

"Stonewall Jackson was a great general, a brave soldier, a noble Christian, and a pure man. May God throw these great virtues against the sins of the secessionist."[41]

President Abraham Lincoln wrote the editor concerning his comments, calling them both "excellent and manly."[42]

Throughout the annals of history, one will only find a handful of godly men leading in war like Jackson did. William the Silent, Gustavus Adolphus, and Oliver Cromwell come to mind. When men took God's name in vain in battle, Jackson took great offense at it—greater offense than he would take to the enemy's attack.

Although a courageous man by nature, Jackson's bravery only increased throughout the wars he fought. He feared no one except God. He implicitly trusted the sovereign hand of God, saying, "My religious belief teaches me to feel as safe in battle as in bed. God has fixed the time for my death. I do not concern myself about that, but to be always ready, no matter when it may overtake me. That is the way all men should live, and then all would be equally brave."[43] When a cannonball ripped off a branch of a tree under which he was standing, Stonewall Jackson completely ignored it, to the amazement of his men standing nearby. Instead of reacting to this near-death occurrence, Thomas merely continued giving instructions to his men in his slow, quiet, and commanding manner.

The Civil War was a sad chapter in American history. But God always has His men in position here and there to give Him the glory and to speak His truth even when the world has corrupted itself. In the thick of war, there is a little peace, righteousness, and joy in the Holy Spirit here and there. There is redemption to be found. There is the kingdom of the Lord Jesus Christ to be seen for those that seek it. It is the best kingdom of all—a kingdom that will never pass away.

> Now when [Jesus] was asked by the Pharisees when the kingdom of God would come, He answered them and said, "The kingdom of God does not come with observation; nor will they say, 'See here!' or 'See there!' For indeed, the kingdom of God is within you." (Luke 17:20-21)

> For the kingdom of God is not eating and drinking, but righteousness and peace and joy in the Holy Spirit. (Romans 14:17)

UNIT 4

National Prosperity and the Rise of Secularism (1865-1920)

*Or do you despise the riches of His goodness,
forbearance, and longsuffering, not knowing that
the goodness of God leads you to repentance? But
in accordance with your hardness and your
impenitent heart you are treasuring up for yourself
wrath in the day of wrath and revelation of the
righteous judgment of God.*

—Romans 2:4-5

The United States emerged from the Civil War as a different country altogether. The irreligious, secular, and Unitarian North had won. The more religious South, populated by more evangelical and orthodox Southern Baptist and Southern Presbyterian churches had lost. By this means, Americans came to view the orthodox Christian faith as hypocritical, racist, and grossly immoral. This view would taint American thinking for generations. Since our Lord was accused of planning to "destroy the temple in three days," Christianity has constantly been the object of false reports and misinterpretation (Mark 14:58).

In order to gain a fair understanding of history, Christian students of history must know God's law. This helps them to recognize the sins of the day and to properly identify the "good guys" and "bad guys." It is also important to obtain an accurate and balanced view of what was going on at the time. It is helpful to look at the faith and life testimonies of a country's leaders. Did they believe in Christ and repent of their sin? Where were the Christians in history and how did they react to the sins of their day?

During this period of national prosperity and the rise of secularism, many of America's leaders became increasingly profane and they would not fear God. Others like Benjamin Harrison, James Garfield, and William McKinley did fear God and acknowledged Christ.

The Reconstruction years were difficult for the South, and animosity between blacks and whites, North and South continued strong in many instances. The radical Republicans and the Marxists pushed for confiscation of property and heavy taxes on the impoverished South.

Between 1865 and 1930, the nation became increasingly immoral. Criminal activity skyrocketed, and biblical Christianity exerted less and less influence on the nation's educational and cultural institutions. Roman Catholicism became the largest denomination in the country—and the Protestants largely gave way to Liberalism, bringing about more denominational fracturing.

Nevertheless, God poured out His blessing upon America between 1865 and 1900. The nation became prosperous. Inventive Americans, many of whom were professing Christians, developed natural resources, built automobiles and steam ships, and introduced electricity to the world. God was giving America another opportunity to repent of her sins and obey His laws. American families enjoyed an increase in wealth and comforts. However, the nation did not repent and give the glory to God. Instead, the federal government focused on increasing its powers, and America grew into a great world empire, proud of its achievements and confident in its own strength.

Everyone proud in heart is an abomination to the LORD; though they join forces, none will go unpunished. (Proverbs 16:5)

Timeline of Important Events

1866   Civil Rights Act of 1866 is passed by Congress.

1867   The United States purchases Alaska from Russia.

1871   The Great Chicago Fire burns down much of the "windy city."

1872   Dwight L. Moody travels to England to conduct revivals there.

1876   General Custer fights the Battle of the Little Bighorn.

1890   North Dakota, South Dakota, Montana, Washington, and Idaho are admitted to the US.

1898   The Spanish-American War takes place in Cuba and the Philippines.

1914   World War I begins, and the United States enters the war in 1917.

1919   The Treaty of Versailles formally ends World War I.

1920   The first radio broadcast takes place in Pittsburgh, Pennsylvania.

Charles Hodge (1797-1878)

CHAPTER 20

Charles Hodge: Contending for the Truth

Beloved, while I was very diligent to write to you concerning our common salvation, I found it necessary to write to you exhorting you to contend earnestly for the faith which was once for all delivered to the saints. For certain men have crept in unnoticed, who long ago were marked out for this condemnation, ungodly men, who turn the grace of our God into lewdness and deny the only Lord God and our Lord Jesus Christ.

—Jude 3-4

Every generation of Jesus' followers must earnestly contend for the faith, as the Apostle Jude admonishes. It was the duty of Charles Hodge to contend for the faith during the great apostasies of 19th century America. He kept the faith and passed it along to future generations. As a professor of theology and as a writer, Charles Hodge made a unique contribution to American history by training thousands of students in the doctrines of the Christian faith. His influence and legacy continue to this day.

America During the Life of Charles Hodge

Charles Hodge lived through some of the most formative years of the American nation. When Charles was born in 1797, the United States of America was only twenty-one years old and John Adams was president. He would live through eighteen different presidencies. During his eighty years of life (1797-1878), the world entered modernity and this nation changed in many profound ways. Charles Hodge witnessed the War of 1812, the Mexican War, and the most pivotal event in American history—the Civil War.

With the 19th century came technological progress, industrialization, and life-changing inventions. These would include the telegraph (1837), the stapler (1841), the sewing machine (1845), dynamite (1866), the typewriter (1867), traffic lights (1868), the telephone (1876), and many more. During Charles Hodge's lifetime, the population of the United States increased ten-fold, from some five million in 1800 to almost fifty million in 1880.

Hodge's Early Life

Charles was born in Philadelphia on December 27, 1797 to Hugh and Mary Hodge. The couple had faced multiple tragedies. Their eldest three sons died in the yellow fever epidemic of 1793. Two years later, another son died of the same pathogen. Born in 1796, their son Hugh Jr. was the first to survive childhood. Shortly after Charles was born in 1797, Hugh Sr. passed away, and Mary was left to raise the two boys by herself.

> *When my father and my mother forsake me, then the LORD will take care of me. (Psalm 27:10)*

The Lord graciously provided a godly upbringing for Charles after his father's death. Mary committed herself to passing on the Christian faith, attending church weekly and drilling her sons regularly in doctrine using the Westminster Shorter Catechism. The pastor of Philadelphia's Second Presbyterian Church, Ashbel Green, aided Mary with this discipleship as well.

The boys also learned lessons of personal piety and devotion through the teaching and example of their mother. Charles later recalled his early life as a young Christian:

There has never been anything remarkable in my religious experience, unless it be that it began very early. I think that in my childhood I came nearer to conforming to the apostle's injunction: "Pray without ceasing," than in any other period of my life. As far back as I can remember, I had the habit of thanking God for everything I received, and asking him for everything I wanted. If I lost a book, or any of my playthings, I prayed that I might find it. I prayed walking along the streets, in school and out of school, whether playing or studying. I did not do this in obedience to any prescribed rule. It seemed natural. I thought of God as an everywhere-present Being, full of kindness and love, who would not be offended if children talked to him.[1]

Westminster Shorter Catechism: A 107-question and answer manual of Christian doctrine and practice. The Westminster Shorter Catechism was produced in 1647 by an assembly of pastors and theologians meeting in London, England during the English Civil War. The Shorter Catechism was used primarily in Presbyterian churches, but was also employed in many other churches in America as a tool for Christian instruction.

As a single mother, Mary worked hard to provide for her two sons, and through a variety of pursuits she managed to raise enough money to send them both to college. Hugh studied medicine at the University of Pennsylvania and Charles studied for the ministry at Princeton. Though he did not know it at the time, Charles would spend most of his life at Princeton as a professor and then as the president of the seminary.

Charles' Education at Princeton

Charles enrolled as a sophomore at Princeton College in September 1812, and it was during his years at college, that Charles and other members of his class experienced a remarkable revival. Writing to his brother Hugh, Charles described what was happening during the school year of 1814-1815:

> I cannot but think that all who see the present state of the College must also feel that this is indeed the harvest, the accepted time, the day of salvation. O! my brother! Though it is only your little Toby who is writing to you, yet he loves you . . . and shudders at the thought of your wanting [lacking] the one thing needful.[2]

Young Charles Hodge and hundreds of other students made public professions of their faith and became zealous in attending Bible studies, worship services, and prayer meetings. After graduating from Princeton College, Charles enrolled in Princeton Seminary in 1816. During his time there, he found in the seminary's president Archibald Alexander the father he never had. Dr. Alexander served as a Paul to Timothy for Charles. In fact, he would name his first son after his mentor—Archibald Alexander Hodge.

Biographer Andrew Hoffecker explains this important relationship between mentor and student:

Nassau Hall, Princeton University

Hodge found in Alexander the maturity and counsel that he had lacked in his youth and adolescence because of the early death of his father . . . Although Alexander fathered several sons of prodigious ability who also became professors at Princeton, he took special interest in young Hodge.[3]

At Princeton Charles found an environment where he grew in both knowledge and in his spiritual devotion to the Lord. Some academic environments are dangerous for spiritual growth because they do not encourage habits of prayer, Bible study, and acts of love towards others. It is a dangerous form of knowledge that only puffs up, but produces little love that edifies (1 Cor. 8:1). Yet, at Princeton Seminary, Charles experienced growth in both knowledge and personal piety. The charter documents of Princeton Seminary during those years described the importance of teaching students in a variety of subjects, but also recognized the importance of encouraging a love for the Lord and personal piety. The seminary's purpose was stated:

. . .to form men for the Gospel ministry, who shall truly believe and cordially love, and therefore endeavour to propagate and defend . . . that system of religious belief and practice which is set forth in the Confession of Faith, Catechisms, and Plan of the Government and Discipline of the Presbyterian Church; and thus to perpetuate and extend the influence of true evangelical piety, and Gospel order.[4]

Charles Hodge gave most of his life over to either studying or teaching. Shortly after his graduation from Princeton, the young scholar was invited to teach biblical languages of Hebrew and Greek at the seminary. After accepting Dr. Alexander's invitation, he spent the following months studying Hebrew with Dr. Joseph Banks in Philadelphia.

Charles Hodge's Early Teaching Career at Princeton   May 1820

Starting out, Charles' annual salary amounted to about $400 per year, (equivalent to about $8000 in today's money). Shortly after he began his teaching career at Princeton, Charles married Sarah Bache, the great-granddaughter of Benjamin Franklin. Within two years the young couple moved into a house near the campus of Princeton Seminary that would serve as their home for the rest of Charles' life. Within their first four years of marriage the Hodges had two children: Archibald Alexander and Mary Elizabeth. The couple would be blessed with a total of six children. Charles was known by his children as a loving and caring father.

In a letter to his mother, Charles explained the responsibilities of a Christian father, as he saw it:

> Our dear little children we have promised to educate for heaven, and as God shall enable us, we mean to perform our vows. To this every thing must be made secondary . . . We feel, therefore, determined, if God shall render us faithful to our purposes, to bring up your dear little grandchildren, as we are sure you would have us to, with the one object supremely in view of fitting them for heaven.[5]

Indeed Scripture reminds parents that it is their first responsibility to point their children to God, as He reveals Himself in His Word.

> And these words which I command you today shall be in your heart. You shall teach them diligently to your children, and shall talk of them when you sit in your house, when you walk by the way, when you lie down, and when you rise up. (Deuteronomy 6:6-7)

> We will not hide them from their children, telling to the generation to come the praises of the LORD, and His strength and His wonderful works that He has done. (Psalm 78:4)

> And you, fathers, do not provoke your children to wrath, but bring them up in the training and admonition of the Lord. (Ephesians 6:4)

European Sojourn

Beware, brethren, lest there be in any of you an evil heart of unbelief in departing from the living God; but exhort one another daily, while it is called "Today," lest any of you be hardened through the deceitfulness of sin. (Hebrews 3:12-13)

During his early years of teaching, Charles Hodge felt that he was not sufficiently prepared for the job. His knowledge of the original biblical languages was insufficient he thought, to continue in his role as a teacher of ministry students. He requested a two-year break from the board of directors at Princeton so that he could travel to Europe and engage in further study. He was also interested in the latest developments in biblical studies in Europe, hoping to gain some knowledge of the German and French languages as well.

During the 18th and 19th century, Western Europe, and Germany in particular became the birthplace of many modern developments in theology, philosophy, and science. Much of this secular humanist thinking eroded belief in the supernatural and undermined the Christian faith. The teachings of Scripture were criticized and in some cases completely rejected. This wider movement in the universities and churches of Europe was known as "liberal theology."

Because this shift towards rejecting the fundamental doctrines of the faith was occurring in Europe at the time, many of Charles' colleagues at Princeton warned him about the influence that such false teachings might have upon him. His close mentor Archibald Alexander warned him that within Europe he would "breathe a poisoned atmosphere. If you lose the lively and deep impression of divine truth—if you fall into skepticism or even into coldness, you will lose more than you gain from all the German professors and libraries."[6]

Liberal Theology: Several movements that describe themselves as Christian but which reject fundamental biblical doctrines that form the core of the Christian faith. Over the centuries liberal theology has developed into many different movements, but every form agrees in rejecting the complete inspiration and infallibility of the Holy Scriptures.

In October 1826 Charles departed America for the shores of Europe. Regrettably, because of financial limitations, he was unable to take his wife Sarah and their two children with him. For two years Charles was separated from his family, corresponding only by letters. He communicated deep affection in letters to his wife: "If you were with me, my heavy heart would be light."[7] In another he exclaimed, "My eye is not always dry when it turns westward. Keep yourself occupied and keep your heart my dear Sarah in the work of God and you will be happy."[8]

Sure enough, while in Paris and Berlin Charles faced a hostile spiritual environment, especially in the apostate universities. But the upbringing he received through his mother and pastor's faithful teaching gave him a solid foundation to stand upon amid the quicksand of liberal theology. Charles was rooted and grounded in the truths of the Bible and he was not about to abandon the faith. His long-time mentor, Archibald Alexander, encouraged him in a letter:

> The air which you breathe in Germany will either have a deleterious [harmful] effect on your moral constitution, or else by the strength of faith required to resist its effects your spiritual health will be confirmed. I pray God to keep you from the poison of Neology! I wish you to come home enriched with Biblical learning, but abhorring German philosophy and theology.[9]

In another letter, the college president told him: ". . . it will be worthwhile to have gone to Germany to know that there is but little worth going for."[10]

Charles often found himself standing alone in European classrooms defending biblically faithful theology. Not only was much of the teaching in the universities and churches shifting away from biblical truth, but the educational model in the European universities was quite different than Princeton's. There was no real interest in life application and personal piety in these classes. There was little respect for biblical revelation and God's authoritative truth. Professional scholars taught students that knowledge was in the process of development. Students learned to join in the task of theological innovation and the heresy manufacturing process. This liberal theology disconnected itself from the fixed truths of God's Word, and surrendered itself to constant change and terrible error. Airing his concerns about the European model of education, Charles Hodge summarized what he learned: "Beware of any course of study which has a tendency to harden your hearts and deaden the delicate sensibility of the soul to moral truth and beauty."[11]

Charles returned home to Princeton in 1828. His sojourn in Europe had deepened his convictions concerning the truths of God's Word. He returned to his post as a professor at Princeton and stayed there until the end of his life. From this position, he would influence thousands of students and leave an indelible mark upon the whole American church.

> **The Westminster Standards:** The "Westminster Standards" consist of the Westminster Confession of Faith, the Westminster Larger Catechism, and the Westminster Shorter Catechism. These documents were produced by an assembly of theologians and ministers in the mid-1600s in England. For two centuries these had served as a summary of the faith for the Presbyterian churches in Great Britain and America.

Professor of Theology at Princeton

Charles Hodge was also influential through his theological journals edited and reproduced for American Christian readers. Princeton Theological Seminary served the American Presbyterian church, and this meant that all the faculty were required to subscribe to the Westminster Standards and to teach in agreement with these standards. In a day of theological slippage and apostasy, this was highly significant for the nation.

Over the course of his long professorship at Princeton, Charles Hodge personally taught over 2,700 students. One of his former students, Dr. W.M. Paxton, described what it was like to be in the classroom with Charles Hodge:

> *The first impression which he made upon the student was his deep sincerity. It was his custom to introduce each lecture with a short prayer, which was so simple, so humble, and so manifestly the expression of a heart in close fellowship with God, as*

to impress upon our minds the conviction—This is not a perfunctory professor, but a man of deep experience, who comes to "testify what he knows." The whole spirit and tone of the lecture was such as to deepen this impression. He did not teach a system which he had wrought out, but truths the power of which he had felt in his own soul.[12]

This was a time in which seminaries and colleges like Harvard and Yale were fast turning away from biblical truth. However for the most part, Princeton held fast. One of Charles' most famous sayings about Princeton came at the end of his life as he reflected on decades of teaching: "I am not afraid to say that a new idea never originated in this Seminary."[13] While many seminaries become breeding grounds for new and novel ideas, Charles wanted Princeton to be a place of learning where the deposit of truth was safeguarded and where the authority of God's Word was supreme.

Upon his return from Europe he was appointed professor of theology at Princeton. It was his task to train students to summarize the "whole counsel of God" and to explain how the various truths of Scripture relate to one another. This field is typically referred to as "Systematic Theology." This discipline seeks to show how the teachings of Scripture form a coherent system and how all the truths of Scripture are consistent with one another. Our God is a God of order; therefore the truth of Scripture will not contain contradictions. Though there are mysteries in Scripture that far surpass the ability of humans to comprehend, the Bible is the infallible Word of God, without change, error, or contradiction. It is our responsibility to seek to understand, explain, preach, and defend that truth.

Over his decades of teaching, Charles also wrote many important books that contributed to the edification and instruction of the church. Some of his books were directed toward students of theology, such as his three-volume *Systematic Theology*. But Charles also wrote for the wider church. One of his most popularly accessible books was written at the request of the American Sunday School Union, for the instruction of young people and called *The Way of Life*.

Views on Slavery and the Civil War

I, therefore, the prisoner of the Lord, beseech you to walk worthy of the calling with which you were called, with all lowliness and gentleness, with longsuffering, bearing with one another in love, endeavoring to keep the unity of the Spirit in the bond of peace. There is one body and one Spirit, just as you were called in one hope of your calling . . . (Ephesians 4:1-4)

Charles Hodge was particularly careful to avoid extremes, and he proved himself to be the "man of the middle" on a variety of issues. When it came to controversial matters, Charles looked for that which was true and good about both positions and then he would set forth a reasoned explanation of what he saw to be the right position. This was the case with his treatment of slavery in America. Within his lifetime Charles witnessed not only the fracturing of the nation but also the dividing of the Presbyterian Church over this issue.

Though the conflict between the Northern and Southern states extended far beyond disagreements over slavery, it was one of the primary concerns. Since the church of Jesus Christ exists in the world though "not of it," social and moral issues in society are very much the concern of this body.

Professor Hodge thought it important for Christians to analyze politics, society, and culture by the Word of God. Slavery for him was not just a political matter but also a moral issue to which the Bible directly speaks. He published several essays as the controversy raged through the Presbyterian Church.

As early as 1818, the General Assembly of the Presbyterian Church went on record to declare its opposition to the institution of slavery, calling it "a gross violation of the most precious and sacred rights of nature . . . utterly inconsistent with the law of God . . . totally irreconcilable with the spirit and principles of the Gospel of Christ."[14] Yet, because of disagreements amongst members of the Assembly, in the following decades the Church avoided addressing the matter directly. Some Presbyterians called for an immediate abolition of slavery. Others, such as James H. Thornwell, argued that slavery should be continued and that the Bible did not forbid the practice.

Charles Hodge, however, wanted the institution of slavery abolished. He argued that the practice was a lower form of civilization and he projected that slavery would disappear with advanced forms of social progress. Charles wanted to see a gradual and final end to the institution in America, but he rejected the idea of bringing it about by war and revolution. While he recognized that the Bible allowed for the institution of slavery as long as it was regulated according to just laws, he still did not believe the institution should be perpetual.

Once the Civil War began, Hodge wholeheartedly endorsed the efforts of Abraham Lincoln and the Union North to stop what they considered the rebellion of the Southern states in secession. When the Emancipation Proclamation was issued by Abraham Lincoln, Hodge registered his support for the immediate abolition of slavery.

Despite Charles Hodge's attempts to maintain the unity of the Presbyterian Church through the Civil War, the split took place in December 1861. The General Assembly of the church first met on April 12, 1861 in Philadelphia, the very day the first shots between North and South were fired at Fort Sumter in Charleston, South Carolina. By this time many of the Southern states had already seceded from the Union. What was the Presbyterian Church to do? The Baptists and the Methodists had already divided years earlier.

Charles continued advocating a unity in the church despite the national conflict. Surely, the church, as the family of God, should remain united through national conflicts. In the April 1861 edition of the *Presbyterian Review*, Hodge explained why the church should maintain the unity of the Spirit in the bond of peace:

We are prepared to say, that notwithstanding this deplorable state of things, we are

General Assembly: In Presbyterian churches, the General Assembly refers to a gathering of pastors and elders representing all the churches that form part of the denomination. In most cases, the gathering of the General Assembly occurs once a year. During these meetings pastors and elders report on the work of the churches and make decisions on important matters that affect all the churches.

> *bound to hold together as a church, because the grounds of difference, important as*
> *they are, do not relate to the divinely appointed terms of Christian or ministerial*
> *communion.*[15]

Some Presbyterians wanted all pastors to take an oath of allegiance to
the Union. After five days of heated debate, the General Assembly passed the
following resolution:

> *That this General Assembly, in the spirit of that Christian patriotism which the*
> *Scriptures enjoin, and which has always characterized this church, do hereby*
> *acknowledge and declare our obligation to promote and perpetuate, so far as in us*
> *lies, the integrity of the United States, and to strengthen, uphold, and encourage*
> *the Federal Government in the exercise of all its functions under our Noble*
> *Constitution.*[16]

Charles voted against this resolution. His son A.A. Hodge clarifies the
circumstances of the situation.

> *These resolutions called upon all Presbyterians, ministers and churches subject to*
> *the General Assembly, to support the General Government in the civil war which*
> *had then commenced. The Northern and Southern Presbyterians then constituted*
> *one body. It was evidently proper to exhort the churches in the non-seceding states*
> *to support the government, for that was an acknowledged moral duty. But to*
> *address the same injunction to Southern Presbyterians, was to assume that their*
> *allegiance was primarily due to the General Government and not to their respective*
> *States; and that was to assume that the United States constituted a nation and not*
> *a confederacy; and that assumed a given interpretation of the constitution. As that*
> *was a political question, a large minority of the Assembly, as loyal as the majority,*
> *deemed that no Church court had a right to decide it.*[17]

Charles personally lent his support to the Union cause, but he would not
compromise when it came to the unity of the church. Politics and the secular
debates and divisions were too powerful to retain unity in the church, however.
In December 1861 a group of Southern Presbyterians formed the General
Assembly of the Presbyterian Church of the Confederate States. The two
Presbyterian churches would remain separate until 1983.

Science and Evolution

In November 1859 Charles Darwin's *On the Origin of the Species* was published, a development of seismic importance. Although Darwin was not the first to propose the theory of evolution, he was the most influential popularizer of this scientific and philosophical revolution. Darwin argued that all species evolved through a process of natural selection, without the direct involvement of a Creator. More significantly, he proposed that man had not been created supernaturally as man and woman, Adam and Eve. Rather, he postulated that mankind had evolved over many millennia out of the lower animal kingdom. This radical position was immediately welcomed by the academic world, for this was a world looking for an intellectual means of escaping moral responsibility to a Creator.

Charles Darwin

Between 1860 and 1920, Darwin's book influenced almost every institution in America, including seminary professors, law schools, judges, and American presidents. As modern nations were running away from God, they were looking for an intellectual basis for their apostasy, and Darwin gave them one. The book codified anti-supernatural humanism for the modern world. Darwin's doctrine of evolution quickly became a formidable challenge to the Christian faith in America.

Charles Hodge had a great personal interest in science. As editor of the *Presbyterian Review*, he sought to include a number of scientific articles in the journal that would be of interest to Presbyterian Christians. However, from the outset Charles sought to defend the doctrine of creation against Darwin's theory. In 1874 he wrote a book titled *What is Darwinism?* in which he concludes:

> *What is Darwinism? It is Atheism. This does not mean, as before said, that Mr. Darwin himself and all who adopt his views are atheists; but it means that his theory is atheistic; that the exclusion of design from nature is . . . tantamount to atheism.*[18]

Charles saw right through Darwin's theory, where there was no place allowed for God as designer, creator, or providential sustainer. He wisely foresaw the devastating consequences that Darwin's doctrine of evolution would have upon the Christian faith and the gospel itself. If mankind did not all descend from the first Adam, then how could Christ, the second Adam, overcome the curse of sin and death for mankind through His act of obedience?

> *Therefore, just as through one man sin entered the world, and death through sin, and thus death spread to all men, because all sinned—For until the law sin was in the world, but sin is not imputed when there is no law. Nevertheless death reigned from Adam to Moses, even over those who had not sinned according to the likeness of the transgression of Adam, who is a type of Him who was to come. But the free gift is not like the offense. For if by the one man's offense many died, much more the grace of God and the gift by the grace of the one Man, Jesus Christ, abounded to many. (Romans 5:12-15)*

Even though Charles Hodge rejected Darwinism, he was influenced by the scientific theories associated with it, and he accepted the proposition that the universe and the earth were much older than 6,000 years. Although he recognized that Genesis 1 seemed to teach that the days of creation were ordinary 24-hour days, he attempted to harmonize the Genesis account with the common geological perspective of his day—that the earth had "existed for countless ages."[19]

Charles admitted that it would be "most natural to understand the word ["Day" in Genesis 1] in its ordinary sense; but if that sense brings the Mosaic account into conflict with facts, and another sense avoids such conflict, then it is obligatory on us to adopt that other."[20] He concluded that the days of Genesis 1 should be understood as "indefinite periods of time," adopting the Day-Age view. Thus, the seminary professor surrendered the epistemological authority of the Scripture speaking for itself to accommodate a scientific hypothesis produced by atheists and agnostic scientists. Should the Christian interpret rock layers according to the Scriptural record? Or should the Christian reinterpret the "ordinary sense" of the word "Day" by the latest theories of scientists who are interpreting the data via a biased and wrong worldview perspective? Sadly, Charles Hodge took the latter approach.

In an age of rank apostasy, Charles Hodge was one of the staunchest defenders of biblical truth. He defended biblical teaching against many varied attacks, whether from liberal theology or from science. Yet he failed to recognize that his acceptance of the Day-Age theory of Genesis 1 was unfaithful to the clear teaching of Scripture.

Life Lessons

Charles Hodge is still recognized as holding steadfastly to Christian orthodoxy in a day of severe faith retrograde for American and European Christianity. Surely, it was the grounding he had received from his mother and pastors early on which stood him in good stead for many years. Memorizing the 107 questions of the Westminster Shorter Catechism as a child gave him a good foundation for his future ministry.

> [W]e should no longer be children, tossed to and fro and carried about with every wind of doctrine, by the trickery of men, in the cunning craftiness of deceitful plotting, but, speaking the truth in love, may grow up in all things into Him who is the head—Christ. (Ephesians 4:14-15)

But also, we see in the life of Charles Hodge an example of standing firm on the truth even when academic forces and popular culture are turning away from the truth in increasing numbers. He was firmly committed to the truth of God found in Scripture. Man changes. Societies change. Ideas concerning right and wrong change. But the Word of God never changes. Princeton began teaching a few ideas which were new and contrary to Scripture during Charles Hodge's watch (as for example his views on the age of the earth). Yet as a whole, Princeton Seminary continued to hold fast to the biblical faith in a time of increasing apostasy. Princeton's departure from the faith would not come until the next century.

Jesus Christ is the same yesterday, today, and forever. Do not be carried about with various and strange doctrines. (Hebrews 13:8-9)

George Washington Carver (1864-1943)

CHAPTER 21

George Washington Carver: A Scientist in Awe of God

For You, LORD, have made me glad through Your work; I will triumph in the works of Your hands. O LORD, how great are Your works! Your thoughts are very deep.

—Psalm 92:4-5

George Washington Carver dearly loved the works of God. He saw the fingerprints of the Creator everywhere around him, and he was constantly enthralled. Few scientists have ever enjoyed God's works of nature as much as he did. In many ways George Washington Carver was both the exemplar Christian scientist and the quintessential Christian artist. As he could see the works of God and as he would experience such profound feelings at viewing these mighty works, he was drawn in to study more of these works and find more creative expressions of them through teaching, science, and art. Carver looked at nature as "unlimited broadcasting stations, through which God speaks to us every day, every hour and every moment of our lives."[1] Here was a man who enjoyed the works of God more than anyone else in recorded American history. Truly he was a man who lived in awe of God.

Background

Deliver me, O my God, out of the hand of the wicked, out of the hand of the unrighteous and cruel man. For You are my hope, O Lord GOD; You are my trust from my youth. By You I have been upheld from birth; You are He who took me out of my mother's womb. My praise shall be continually of You. I have become as a wonder to many, but You are my strong refuge. Let my mouth be filled with Your praise and with Your glory all the day. (Psalm 71:4-8)

George Washington Carver was born in the state of Missouri sometime between 1861 and 1863, during the War Between the States. Both Kansas and Missouri were uncommonly dangerous places around the war years. As early as 1856, John Brown raided homes in Pottawatomie Creek, Kansas, killing four men and boys in cold blood. These were the early beginnings of modern terrorism, in which innocent people were killed over political causes. The argument in Kansas and Missouri was over slavery—whether Kansas would allow it or ban it. John Brown's anarchical killings provoked more anarchy from the pro-slavery outlaw bands, and the vicious cycle continued for at least ten years. The pro-slavery outlaws or "bushwhackers" would kidnap slaves or freed slaves in Missouri and Kansas and sell them for profit in other slave states. Meanwhile, the anti-slavery outlaws kidnapped slaves from Missouri and released them in Kansas. Families were hardly secure and safe where there was such little law and order in these western settlements. These were dangerous times.

Moses and Susan Carver lived in Newton County, Missouri, in the very heart of all of this bushwhacking and kidnapping. The couple was childless but they had raised an orphaned niece and two nephews. In 1855 Moses Carver bought a thirteen-year old slave woman named Mary from a neighboring farm. Mary brought with her a son named Jim, and while at the home of the Carvers she bore another son named George. The boy's father was a slave from the neighboring farm who was killed in a tragic farm accident shortly after George was born.

Twice, bushwhackers raided Moses's farm in Newton County. The first time they hung Moses over a fire and tried to force the stubborn farmer to tell them where he hid his money. On the second time, however, they kidnapped little George and his mother. Moses Carver hired a neighbor, a man named Sergeant Bentley, to track down the kidnappers. Immediately Bentley pulled together a small posse of men and they all set out into the night to find George and his mother. The men came upon George in a nearby cabin but they were never able to find Mary. That was the last anyone ever saw of her. Late that night, Bentley brought the infant George to his house and put him in the crib next to his own baby son. Then Moses and Susan Carver decided to bring both George and his older brother Jim into their own home and raised them as their sons.

Throughout his childhood George Carver was sickly and often suffered from bronchitis or whooping cough. His repeated coughing may have affected his vocal cords, as his voice remained high-pitched for his entire life.

God Calls George Carver

Now therefore, thus shall you say to My servant David, "Thus says the LORD of hosts: 'I took you from the sheepfold, from following the sheep, to be ruler over My people, over Israel. And I have been with you wherever you have gone, and have cut off all your enemies from before you, and have made you a great name, like the name of the great men who are on the earth.'" (2 Samuel 7:8-9)

As a little boy, George was fascinated with every square inch of the Carver farm. He collected rocks, planted a flower garden, and developed a knack for nurturing sick plants back to health. His mother would have to check his pockets pretty regularly for frogs and other small animals before he came inside. When he was ten years old, George underwent something of a conversion experience. Later in his life he wrote about it in a letter:

I was just a mere boy when converted, hardly ten years old. There isn't much of a story to it. God just came into my heart one afternoon while I was alone in the loft of our big barn while I was shelling corn to carry to the mill to be ground into meal. A dear little white boy, one of our neighbors, about my age came by one Saturday morning, and in talking and playing he told me he was going to Sunday school tomorrow morning. I was eager to know what a Sunday school was. He said they sang hymns and prayed. I asked him what prayer was and what they said. I do not remember what he said; only remember that as soon as he left I climbed up into the loft, knelt down by the barrel of corn and prayed as best I could. I do not remember what I said. I only recall that I felt so good that I prayed several times before I quit.[2]

Although his parents weren't churchgoers, George found his way to a small country church about a mile from the house, where a Sunday school teacher named Flora Abbot took an interest in him. She helped him memorize Bible verses and learn a few hymns. Meanwhile, Susan Carver homeschooled him using Noah Webster's *Blue Back Speller*. For a while he received some tutoring from an educated black teacher who had moved into the area. It was clear from the outset, that George Washington Carver loved to learn. When the Carvers found a school in nearby Neosho which accepted "colored" students, George was enrolled and boarded with Andrew and Mariah Watkins. While living with this Christian family, George attended church regularly and began to read the Bible. It was Mariah who gave him his first Bible as a Christmas gift, a treasure he would keep with him for the rest of his life.

At thirteen years of age, on December 22, 1876, George graduated from the little primary school in Neosho. He then packed up his Bible and his few belongings and walked seventy-five miles to Fort Scott, Kansas in search of further education. For two years George attended school, providing for the tuition by working as a housekeeper and a cook for a blacksmith in the town.

On March 26, 1879 he witnessed a mob on the street outside of his home, attacking an African American man who was accused of sexually abusing a twelve-year-old white girl. The man, Bill Howard, had already served four years at a Missouri Penitentiary for a similar offense.[3] However, this time a large mob of citizens took justice into their own hands and killed the man. Fearing this mob anarchy, George left town immediately for Olathe, Kansas. There he continued his education, attended the local Methodist church, and taught Sunday school. Soon thereafter George moved 200 miles west to Minneapolis, Kansas, where he started his first business, washing clothes in an old shack in Poverty Gulch.

At nineteen years of age he enrolled in a school at the 8th grade level. Still committed and determined to gain a good education, though older than the rest of the class, George found he fit in alright with the younger folk with his small frame, high voice, and young looks.

Pursuing an Education Against all Odds

Those who hate me without a cause are more than the hairs of my head; they are mighty who would destroy me, being my enemies wrongfully; though I have stolen nothing, I still must restore it . . . But as for me, my prayer is to You, O LORD, in the acceptable time; O God, in the multitude of Your mercy, hear me in the truth of Your salvation. (Psalm 69:4, 13)

In Minneapolis George made a little money in real estate and he joined the Presbyterian church. Around 1885, he applied to Highland College, a Presbyterian school. He received an acceptance letter but, when he showed up for school, the college president took one look at him and said, "You didn't tell me you were a Negro. Highland College does not take Negroes."[4] This news was devastating to George, putting an end to his educational journey for some time. He moved out to Western Kansas and staked a claim on 160 acres, but he was unable to make a go of it. So he sold it and moved to Iowa, where he enrolled in Simpson College. At twenty-seven years of age, George was the only student on campus of African descent. Once again he opened a laundry business to fund his education. Gifted in both artistic talent and science, George signed up for a wide variety of classes including painting and music. He eagerly attended church services and revival meetings, always with a hunger and thirst after the things of God. In a letter to friends, he wrote, "I am learning to trust and realize the blessed result from trusting [God] everyday . . . I realize that God has a great work for me to do."[5]

From Simpson, George transferred to Iowa State College, once again he was the only black enrollee in the school. Nobody seemed to want to bunk with him, so a professor named James Wilson let George sleep in his office. With Professor

Wilson's help, George started three prayer groups on campus, and he continued to develop his artistic talents, even winning national art contests. One of his paintings was displayed at the Chicago World Fair in 1894. Finally, at thirty-one years of age, George obtained his Bachelor's degree in agricultural sciences. He went on to get his Master's degree, and the college offered a well-paying job for him upon his graduation.

However, it was about this time that he received an offer from Booker T. Washington, who was planning an agricultural college at his school in Tuskegee, Alabama. Washington's offer was a lower-paying position, but George was finally persuaded to accept it so as to provide educational opportunities for "my people," as he said.

Booker T. Washington

But take careful heed to do the commandment and the law which Moses the servant of the LORD commanded you, to love the LORD your God, to walk in all His ways, to keep His commandments, to hold fast to Him, and to serve Him with all your heart and with all your soul. (Joshua 22:5)

Born into slavery himself in 1856, Booker T. Washington was slightly older than George Washington Carver. Early on, he was educated using the same *Blue Back Speller* George had used as a child. At sixteen years of age, Booker traveled 500 miles from his home in West Virginia to get an education at Hampton Institute in Virginia. The Institute was formed by the American Missionary Association and was directed by General Samuel Chapman Armstrong, a Presbyterian.

After graduating from Hampton, Booker T. Washington took a job working with General Armstrong to provide a school for Native American Indians. In 1881 Washington moved to Tuskegee, Alabama to help found another college for freed slaves. Within four years, the school counted almost 1,000 students attending. But it wasn't until 1896 that the school received funds to begin an agricultural college.

Booker T. Washington

Washington taught his students to "read the Bible everyday."[6] He wrote, "We must learn to incorporate God's laws into our thoughts and words and acts. Frequent reference is made in the Bible to the freedom that comes from being a Christian. A man is free just in proportion as he learns to live within God's laws . . . As we learn God's laws and grow into His likeness we shall find our reward in this world in a life of usefulness and honor. To do this is to have found the kingdom of God, which is the kingdom of character and righteousness and peace."[7]

George Washington Carver's Contributions to Farming

The works of the LORD are great, studied by all who have pleasure in them. (Psalm 111:2)

Upon his arrival at Tuskegee, George Washington Carver immediately began laboring to create an agricultural program at the Institute. His work was especially useful to small farmers in the South. George would publish an agricultural bulletin which provided ideas for farmers to help them increase yields and save money. For example, he advised mixing wild acorns with corn to feed chickens and cows and he recommended a certain mixture of phosphate and

George Washington Carver with his colleagues at the Tuskegee Institute, 1902

potash to fertilize sweet potatoes. According to his experiments, this fertilizer application increased the yield about fifty-fold! Obviously, farmers were excited to receive these helpful tips from a very practical-minded agricultural scientist.

George Washington Carver and Booker T. Washington did not get along very well at Tuskegee. The problem was mainly a clash of personalities. While Carver was fairly unorganized and sloppily dressed, Washington was more structured and committed to an extremely high level of discipline. Yet, by the mercy of God, the two were somehow able to work together for almost twenty years. Multiple times Carver threatened to resign from the college, but he never quite followed through on his threats. Booker T. Washington traveled internationally and arguably became the most famous man of African descent in the world, yet he lavished praise on his somewhat uncooperative professor of agriculture. In an article he wrote for the *Atlantic Monthly*, Washington wrote, "I have always said that the best means . . . for destroying race prejudice is to make [oneself] a useful, and if possible, an indispensable member of the community in which he lives. I do not know of a better illustration of this than may be found in the case of Professor Carver."[8]

Booker T. Washington's strenuous schedule caught up with him, and he died on November 13, 1915. George Washington Carver's love and respect for Washington was well understood when he turned over $1,000, almost a year's salary, to a memorial fund in honor of his superior at the college.

Carver taught the chemistry and agriculture classes at Tuskegee. He also managed the experimental farming for the school, which included about 170 acres of crops. He even ran the college dairy and poultry business. These ventures not only provided a practical education for the students but also helped to feed them.

Classes at the Tuskegee Institute in 1902

Beginning around 1894, the boll weevil made its way across the Mexican border into the American South. Over the next twenty-five years this little pest devastated the cotton crop. The Tuskegee Institute began offering conferences for farmers during these years, providing them with scientific information and alternative crop ideas. These conferences virtually saved farming in the South in the early 20th century. During the summer months, George traveled in a wagon across the South with the goal of getting more instruction and practical information into the hands of more farmers.

Professor Carver in the Classroom

O LORD, how manifold are Your works! In wisdom You have made them all. The earth is full of Your possessions—this great and wide sea, in which are innumerable teeming things, living things both small and great. (Psalm 104:24-25)

Above all things, George Washington Carver loved God. He loved to speak of the Creator when he taught on the creation. Often his botany lectures appeared more like sermons than lectures. He wasn't afraid to speak of God . . . all the time.

George's classes quickly became the most popular on campus—mainly because he carried with him such a sense of wonder. All of God's creation was exciting to him, and this excitement was contagious. All the world held meaningful and important discoveries for George Washington Carver and any who would seek them out. Out of God's infinite wisdom, He has created a world that is discoverable by those made in His image. He has hid these things in the world for men and women to find out. Since Christians are certain that this creation is not a product of random chance, more than anybody they should be aware of the fact that there are useful scientific breakthroughs in this world, still awaiting discovery. When scientists discover these hidden secrets, they provide helpful solutions to people's problems and more cause to glorify God, the source of all these good things.

It is the glory of God to conceal a matter, but the glory of kings is to search out a matter. (Proverbs 25:2)

More than that, George found nature to be a means by which God communicates to man concerning His own nature. "To me nature in its varied forms are the little windows through which God permits me to commune with him and to see much of his glory, by simply lifting the curtain, and looking in. I love to think of nature as wireless telegraph stations, through which God speaks to us every day, every hour, and every moment of our lives."[9]

Beginning in 1907, George began teaching Bible classes on Sunday evenings at the college, and these continued for several decades. When asked to provide a few words to young men and women in the 1920s, Carver wrote:

> I want them to find Jesus and make Him a daily, hourly, and monthly part of themselves. O how I want them to get the fullest measure of happiness and success out of life. I want them to see the Great Creator in the smallest and apparently the most insignificant things about them.[10]

The secret to George's teaching ability was found in his real-life illustrations. He took his students on walks in the woods. He brought plants into his classroom and described them in artistic language instead of relying on boring scientific terms.

Relationships were important to Carver as well. He tried to learn the history and background of each of his students. He was known to get into play wrestling matches with the young men. Years after the students left Tuskegee, they would receive letters from Professor Carver. Inevitably he would begin these letters with a fatherly tone: "My dear boy . . ."

Carver the Scientist

> You visit the earth and water it, You greatly enrich it; the river of God is full of water; You provide their grain, for so You have prepared it. You water its ridges abundantly, You settle its furrows; You make it soft with showers, You bless its growth. You crown the year with Your goodness, and Your paths drip with abundance. They drop on the pastures of the wilderness, and the little hills rejoice on every side. The pastures are clothed with flocks; the valleys also are covered with grain; they shout for joy, they also sing. (Psalm 65:9-13)

On January 20, 1921 Professor Carver was invited to testify before the United States Congress Ways and Means Committee on the benefits of the peanut. He explained to the most powerful body of governors in the country that peanuts and sweet potatoes were "two of the greatest products God has ever given to us."[11] Then he demonstrated a number of products which he had developed from the peanut. Wrapping up his testimony to the committee, Carver said,

> If you go to the first chapter of Genesis, we can interpret very clearly, I think, what God intended when he said, "Behold I have given you every herb that bears seed upon the face of the earth, and every tree bearing seed. To you it shall be meat" [Gen. 1:29]. That is what he means about it. "It shall be meat." There is everything there to strengthen and nourish and keep the body alive and healthy.[12]

During a period of questioning, the committee chairman asked:

"Dr. Carver, how did you learn all of these things?"

Carver answered: "From an old book."

"What book?" asked the Chairman.

Carver replied, "The Bible."

The Chairman inquired, "Does the Bible tell about peanuts?"

"No, sir," Dr. Carver replied, "but it tells about the God who made the peanut. I asked Him to show me what to do with the peanut, and He did."[13]

Towards the end of his life, Carver developed a treatment for polio using peanut oil. It turned out that the oil was an excellent aid to rebuild muscle tissue for those who were afflicted with this disease. George used this oil to treat a young man named Emmett Cox, Jr. who had suffered from polio since he was two. Within six months of treatment using Carver's peanut oil, Cox was able to walk without braces on his legs. President Franklin D. Roosevelt, himself a victim of the disease, came to visit George Washington Carver in his lab in 1939.

In a letter to Professor Carver, the president said, "I am sure that it helps."[14]

Over the years, Carver developed 265 uses for the peanut and 118 uses for the sweet potato. Although many of his products did not sell well commercially, poor families were able to make use of them during World War I and later during the Great Depression. In the 1920s, George's research saved peanut crops in the South which had been attacked by a certain fungus.

When a British botanist named Sir Harry Johnson met George Washington Carver, he was impressed. Based on the "soundness of his science," Johnson thought Carver could just as well be a professor at Cambridge or Oxford.[15]

George Washington Carver's Faith

Yes, if you cry out for discernment, and lift up your voice for understanding, if you seek her as silver, and search for her as for hidden treasures; then you will understand the fear of the LORD, and find the knowledge of God. For the LORD gives wisdom; from His mouth come knowledge and understanding. (Proverbs 2:3-6)

The turn of the 20th century marked a turning away from God for the university and the scientist in America. Charles Darwin had made his mark, and Europe and America didn't think they needed God anymore. According to the evolutionary theory, God didn't create man but rather humans evolved by chance and appeared on the earth over a period of millions of years. If evolution were true, there was no longer any need to fear God or to obey Him. After all, man did not need God to create him in the first place. And he didn't think he needed God to understand the world and to improve life for himself on the earth.

George Washington Carver's view of science flew smack in the face of this popular evolutionary thinking. In November 1924 George spoke at the Marble Collegiate Church in New York City. It was a speech that would quickly besmirch his reputation with the secular world. He told the crowd, "God is going to reveal things to us that He never revealed before if we put our hands in His . . . Without God to draw aside the curtain I would be helpless."[16]

Although the Christians hearing Carver were very enthusiastic about his talk, the press was appalled by his unscientific language. The *New York Times* published an article chastising George, entitled, "Men of Science Never Talk That Way." The writer accused George of demonstrating "a complete lack of the scientific spirit."[17] The editorial went on to criticize Christianity, establishing a separation between modern science and faith. Shortly thereafter, George wrote an article in response to the attack. He told the world, "I thoroughly understand that there are scientists to whom the world is merely the result of chemical forces or material electrons. I do not belong to this class."[18] He explained that scientific discovery was a combination of information and divine inspiration. He quoted Galatians 1:12, "For I neither received it from man, nor was I taught it, but it came through the revelation of Jesus Christ."

In the following days and weeks, newspapers throughout the country covered the story of Carver's recognition of God and dependence on Him in his science. Much of the coverage was coated in mockery.

Unlike many academics and scientists who give way to pride as if they had obtained the knowledge of the universe all by themselves, George Washington Carver always maintained a humble approach to science. He even went as far as to say, "I didn't make these discoveries. God has only worked through me to reveal to his children some of his wonderful providences."[19] George's favorite story (told in various ways to various audiences) is an exchange between himself and God regarding the mysteries of the peanut.

> Years ago I went into my laboratory and said, "Dear Mr. Creator, please tell me what the universe was made for."
>
> The Great Creator answered, "You want to know too much for that little mind of yours. Ask something more your size, little man."
>
> Then I asked, "Please, Mr. Creator, tell me what man was made for."
>
> Again the Great Creator replied, "You are still asking too much. Cut down on the extent and improve the intent."

So then I asked, "Please, Mr. Creator, will you tell me why the peanut was made?"

"That's better, but even that's infinite. What do you want to know about the peanut?"

"Mr. Creator, can I make milk out of the peanut?"

"What kind of milk do you want? Good Jersey milk or just plain boarding house milk?"

"Good Jersey milk."

And then, the Great Creator taught me to take the peanut apart and put it together again. And out of the process have come forth all these products.[20]

George Washington Carver did not possess a covetous bone in his body. He was generous to a fault, and especially during the Great Depression gave up much of his own finances to "keep the wolf from the door."[21]

At times George turned down gifts of money from the wealthy. Upon receiving one check, he said he knelt down by his bedside and "prayed for light and direction." He explained in a letter to the donor: "I said, 'Oh God. This is your money.' What shall I do with it to bring the greatest return for Him?"[22] So George decided to return the check so that the money could be distributed to others more needy than he.

In his late seventies, George traveled to New York to meet with a publisher who was working on his biography. When he tried to book a room at the New Yorker Hotel, he was at first turned down. The hotel clerk told him to wait in the men's restroom. So for six hours Carver sat quietly waiting for his room. It wasn't until the publisher threatened to sue the hotel that he was finally shown to his room. Ethnic prejudice was to die hard in America in the 20th century.

Nevertheless, George never complained about the hardships he faced as an ethnic minority, nor did he grow bitter or prejudiced himself. He never let oppressive persecution discourage him in his labors. Instead, he pressed on with constant faith, unrelenting diligence, uninhibited joy and gratitude to God, and an unflagging, optimistic, and bold spirit.

Rather, his magnanimous spirit was infectious and contributed positively to reduce ethnic prejudice. A young man once remarked to him, "You are surely making a great contribution to your race, Professor." His response was noteworthy: "My son, I am only God's helper in this work. And I am certain He has not had in mind any particular race, but the needs of all humanity."[23]

End of Life

Towards the end of his life George entered into a close friendship with Henry Ford, the owner of the most successful automobile company in America. He was offered a job with the company at many times the $1,500 annual salary he was paid at Tuskegee. Needless to say he refused the offer. However, he did spend months at Ford's palatial mansion in Detroit, and the carmaker even built a private cabin where the professor could stay on his visits. He also built a school in Georgia for African American children called "The George Washington Carver School."

George Washington Carver died (probably of heart failure) on January 5, 1943. He was somewhere between 80 and 82 years of age. For his funeral, the congregation sang "The Old Rugged Cross" and "My Faith Looks Up to Thee."

Legacy

Then I heard a voice from heaven saying to me, "Write: 'Blessed are the dead which die in the Lord from now on.'" "Yes," says the Spirit, "that they may rest from their labors, and their works follow them." (Revelation 14:13)

Before he died, George left his life savings of $32,374.19 to an endowment fund assigned to carry on his research. In today's money, that would amount to about $500,000—not bad for a man who never earned more than $1,500 per year teaching at Tuskegee.

To better understand the contribution of this godly man of science, it would be helpful to compare the science of George Washington Carver with the science of Charles Darwin. For one thing, Darwin only produced a hypothesis (or guess) about man's origins, which turned out to be wrong. Man did not evolve from an ape or some other matter by a process of natural selection. Darwin's science was also impractical, in that it could not be used for much of anything. Conversely, George Washington Carver's science produced hundreds upon hundreds of various cosmetics, household products, paints, glues, foods, beverages, and medicines.

US World War II Poster featuring George Washington Carver, 1943

George Washington Carver was a truly unusual man. He never let fame get in the way of his commitment to God. From hundreds of testimonies of students, friends, and biographers, what emerges is a portrait of a man who was humble, loving, lovable, generous, hard-working, and instinctively and perpetually creative. He was a true genius. His best friend, Harry Abbott, summarized the character of Carver shortly after his death in these words:

> *I grant without question all the appraisals of your scientific accomplishment. But all that pales into insignificance when compared with your magnificent stature as a simple, lovable, kind-hearted soul, whose very presence is a benediction and whose interest is a blessing.*[24]

> *Though I speak with the tongues of men and of angels, but have not love, I have become sounding brass or a clanging cymbal. And though I have the gift of prophecy, and understand all mysteries and all knowledge, and though I have all faith, so that I could remove mountains, but have not love, I am nothing . . . And now abide faith, hope, love, these three; but the greatest of these is love. (1 Corinthians 13:1-2, 13)*

Dwight L. Moody (1837-1899)

CHAPTER 22

Dwight L. Moody: Evangelist and Entrepreneur

For I am not ashamed of the gospel of Christ, for it is the power of God to salvation for everyone who believes, for the Jew first and also for the Greek. For in it the righteousness of God is revealed from faith to faith; as it is written, "The just shall live by faith."

—Romans 1:16-17

Two world-changing events occurred in 1837. Queen Victoria ascended the British throne and Dwight Lyman Moody was born. These two persons impacted the world in very different ways and they were almost equally famous. Dwight Moody died in 1899, and Queen Victoria in 1901. Today, Moody is remembered for his evangelistic efforts to preach the gospel and make disciples throughout Great Britain and America. Church historian Mark Noll claims that "no evangelist was better known [in the 19th century] than Dwight Lyman Moody."[1] During his lifetime this American evangelist preached the gospel to millions of people, and through the institutions he founded, his influence has reached countless others to the present day.

Dwight L. Moody's humble beginnings would never have suggested such a world-changing impact. What is despised in the eyes of the world, God has the power to use to the maximum benefit of His kingdom. The Lord God raises up one and brings down another, and He sovereignly uses humble people to accomplish His eternal purposes. To this day, Dwight Moody's legacy continues through the Moody Church in Chicago, the Moody Bible Institute, and the numerous other institutions that bear some connection to his life's work.

Early Life in Northfield

For the LORD your God is God of gods and Lord of lords, the great God, mighty and awesome, who shows no partiality nor takes a bribe. He administers justice for the fatherless and the widow, and loves the stranger, giving him food and clothing. (Deuteronomy 10:17-18)

Dwight L. Moody was born on February 5, 1837 to Edwin and Betsy Moody in Northfield, Massachusetts. This would remain his hometown until he died. He was the sixth child in the home, where his father struggled with ongoing problems with drunkenness and financial irresponsibility and debt. Tragedy struck the family on May 28, 1841, when Edwin died of what may have been a heart attack.[2] Dwight was only four years old at the time.

Left a widow with nine young ones, Betsy was instantly confronted with her husband's creditors. Dwight L. Moody later recalled these early memories:

It brings the tears to my eyes every time I think of it . . . My father died before I can remember. There was a large family of us. Twins came after his death. [Now there were] nine of us in all. He died bankrupt, and the creditors came in and took everything – as far as the law allowed. We had a hard struggle. Thank God for my mother! She never lost hope.[3]

Betsy was cruelly treated by Edwin's many creditors. A man named Ezra Purple was particularly unfeeling towards her, bursting into the house while she was still recovering in bed from the birth of twins. Betsy explained that she

Railroad station in Northfield, Massachusetts

didn't have any way to make the payment at the moment, but would follow up with the money later. Biographer Kevin Belmonte adds, "With a severity Scrooge would have admired, Ezra Purple castigated Betsy in coarse language and stormed from the house."[4]

Betsy's brother Cyrus and another brother saved the day, pooled their resources and made the necessary mortgage payment. Cyrus would bring firewood for the family, and a local pastor, Oliver Everett showed the compassion of Christ by providing food and assisting with the education of the Moody children.

> *Pure and undefiled religion before God and the Father is this: to visit orphans and widows in their trouble, and to keep oneself unspotted from the world. (James 1:27)*

Many a great man has a great mother behind him, and Dwight L. Moody was no exception to the rule. A poor woman herself, she was known for taking care of the poor that entered her home. She planted fields. She made her children's clothes, first by spinning the yarn and weaving the cloth. Lacking wood for heat, she would tell the children to stay in bed in the mornings until it was time to leave for school. Dwight L. Moody writes of his mother's charity:

> *There was one time we got down to less than a loaf of bread. Someone came along hungry and she said, "Now children, shall I cut your slices a little thinner, and give some to this person?" And we all voted for her to do it. That is the way she taught us.*[5]

When Betsy died at 91 years of age, her grateful son rose up and called her blessed. He described his mother's simple faith at her funeral:

> *I want to give one verse—her creed. Her creed was very short. Do you know what it was? I will tell you what it was. When everything went against her, this was her stay. "My trust is in God. My trust is in God." And when the neighbors would come in and tell her to bind out her children, she would say, "Not as long as I have these two hands. "Well," they would say, "you know one woman cannot bring up seven boys; they will turn up in jail or with a rope around their necks." She toiled on and none of us went to jail, and none of us had a rope around his neck . . . and if everyone had a mother like that mother . . . there would be no use for jails.*

> *Here is a little book (a little book of devotions); this and the Bible were about all the books she had in those days; and every morning she would stand us up and read out of this book. All through the book I find things marked . . . And on Sunday she always started us off to Sunday School. It was not a debatable question whether we should go or not. All the family attended.*[6]

Pastor Everett continued in the discipleship of the family and baptized all of them in 1842. Dwight began working to support the family while he was still very young. At ten years of age, he took a trip to a nearby town for a temporary job. Here in Greenfield, Massachusetts he met a kind old man who placed a blessing on him.

> *He was a feeble, old, white-haired man, and I was so afraid that he would pass me by that I planted myself directly in his path. As he came up to us, my brother spoke to him, and he stopped and looked at me. "Why I've never seen you before. You must be a new boy," he said. He asked me about my home, and then, laying his trembling*

hand upon my head, he told me that, although I had no earthly father, my Heavenly Father loved me, and then he gave me a bright new cent . . . I don't remember what became of that cent, but that old man's blessing has followed me for over fifty years; and to my dying day I shall feel the kindly pressure of that hand upon my head.[7]

These hardships produced a different upbringing for Dwight L. Moody. He grew up working instead of attending school. His limited education would handicap him a little later on in life. His teenage years were something of a lost opportunity when Pastor Everett moved away and another pastor failed to follow up with the young boy. In fact, the man came across as unfriendly and unloving as Moody later recounts:

I don't know that the new minister ever said a kind thing to me . . . or even once put his hand on my head. I don't know that he ever noticed me, unless it was when I was asleep in the gallery, and he woke me up. That kind of thing won't do; we must make Sunday the most attractive day of the week; not a day to be dreaded, but a day of happiness . . . I used to look upon Sunday with a kind of dread. Very few kind words were associated with that day.[8]

Lacking the discipleship of a father figure in his life, Dwight began to develop ungodly habits. He became prideful and resisted authority, particularly in his schooling. He took on the habit of cursing and frequent fighting with other boys. On one occasion Dwight joined a group of other delinquents in stampeding the cattle of one of his neighbors.[9]

Life in Boston

Then Jesus said to His disciples, "If anyone desires to come after Me, let him deny himself, and take up his cross, and follow Me. For whoever desires to save his life will lose it, but whoever loses his life for My sake will find it." (Matthew 16:24-25)

Discontented in the small town, Dwight L. Moody decided to move to Boston in his seventeenth year. Against his mother's better wishes, he traveled to the big city on 5 dollars he scarfed off his brother.

Upon arriving in Boston in the spring of 1854, Dwight sought out his uncle, Samuel Holton, who was running a successful shoe store in the city. It was a complete surprise for Uncle Samuel to receive this visit from his penniless nephew. Out of pride, Dwight didn't ask for the job hoping his uncle would offer him one right off the bat.

In God's good providence however, another uncle, Lemuel Holton offered a room to the seventeen-year-old boy until he was able to make his own living. Over the next week, Dwight was unsuccessful at finding work, but finally humbled himself and returned to the shoe store to ask for the job. His Uncle Samuel gave it to him on condition that he would submit to Samuel's authority and attend church regularly. This job turned out to be a lifesaver for young Dwight L. Moody, and he was always grateful to his uncle for the opportunity. Later in his life, he would send money when his uncle encountered financial setbacks, one time attaching this note:

> You gave me work & good advice & I look back to that hour as the turning point in my life & I feel as if I owe you a debt I can never pay, so the money I send you is not a loan but a part payment of what I owe you.[10]

Lonely and single in Boston, Dwight decided to join the Young Men's Christian Association (YMCA). Membership in the association cost only $1 per year. But one of the benefits offered was access to a large library. Dwight improved his education there, devouring book after book. He attended church regularly with his Uncle Samuel at Mt. Vernon Congregational Church, but he didn't get much out of the sermons, sometimes falling asleep during the service. However, he did connect with his Sunday school teacher, a man by the name of Edward Kimball. Here Dwight came to a deeper understanding of the Christian faith, but he did everything he could to put off the demands of Christ on his life. He didn't want to be a Christian. Dwight wrote: "I thought I would wait till I died, and then become a Christian. I thought if I had the consumption, or some lingering disease, I would have plenty of time to become one, and in the meantime, I would enjoy the best pleasures of the world."[11]

Nevertheless, Edward Kimball was committed to this young man and deeply hoped for his conversion. One morning, Mr. Kimball decided to confront Dwight and "speak to Moody about Christ, and about his soul."[12] He dropped in at the store, and found Dwight in the back of the store putting shoes on shelves. With tears in his eyes Mr. Kimball told Dwight "of Christ's love for him, and the love Christ wanted in return."[13] Right then and there, Dwight responded to his teacher's fervent, loving appeal and committed himself to following Christ. This turned out to be such an influential moment in Dwight's life and in the history of America that the city of Boston affixed a bronze plaque commemorating the date and location on Court Street. The plaque reads:

D.L. Moody
Christian Evangelist,
Friend of Man,
Founder of the Northfield Schools,
Was Converted to God
In a Shoe Store on
This Site
April 21st, 1855

It was Edward Kimball's heartfelt appeal and direct evangelism that influenced Dwight to become an evangelist. He always remembered the sincere and loving appeal of a friend who brought him to the faith, and he wanted to do the same for others.

Life and Ministry in Chicago

He has shown you, O man, what is good; and what does the LORD require of you but to do justly, to love mercy, and to walk humbly with your God? (Micah 6:8)

Dwight learned something about himself while he worked in Boston for two years: he enjoyed business and he had a gift for doing it well. Because of his successes, the young man was eager to do more in business. He decided to look

Plaque near the old shoe store in Boston, where Dwight L. Moody was converted

for opportunities in Chicago. On September 15, 1856 Dwight purchased a train ticket and departed for the windy city.

Chicago was a booming town in the 1850s. In that decade, Chicago's population grew from 30,000 to 109,000.[14] Business and industry were on the rise, and Dwight could see this was the place for anybody who wanted to grow rich. Yet still, he did not forget what God had done for him through the influence of Edward Kimball. While he pursued business, Dwight L. Moody began evangelizing on the streets of Chicago. He would "hail young men on the street corners, visit their boarding-houses, or even call them out of saloons."[15]

About this time, Dwight started up a small Sunday school for rough-hewn boys off the street. Because of his own difficult upbringing, he could relate to the fatherless boys growing up in the city. He would invite them to attend his Sunday school, where he would provide food and clothing, and share the gospel. Out of this early ministry came a mission school for needy boys in Chicago's North Market Hall. The school eventually expanded to accommodate over 1,500 children.

It wasn't long before news about this very active ministry was broadcast about the city and the nation. Shortly after the 1860 election, Abraham Lincoln visited Chicago and even addressed an audience at Dwight L. Moody's Sunday school.

As the American Civil War broke out, Chicago was mobilized for the Union cause. Dwight L. Moody strongly opposed slavery, and he was firmly committed to the Union cause. However, he was conscientiously opposed to military service, unwilling to ever use a weapon against a fellow human being—in his words, "in this respect I am a Quaker."[16] Nonetheless, he still wanted to be involved in some way with the war effort so he worked with the YMCA throughout the war years. While providing material relief to men on the frontlines, Dwight was also able to share the gospel with the sick and the dying. He went to the frontlines of battle at least nine times during the Civil War. This experience, according to biographer Kevin Belmonte, "brought a sad and singular wisdom to his heart."[17]

While serving with the YMCA, Dwight married a nineteen-year-old young lady named Emma Revell. Dwight had first met her shortly after he arrived in

Chicago, and over four years they developed a relationship. Shortly after their engagement, Dwight demonstrated his characteristic impulsiveness when he stood up after a church service and announced to the whole congregation that he was now engaged "to Miss Emma Revell and therefore [I] cannot be depended upon to see the other girls home from meeting."[18] Dwight and Emma married in 1860.

Through the 1860s, God blessed Dwight L. Moody with a great deal of success in business. He built up substantial wealth through various entrepreneurial endeavors in Chicago. The tension between business and ministry only heightened as the years went by, and it became increasingly difficult to focus on both at the same time. Finally, the day came when a decision had to be made. He later confessed, "The greatest struggle I ever had in my life was when I gave up business."[19] The catalyst that brought him to this decision was the day he came to minister at the bedside of a dying friend. Eternal matters became more critical in his mind than the temporal, and he realized that he must from here on out focus on full-time evangelistic ministry. His business skills did not go to waste though, as he would find great opportunity to employ them throughout his future ministries.

The Great Chicago Fire of 1871

If a trumpet is blown in a city, will not the people be afraid?
If there is calamity in a city, will not the LORD have done it? (Amos 3:6)

Throughout the 1860s, Dwight L. Moody was becoming better known in Chicago as a preacher, evangelist, and Sunday school teacher. He founded Moody Church in 1864 and helped raise funds for various YMCA efforts and church building projects. It was at a Sunday school convention in June 1871 where Dwight met Ira Sankey, a talented gospel singer. Shortly afterward, Dwight and Ira began to collaborate in evangelistic meetings. Dwight would preach and Ira would sing. Then they would invite sinners to believe in the Lord Jesus Christ and receive God's forgiveness for sins.

On Sunday night, October 8, 1871, a small farm fire broke out and it quickly grew into a gigantic conflagration, destroying a large part of Chicago. Dwight was preaching that evening in Farwell Hall, a facility of the YMCA. As the fire continued to spread, he kept preaching. Ira Sankey later recalled his experiences that night:

Mr. Moody asked me to sing a solo . . . Standing by the great organ at the rear of the platform I began the old, familiar hymn, "Today the Savior Calls." By the time I had reached the third verse, my voice was drowned by the loud noise of the fire engines rushing past the hall, and the tolling of bells . . . we could hear . . . the deep, sullen tones of the great city bell, in the steeple of the old court house . . . ringing out a general alarm.[20]

After the service, Dwight rushed home just in time to save the family and a number of the family's valuables. The parents dressed their children, grabbed a few possessions, and fled as the flames engulfed their home. By the mercies of

The Great Fire of Chicago, 1871

God, the entire Moody family was safe, but the loss of homes and businesses in Chicago was devastating. The fire destroyed over 17,000 structures including the Moody Church building, and killed around 300 people. Not to be daunted by these setbacks, Dwight immediately returned to the task of fundraising and rebuilding the Christian churches and organizations that were lost in the fire.

An Expanding Mission to America and Great Britain

The prayer of a righteous person has great power as it is working. Elijah was a man with a nature like ours, and he prayed fervently that it might not rain, and for three years and six months it did not rain on the earth. Then he prayed again, and heaven gave rain, and the earth bore its fruit. (James 5:16b-18 ESV)

Over the previous years, Dwight L. Moody had developed close relationships with the leading evangelical pastors in England including Charles H. Spurgeon and G. Campbell Morgan. In 1872, he took his family to England, hoping to learn from these brothers and witness firsthand what the Lord was doing in the British Isles. What initially began as a study visit turned into a preaching tour as Moody quickly received invitations from English pastors to fill their pulpits.

His first preaching invitation came from Pastor John Lessey in a North London church. He was reluctant to accept it at first, but eventually agreed to preach for the morning and evening Sunday service. It was during the evening service that a tremendous spiritual interest became visible. People crowded into the "inquiry room" to speak with Dwight and Pastor Lessey about the condition of their souls.

The next day Moody sailed to Ireland, but while he was there Pastor Lessey sent a message, requesting him to return to London for more spiritual work there. Upon his return to London, he ministered for ten full days, during which time over four hundred people made professions of faith and joined Pastor Lessey's church. Astonished at this response to the gospel, Dwight wondered whether someone had prayed for such an outpouring of the Spirit. "I wanted to know what this meant. I began making inquiries."[21] He came to find out that there was a certain woman from Pastor Lessey's congregation named Marianne Adlard. Bedridden for a very long time, this woman of God had spent many hours each day in prayer that the Lord would send revival to the congregation. When she had heard of Dwight Moody's work in America, she simply prayed "O Lord, send this man to our church."[22] When Dwight learned of this, he was convinced that it was these prayers that brought him to minister in Great Britain at just the right time. In his words, "[God] had heard her, and [He] brought me over four thousand miles of land and sea in answer to her request."[23]

As Dwight traveled through Great Britain, he received one invitation after another to preach in Anglican, Presbyterian, and Baptist churches. A great spiritual interest in the things of God was sweeping through the nation. Convinced that there was a great harvest ready in the British Isles, Dwight returned to Chicago and recruited Ira Sankey for a return trip to Britain. Between 1873 and 1875, they conducted an evangelistic tour that brought about a great spiritual harvest.

Biographer Lyle Dorsett explains, "It is sometimes said that Moody and Sankey brought revival to the United Kingdom. It is more accurate to say that they were mightily instrumental in helping turn an already existing small flame into a raging fire."[24] Whatever lasting spiritual fruit came from the ministry of Dwight Moody and Ira Sankey was the work of God. He uses humble instruments in His hands to save sinners, but those instruments themselves are only effective when the Spirit of God is at work changing hearts along the way.

> But as many as received Him, to them He gave the right to become children of God, to those who believe in His name: **who were born, not of blood, nor of the will of the flesh, nor of the will of man, but of God.** (John 1:12-13, emphasis added)

Together, Dwight and Ira ministered to hundreds of thousands of people throughout the British Isles. As people listened to Dwight preach, they heard a simple message, filled with illustrations, easily understood by the common person, and earnest in appeal. Dwight's sermons were simple, and he organized most of his teaching around what he called "the three R's"—"Ruin by sin, Redemption by Christ, and Regeneration by the Holy Ghost."[25] His gift was discovered in the presentation of a simple and clear gospel message. He rarely talked about other doctrines of the faith in public preaching, but rather believed it was his primary gifting to call men and women to faith in Jesus Christ. Although, he would on occasion speak about the new life that a disciple of Jesus ought to live, and he urged those who became converted to join a local church and participate in the body life of the church.[26] Dwight wrote, "It is not only a duty but a glorious privilege to be in the bosom of some church."[27]

Founder of Schools

Come, you children, listen to me;
I will teach you the fear of the LORD.
Who is the man who desires life,
And loves many days, that he may see good?
Keep your tongue from evil,
And your lips from speaking deceit.
Depart from evil and do good;
Seek peace and pursue it. (Psalm 34:11-14)

Moody finally decided to return to his hometown of Northfield, Massachusetts in 1876. He would continue to visit Chicago for the rest of his life to oversee the churches and institutions he had helped form, including Moody Bible Institute. Northfield remained his "home base" while he would take up preaching opportunities throughout America and around the world.

Recalling his own challenging upbringing in Northfield, Dwight felt a burden for the children of his hometown who faced similar trials. He wanted to provide a Christian education for the youth. In 1879 Dwight founded Northfield Seminary, a school for girls. He explained his purpose: "The Lord laid it upon my heart some time ago to organize a school for young women in the humbler walks of life, who never would get a Christian education, but for a school like this."[28] At its initiation ceremony, Moody offered up this prayer to God on behalf of the school:

> *O Lord, we pray that no teacher may ever come within its walls, except as they have been taught by the Holy Spirit; that no scholars may ever come here, except as the Spirit of God shall touch their hearts. O God, we are Thine; this building is Thine! We give it over to Thee. Take it, and keep, and bless it, with Thy keeping power.*[29]

After this, he set out to establish a similar school for boys and in 1881, the Mount Hermon School was opened four miles from Northfield Seminary. The school's format would be unique: the boys would both study and work. Mount Hermon would be a place where underprivileged boys could receive a basic education, learn the Christian faith through their studies, and gain practical work skills.

In an amazing turn of God's providence, the school was built on land once owned by the Moody family's old miserly landlord Ezra Purple. Before the building commenced, Dwight took a group of his friends to the land and they prayed for God's blessings upon the work. There he told them of the story of "old man Purple"[30] and how this miser had acted so mercilessly towards his family in their time of need. Years ago, as he gained success in business himself, Dwight had committed himself to purchase the land one day, and now he thanked God that "instead of owning the farm itself, he could lay it at the feet of the Saviour."[31]

God's Merciful Deliverance at Sea

> *Those who go down to the sea in ships,*
> *Who do business on great waters,*
> *They see the works of the LORD,*
> *And His wonders in the deep. (Psalm 107:23-24)*

The Word of God tells us that we ought not to forget "all His benefits" (Ps. 103:2) because it is the Lord who "redeems our life from destruction" (Ps. 103:4). These consoling truths came home with great force upon Dwight L. Moody as he was delivered from the jaws of death in November 1892.

Having spent some time preaching in Great Britain, he was on board the SS *Spree* heading home to New York City. After three days at sea, the passengers heard "a terrible crash and shock."[32] Dwight's son Will rushed out to discover the reason for the interruption and returned with the dire news that the propeller shaft of the ship was broken and the ship was about to sink. The crew of the *Spree* did everything they could to save the ship, but it seemed a lost cause. Moody recounted, "We were utterly, absolutely helpless . . . We could only stand still on the poor, drifting, sinking ship, and look into our watery graves."[33]

For an entire day, Dwight L. Moody and the other passengers waited in suspense as the captain and crew deliberated on a solution. No one slept very well that night. On the following day Dwight organized a prayer meeting to beseech the Lord for deliverance. In the midst of such dire circumstances, "everybody prayed."[34] As the ship rocked back and forth, Dwight read aloud from Psalm 91 and Psalm 107.

> *For He shall give His angels charge over you, to keep you in all your ways. (Psalm 91:11)*

After the prayer meeting, the ship continued its slow descent into the ocean while the seven hundred passengers went to sleep. Around 3 a.m. the next morning Dwight was awakened by his son Will calling him to come out on deck. There shining through the night sky over the Atlantic came a light—another ship approaching. It was the *Lake Huron*. Evidently, the crew had seen the rockets shot off from the *Spree* and had come to rescue the helpless passengers. Over the next eight days, the *Lake Huron* towed the *Spree* back to Ireland. Though the New York City newspapers ridiculed him for it, Dwight testified that God had delivered the ship in answer to prayer. It was God who answered by delivering the passengers from the jaws of death.

Moody confessed later that this life-changing trial worked steadfastness in him unlike anything he had ever experienced before. Though he felt like "it was the darkest hour of my life,"[35] yet he was firmly convinced of God's sovereign care in that moment. He explained, "God heard my cry, and enabled me to say, from the depth of my soul: 'Thy will be done!' Sweet peace came to my heart. Let it be 'Northfield or Heaven,' it made no difference now."[36]

The World Fair of 1893

Then the master said to the servant, "Go out into the highways and hedges, and compel them to come in, that my house may be filled." (Luke 14:23)

Between May 1 and October 30, 1893, over 27 million visitors from all over the world passed through Chicago to visit the World Fair. Dwight saw this historic event as a once-in-a-lifetime evangelistic opportunity. Over the years he had built many relationships with Christian organizations, churches, and individuals throughout the United States. Taking advantage of these connections, he worked with numerous volunteer secretaries to write appeals for funds for a massive evangelistic campaign in Chicago that would continue throughout the entire six-month fair. Dwight estimated that daily expenses would run about $20,000 for a total of $3.8 million (in modern-day money) to bring about what he envisioned.[37]

The Chicago World Fair, 1893

Services were hosted in local churches and within the various tents and facilities used for the World Fair. Dwight was willing to take any and every opportunity to preach the gospel. He wanted the good news to reach every person who came through the fair. He even made use of the rodeo space "Tattersall's Hall" and the giant tents of "Forespaugh's Circus." As many as 10,000 to 20,000 people gathered for Sunday morning services in the tent, and a grand total of 2 million people attended these evangelistic campaign efforts at the 1893 World Fair.[38]

Final Campaign

I have fought the good fight, I have finished the race, I have kept the faith. Finally, there is laid up for me the crown of righteousness, which the Lord, the righteous Judge, will give to me on that Day, and not to me only but also to all who have loved His appearing. (2 Timothy 4:7-8)

Though Dwight outlived his dear friend and fellow preacher Charles H. Spurgeon by about six years, he also died at the relatively young age of 62. In his last five years of life, Dwight continued traveling, preaching, and writing, but he would spend increasing lengths of time at home in Northfield. In 1894 he and Emma were delighted to see their two oldest children married and grandchildren soon followed.

By 1899, Dwight's health began to decline. Late in the year, he embarked on another evangelistic campaign in the western United States, culminating with a week of meetings in Kansas City, Missouri towards the middle of November. The meetings were well attended, and Dwight preached on the hope of heaven:

We say this is the land of the living! It is not. It is the land of the dying. What is our life here but a vapor? . . . But look at the other world. No death, no pain, no sorrow, no old age, no sickness, no bending forms, no dimmed eyes, no tears. But joy, peace, love, happiness . . . Think of it! Life! Life! Life without end! And yet so many choose this life on earth, instead of the life in Heaven. Don't close your heart against eternal life. Only take the gift, only take it.[39]

On Friday night, November 16, Dwight preached his final sermon. After the message he collapsed, utterly exhausted. A doctor was called, and he advised that the worn evangelist return home immediately to rest. Two days later Dwight arrived at the train station near Northfield. In the weeks that followed, his health continued to decline. As the end approached, he testified to his family, "This is my triumph; this is my coronation day! I have been looking forward to it for years."[40] And on Friday, December 22, 1899, Dwight L. Moody entered eternity.

Some years before his death, Dwight recorded the message he wanted others to hear on the day he died, in hope they might be prepared for that great day:

Some day you will read in the papers that D.L. Moody, of East Northfield, is dead. Don't you believe a word of it! At that moment I shall be more alive than I am now. I shall have gone up higher, that is all – out of this old clay tenement into a house that is immortal; a body death cannot touch, that sin cannot taint, a body fashioned like unto His glorious body. I was born of the flesh in 1837. I was born of the Spirit in 1856. That which is born of the flesh may die. That which is born of the Spirit will live forever.[41]

William McKinley (1843-1901)

CHAPTER 23

William McKinley: Humble President, Faithful Husband

By humility and the fear of the LORD
Are riches and honor and life.

—Proverbs 22:4

A t the turn of the 20th century, America's place in the world was about to change dramatically. The United States would come to fill a much larger role in world politics. And God, who raises up rulers and bring others down, chose to call a humble Christian believer to center stage at this key moment in American history. Though he would take a position of power and greatness, William McKinley demonstrated a humility unlike many other American presidents. Few were so outspoken about their trust in God or relied upon God so much for guidance. McKinley is also known for his great care for his infirm wife over several decades even as he carried on with his weighty responsibilities as an American leader. He was a man of the Word and prayer. He once remarked, "The greatest discovery a man or a nation can make, is to find the truth of God's Word."[1] He also testified that, "I pray to God every day to give me strength to do this work."[2] As he reached the heights of fame and political position, President McKinley never slackened in his commitment to seek the face of the Lord.

Childhood Years and Military Service

Again, the kingdom of heaven is like a merchant seeking beautiful pearls, who, when he had found one pearl of great price, went and sold all that he had and bought it. (Matthew 13:45-46)

William McKinley was born on January 29, 1843. When he was nine years old, his family settled in Poland, Ohio and it was at the Methodist church where William professed faith in Christ. As a twelve-year-old little boy, he confessed that, "I have sinned. I want to be a Christian. I give myself to the Savior who has done so much for me. I have found the pearl of great price."[3] From that point on, William walked with the Lord, continuing in the diligent study of the Scriptures, earnestly seeking God in prayer, and assembling with God's people for worship. Unlike many US presidents, William McKinley would not allow the responsibilities of the presidency to interfere with his devotion to the Lord.

At age seventeen, William entered Allegheny College in Pennsylvania after which he returned to Ohio to work as a school teacher earning a meager $25 a month.[4] When the Civil War broke out, William quickly enlisted to fight for the Union cause, on June 11, 1861. He was personally committed to putting an end to slavery in the American South. During the War, William served alongside his superior officer, Rutherford B. Hayes, who would later become the 19th president of the United States (in 1877).

His military service in the Civil War were important years of personal growth. The war produced untold human suffering and exposed much of the evils of the human heart. Nevertheless, many men came to saving faith in the Lord Jesus Christ through the faithful efforts of pastors and evangelists by the preaching of the Word. Young William McKinley participated in numerous prayer meetings with his fellow soldiers. He wrote in his diary of his commitment to serve the Lord first and foremost, and his hope in Christ:

> Should this be my fate I fall in a good cause and hope to fall in the arms of my blessed redeemer. This record I want to be left behind, that I not only fell as a soldier for my Country, but also as a soldier of Jesus . . . In this emergency let . . . my parents, brothers and sisters, and friends have their anxiety removed by the thought that I am in the discharge of my duty, that I am doing nothing but [that which] my revolutionary fathers before me have done, and also let them be consoled with the solacing thought that if we never meet again on earth, we will meet around God's throne in heaven.[5]

McKinley's mentor and later President, Rutherford B. Hayes

The war experience shaped his abilities in administration, leadership, and courageous and wise risk-taking, a preparation that would stand him in good stead for his later service for his country.

Marriage to Ida, Family Afflictions, and First Years in Politics

It is good for me that I have been afflicted, that I may learn Your statutes. (Psalm 119:71)

As the War ended, young William McKinley returned home to Ohio and began preparations for a legal career by enrolling at the Albany Law School in New York. After a year of study, he returned to Ohio, and passed his legal exam in 1867. While he did faithfully participate in the ministry of his local Methodist church and in Christian service at the local YMCA, he also joined the local Masonic lodge.[6] Membership with the Freemasons was an all-too-common inconsistency for Christians in the 19th century.

William McKinley established his legal office in Canton, Ohio, and it wasn't long before he had built a reputation of consistent, principled integrity, earning the respect of his community. Though he was first committed to a career in law, he always had his sights set on state and national politics. His goal was to gain a seat in Congress as a member of the US House of Representatives. Four years into his law work, William had established himself well, earning a solid income of $10,000 a year.[7]

Following the war, William met his wife Ida, daughter of the wealthy businessman James Saxton, who made his wealth through banking, mining, and other business efforts. This was one of the wealthiest families in Canton. In the fall of 1870 William proposed marriage to Ida and, with her father's blessing, they were married. Within two years, the couple were blessed with two daughters—Katie and Ida. However, God humbled the family with several difficult providences in the wake of these births. Mrs. McKinley's mother died of cancer, and soon afterwards, Baby Ida passed away at the tender age of five months. Then, Mother Ida suffered a fall which left her

Ida Saxton McKinley

bedridden for months; and she began to suffer from epileptic seizures. She would face this medical condition for the rest of her life, and this would come to define the political life of the McKinley family. The condition of epilepsy was poorly understood at the end of the 19th century. Many considered such a condition a sign of mental instability or insanity, and this public perception would press William McKinley towards concealing Ida's struggles from the public for most of his years of national service.

Even as Ida was suffering with her own health challenges, four-year-old Katie also died of scarlet fever. A dark cloud of despair seemed to descend over the McKinley home. For a time Ida refused to eat. Nevertheless, through each and all of these agonizing afflictions, William patiently encouraged his wife towards faith and hope. In time Ida emerged out of her bout with depression and despair.

William's political aspirations to serve in Congress came to fruition when he was elected in October 1877 to represent Ohio's seventeenth congressional district. Over time his political influence grew, but he was always careful to attend to his wife's needs the whole time he served in Washington.

During his years as a congressman, William became known as a "Protectionist" because he advocated raising tariff rates. He believed this would boost the strength of the economy and protect American businesses. The Republicans also found this to be a good way to increase the budgets and the power of the federal government. This was in contrast with those in the Democratic Party such as Grover Cleveland, who were committed to free trade and smaller government at this time.[8]

Having served in Congress for four years, William McKinley ran for governor of the state of Ohio in the 1891 election. He was elected the 39th governor of Ohio, and was inaugurated on January 11, 1892. Mr. and Mrs. McKinley moved into the Chittenden Hotel, directly across from the state capitol

> **Protectionist:** A Protectionist is primarily interested in raising taxes on goods imported into a country. This is intended to protect the country's businesses against competition from foreign products.

building in Columbus. It was a strategic location, in that William McKinley could visually communicate with Ida at a set time twice a day from the front steps of the capitol building. Each morning he would walk to the capitol and before entering the building wave his hat towards the hotel window. Ida would wave a handkerchief back at him, and then again at 3 p.m., he would step outside and repeat the ritual. Many Ohioans were touched by William's show of affection and devotion to his wife.

"Husbands, love your wives, just as Christ also loved the church and gave himself for her." (Ephesians 5:25)

First Presidential Term

Now give me wisdom and knowledge, that I may go out and come in before this people; for who can judge this great people of Yours? (2 Chronicles 1:10)

With the encouragement of his friend and close advisor, Ohio businessman Mark Hanna, William McKinley began to set his sights on the US presidency. At the Republican National Convention of 1896, he won the Republican nomination. However, at this point in his political career he faced something of a challenge. Candidates for the presidential office were expected to conduct an aggressive campaign by traveling through the country meeting with groups of Americans, giving speeches, and interviewing with local newspapers. This William McKinley could not do, given his need to care for Ida with her medical condition. So instead, he conducted what became known as the "front porch campaign," where he invited the nation to visit him at his home in Canton, Ohio. An astounding 750,000 Americans came to visit the McKinley home from all over the country during the campaign.

In the providence of God, William McKinley won the general election against his Democratic rival William Jennings Bryan, securing 51% of the popular vote. As he took the oath of office on March 4, 1897, William McKinley placed his hand on 2 Chronicles 1:10, in which Solomon asks for wisdom to rule the people of God.[9]

Once again, his allegiance to his wife was tested during the inaugural ball—a celebration conducted in his honor. Ida experienced an epileptic seizure during the festivities. Immediately, William McKinley, the president of the United States took his wife home with him, and remained there by her side as the band played on. Ida was often temperamental and easily irritated throughout his presidential term. In spite of her physical and emotional challenges, William continued to patiently love and care for her through it all.

> *Husbands, likewise dwell with your wives with understanding, giving honor to the wife, as to the weaker vessel, and as being heirs together of the grace of life, that your prayers be not hindered. (1 Peter 3:7)*

The Spanish-American War

> *Woe is me, that I dwell in Meshech, that I dwell among the tents of Kedar! My soul has dwelt too long with one who hates peace. I am for peace; but when I speak, they are for war. (Psalm 120:5-7)*

As William McKinley took the office of president, the United States was feeling its economic and political strength in the world arena. Now this burgeoning young nation was in a position to compete with the great powers of Europe, such as the old decrepit Spanish empire. The sovereign God over all the kings of the earth had blessed the nation with riches, honor, and power, and America was about to reach its zenith over the next fifty years. Thus, the temptation to imperialism was strong. As our Lord Jesus warned us, "Gentile leaders" always tend to lord it over their constituents (Matt. 20:25).

President William McKinley found himself right at the center of these debates over imperialism. Initially, he spoke against foreign intervention and imperial domination. In some ways, he moderated America's approach but the temptation to "rule the world" was very strong. The president quickly capitulated to the American businessmen who had wrested control of the Hawaiian Islands from Queen Liliuokalani (1838-1917). Earlier in 1893, American troops had backed the revolution started up by the American financiers against the Hawaiian queen. Hawaii was finally annexed as a United States territory in 1898.

> **Imperialism:** Imperialism is a foreign policy that involves extending a country's power and influence, especially over other countries, either through diplomacy or by military force.

The primary event which would come to define William McKinley's presidency was the Spanish-American War. Over the previous fifty years, Cuban revolutionaries had attempted to overthrow their Spanish rulers on several occasions. Americans generally considered the continued presence of Spain in Cuba a danger to the United States and an act of oppression against the Cuban people. In 1896, General Valeriano Weyler, a military hero and former governor of several Spanish colonies, was sent by Spain to put down the rebellion in Cuba. He opened concentration camps on the principle that the rebels, with their hit-and-run tactics, could only be stopped by separating them from the rest of the Cuban people. However, many thousands died in the camps, as the Cuban revolutionaries continued their campaign against the Spanish. Diplomatic pressure from the United States resulted in General Weyler's recall to Spain in 1897. The Cubans' desire for independence and the American sympathy for the rebels eventually resulted in the tragic Spanish-American War. The anti-interventionism of John Quincy Adams and James Monroe was quickly dissipating.

In his inaugural address to the nation on March 4, 1897, President William McKinley had announced, "We want no wars of conquest; we must avoid the temptation of territorial aggression."[10] But the political pressure and temptations were too strong to resist. By the end of 1897 it became clear that Americans were looking for a war with Spain over Cuba. All that was required for a war between the nations was a "trigger" event that would justify immediate military action. In God's providence, an incident occurred that did provide adequate justification for the American public.

On February 15, 1898, an explosion on the Battleship USS *Maine* sitting at harbor in Santiago, Cuba, killed more than six hundred US sailors and sank the ship. The American press quickly jumped to the conclusion that the explosion was caused by an intentionally planted Spanish mine and should be considered an act of war. Spanish engineers disputed this conclusion and determined the blast was "outward," indicating the explosion of powder came from within the ship. On the other hand, American investigators claimed the blast was "inward," indicating an attack from outside.

While the President of the United States met with the cabinet to determine the proper response, Assistant Secretary of the Navy Theodore Roosevelt ordered the American Asiatic fleet to Manila Bay in the Philippines. His concern was that in case of war America would want to keep European navies from seizing control of that Spanish colony. President McKinley presented a list of demands to Spain, but the Spanish government was unwilling to comply.

The Republican Party, numerous journalists, and important church leaders were calling for "a righteous crusade against Spain on behalf of humanity, democracy, and Christian progress,"[11] and this was enough to persuade the President to act. On April 11, 1898, President McKinley's appeal to Congress for a declaration of war was granted and Congress declared war against Spain by a vote of 311-6.

Eager to participate in the glory of battle himself, Theodore Roosevelt helped raise a regiment of cavalry in San Antonio, Texas called the "Rough Riders." On July 1, 1898, Roosevelt led his regiment to victory at the Battle of San Juan Hill outside Santiago, Cuba. Roosevelt himself wrote what became a best-selling book entitled *The Rough Riders* in which he recorded the battle that came to symbolize the Spanish-American War. The Americans won every battle in this war against the undermanned and out-gunned Spaniards in Cuba and the Philippines. Only about 300 Americans died in battle, but more than 2,000 died of disease, mostly yellow fever. The Spaniards lost about 1,000 in battle and more than 15,000 by disease.

According to the terms of the peace treaty, the United States acquired Guam, Puerto Rico, and the Philippines (for a price of $20 million). Congress then passed the "Teller Amendment" promising the Cubans their independence and American withdrawal of troops. The Filipinos were also promised independence (when the American government deemed them ready for it). But between 1899 and 1902 the United States fought a vicious and costly war with the Filipinos who were seeking a more immediate independence. Tens of thousands of combatants died in the ensuing conflicts along with more than 100,000 civilians. The acquisition of the Philippines was costly for both countries. The Philippines would not receive their independence until 1946, after the conclusion of World War II.

President William McKinley spoke of how God directed him towards moving ahead with the annexation of the Philippines. In his words:

Roosevelt's Rough Riders

The Battle of San Juan Hill, 1898

I walked the floor of the White House night after night until midnight; and I am not ashamed to tell you, gentlemen, that I went down on my knees and prayed Almighty God for light and guidance more than one night. And one night late it came to me this way—I don't know how it was, but it came: (1) That we could not give them back to Spain—that would be cowardly and dishonorable; (2) that we could not turn them over to France and Germany—our commercial rivals in the Orient—that would be bad business and discreditable; (3) that we could not leave them to themselves—they were unfit for self-government—and they would soon have anarchy and misrule over there worse than Spain's was; and (4) that there was nothing left for us to do but to take them all, and to educate the Filipinos, and uplift and civilize and Christianize them, and by God's grace do the very best we could

by them, as our fellow-men for whom Christ also died. And then I went to bed, and
went to sleep, and slept soundly, and the next morning I sent for the chief engineer
of the War Department (our map-maker), and I told him to put the Philippines on
the map of the United States (pointing to a large map on the wall of his office), and
there they are, and there they will stay while I am President![12]

What President McKinley may not have realized was that the Christianization of the Philippines was more dependent on how many gospel-preaching missionaries actually reached the Filipinos rather than on how the American government intervened in their civil affairs. It turned out that the role of the American government was very small when it came to this "Christianizing" process.

Nonetheless, the United States' mission agencies did send Protestant missionaries into the Philippines following the war. After the first Protestant service was conducted in the Philippines on August 28, 1898, missionaries flooded into the country from Presbyterian, Methodist, Baptist, Congregationalist, Brethren, and Christian and Missionary Alliance denominations. By the year 2010, Protestants made up about 8% of the Filipino population, or roughly 8,000,000 souls. On July 4, 1946, America granted the Philippines complete independence to govern themselves. The acquisition of the Philippines during the presidency of William McKinley began a major shift in American foreign policy that would lay the foundation for future military and political interventions into foreign nations throughout the 20th century.

President McKinley's Second Term and Assassination

Daniel answered and said: "Blessed be the Name of God forever and ever, for
wisdom and might are His. And He changes the times and the seasons; he removes
kings and raises up kings . . . " (Daniel 2:20-21)

God raises up leaders and He brings them down, including those who rule the most powerful nations in the world. This is the lesson learned by Kings Nebuchadnezzar and Belshazzar in Daniel chapters four and five. Such is the case with every nation and every leader in every era of world governance.

After a popular reelection for a second presidential term, William McKinley had achieved the height of his popularity and the most powerful position over the country. His firm hand of leadership through the Spanish-American war had given the American people confidence in his guidance as the leader of the nation. He had won the election of 1900 handily, with the war-hero Theodore Roosevelt as his Vice-Presidential running mate. However, President McKinley's second term would be short-lived. According to the providential ordination of Almighty God, his presidency would come to an end by an assassin's bullet on September 6, 1901.

McKinley had always insisted that he should be approachable by the American people. He wanted to be accessible so that he could shake hands and speak with any and all Americans. Yet, the Secret Service had expressed concern over his safety, especially after hearing of other recent assassinations going on in Europe at the time.

President McKinley was attending the Pan-American Exposition in Buffalo, New York on the fatal day. A young factory worker from Cleveland, Ohio, named Leon Czolgosz had imbibed deeply of a political philosophy known as anarchism. This young man had been drawn into this philosophy, when he attended a lecture by a radical anti-Christian philosopher and dangerous anarchist named Emma Goldman. Leon was especially inspired by her call to assassinate all political leaders, and this became the impetus to follow through on the assassination of the President.

On the evening of September 6, 1901, President McKinley entered the Temple of Music at the exposition in Buffalo and began greeting the local

Anarchism: Anarchism is a political philosophy that teaches that there should be no government and that the individual should be absolutely free from any govering authority.

1900 re-election poster featuring William McKinley

residents who had gathered to meet him. As he reached out to grasp the hand of Leon Czolgosz, the assassin pressed a hidden revolver against the President's chest and fired twice. The Secret Service agents immediately subdued the assassin as the President reeled backwards from the force of the shots.

Immediately, William McKinley told his cabinet secretary George Cortelyou not to share the news of his injuries with his wife, fearing that this might further endanger her health. As an angry crowd was gathering around Leon Czolgosz, the president quickly interceded. Raising a bloodied hand, he called out: "Let no one hurt him; may God forgive him."[13]

President McKinley was taken to a nearby home for a medical examination. The doctors were unable to locate the second of the two bullets that had entered his chest. Initially it seemed that the President would recover, but by September 13 his condition had deteriorated. Gangrene had appeared on the walls of his stomach. That night it was clear to all that President McKinley was dying.

In his last hours, William told Ida, "It is God's way. His will, not ours, be done." Ida responded, "I want to go with you." To which William answered, "We are all going, my dear." [14]

As he faded away, President McKinley whispered the words of his favorite hymn, "Nearer, My God, to Thee."

Then, with my waking thoughts bright with thy praise,
Out of my stony griefs Bethel I'll raise;
So by my woes to be nearer, my God, to thee;
Nearer, my God, to thee, nearer to thee!

Or if, on joyful wing cleaving the sky,
Sun, moon, and stars forgot, upward I fly,
Still all my song shall be, nearer, my God, to thee;
Nearer, my God, to thee, nearer to thee![15]

Thus, in his last words, President McKinley confessed his faith in the providence of God and humbly submitted himself to the will of God. Journalist

Frederick Barton wrote that no president "ever regarded himself more directly under Providential destiny as ruler of the nation than William McKinley."[16]

It is clear from his speeches, diaries, and biographical material, that this was a man who feared God, and sought to humble himself and the nation before Him. President McKinley would call out for God's mercy on the nation in his prayers, his Thanksgiving proclamations, and inaugural addresses. In his First Inaugural Address, the newly-elected president provides these remarkable words, hardly ever used by any political leader in the history of the United States:

> *Our faith teaches that there is no safer reliance than upon the God of our fathers, who has so singularly favored the American people in every national trial, and who will not forsake us so long as we obey His commandments and walk humbly in His footsteps.*[17]

President McKinley clearly understood the need for a nation to keep the commandments of God and remain humble before Him. However imperfectly he followed through on this during his political career, it is clear that this was his intention. Most importantly, William McKinley the husband understood the clear commands of Ephesians 5:25 and 1 Peter 3:7. To the very end, he really did seek to love his wife as Christ loved the church and gave Himself for her. William McKinley stands out among the American presidents for his firm faith in the Lord Jesus Christ, his fear of God, and his steadfast belief in the providential hand of God.

> *Now before [Josiah] there was no king like him who turned to the LORD with all his heart, with all his soul, and with all his might, according to all the law of Moses; nor after him did any arise like him. (2 Kings 23:25)*

UNIT 5

Remnant Revivals and Spiritual Decline (1920-Present)

Even so then, at this present time there is a remnant
according to the election of grace.

—Romans 11:5

During the first half of the 20th century, Europe and America were wrapped up in two massively destructive world wars. These marked ultimate outworkings of humanist pride and Darwinian evolution that had engulfed a world that had walked away from Christ.

Almost the entire world had embraced Darwinian evolution as the best theory of origins. This evolutionary theory provided much encouragement to the racism of Nazi Germany and Japan (who wanted to believe that their races were superior to all others). It was these ideas, popularized by Charles Darwin and others who had rejected the Christian faith, that produced the devastation of the 20th century. Two horrible world wars yielded a hundred million dead soldiers and citizens and too many bombed-out cities to count.

So, the Lord of heaven and earth humbled the nations of the world, but most continued in their pride. After World War II the United States became the most powerful nation on earth and remained so until the 2010s. After the war, a technology revolution provided for strengthened economies all over the world. Yet this did not produce gratitude and service to the true and living God. America instead removed the Bible and prayer out of schools in the 1960s. The nation approved the killing of babies in 1973, and sixty million babies would lose their lives over the next forty years. The schools and colleges of the nation would teach children perverted lifestyles similar to what was seen in Sodom and Gomorrah, Pompeii, or other places destroyed by our righteous and holy God.

The 20th century marked the largest apostasy in the history of the Christian Church in the West. By 1930, almost every Christian denomination had accepted Darwinism. These churches questioned the authority of God speaking through His Word. They rejected God's laws. Many refused to believe in the miracles of Jesus or the miracle of the virgin birth. The gospel itself was lost in a sea of moralisms and confusion.

However, several revivals breathed a little life into the Christian church along the way. Through the terrible years of the 20th and early 21st centuries, the Lord did not leave His church without some visitation of the Holy Spirit and spiritual faith and life.

Thanks to the faithful work of J. Gresham Machen in the 1930s, a remnant of Presbyterians held on to the faith. The Conservative Baptists and the General Assembly of Regular Baptists emerged from the liberal Baptist denominations. Some of the evangelical and Pentecostal denominations maintained a commitment to a supernatural worldview. Billy Graham led the evangelical world with his revival services in the 1950s, 1960s, and 1970s.

Then, the Jesus Movement of the 1960s and 1970s aroused an interest in Bible study among the nation's youth. In popular history books, this period will be remembered as the age of drugs, sexual sin, and rebellion. However, God was working in the hearts of hundreds of thousands of young men and women who flocked into revival meetings to hear the preaching of men like David Wilkerson or Chuck Smith. College ministries like Campus Crusade and the Navigators brought discipleship programs to millions of college students. Largely because of these little revivals, church attendance among evangelicals continued strong into the 2010s.

However, the revivals failed to reach the millennial generation (those children born between 1980 and 2000). Millions of these young people left the church. This generation has failed to retain a biblical perspective on most issues. They were not discipled by their churches because the churches were more committed to entertainment and music than to preaching and teaching the Word. Nor had the young people been properly instructed in the Word of God by their own parents. Receiving their training from ungodly teachers in school and popular media, this generation very much turned away from the Lord Jesus Christ and left the church.

Nonetheless, every Christian in the world must be thankful for the remnant of serious Christians who remained true to Christ and His Word in the 21st century. Christian authors, reformers, and teachers like J. Gresham Machen, Henry Morris, David Wilkerson, and Elisabeth Elliot made crucial contributions to the faith at this time. Thanks be to God for those who keep the faith during periods of serious retrograde!

> Hold fast the pattern of sound words which you have heard from me, in faith and love which are in Christ Jesus. (2 Timothy 1:13)

Timeline of Important Events

1927	Charles Lindbergh flies solo across the Atlantic Ocean.
1929	The Great Depression begins after the stock market crashes.
1931	The Empire State Building opens.
1935	President Franklin D. Roosevelt gets a Social Security Act passed through Congress.
1939	Germany invades Poland and World War II begins.
1941	Japan attacks Pearl Harbor and the United States joins World War II.
1945	The United States drops atomic bombs on Hiroshima and Nagasaki ending World War II.
1946	The Cold War begins between two world superpowers: the United States and the Soviet Union.
1949	NATO forms and Germany is divided in two.
1962	The Cuban Missile Crisis threatens a war between Russia and the United States.
1963	President John F. Kennedy is assassinated.
1964	Congress approves the Civil Rights Act of 1964.
1969	Neil Armstrong walks on the moon.
1973	The Vietnam War ends as the United States pulls out.
1974	Richard Nixon resigns presidency over Watergate Scandal.
1980	Ronald Reagan is elected to the presidency.
1991	The First Gulf War begins.
2001	America witnesses terrorist attacks on the World Trade Center and the Pentagon. The Second Gulf War and the invasion of Afghanistan begin.
2005	Hurricane Katrina, the most devastating natural disaster in recent history, strikes Louisiana.

J. Gresham Machen (1881-1937)

CHAPTER 24

J. Gresham Machen: Valiant for Truth

For I delivered to you first of all that which I also received: that Christ died for our sins according to the Scriptures, and that He was buried, and that He rose again the third day according to the Scriptures, and that He was seen by Cephas, then by the twelve.

—1 Corinthians 15:3-5

How important is the historical fact that Jesus was born of a virgin or that He rose from the dead? Can one still be a Christian and disbelieve these historical realities? Is there such a thing as Christianity without the physical resurrection? The raging hurricane of modernism and anti-supernaturalism had already swept across Europe and America by the 1920s, and there weren't many Christian leaders left who were willing to take a strong stand against the academic elite. Almost every denomination quickly compromised with the onslaught of Darwin's evolution and the religion of scientism. Although a large portion of the Christian West had apostatized into atheism, others wanted to hold on to a veneer of Christianity. They wanted to retain the pretense of the Christian faith, while compromising with the world on key doctrines. They thought that one could be a true Christian and yet disbelieve such essential truths as the virgin birth and the resurrection.

One man will always be remembered for standing "valiant for truth" in this age of terrible theological retrograde—J. Gresham Machen (pronounced "may-chen"). Having a strong academic mind himself, he argued vigorously that Christianity could not exist without the virgin birth, the resurrection, and numerous other central Christian beliefs. If you don't believe in the resurrection of Jesus Christ, Machen argued, you are simply not a Christian. If the resurrection of Jesus Christ is defined as the very heart of the gospel in 1 Corinthians 15, then this must be a fatal compromise of the faith. Thus, J. Gresham Machen was very much contending for the faith "once for all delivered to the saints" (Jude 3). He was waging war for the truth of the faith against compromising church leaders who preferred to make Christianity acceptable to a world which is always hostile to the faith.

Early Years

But you must continue in the things which you have learned and been assured of, knowing from whom you have learned them, and that from childhood you have known the Holy Scriptures, which are able to make you wise for salvation through faith which is in Christ Jesus. (2 Timothy 3:14-15)

J. Gresham Machen's father Arthur was 55-years old when Gresham was born, and his mother Mary was 35. Known to most of her friends as "Minnie," Mary had grown up in a wealthy family in Macon, Georgia. Arthur Machen was a Harvard-educated lawyer in Baltimore, Maryland. He had paid his way through college by writing detective novels and started practicing law in 1853.

The Machens had three sons, Arthur Jr., J. Gresham, and Thomas, born in that order. The family was wealthy, but that wasn't what mattered most to them—the parents sought the kingdom of God and His righteousness first, and the discipleship of their sons was preeminent in the home. Biographer Ned

Baltimore, Maryland in the early 1900s

Stonehouse notes how Minnie especially was careful and thorough in teaching the Word of God to her son:

> *In mature life Machen often paid tribute to the instruction in the Bible that he received at his mother's knee. At twelve years of age his knowledge of its contents, including the names and character of all the kings of Israel and Judah, he later observed, surpassed that of the average theological student of his day.*[1]

Gresham's early instruction centered primarily around the Bible, the *Westminster Shorter Catechism*, and Bunyan's *Pilgrim's Progress*. He attended private school, and according to transcript records for his freshman year in high school, he received a 99 grade in Geometry, Algebra, Latin, Greek, and Natural Science.[2]

Machen matriculated to Johns Hopkins University after high school, and graduated in 1901 at only twenty years of age. As a graduation present, his parents sent him with his cousin Loy and brother Arthur off to Europe. This was the first of many visits that Gresham would make to Europe in his life. He enjoyed sports and the outdoors, especially mountain climbing.[3] On this first trip to Europe, Gresham made the ascent up Monte Rosa, a 15,000-foot mountain situated between Switzerland and Italy. From there he took in the view of the great beauty and majesty of the Matterhorn, which he would conquer some thirty years later.[4]

Studies at Princeton Seminary and Abroad

Upon his return from Europe, Gresham was unsure of his calling, and for a brief while considered further studies in economics or law. He wrote to his father:

> I am still very doubtful about studying economics. I wish that instead of thinking about these special fields, I were led to something eminently regular—like practicing law. The ministry I am afraid I can't think of.[5]

In spite of his reservations about pursuing the ministry, young Machen decided to enter Princeton Seminary in 1902. Though excelling in his seminary work, he was still unsure of his calling to the ministry. After spending additional time studying in Europe, he returned to take on a position as an instructor at Princeton, which he would continue with for the next fifteen years. Finally, he was ordained as a minister in the Presbyterian church in 1914. Through these many years of study and teaching, Gresham's convictions were further established in the truths of Scripture and his own sense of calling to the ministry solidified.

Teaching Labors at Princeton

During his time abroad Machen studied under many of the most renowned professors of theology and biblical studies. These were the instructors who were training the next generation of pastors, and they were for the most part systematically tearing down the Christian faith in the Western world. Yet, J. Gresham Machen was equipping himself during these early years to better address the difficult historical and theological questions that scholars were posing against the biblical faith. Many of Machen's later works would defend the historical reliability of the New Testament. J. Gresham Machen began teaching New Testament and elementary Greek at Princeton Seminary in 1906, and continued in that position until he founded his own seminary decades later.

Christian Service

Although he lived in an academic world, J. Gresham Machen should not be seen as merely some intellectual who had little familiarity with the Christian life and the real, practical service to others. Biographer Ned Stonehouse describes the heart of this man of God of the 20th century:

> *Let no one, however, conclude . . . that Machen was out of touch with life, disinterested in the practice of Christianity, or without compassion upon men in their suffering and temptations. The evidence to the contrary is overwhelming. The record is one of countless acts of humble service and of devoted ministry to the needy and distressed.*[6]

Machen would demonstrate love and compassion for those suffering, by making generous gifts. For example, he paid in full for the cataract surgery of a janitor at Princeton Seminary. In a letter to his mother, he wrote:

> *In the early part of the afternoon I went to the Mercer Hospital in Trenton to see Charlie Wykoff, the colored janitor of Alexander Hall, who has undergone an operation for cataract. I am financing the operation and standing for the modest hospital charges. Charlie has been here for some thirty years at the seminary, and he*

and I are old friends. We get along very finely together. I hope the operation may be
successful, since it would be sad for poor old Charlie to get blind.[7]

He also invested a great deal of his life into a man named R.H. who came to faith out of a life of drunkenness. For over twenty years Gresham Machen continuing caring for the man, writing him numerous pastoral letters and helping with financial needs from time to time. He recorded some of his early more trying experiences in his work with R.H.:

I have taken up with an old fellow by the name of H., who has been a drunkard most
of his life, but was converted a year or so ago (before I knew him) and came into the
First Presbyterian Church. He has a hard time with his old failing, but is trying to
do better. For the last few weeks, he has spent a considerable part of the time in my
room reading Pilgrim's Progress . . . *About a month ago he had a terrible lapse,*
when two nice suits of clothes that I gave him were sold to get money for drink.
That was discouraging, and has made me very cautious about helping him in a
pecuniary [financial] way, but we are paying for his board and lodging till he gets
regular work.[8]

Machen continued to care for the man until his death in 1933 at the age of 84.[9]

World War I and Service with the YMCA

Sometimes referred to as "The Great War", World War I commenced in 1914. Although the United States was at first committed to neutrality in this European conflict, tensions escalated between America and Germany especially after the sinking of the RMS *Lusitania* in 1915 (where 128 Americans lost their lives). The disruption of trade and the killing of innocent Americans was the main reason for America's involvement in World War I. By 1917, the United States had lost about 25% of her merchant ships[10] before Congress declared war on Germany (on April 6, 1917).

Too old for the military draft, J. Gresham Machen still felt an obligation to help his country out in some way. He considered working as an ambulance

Trench warfare in World War I

driver or as a chaplain, but eventually settled on volunteering with the YMCA (Young Men's Christian Association). This American charitable organization would construct small huts near the front lines, offering various book resources and food items to the soldiers, including sandwiches, coffee, and hot chocolate. They also provided Bible studies and counseling for interested soldiers.

Machen found himself operating one of these huts for the YMCA, serving food and beverages to the men near the front lines in St. Mard, France. Biographer, Stonehouse describes the day-to-day menial work involved:

> *To an astonishing extent, in fact, his activity for months seemed to consist largely in manufacturing and selling chocolate for twenty centimes per "quart" or one fourth of a liter. The daily task of preparing the chocolate was a singular one for any ordained professor and doubly so for Machen. The process was quite involved. First large bars of sweet chocolate had to be shaved up; a fixed quantity of water*

was boiled, the chocolate mixed in, a larger quantity of water added, the whole brought again to a boil, condensed milk added and the process concluded with a final boiling.[11]

J. Gresham Machen's hot chocolate output increased rapidly, and he was moving over 510 cups a day![12] When the Armistice was signed in November 1918, Machen chose to remain in France as new opportunities for ministry were opening up. Here he could use his preaching and teaching gifts to share the gospel of Jesus with a broken people living in a broken land. For the next three months Machen brought the Word to military camps, returning to Princeton seminary in March 1919.

Conflicts with Liberal Theology

Now I urge you, brethren, note those who cause divisions and offenses, contrary to the doctrine which you learned, and avoid them. For those who are such do not serve our Lord Jesus Christ, but their own belly, and by smooth words and flattering speech deceive the hearts of the simple. (Romans 16:17-18)

Princeton University had been dallying with liberalism and evolution since the days of the presidency of Woodrow Wilson. Although Wilson had descended from rich Christian roots (in the Southern Presbyterian tradition), when he assumed the presidency of Princeton in 1902 he put a stop to the college's regular Bible instruction classes.[13] In 1907, Woodrow Wilson and his wife Ellen appealed to a Ouija board hoping to conjure up James McCosh (dead for 13 years), on matters relating to Princeton politics.[14] Not surprisingly, by 1908 Wilson had become a liberal progressive in his ideas. His rationale for his progressivism was contained in a book called "The Constitutional Government of the United States." He argued for an evolutionary view of government and a rejection of fixed law or absolutes, writing: "In our own day, whenever we discuss the structure or development of anything, whether in nature or in society, we consciously or unconsciously follow Mr. Darwin . . . Living political constitutions must be Darwinian in structure and practice."[15]

At the same time, higher critical theories from Germany were seeping into Princeton Seminary. German theologians like Albrecht Ritschl (1822-1889) and Adolf von Harnack (1851-1930) had rejected certain books of the Bible (like the Gospel of John) calling the Scriptures "inauthentic" from their arrogant perspectives. They went so far as to teach that the Apostle Paul invented "Christianity" and they insisted that this imposition was very different from the "simple, ethical monotheism" taught by Jesus. Such teachings undermined the authority and unity of Scripture in the most sinister, demonic way, and infected the churches and seminaries in America in the early 20th century.

J. Gresham Machen released his first book in 1921, entitled *The Origin of Paul's Religion*. He convincingly argued the case that Paul's theology could not have been self-conceived but it was rather a faith that was revealed to him by a revelation of the Lord Jesus Christ. Against the skeptics and the higher critics of the day, Machen affirmed the New Testament record. On the Damascus Road, Paul encountered the risen and ascended Christ (Acts 9), and he was truly and dramatically converted to the faith he once tried to destroy (Gal. 1:11-17). This was the first of many books that Gresham would write so as to defend orthodox historic Christianity against the anti-supernatural, liberal attacks on the faith.

Two years later Gresham wrote his two most famous books: *New Testament Greek for Beginners*, an easy-to-use textbook for students, and *Christianity and Liberalism*. This was the book that would make the greatest impact upon the American church.

In the early 1900s, the humanist teachings of higher criticism and evolution opened up a trend towards liberal theology among many of the Christian denominations in America. Across the nation Christians were tempted to compromise on essential doctrines such as the resurrection of Christ, the virgin birth of Christ, the miracles of Jesus, and the inspiration and perfection of the Scriptures. In many cases, seminary professors and pastors who were abandoning biblical teaching were allowed to continue as teachers in the churches and on the mission field. J. Gresham Machen became gravely concerned because he saw these departures from biblical orthodoxy as deadly to the church in the Western world.

The theologian Richard Niebuhr once summarized liberal theology in this very succinct way: "A God without wrath brought men without sin into a kingdom without judgment through the ministrations of a Christ without a cross."[16] Obviously, this sort of theology was diametrically opposed to the biblical faith.

The controversy between those who held fast to biblical teaching—the "Fundamentalists" and those who advocated a liberal theology—the "Modernists" reached a critical point when a pastor in New York preached a sermon called "Shall the Fundamentalists Win?" This message came in 1922 from a Baptist pastor, Harry Emerson Fosdick, who was filling the pulpit of the First Presbyterian Church in New York City. In his sermon, Fosdick called for tolerance of those who could not believe that the Bible was inspired, that Christ died a substitutionary death on the cross, that Christ was born of a virgin, and other basic doctrines. Fosdick described the "Fundamentalists" as intolerant and unkind, quite different from the way Scripture speaks of heretics and schismatics. From a biblical standpoint, it is those who deny the basic truths of God's Word who are the divisive and unloving ones.

> *If anyone teaches otherwise and does not consent to wholesome words, even the words of our Lord Jesus Christ, and to the doctrine which accords with godliness, he is proud, **knowing nothing, but is obsessed with disputes and arguments over words, from which come envy, strife, reviling, evil suspicions, useless wranglings of men of corrupt minds and destitute of the truth, who suppose that godliness is a means of gain. From such withdraw yourself.** (1 Timothy 6:3-5, emphasis added)*

Harry Emerson Fosdick and the other liberals were striking at the very heart of the Christian faith and J. Gresham Machen boldly labeled these liberal ideas as the substance of a false religion, something very different from the Christian faith as communicated by the Lord Jesus Christ Himself. Machen explained the purpose of his powerful little book, *Christianity and Liberalism*, in an advertisement blurb:

*What is the difference between modern "liberal" religion and historic Christianity? An answer to this question is attempted in the present book. The author is convinced that liberalism on the one hand and the religion of the historic church on the other are not two varieties of the same religion, **but two distinct religions proceeding from altogether separate roots**. This conviction is supported by a brief setting forth of the teachings of historic Christianity and of the modern liberalism with regard to God and man, the Bible, Christ, salvation, the Church, and Christian service. If Christianity, in its historic acceptation, is really to be abandoned, it is at least advisable that men should know what they are giving up and what they are putting in its place.[17] (emphasis added)*

To the liberal argument that Christianity was nothing but a lifestyle taught by Jesus, Machen pointed out that this faith as recorded throughout the entire New Testament was based upon a message to be believed—the message of the gospel. He consented that following Jesus does entail a certain way of life, but at root the faith required the belief of certain objective truths. The gospel of Jesus Christ is primarily a message about real acts of God performed in real human history, centered on the incarnation of the Son of God, his death and resurrection. Machen wrote:

Christian doctrine, I hold, is not merely connected with the gospel, but it is identical with the gospel, and if I did not preach it at all times, and especially in those places where it subjects me to personal abuse, I should regard myself as guilty of sheer unfaithfulness to Christ. It is, I hold, only as He is offered to us in the gospel – that is in the "doctrine" which the world despises – that Christ saves sinful men; and never will I create the impression that there can be Christian prayer or Christian service except on the basis of those redeeming facts.[18]

If professing "Christians" were to deny that Jesus is the Son of God, that He was born of a virgin, that He died on the cross for the sins of the world, and that He rose again on the third day, then we can go so far as to say what the Apostle Paul said—their faith is in "vain" (1 Cor. 15:12-15). In other words, if what the liberals of Machen's day were saying is true, then faith in Jesus Christ is pointless.

He further explained:

> *If Jesus was only what the liberal historians suppose that He was, then trust in Him would be out of place; our attitude toward Him could be that of pupils to a Master and nothing more. But if He was what the New Testament represents Him as being, then we can safely commit to Him the eternal destinies of our souls."*[19]

The questions which arose during this time of unbelief and skepticism are just as important today: who is Jesus? Is He merely a good teacher? Or is He the Savior of the world? How we answer that question and what we believe about Jesus Christ is a matter of eternal life or eternal death.

> *He who believes in the Son has everlasting life; and he who does not believe the Son shall not see life, but the wrath of God abides on him. (John 3:36)*

Founding of a New Seminary and a New Church

The destructive false teaching disrupting the American Christian church as a whole was taking the Presbyterian Church by storm. The conflict also erupted within Princeton, leading eventually to J. Gresham Machen's resignation from the seminary in 1929. Several other biblically-minded teachers joined with him to form a new seminary in Philadelphia called Westminster Theological Seminary, an institution dedicated to training students to be faithful interpreters of the Word of God.

After his departure from Princeton, Machen remained within the Northern Presbyterian church for awhile, but that also was to change in God's good providence. For a number of years the Board of Foreign Missions of the Presbyterian Church had been funding numerous missionaries who openly denied foundational Christian doctrines. Instead of proclaiming the truth of the gospel, these missionaries were only interested in alleviating poverty and sickness and other humanitarian efforts. A missions report titled *Rethinking Missions*, funded by John D. Rockefeller and published in 1932, was promoted by the Presbyterian Church and reviewed by one of the Presbyterian Church's most well-known missionaries, Mrs. Pearl S. Buck. In her own words, she called the report "the only book I have ever read which seems literally true in its every observation and right in its every conclusion."[20] She went on to explain:

> *Let the sole question about that missionary be whether or not he is beloved in the community, whether the people see any use in his being among them, whether or not the way he has lived there has conveyed anything to the people about Christ – not mind you, whether or not he has preached, for that is of no value, but whether by the way he has lived he has conveyed anything . . . **But above all, let the spread of the spirit of Christ be rather by mode of life than preaching.** I am weary unto death with this incessant preaching. It deadens all thought, it confuses all issues.* [21] *(emphasis added)*

Mrs. Buck's spite for the "foolishness of preaching" was faithless and fatal, for she failed to realize that this was the power of God unto salvation (1 Cor. 1:18). The Apostle Paul vastly disagreed with this corrupted faith and its corrupted vision of missions:

> *How then shall they call on Him in whom they have not believed? And how shall they believe in Him of whom they have not heard? And how shall they hear without a preacher? And how shall they preach unless they are sent? As it is written: "How beautiful are the feet of those who preach the gospel of peace, who bring glad tidings of good things!" But they have not all obeyed the gospel. For Isaiah says, "Lord, who has believed our report?" So then faith comes by hearing, and hearing by the word of God. (Romans 10:14-17)*

J. Gresham Machen pulled out all the stops in his condemnation of the report and Mrs. Buck's review of it. He insisted that this *Rethinking Missions* was "from beginning to end an attack upon the historic Christian Faith."[22] A significant number of members in the Presbyterian church could no longer in good conscience provide financial support to the Board of Foreign Missions that had taken such a position against the preaching of the gospel. Therefore a number of leaders came together to form an Independent Presbyterian Board of Foreign

Faculty of Westminster Theological Seminary with J. Gresham Machen at the center

Missions, which would henceforth support missionaries who were committed to the faithful deposit of biblical truth and the communication of the gospel to the nations.

Subsequently, J. Gresham Machen's New Brunswick Presbytery proceeded to remove his ministerial credentials without ever holding a trial or giving him the opportunity to defend his actions. Along with a number of other pastors and elders in the Northern Presbyterian church, Machen helped to form "the Presbyterian Church of America" (later renamed the "Orthodox Presbyterian Church"). This new group of churches committed themselves to the Word of God as the only infallible rule of faith and practice.

Final Days

I have fought the good fight, I have finished the race, I have kept the faith. Finally, there is laid up for me the crown of righteousness, which the Lord, the righteous Judge, will give to me on that Day, and not to me only but also to all who have loved His appearing. (2 Timothy 4:7-8)

J. Gresham Machen's last few years of life were consumed with many pressures that broke down his physical condition. For most of his years he enjoyed good health thanks to his general habits of fitness and recreation, and his lifelong love of mountain climbing. But his load of responsibilities had increased dramatically. Forming a seminary and developing a new denomination took a heavy toll.

During the Christmas break of 1936, Machen accepted an invitation to speak in North Dakota at several of the churches which had affiliated themselves with the Orthodox Presbyterian Church. He had been suffering from illness, and when he arrived in Bismarck the thermometers were bottomed out at 20-below-zero. After preaching in Bismarck, Carson, and Leith, his health failed. Pastor Sam Allen, who was with Gresham Machen during these final days, recorded what happened:

> *Almost immediately after his talk he was stricken with pleurisy. He could not walk up the steps by himself. The pain was intense. He was in agony. From Leith to Bismarck (75 miles) he groaned with pain and had a terrible thirst . . . This was the saddest and most grievous trip I ever made . . . At last, after what seemed an age, we arrived in Bismarck about 7:17PM. He had to be helped from my car to his room. At first he wouldn't consent to the calling of a doctor, but the pain was so intense that he finally yielded on the point.[23]*

He checked into a hospital, and there he was diagnosed with pneumonia. On New Year's Eve 1936, Sam Allen came in to pray with him. Machen shared with the pastor a vision he had had of heaven, saying, "Sam, it was glorious; it was glorious."[24] Sensing the end was near, he sent off a telegram to his friend and fellow teacher at Westminster Seminary, John Murray, letting him know, "I'm so thankful for the active obedience of Christ. No hope without it."[25] It was the "active obedience of Christ" that provides for a righteousness we could never have gained for ourselves—achieved by the obedience of our Lord Jesus Christ.

> *For as by one man's disobedience many were made sinners, so also by one Man's obedience many will be made righteous. (Roman 5:19)*

> *For He made Him who knew no sin to be sin for us, that we might become the righteousness of God in Him. (2 Corinthians 5:21)*

J. Gresham Machen died with a certain confidence that "there is therefore now no condemnation to those who are in Christ Jesus" (Rom. 8:1). He was certain that he was soon going to "be with Christ, which is far better" (Phil. 1:23). On January 1, 1937, around 7:30 p.m., this defender of the faith entered into the presence of His Lord. He was faithful unto death.

A Faith Worth Fighting For

Every age presents its own battles and tests of faith for men and women of God. During an age of severe breakdown of faith, where leaders are abandoning the field on the right and on the left, God is testing the faith of those who still remain. When Shammah continued to stand and fight in the field of lentils, after the other fighting men had scattered in fear, he proved his faithfulness and courage for future posterity to emulate (2 Sam. 23:11-12). This is what we find with J. Gresham Machen. By the grace of God, he continued to stand and fight in the field of lentils when many others had already given up. Eventually, a faithful, evangelical church emerged in the following decades of the 20th century.

J. Gresham Machen's life remains a testimony to the church in the present day. He was a man committed to the truth of the Bible. The Apostle Paul urged Timothy to "guard what was committed to your trust" (1 Tim. 6:20), and this continues to be the call for each and every generation of Christians. We must earnestly contend for the truth of the gospel. Eternal souls are at stake. The Lord

Jesus Christ is the only way to the Father (John 14:12). The Bible is inspired by God (2 Tim. 3:16-17). There is only one God (Isa. 45:22). Salvation is by faith in Jesus Christ alone (Acts 4:12). These are truths worth fighting for, even at the cost of our own lives.

We learn from Gresham's life that there are some battles more critical than others. While there are doctrinal issues over which Christian people should avoid arguing (1 Tim. 1:5-6; 4:7), there are also those doctrines of the faith which are absolutely essential and they must be defended at all costs. What we believe about God, the Bible, Jesus Christ, and salvation are essential matters. If we will be faithful to our Lord Jesus Christ, we must "contend earnestly for the faith which was once for all delivered to the saints" (Jude 3). May the Lord make us faithful to speak the truth in love (Eph. 4:15), never turning away from the gospel by which we are saved (1 Cor. 15:1-2).

Elisabeth Elliot (1926-2015)

CHAPTER 25

Elisabeth Elliot:
A Life of Gospel Sacrifice

Therefore I endure all things for the sake of the elect,
that they also may obtain the salvation which is in
Christ Jesus with eternal glory.

—2 Timothy 2:10

What would it cost to bring the gospel of Jesus Christ to the fierce Auca tribe of Ecuador? In January 1956, five young missionary wives learned that the advance of the kingdom often comes at great cost. Walking in the footsteps of the suffering Savior requires suffering for His disciples. In the case of these five missionary wives, it would cost the lives of their five husbands. But, as one of the early Christians, Tertullian, once said, "the blood of the martyrs is the seed of the church."[1] The aphorism remains true and applicable even in the dense, humid jungles of Ecuador. The blood of those five faithful men of God would fall to the ground as seed and produce eternal fruit to the glory of God.

Elisabeth Elliot was one of these five women who lost their husbands on that memorable day in 1956. Yet, God would use this woman of faith to tell the story of the critical mission work with the lost peoples of Ecuador and inspire thousands of others to live lives of faith. Elisabeth, who went by the name "Betty," wrote numerous books recording the amazing providences of God who, through the blood of His Son, redeems people from every tribe, tongue, and nation (Rev. 5:9).

Early Years at the Feet of Christ

Your eyes saw my substance, being yet unformed. And in Your book they all were written, the days fashioned for me, when as yet there were none of them. (Psalm 139:16)

Elisabeth Elliot was born Elisabeth Howard in Brussels, Belgium to American missionary parents in 1926. Within a few months of her birth, the family returned to the United States and lived in Germantown, Pennsylvania for Betty's early childhood years. Her father worked as an editor for the *Sunday School Times* in Germantown. By God's grace, Betty heard the words of Scripture read from her earliest years. Each morning the family gathered to sing from the hymnal after breakfast, and Mr. Howard would read Scripture to the children around at dinner time. This routine was consistently observed through Betty's entire childhood.

Elisabeth's aspirations for missionary work were instilled from her earliest years. The family moved to Moorestown, New Jersey where missionaries would often lodge with the family, sharing their stories of adventure and gospel power with Betty and her siblings. Young Elizabeth Howard was especially impressed with the story of the Chinese missionaries John and Betty Stam, murdered in 1934 by the communists. At age thirteen she had read a newly-published biography of the Stams, where she came across these words of Betty Stam:

Lord, I give up all my own plans and purposes, all my own desires and hopes, and accept Thy will for my life. I give myself, my life, my all utterly to Thee to be Thine, forever. Fill me and seal me with Thy Holy Spirit. Use me as Thou wilt, work out Thy whole will in my life at any cost, now and forever.[2]

The young woman copied this prayer into the front of her Bible and often returned to it to ponder what it meant to make such a sacrifice. Increasingly as Betty grew older, she was drawn to spiritual things, she was less and less interested in her peer group at school, and more drawn to form relationships with visiting missionaries.

In 1941 Betty's father was promoted to be the general editor of the *Sunday School Times*. With the additional income made available, the Howards decided to send Betty to a boarding school, the Hampden DuBose Academy in Florida, where she would study for three years. There she built a friendship with the principal's wife, Mrs. DuBose, who introduced Betty to the writings of Amy Carmichael. This Irish missionary to India was a great inspiration to Betty, and years later she would publish her own biography of this remarkable woman. God often uses the stories of saints of the past to inspire saints in the present, and such was the case for Betty Howard.

College Years

Trust in the LORD with all your heart, and lean not on your own understanding;
in all your ways acknowledge Him, and He shall direct your paths. (Proverbs 3:5-6)

Upon her graduation from high school, Betty Howard entered Wheaton College in Wheaton, Illinois; her father at the time was a member of the Board of Trustees of the college. While at Wheaton, Betty joined the Foreign Mission Fellowship with an eye towards involvement in missions herself. She changed her major twice, eventually settling on Greek, in order to better prepare herself for future work in translating the Word of God into a foreign language.

While studying New Testament Greek at Wheaton, Betty connected with a fellow Greek student named Jim Elliot who was also pursuing a calling to foreign missions. Friends informed Betty that no one else knew so much Scripture as Jim Elliot, and she noticed that "a Bible always rested on top of his stack of textbooks when he entered the classroom."[3] Her biographers explained their commonalities: "They had so much in common: they were both studying Greek,

Blanchard Hall, Wheaton College in Wheaton, Illinois

they both wanted to be missionaries, and they both loved learning about the Bible and reading about great saints like Amy Carmichael and Hudson Taylor."[4]

Though Betty and Jim were involved in something of a budding relationship, they weren't sure whether they were supposed to be married. It seemed that their calling to serve the Lord overseas was in conflict with their desire to be married. The question that kept passing through their minds was, "Should we serve as single missionaries and be wholly devoted to the cause of Christ?"

After graduating from Wheaton, Betty Howard continued her language studies at the Summer Institute of Linguistics, a training center in Norman, Oklahoma under the auspices of Wycliffe Bible Translators. The Institute would teach missionaries how to master an unwritten language of a people group, create a writing system, and then translate Scripture into the language. Students at the Institute would spend time interacting with Native Americans. They would attempt to learn the language, reduce it to a written form, and then translate portions of the Bible into the foreign language. From Oklahoma, Betty moved on to Prairie Bible Institute in Alberta, Canada for further study.

During these years, Betty and Jim continued corresponding by letters, both still unsure about what to do about marriage. In 1950, Jim Elliot wrote of his plans to become a missionary to Ecuador, and he informed her that he could not consider marriage until he was well-established in his mission work. At first Betty thought that her calling would be to go to the other side of the world and it seemed that South America was *too close* to the United States. Now twenty-four years of age, young Betty Howard continued diligently in prayer for direction and wisdom.

> *Ask, and it will be given to you; seek, and you will find; knock, and it will be opened to you. For everyone who asks receives, and he who seeks finds, and to him who knocks it will be opened. (Matthew 7:7-8)*

In God's providence, Betty met Catherine Morgan, a missionary from Bogotá, Columbia who had recently returned from the field when her husband was taken ill. Upon their return, Mr. Morgan died and Catherine continued working for a missionary magazine. She urged Betty to service in South America, pointing out the great needs for gospel witness in that area of the world. That was the encouragement she needed, and Betty began to study the Spanish language and made plans to go minister in Ecuador and serve as a missionary translator.

Missionary Life in Ecuador

> *Let the peoples praise You, O God; Let all the peoples praise You. Then the earth shall yield her increase; God, our own God, shall bless us. God shall bless us, and all the ends of the earth shall fear Him. (Psalm 67:5-7)*

Jim Elliot and his friend Pete Fleming journeyed to Quito, the capital city of Ecuador, in 1952. They would begin their studies in Spanish before moving to the missionary station in Shandia, where they would join the retiring missionary Dr. William Tidmarsh working with the Quichua people. Located near the

Modern-day Quito, Ecuador

Equator at 9,350 feet above sea level, Quito is one of the highest national capitals in the world. Shandia was located about 150 miles southeast of the capital city.

Meanwhile, Betty arrived in Ecuador in September of the same year, ministering with another missionary team at San Miguel de Los Colorados, Ecuador. The Colorado language had yet to be put in written form, and there Betty helped the other missionaries learn the language and translate portions of the Bible. As she settled into this jungle setting, Betty found that missionary life was not as glamorous as she had supposed. Her biographer writes that she was "astonished at how much time and energy was taken up as a missionary just doing what was necessary to stay alive."[5] At first, it was hard slogging as she worked to master the extremely difficult Colorado language. The Lord answered her prayers for help, sending a man named Don Macario who could speak both Spanish and the native language. Although not a member of the Colorado tribe, he had grown up alongside the tribal children and was fluent in their language. By the mercies of God, Don Macario was also a Christian and he was eagerly hoping this tribal people would come to faith. Day after day, the two worked together unraveling the difficult spoken language so as to provide a written form. However, on January 25, 1953, the project suffered a severe setback when Don Macario was murdered over a property dispute. Unsure what God's plans were for this project, it wasn't long before Betty realized that He had a different path set out for her life. She received a telegram from Jim Elliot three days later, bearing the words: "Meet me in Quito. Love, Jim."[6]

Betty and Jim reunited at the Tidmarsh house in Quito, and they shared about their recent adventures in Shandia and San Miguel de Los Colorados. Jim finally popped the question, "Betty, will you marry me?"[7] To which Betty answered with an enthusiastic "Yes!" The two were joined in marriage on October 8, 1953 in a small civil ceremony in Quito attended by a few other missionary couples. Afterwards they returned to the mission station at Shandia and continued an evangelistic ministry among the Quichua people.

Traveling through the jungles of Ecuador was not an easy task. Betty Elliot wrote of the isolation of missionary life: "The missionary and his family would be completely cut off from the outside world long months at a time – four, six, eight days of heartbreaking struggle on dangerous jungle trail separated him from medical and other help."[8] However, travel was made drastically easier when Jim and Betty met up with a missionary pilot named Nate Saint. The Missionary Aviation Fellowship sent Nate as a pilot to Ecuador to assist missionaries on the ground with food, supplies, and transportation. Nate was a gifted pilot and mechanic, handling all necessary maintenance of the plane himself. He quickly became an invaluable asset to the other missionaries.

Nate Saint was meticulous with his preparations for each trip, carefully weighing every item taken on the plane down to the ounce, being sure there was enough fuel to reach the planned destination. Though careful, he also understood the risks. In his words, "I'm concerned about safety, but I don't let it keep me from getting on with God's business. Every time I take off, I am ready to deliver up the life I owe to God."[9] Nate was also an aviation innovator. He developed a method for lowering items to the ground in a bucket while the plane was in mid-flight. This enabled the transport of goods to missionaries on the ground without having to land in inaccessible areas. This innovation would prove important in reaching the reclusive Auca tribe.

Operation Auca

How beautiful upon the mountains are the feet of him who brings good news, who proclaims peace, who brings glad tidings of good things, who proclaims salvation, who says to Zion, "Your God reigns!" (Isaiah 52:7)

Through the 1950s, Jim and Betty Elliot pursued ministry with the Quichua people. Together with missionary associates Nate Saint and Ed McCully, they also sought to bring the gospel to the Jivaros, a dangerous head-hunting tribe known for their practice of shrinking human skulls. Yet, there was still another tribe that had not been reached. For years the Elliots heard harrowing stories of the vicious Auca tribe. This reclusive people group avoided all outsiders, and was known to murder anybody who would enter their territory. They would kill

Nate Saint fixing his plane

without warning or provocation. Nate Saint wrote, "For a number of years . . . the Aucas constituted a hazard to explorers, an embarrassment to the Republic of Ecuador, and a challenge to missionaries of the Gospel."[10]

In the 1940s the Shell Oil Company looked into investing drilling projects in the area, but abandoned the effort due to Auca violence. Betty explained the way of the Auca: "From an early age on, young boys are trained in the accurate use of their nine-foot hardwood lances."[11] Reaching the Auca people with the gospel would be a risky mission, but Jim and Betty Elliot loved these peoples and very much wanted to see them join the "assembly of the firstborn whose names are written in heaven" (Heb. 12:23). Five missionary couples committed together to seek out this objective: Jim and Betty Elliot, Pete and Olive Fleming, Ed and Marilou McCully, Nate and Marjorie Saint, and Roger and Barbara Youderian.

The mission began with Nate Saint piloting several aerial visits over the area, dropping various gifts to show their goodwill to the Auca people. Each week they would leave a different gift, something that would make the tribal peoples more curious about these foreign visitors from the sky. As the weeks passed and the gifts continued, they would watch increasing numbers of Aucas down below awaiting the arrival of the plane. After several months of these gift drops, the five men finally decided to make a landing in Auca territory and attempt a face-to-face meeting. The date was set for January 3, 1956. There was great uncertainty in this mission, especially given the reputation of the tribe. All were aware of the dangerous risk involved. Betty wrote of what the five women were thinking:

> The other wives and I talked together one night about the possibility of becoming widows. What would we do? God gave us peace of heart, and confidence that whatever might happen, His Word would hold . . . God's leading was unmistakable up to this point. Each of us knew when we married our husbands that there would never be any question about who came first—God and His work held first place in each life. It was the condition of true discipleship; it became devastatingly meaningful now.[12]

As the men departed for the first flight to make contact with the Auca tribe, together the women sang one of their favorite hymns, "We Rest on Thee."

We rest on Thee, our Shield and our Defender!
Thine is the battle, Thine shall be the praise;
When passing through the gates of pearly splendor,
Victors, we rest with Thee, through endless days.

The first visit occurred on Friday morning, January 6. As the plane landed on a sandbar, three Aucas, a man and two women, emerged from the jungle and met with the five missionaries. The men shouted in Auca *"Puinani!"* ("Welcome"). It was apparent that the Aucas were uneasy, yet the missionaries pursued attempts to communicate. As the Americans handed them gifts (a model airplane, a machete, and a copy of *Time* magazine), the Aucas warmed up. Nate Saint took the man for a flight while the Auca women continued to study the strange objects the missionaries had brought to them.

The first encounter with the three Auca appeared to be a success. Returning the next day, this time the men encountered no one. The following day was Sunday, and once again, the missionaries planned another visit. Over the radio, they passed the message on to the wives eagerly waiting at the mission station: "This is the day! Will contact you next at four-thirty!"[13]

Through the Furnace of Affliction

All this has come upon us; but we have not forgotten You, nor have we dealt falsely with Your covenant. Our heart has not turned back, nor have our steps departed from Your way; but You have severely broken us in the place of jackals, and covered us with the shadow of death. (Psalm 44:17-19)

The message never came. The five women spent the rest of the day waiting by the radio, anxious for news, praying for God's protection. The following day was Monday, January 9, 1956, and another Missionary Aviation Fellowship pilot was dispatched to search for the plane and the men. The pilot reported seeing the plane on the sandbar with the fabric of the wings stripped off. There was no sign of the men to be seen anywhere. News of the missing missionaries spread quickly, and the United States Air Rescue Service based in Panama, along with a number of Ecuadorian soldiers, conducted a search of the area where their plane was found.

The missionary women continued to pray, and wait for news by the radio. It wasn't long before the sad news came through. One by one, the rescuers identified the bodies of the missionary men—all five had been speared to death. It was devastating for the women, who had hoped against hope that the gifts would have made a difference. Why had the Aucas still attacked the missionaries who had only communicated goodwill to the tribal people?

As the wives adjusted to the new hard reality of widowhood, many of them caring for young children, the news of the tragedy spread all over the world. Letters of condolence came from everywhere. The people of God joined together in fervent prayer for the widowed missionaries in Ecuador, and for the Aucas to be converted to God. Betty Elliot wrote:

> *Only eternity will measure the number of prayers which ascended for the widows, their children, and the work in which the five men had been engaged. The prayers of the widows themselves are for the Aucas. We look forward to the day when these savages will join us in Christian praise.*[14]

The sacrifice of five lives for such a violent and ungrateful people as the Auca tribe didn't make sense to many outsiders. Why would anyone hazard their own life to reach the Auca people who clearly did not want to be reached? Elisabeth explained:

> *The massacre was a hard fact, widely reported at the time, surprisingly well remembered by many even today [1996]. It was interpreted according to the measure of one's faith or faithlessness – full of meaning or empty. A triumph or a tragedy. An example of brave obedience or a case of fathomless foolishness.*[15]

It was best put by Jim Elliot himself, who years earlier had written in his journal, "He is no fool who gives up what he cannot keep to gain what he cannot lose."[16] This would become a life motto for many young persons of faith over the following half century.

Though Betty and the other wives would face immense grief in the days that followed, God's good purposes were soon to be better understood. The death of the five missionaries would not be in vain. In time, the sacrifice of the Elliots, the Saints, the Flemings, the McCullys, and the Youderians would bear fruit. Their sacrifice would ultimately lead to the salvation of the Auca people, and to the glory of the Name of the risen Christ.

> *And we know that all things work together for good to those who love God, to those who are the called according to His purpose. (Romans 8:28)*

Living Among the Waorani

> *But I say to you, love your enemies, bless those who curse you, do good to those who hate you, and pray for those who spitefully use you and persecute you, that you may be sons of your Father in heaven; for He makes His sun rise on the evil and on the good, and sends rain on the just and on the unjust. (Matthew 5:44-45)*

In 1957, one year after the martyrdom of the five missionaries, Betty released her most well-known book, *Through Gates of Splendor*. The first edition of the book ended with the martyrdom of the five missionaries. However, this book did not tell the story of what happened in the years that followed. In 1958 a second edition was released and here Betty included a new epilogue that detailed what had happened to the missionaries over the previous two years.

The Missionary Aviation Fellowship continued with more gift drops to the Aucas, demonstrating even more love and goodwill after the violent murder of the five missionaries. Betty stayed on with her daughter Valerie, continuing her work among the Quichua people. But then, she moved on to minister to the Auca people, the very tribe that killed her husband. Once she had made contact with the Auca, she learned that these were really known as the "Waorani" people. The name "Auca," which means "savage," was given to them by outsiders. Two years after her husband was killed, she wrote of her mission work with the tribe:

> *In another leaf house, just about ten feet away, sit two of the seven men who killed*

my husband. Gikita, one of the men, has just helped Valerie, who is now three and one-half, roast a plantain. Two of his sons have gone to the forest, shouldering their skillfully-made blowguns in search of meat to feed the fifteen or twenty Auca Indians who are at present in this clearing. How did this come to be? Only God who made iron swim, who caused the sun to stand still, in whose hand is the breath of every living thing – only this God, who is our God forever and ever, could have done it.[17]

Betty began to learn the Auca language with the help of an Auca woman named Dayuma. The Holy Spirit opened up the hearts of these people, as the missionaries told them of the one true living God and His Son Jesus Christ. Before Betty Elliot returned to the United States in 1963, she saw her prayers answered with the first baptisms of the tribe. Dr. Everett Fuller baptized nine Waorani as disciples of the Lord Jesus Christ, and many more would be converted in subsequent years. A stronger Man has come into the devil's house, and taken his subjects from him, and once again, the reign of Christ was realized in the jungles of Ecuador.

Return to America

The Lord has appeared of old to me, saying: "Yes, I have loved you with an everlasting love; Therefore with lovingkindness I have drawn you." (Jeremiah 31:3)

Upon her return to the United States, it was clear the Lord had a new ministry for Elisabeth Elliot. There seemed to be a renewed spiritual interest developing in the country during the 1960s and 1970s. She received hundreds of requests to speak in churches and conferences. She remarried on New Year's Day, 1969 to Dr. Addison Leitch, a professor at Gordon-Conwell Theological Seminary. After only four years of marriage, however, Addison was diagnosed with two different forms of cancer and he died in September 1973. It seemed her life was to be attended by more heartbreaks, but God had a purpose for all of this. During the brief spiritual revival of the 1970s and 1980s in America, the Lord would use Elisabeth Elliot to encourage, strengthen, and guide millions of young Christian women in their trials and spiritual struggles through her books and speaking.

In the years that followed, Elisabeth Elliot provided rooms to various boarders in need of a place to live in Hamilton, Massachusetts near Gordon-Conwell Theological Seminary. This is how she met her third husband: Lars Gren. They were married on December 21, 1977—Betty was fifty-one years old and Lars was forty-one.

In 1987 Betty finished a project she had long wished to complete: a new biography of Amy Carmichael. This biography, entitled *A Chance to Die*, became a huge best-seller. Then, in 1988, at the suggestion of many friends, Betty began a radio program called *Gateway to Joy*. This program would reach millions of women all over the world with encouragement and hope. Each broadcast began with the line: "'You are loved with an everlasting love.' That's what the Bible says. 'And underneath are the everlasting arms.' This is your friend Elisabeth Elliot, talking with you today about . . ."[18] The program addressed Scripture, missionary stories, hymns, and more, and it continued in production until Betty's retirement in 2001.

Elisabeth Elliot Gren returned to Ecuador with her husband Lars to visit the Waorani people in 1996. Through the previous three decades, missionary work among the tribe had continued. Nate Saint's son Steve had also come back to minister to the people who had killed his father. During this visit, Betty was overjoyed to see Christ's powerful gospel making major inroads into transforming a savage tribe into God's holy people. The complete New Testament had been translated into the Waorani language, and two of the men who had killed the missionaries, Minkayi and Kimo, had professed faith in Christ. Thirty-two years after the tragic event occurred at the sandbar in the jungles of Ecuador, Betty continued to see and trust God's hand at work:

> *For us widows the question as to why the men who had trusted God to be both shield and defender should be allowed to be speared to death was not one that could be smoothly or finally answered in 1956, nor yet silenced in 1996. God did not answer Job's questions either. Job was living in mystery – the mystery of the sovereign purpose of God.[19]*

In her last years Elisabeth Elliot struggled with dementia and a continuing decline in health. She passed into glory and joined the saints triumphant at the age of eighty-eight in 2015. Her life was a beautiful example of sacrifice, service, and Christian love. She handled her tragedies with faith, grace, and love. She followed in the footsteps of her Master, the Lord Jesus Christ, and through her sufferings she was transformed into the image of Christ from glory to glory. For this generation and others following, Elisabeth Elliot will be an example of faith and a testimony to God's grace.

> *For we who live are always delivered to death for Jesus's sake that the life of Jesus also may be manifested in our mortal flesh. (2 Corinthians 4:11)*

Henry Morris (1918-2006)

CHAPTER 26

Henry Morris:
Father of Modern Creation Science

Then the LORD saw that the wickedness of man
was great in the earth, and that every intent of the
thoughts of his heart was only evil continually.
And the LORD was sorry that He had made man
on the earth, and He was grieved in His heart. So
the LORD said, "I will destroy man whom I have
created from the face of the earth, both man and
beast, creeping thing and birds of the air, for I am
sorry that I have made them." But Noah found
grace in the eyes of the LORD.

—Genesis 6:5-8

In 1959 evolutionists around the world were celebrating. It was the year of the 100th anniversary of the publication of Charles Darwin's revolutionary book *On the Origin of Species*, a work which expounded the theory of the evolution of man from animals. One hundred years later, the world's leading evolutionists gathered at the University of Chicago for a Darwin Centennial

Celebration. At this event Julian Huxley, grandson of "Darwin's Bulldog" Thomas Huxley, triumphantly announced that creationism was dead. Julian was the brother of Aldous Huxley, another famous anti-Christian author who wrote the book, *Brave New World*.

At first glance it appeared that Huxley was right. Around the world Darwin's theory had been accepted as fact by most scientists and scholars in every field of study. Even many Christians accepted evolution. Sometimes called theistic evolutionists, these Christians believed that God must have used evolution to gradually evolve mankind into existence. Even among Christians who rejected theistic evolution, most still believed that the earth itself was millions of years old. Few Christians believed what was straightforwardly recorded in Genesis: that God created everything out of nothing in six literal 24-hour days and that the earth was destroyed by a worldwide flood in the days of Noah.

By the 20th century, modern science had come into its own as a faith. Scientists had become the new priestly and prophetic class for those who had rejected God and replaced God's authority with man's authoritative claims. When scientists emerged out of a laboratory with a new theory or hypothesis, even though backed with the thinnest of evidence, the populace would bow down and accept their reports with a sort of reverential awe. These scientists had provided "scientific" explanations to

Thomas Huxley, "Darwin's Bulldog"

disprove God's existence and His creative power, and that was the sort of science desired by those who wanted to escape God. They were the high priests of the new humanist, materialist religion of the day.

However, the story wasn't finished yet. The Christian faith had not completely disappeared in this "brave new world" without God. Just two years after Julian Huxley made his proud pronouncement, another book came into circulation. It was written by Henry Morris and John C. Whitcomb, a Christian scientist and a Christian theologian. The book, *The Genesis Flood*, would create its own quiet revolution in the Christian world. The Lord would use this publication to call

The Genesis Flood

Christians back to a biblical understanding of the origins of the universe and a literal interpretation of the book of Genesis. After the publication of *The Genesis Flood*, many Christian scientists would seek to study and interpret scientific evidence in light of the Bible. It was especially important that a scientist, a man of the "priestly class" would submit himself to the absolute authority of God's revealed Word. And so, God raised up Dr. Henry Morris as the foremost leader of the Christian creation science movement.

Historical Background

Remember the Sabbath day, to keep it holy. Six days you shall labor and do all your work, but the seventh day is the Sabbath of the LORD your God. In it you shall do no work: you, nor your son, nor your daughter, nor your male servant, nor your female servant, nor your cattle, nor your stranger who is within your gates. For in six days the LORD made the heavens and the earth, the sea, and all that is in them, and rested the seventh day. Therefore the LORD blessed the Sabbath day and hallowed it. (Exodus 20:8-11)

Prior to the 19th century, most Christians believed in a literal six-day creation. The early church fathers held to a young earth, including Augustine who believed that God created all things instantly. The Westminster Confession of the Protestant Reformation period taught that God created all things out of nothing "in the space of six days,"[1] rejecting Augustine's instantaneous creation and maintaining the biblical account. In any case, the Christian church universally accepted the literal biblical account of the genealogies back to Noah and Adam (and held to a young earth) until the 1800s.

At the turn of the 19th century, two geologists named James Hutton and Charles Lyell challenged the young earth view of geology, advocating another perspective called Uniformitarianism. According to this view, the geological layers of the earth were not formed rapidly by a global catastrophe. Instead they were said to have settled gradually over millions of years. However, the Apostle Peter had warned against scoffers who say "things continue as they were from the beginning of creation."

Scoffers will come in the last days, walking according to their own lusts, and saying, "Where is the promise of His coming? For since the fathers fell asleep, all things continue as they were from the beginning of creation." For this they willfully forget: that by the word of God the heavens were of old, and the earth standing out of water and in the water, by which the world that then existed perished, being flooded with water. (2 Peter 3:3-6)

Instead of rejecting Uniformitarian geology, most 19th century Christians came to accept it. Theologians worked hard to harmonize or reinterpret Genesis to fit this new "scientific" perspective. The Gap Theory was one such attempt. According to this view, God created all things as recorded in Genesis 1:1. Then chaos and catastrophe occurred during a long gap period lasting for millions of years. This period was supposed to have taken place in the second verse of Genesis one—"the earth was without form, and void." As the theory goes, God finally initiated a second creation some six thousand years ago as recounted in Genesis 1:3 and following. By positing a gap of millions of years between two different acts of creation, the Gap Theory attempted to harmonize the Bible with an old earth. Thomas Chalmers (1780-1847), an influential Scottish evangelical pastor, seems to have favored it in some of his writings.

An alternative to the Gap Theory developed, known as the Day-Age View. Instead of interpreting the creation days as 24-hour days, this theory taught that each day was a long period of unspecified length. Thus the world would have been created over the course of millions of years. It was another attempt to

> **Geology:** The science that deals with the earth's physical structure and substance, its history, and the processes that act on it. Geology is concerned with the solid earth, the rocks of which it is composed, and the processes by which they change over time.

harmonize Genesis with Uniformitarian geology. Charles Hodge held to this view.

Charles Darwin's theory set forth in *On the Origin of Species* was built off of Lyell's Uniformitarianism. Darwin had to assume an old earth to make enough time for the long process of evolution to occur—at least to make his hypothesis seem reasonable for the masses. Initially, Darwin's views created quite a controversy. In England, Anglican Bishop Samuel Wilberforce, the son of William Wilberforce, argued against evolution with Thomas Huxley in 1860. Meanwhile in America, Charles Hodge denounced Darwinism as "tantamount to atheism."[2] Others rejected Darwin's hypothesis on scientific grounds, but

Darwinian Evolution was widely accepted by the scientific community by the end of the 19th century.

Between 1880 and 1960, most Christians who still believed in creation held to the Gap Theory or the Day-Age View. In 1915 the Gap Theory was given a further boost when it was espoused by the *Scofield Reference Bible*, a popular study Bible used by many American evangelicals. Only a few Christians, mostly Lutherans or Adventists, still believed in six day creation..

In 1925 Tennessee passed a law forbidding the teaching of evolution in state schools. The American Civil Liberties Union (ACLU) immediately challenged this law and hired an anti-Christian attorney named Clarence Darrow to defend a teacher named John Scopes who was charged with teaching evolution in a Tennessee high school. The prosecuting attorney, William Jennings Bryan, was a prominent evangelical and former presidential candidate. Held in the small town of Dayton, Tennessee, the trial drew nationwide interest. Although Scopes was eventually convicted of breaking the law in the trial, evangelical Christians were held up to ridicule and discredited in the press. They were portrayed as anti-scientific and anti-intellectual for believing in biblical creation, a stereotype still common today. After the Scopes Trial, Christian creationists retreated to the sidelines and Darwinism appeared to be triumphant. Clarence Darrow summed up the spirit of the age, when he arrogantly declared:

> *The fear of God is not the beginning of wisdom. The fear of God is the death of wisdom. Skepticism and doubt lead to study and investigation, and investigation is the beginning of wisdom.*[3]

This was the attitude of the 20th century evolutionist. Such testimonies represented the pride of man that would characterize the American populace, the media, and the universities. To this, the Scriptures speak:

> *Why do you boast in evil, O mighty man? The goodness of God endures continually. Your tongue devises destruction, like a sharp razor, working deceitfully. You love evil more than good, lying rather than speaking righteousness. Selah. You love all devouring words, you deceitful tongue. God shall likewise destroy you forever; He*

shall take you away, and pluck you out of your dwelling place, and uproot you from the land of the living. Selah (Psalm 52:1-5)

Early Life

From childhood you have known the Holy Scriptures, which are able to make you wise for salvation through faith which is in Christ Jesus. (2 Timothy 3:15)

It was at such a time as this that Henry Morris was born on October 6, 1918 in Dallas, Texas. He was the eldest son of Henry and Ida Morris, a well-to-do Texan couple with a rough Wild West edge. When Henry was just an infant, the famous evangelist and staunch defender of Scripture R.A. Torrey (1856-1928) came to visit the Morris home. Taking the infant Henry Morris in his arms, Torrey prayed for the child and dedicated him to the Lord's service.

Farm in Texas during the "Great Depression" and the "Dust Bowl"

For generations, the faith had been quite weak in the Morris family. Records indicate that family members had been Freemasons and there had been multiple generations of drunkenness and divorce until the Lord in His mercy intervened. Henry Morris was discipled by his godly grandmother "Mamie" Morris who would read the Bible to the little boy and talk to him often about the Lord. Years later Morris recalled:

> All I know is that I can never recall a time in my life when I did not know about the Lord Jesus and His love for me, and believe in Him. Mother also taught me about Christ, of course, as did my Sunday School teachers, but somehow I especially remember those talks with Grandmother.[4]

Henry Sr. and Ida had two more sons after Henry Jr. When the Great Depression hit in 1929, Henry Sr's real estate business went bankrupt and he fell into the sin of drunkenness. This led to the couple divorcing, and Ida was left to fend for herself as a single mother with three young sons. Thankfully, the family was able to live with Ida's mother Amanda "Muddy" Hunter. Once again by the grace of God, Henry was blessed with a godly grandmother who served as a stabilizing and strong spiritual influence in his life, and he was baptized at the age of ten.

Early on, Henry would work odd jobs to help support the family. He kept up with his studies in school, but he was bullied quite a bit for his godly character, his academic brilliance, and the family's poverty. After graduating from high school in 1935, Henry applied to Rice Institute in Houston. This privately-endowed engineering college required no tuition, but the bar to entry was high. Thanks to his good grades, the young man was admitted into the school to study civil engineering. He graduated four years later, and secured a well-paying engineering job in El Paso, Texas.

Marriage and Family

Henry Morris married Mary Louise Beach in 1940. Although she had been raised in a Lutheran family, Mary Louise had received very little biblical training.

However, the couple found a solid Southern Baptist church early on in their marriage, where they received good biblical preaching and teaching and grew spiritually. The congregation seemed to have a strong hunger for the Word of God and a vibrant love for one another, something Henry and Mary Morris had not previously encountered.

Sixty years earlier, the Lord had used Dwight L. Moody as a preserving element in the American church, especially with the formation of Moody Bible Institute. This influence would carry on through the work of a man named Dr. Irwin Moon, who taught at the Institute in the 1940s. In God's good providence, Dr. Moon visited the Morris' church in 1941. This Christian scientist's lectures instilled greater confidence in the absolute authority and accuracy of the Bible in Henry's heart. Dr. Moon's lecture on the Genesis Flood was especially impacting for the younger scientist. Dr. Moon would become most well known for his "Moody Science Videos" produced in the 1960s.

During these years, Henry Morris became involved in the Gideons organization, where he would find much spiritual strengthening and opportunities for lay ministry. The Gideons distributed Bibles throughout American communities, and encouraged regular, daily participation in the Word and prayer. For the rest of his life, Henry Morris began each day with an hour of dedicated Bible study and prayer.

Over the next several years, Henry and Mary Morris would be blessed with six children. They knew they needed to build their family on the solid rock of God's Word (Matt. 7:24-25) and bring their children up in the nurture and admonition of the Lord (Eph. 6:4). In addition to being members of a solid Bible-believing church and personal students of the Word, Henry Morris was also faithful to lead his family in Bible reading and prayer. His daughter Rebecca recalls:

> His spiritual influence was most strongly felt around the table. With few exceptions, the family ate morning and evening meals together. Someone always read a passage from the Bible, and they took turns praying. None of his children forgot the sounds of his voice as he read the Bible, never faltering or stumbling over words or inflection.

His familiarity with each chapter was so intimate it seemed he must have practiced
and memorized each line. His awe of Scripture left an indelible mark on each child's
heart.[5]

Although he grew up in a broken home with much generational sin and
family disintegration, the Lord poured out His steadfast love abundantly on
Henry Morris and his family. By God's grace, the couple would enjoy sixty-six
years of happy marriage and all six of their children continued faithfully walking
with the Lord. And by the grace of God, Henry's extended family would also
come to know the Lord, including his father, mother, brother, grandfather, and
two uncles.

Therefore know that the LORD your God, He is God, the faithful God who keeps
covenant and mercy for a thousand generations with those who love Him and keep
His commandments. (Deuteronomy 7:9)

Further Education and Flood Geology

For the weapons of our warfare are not carnal but mighty in God for pulling down
strongholds, casting down arguments and every high thing that exalts itself against
the knowledge of God, bringing every thought into captivity to the obedience of
Christ. (2 Corinthians 10:4-5)

In 1942 Henry Morris became a professor of civil engineering at his alma
mater, Rice Institute. Throughout his long career as an engineering professor he
was involved in campus ministry with students, working with the Gideons, the
Navigators, and Inter-Varsity Christian Fellowship. Morris became increasingly
concerned about the stranglehold evolutionary dogma had over college
education in America. He watched many students who entered Rice as Bible-
believing Christians lose their faith by the time they graduated. Bombarded by
constant attacks on the Bible's historical and scientific accuracy, these young
men and women abandoned the Scriptures altogether and became modernists,
agnostics, or atheists.

Profoundly saddened by the growing apostasy he was witnessing, Henry Morris began a more thorough study of origins—creation and evolution. He delved deeply into the Scriptures and poured over as many books as he could find on the subject. Although he encountered many works written by Christians advocating theistic evolution, he rejected them out of hand when he found contradictions with God's revelation in Genesis. More than anything, Morris was firmly committed to the final authority of the Bible as inerrant and infallible. Without qualm or hesitation, he believed "[God's] word is truth" (John 17:17) and he was willing to say "let God be true but every man a liar" (Rom. 3:4).

From the outset then, the young scientist realized that he had to reject the old earth creationist arguments. He didn't know how to reconcile the Genesis account of creation and the global flood with what some were calling "scientific evidence." But, first and foremost, he knew that the Bible was absolutely true, and the scientific evidence must and will agree with the Bible if that evidence is properly interpreted. He didn't have all the answers as he launched into his studies of origins, but he was willing to look for them.

In the course of his studies, Henry Morris came across the writings of George McCready Price, a self-educated Seventh-Day Adventist geologist. Price argued cogently for a literal six-day creation and a young earth. He pointed out that the worldwide flood recorded in Genesis 6-8 could very well explain the formation of the geologic rock layers and fossils. The key to casting down the arguments for evolution and an old earth was flood geology (2 Cor. 10:4-5). He wrote:

The philosophy of evolutionary development is at the center of all anti-Christian and anti-Biblical systems. The theory of evolution draws its only real evidence from historical geology and, in the minds of most people at least, once the orthodox framework of geologic ages is granted, evolution necessarily follows as an implication. Consequently, the reality or non-reality of these geologic ages is a very important problem.

In the last century, Christendom quickly accepted the geologic ages as taught by Cuvier and Lyell, adopting the day-age theory, for the most part, as a supposed means of harmonizing Genesis with geology. This situation made it very easy, then, for the transition into theistic evolution and finally into outright modernism on the part of most of the churches of the immediate past generation. I am afraid that this history will be repeated on the part of present evangelical churches if our present tendency of continual retreat under scientific theories goes on.[6]

With this in mind, Henry Morris moved his family to Minneapolis where he continued his studies of hydraulics, hydrology, and geology at the University of Minnesota. There he earned a master's degree and a Ph.D., and with that he pursued studies in flood geology. In 1951 he became head of the civil engineering

> **Hydrology:** A branch of science dealing with the properties, distribution, and circulation of water on and below the earth's surface and in the atmosphere.

department at Southwestern Louisiana University. While there he engaged in much evangelism of the predominantly Roman Catholic population that lived in the area.

The Genesis Flood

As a committed Christian, who worked in the field of science, Dr. Morris began looking for other Christian scholars and scientists who shared his convictions. At this time there was no such organization of Christians. Several attempts had been made to organize, but all had failed, either dissolving quickly or becoming infiltrated and captured by evolutionists. When Henry Morris joined the American Scientific Affiliation (ASA), he was hoping to find a commitment to the authority of God's Word. He quickly realized however,

> **Hydraulics:** A branch of science and technology concerned with the conveyance of liquids through pipes and channels, especially as a source of mechanical force or control.

that the organization was filled with theistic evolutionists. Nevertheless he presented a paper entitled "Biblical Evidence for a Recent Creation and Universal Deluge" at the 1953 ASA Convention. The paper met with a cool reception from the members of the society, but one man was favorably impressed: John C. Whitcomb, Professor of Old Testament at Grace Theological Seminary. After the convention, Whitcomb wrote to Morris:

> *I greatly appreciated your paper on a Recent Creation and Universal Deluge which you read at the A.S.A. convention. I feel that your conclusions are scripturally valid, and therefore must be sustained by a fair examination of geologic evidence in time to come. My only regret is that so few trained Christian men of science are willing to let God's Word have the final say on these questions . . . I have adopted your views . . . and am presenting them to my class as preferable alternatives to the Gap Theory and the Day-Age Theory.*[7]

This connection would produce a life-long friendship. Henry Morris shared his plans with Whitcomb to write a book that addressed the geological implications of the flood. At the same time, John C. Whitcomb was working on a doctoral dissertation on the flood. Together, the men decided to co-author a book on the Genesis Flood, combining Morris' scientific knowledge with Whitcomb's Old Testament scholarship. This would be the book that would define the battle of ideas between Christ and the world in the latter half of the twentieth century.

Work on the book proceeded slowly, however. Both men had full-time jobs and they were raising large families (Whitcomb had four children of his own). In 1957 Dr. Morris became head of the civil engineering at the prestigious Virginia Polytechnic Institute in Blacksburg, Virginia, where he would serve for the next thirteen years. Moreover, this book was no ordinary book. It required a great deal more research, and the more the authors researched, the more problems they uncovered which required further research. Again and again, they would turn to the Lord for guidance (Jas. 1:5). Morris wrote:

> *The Lord marvelously led in the necessary research and writing of the book. Time*

and again, after encountering a difficult geological (or other) problem, I would pray
about it, and then a reasonable solution would somehow quickly come to mind or
hand, and the manuscript gradually took shape.[8]

After finishing the first draft in 1959, the two authors sent the manuscript of *The Genesis Flood* to several scientists, theologians, and grammarians for review, and incorporated their feedback. In July 1960 the Morris and Whitcomb families met at Winona Lake, Indiana to review the final manuscript. They decided to have a picnic at the lake. The children splashed around in the water while Dr. Morris and Dr. Whitcomb sat on the beach in lawn chairs reviewing the 500-page typewritten manuscript. All of a sudden, the wind picked up, sending the manuscript pages flying across the beach. With dirty and wet hands, parents and children managed to collect all the pages, preventing them from being hopelessly damaged or destroyed.

Finally, the book was completed. But, another problem confronted them—the need for a publisher. Morris and Whitcomb originally planned to publish with Moody Press, but the Moody editors were reluctant to do so. They wanted the book cut down to 300 pages, and they made it clear that they didn't agree with the book's message. They also forewarned the authors of significant time delays in the publication.

However, in the providence of God, a copy of the manuscript had been sent to an Orthodox Presbyterian pastor and theologian named Dr. Rousas J. Rushdoony. Rushdoony received the book with great enthusiasm, recognizing its potential for helping to revive the Christian faith around the world. He recommended that Morris and Whitcomb share the manuscript with a publisher named Charles Craig, the owner of the small Presbyterian and Reformed Publishing Company (P&R). Craig received the manuscript with great enthusiasm and promised to publish the book in its entirety right away. Henry Morris wrote of this publishing relationship:

[Charles Craig] . . . took a special interest in our book, even though he had
never before published a scientific book. His own background was among the
Presbyterians, and all his authors heretofore had been strong Calvinists. Both Dr.

Whitcomb (Grace Brethren) and I (Baptist) seemed a little out of place among these Reformed and Presbyterian writers, but we all shared an absolute commitment to Biblical inerrancy and authority. In eschatology, all the P&R authors were either amillennial or postmillennial, whereas both John Whitcomb and I were (and are) "pretribulation" premillennialists, but we nevertheless had much in common with Craig and got along very well with him.[9]

And so, in 1961, the Presbyterian and Reformed Publishing Company issued *The Genesis Flood*. The book presented strong biblical and scientific arguments for the worldwide flood and challenged Uniformitarian geology head-on. The authors argued that the clear language of the biblical text, the gigantic proportions of Noah's Ark, and the corroborating testimony of 2 Peter 3 all made clear that the flood had to be global (and not a small, local flood). The authors wrote:

If only one (to say nothing of all) of the high mountains had been covered with water, the flood would have been absolutely universal; for water must seek its own level—and must do so quickly![10]

Morris and Whitcomb also pointed out a major problem with Uniformitarian geology, which posited that the fossils were millions of years old and predated Adam. This theory implied that there must have been millions of years of death before the Fall, and such a belief is completely contrary to Scripture.

"Through one man sin entered the world, and death through sin, and thus death spread to all men, because all sinned" (Romans 5:12).

Thus, Dr. Morris and Dr. Whitcomb argued that the massive quantities of fossils found in geological layers of rocks had to have been laid down by a sudden deluge of water—a worldwide flood. The book produced a sound, and more believable scientific explanation for fossils laid down by water in a large and sudden event. But more than anything, the book became a clarion call for Christians to return to the authority of the Bible even when addressing historical and scientific matters. The authors wrote:

Either the Biblical record of the Flood is false and must be rejected or else the system of historical geology which has seemed to discredit it is wrong and must be changed. The latter alternative would seem to be the only one which a Biblically and scientifically instructed Christian could honestly take, regardless of the "deluge" of scholarly wrath and ridicule that taking such a position brings upon him. But this position need not mean at all that the actual observed data of geology are to be rejected. It is not the facts of geology, but only certain interpretations of those facts, that are at variance with Scripture.[11]

One of the greatest contributions of *The Genesis Flood* was to present an alternative system of geology that interpreted the facts in harmony with Scripture.

Of course, the book was largely ignored by the secular scientific community, but it had an immediate impact among Christians. Most of the reviews were favorable, and those Christians who feared God and trembled at His Word were thrilled by what they read in *The Genesis Flood*. However, those Christians who coveted academic respectability and were set on compromising with evolutionists who did not fear God were upset by the book's message. None of the critical reviews, however, ever seriously addressed the book's exegetical and scientific arguments. One of Dr. Morris' chief critics was his own pastor in Virginia, who represented the more liberal wing of the Southern Baptist Convention. The man refused to even read the book because it questioned "science," and eventually, the Morrises and a few other families were forced to leave and plant a more solid Bible-believing church.

Not surprisingly Dr. Henry Morris was also persecuted by fellow faculty members at Virginia Tech. When the university received a new dean, matters grew worse and some of the faculty brought increasing pressure to bear in an attempt to remove Morris from his position at the university. However, the Lord's hand was upon Dr. Morris and his engineering department was the most successful in the university. Nonetheless, the Christian professor was finally forced to resigned in 1970. Before he left, Morris wrote a hydraulic engineering textbook that Virginia Tech students would use for many years.

Beloved, do not think it strange concerning the fiery trial which is to try you, as though some strange thing happened to you; but rejoice to the extent that you partake of Christ's sufferings, that when His glory is revealed, you may also be glad with exceeding joy. If you are reproached for the name of Christ, blessed are you, for the Spirit of glory and of God rests upon you. On their part He is blasphemed, but on your part He is glorified. (1 Peter 4:12-14)

Institute for Creation Research and Final Days

You will have tribulation ten days. Be faithful until death, and I will give you the crown of life. He who has an ear, let him hear what the Spirit says to the churches. He who overcomes shall not be hurt by the second death. (Revelation 2:10b,11)

Henry Morris was not at all disheartened by the persecution he received from the Christian community and the secular world. Instead, he turned his attention to a new work God was calling him to—the fortification of the Christian faith and the faithful Christian church in the midst of a very hostile world. After publishing *The Genesis Flood*, Drs. Morris and Whitcomb began to receive many speaking invitations from various groups of Christians around the country. The need for networks and organizations of Christian scientists and scholars committed to literal biblical creationism was even more urgent. Christian youth in particular needed a robust Christian creationist education.

As genuine believers began to discern the vast difference between the Christian view of knowledge, origins, and science and that of the non-Christian unbelieving world, a new movement began. Christians parents and churches realized they must organize special schools and colleges for their own children. They must abandon the godless, materialist form of public education, and raise their children "in the nurture and the admonition of the Lord" (Eph. 6:4). The Christian home schooling movement had its start in the 1970s and 1980s, largely propelled by this commitment to a Christian view of knowledge and science.

Dr. Henry Morris helped found the Creation Research Society in 1963, and seven years later he moved his family to San Diego, California and founded the Institute for Creation Research (ICR). For the rest of his life he worked with ICR, researching, writing, speaking, and teaching. Moving from a well-paid professorship at a prestigious university to the presidency of a fledgling Christian ministry was a step of faith. But Henry trusted God to supply his needs "according to His riches in glory by Christ Jesus" (Phil. 4:19).

The Lord brought together a gifted team of workmen at ICR. Dr. Duane Gish was a talented biochemist and gifted debater. Henry's son, Dr. John Morris became a biologist and led several expeditions to Mount Ararat in search of Noah's Ark. A gifted Australian speaker and teacher named Ken Ham joined the team in the 1980s. He had been greatly impacted by reading *The Genesis Flood* as a university student and would go on to found the world's largest creation ministry, Answers in Genesis (AIG), which would construct a Creation Museum and the Ark Encounter (a life-sized ark) in Kentucky.

As he grew older, Dr. Morris came to deplore what he called "the attitude of pietistic defeatism that had characterized evangelical Christianity for several generations."[12] Yet, he lived long enough to see how the Lord had used his work to sustain the Christian faith and to grow a worldwide creationist movement and bring reformation to large portions of the evangelical church on this issue. He was also overjoyed to see his physical and spiritual children walking in the truth (3 John 4). On February 25, 2006, Henry Morris died peacefully at home and went to be with the Lord in heaven.

> *"Blessed are the dead who die in the Lord from now on." "Yes," says the Spirit, "that they may rest from their labors, and their works follow them." (Revelation 14:13)*

Life Lessons from Henry Morris

First and foremost, Dr. Henry Morris displayed an unwavering commitment to the Bible as the inerrant and infallible Word of God. Whereas previous generations of Christians had lost faith in God's revelation, and had relegated it to a shallow one-day-a-week experience, Henry Morris took the Word of

God as authoritative for all of life. He believed it was absolutely true not just in matters of salvation but for all of life, including history and science. Whereas, the half-hearted "Christian" did not want God to speak to real life, right and wrong, science, and origins, Henry Morris bowed himself before the Lord and cried out, "Speak Lord, for your servant hears!" (1 Sam. 3:9) With this attitude and presuppositional framework, he set out to examine the evidence. When he was struggling with a problem, he asked God for help, and the Lord gave Him wisdom to understand the evidence in the light of His Word.

This commitment produced in him an unwavering courage. Unquestionably, Dr. Henry Morris was not afraid to be called a fool for Christ's sake. Unlike many Christians of his day, he did not compromise the truth of God's Word for the sake of academic respectability. He knew that the wisdom of the world is foolishness with God. He trusted that "the foolishness of God is wiser than men, and the weakness of God is stronger than men" (1 Cor. 1:25).

And finally, Dr. Morris took the faith as more than an intellectual pursuit—it was a life to be lived out in obedience and love for God. If anything could be said about this 20th century Christian scientist—he was a godly man. He was a worshipful man, a praying man, and a faithful husband and father who led his family in worshiping the Lord every day. He took his place as a regular member of his local church, and he was zealous in sharing the gospel with unbelievers. This is a life that serves as an example for ordinary Christians in the modern world—faithful to Christ in personal life, church life, university life, and professional life no matter the cost. May God raise up more Christian men and women like Henry Morris in this time!

> *Therefore, my beloved brethren, be steadfast, immovable, always abounding in the work of the Lord, knowing that your labor is not in vain in the Lord. (1 Corinthians 15:58)*

David Wilkerson (1931-2011)

CHAPTER 27

David Wilkerson: Spiritual Revival During an Age of Apostasy

Will you not revive us again, that your people may rejoice in you?

—Psalm 85:6

S ome have called the 1940s and 1950s the lowest time in the Christian life of the West. A spiritual malaise had spread through the Christian faith in the Protestant countries of Britain, the Netherlands, Germany, Canada, and America. This breakdown of faith would also have ill effects on other nations around the world as churches, ministries, and mission boards turned liberal and lost touch with the power of the gospel.

Those leaders with a heart for reformation and spiritual life were saddened when no revival of any real lasting effect came about. When a revival appeared, there was only a little temporary excitement, a gathering of a crowd, and some outward professions, but there was little or no change of life and culture. Here and there were to be found voices crying in the wilderness: men like Leonard

Ravenhill (1907-1994), D. Martyn Lloyd-Jones (1900-1981), and A.W. Tozer (1897-1963). Mercifully, the Lord did sustain a little spiritual life in Britain and America during these dark years. He brought a small revival in the 1960s and 1970s. However, it was slight compared to the 16th century Reformation or the 18th century Great Awakening. Nonetheless, small blessings are still to be counted.

The British evangelist Leonard Ravenhill gave the spiritual answer to the false conception of the Christian faith in these simple words: "Jesus did not come into the world to make bad men good. He came into the world to make dead men live!"[1] These were powerfully insightful words and they came to correct the thinking of a few men of God in that era, including that of American evangelist David Wilkerson.

The spiritual malaise in the West was the product of a long and painful decline that continued from the late 1700s to the 1960s. It consisted of a thorough-going theological weakness, division over minor things (creating a plethora of denominations), spiritual disempowerment, faithlessness, a very low view of the church, moral decline, and generational apostasy.

To put it in simple terms, God was too small. In the mind of the modern Christian, the character and works of the true and living God had been set aside and marginalized. This widespread perspective came about by the rise of humanism and the glorification of man in the schools, as well as by the teaching and the books produced by the American church. Man's choices had become more important than God's purposes and power. Man's works had become more impressive than God's works. God's law had been replaced by man's laws. External obedience and external appearances were considered more important than heart-deep love for God and the true worship of God. Much of Christianity was reduced to the rousing up of an emotional excitement. Sometimes the faith was no more than a thin-coated sentimentality. Sometimes Christianity was reduced to an intellectual consent to doctrines without any real love for God and faith. The Christian faith seemed to be unraveling in a hundred different ways. It was a sad time for American Protestantism. To make things worse, from the 1960s into the 2010s, many terrible moral scandals both among Protestants and Roman Catholics smeared the name of Christ in the eyes of the world.

At the same time church growth experts rushed in with new and innovative ideas to increase the size of churches. Large choirs at first became popular and then they were later replaced by professional rock bands in most churches. Religious activity reached an all-time high, yet the preaching of the Word was little valued. A genuine Christian faith seemed far removed from much church experience in the latter half of the 20th century. No Christian denomination was entirely immune from the problems.

However, God was still working at this time in the history of the American church. One man's journey provides a good picture of how God's mercy still works in times of spiritual decline. David Wilkerson was one of the key leaders in a small revival called the "Jesus Movement" of the 1970s. His life offers a good picture of how God transforms a man from an external form of lifeless religion into something more life-giving and substantial. In an otherwise rather cold world, David Wilkerson demonstrated the love and compassion of Christ. At times, this evangelist and pastor spoke to the moral and religious situation with laser-sharp precision and a prophetic voice hardly matched by anyone else in America at the time. His beginnings were rooted in the Pentecostal Assemblies of God denomination. David Wilkerson was best known for his ministry to the gangs in New York City in the late 1950s. He carried the Cross to those who carried switchblades. His story, *The Cross and the Switchblade*, became a popular motion picture with Christian churches in the 1970s. Something about his story woke up the Christian church.

The Flaw in David Wilkerson's Christian Heritage

You did not choose Me, but I chose you and appointed, that you should go and bear fruit, and that your fruit should remain, that whatever you ask the Father in My name He may give you. (John 15:16)

David Wilkerson's Christian heritage was evangelical, conservative, fundamentalist, legalistic, and Pentecostal. These adjectives were very familiar to children raised in Christian churches from the 1920s through the 1990s. This "conservative" heritage was fading at the turn of the 21st century. By the 1930s, evangelicalism had become became a conservative half-way house with the goal of salvaging the Christian faith from the liberals. First, the liberals had tried to destroy the faith in the 1900s by rejecting the authority of God's Word. To counter this liberalism, many Christians reacted by adopting a conservative approach to the faith which focused more so on externals. It turned out to be another path towards apostasy for many. For the most part, it was still too shallow, too man-centered, and too faithless at root.

David Wilkerson was born to Kenneth and Ann Wilkerson on May 19, 1931 in Hammond, Indiana. David's grandfather was a Pentecostal evangelist who was known for his wild theatrics on stage. His father was also a preacher and worked as a pastor in Turtle Creek, Pennsylvania during David's adolescent years. The Wilkerson children were not allowed to attend the local high school football games or participate in gym class. Card games were strictly forbidden, and rarely did the family do much together (except for family worship). Relationships were stiff and communication poor. Yet God, in His mercy, laid His hand on David at nine years of age. During a church family camp, the young man professed faith in Christ. Two years later he heard a sermon about serving the Lord in ministry, and he responded by running down the aisle, crying out, "Jesus use me! Put your hand on my life!"[2] To commemorate this early calling on his life, his father gave him a copy of *Foxe's Book of Martyrs*, and he was allowed to preach his first sermon at the church at the tender age of fourteen.

David's later teen years were marked with trauma as his father suffered from bleeding ulcers that rendered him almost an invalid. There were multiple near-death incidents and, as his biographer and son Gary Wilkerson writes, they were "full of agonized screams, bloody bed sheets, and bloody floors."[3] Still as a young seventeen-year-old boy, David worked at the local market and preached at various venues around town to provide extra income for the family. His son Gary tells the story of how young David Wilkerson was depended upon for the family's sustenance. The family was sitting at the table eating dinner, and David announced to the family: "I'm thinking about quitting Harkins Market."

His father stopped eating, and sat there staring down at his plate. Finally, he said, "David, we won't make it."[4]

Young David felt a keen responsibility for providing for his family while his father suffered severe bodily affliction. After attending a Bible school for eighteen months, David was ordained as a pastor in the Assemblies of God. During his first years of ministry he tried the traveling life of a Pentecostal healing evangelist and ventriloquist. Then, after his marriage to Gwen, he accepted a church pastorate in Philipsburg, Pennsylvania.

Awakening

> *Now the Lord spoke to Paul in the night by a vision, "Do not be afraid, but speak,*
> *and do not keep silent; for I am with you, and no one will attack you to hurt you;*
> *for I have many people in this city." And he continued there a year and six months,*
> *teaching the word of God among them. (Acts 18:9-11)*

Four years into his ministry at Philipsburg, David Wilkerson's little congregation had increased numerically, and the church also sponsored a television broadcast which aired his preaching. However, David was not at peace with the spiritual condition of the church. There was little zeal in the church, very little outreach, and no ministry of mercy. Though it was a Pentecostal church, he had to admit to himself this was no Pentecost.

So David prayed in these early years of his ministry: "Lord, if this is pentecost, I don't want it. If it's having a 'bless me' club every week, I'll have nothing to do with it."[5] About this time in his life, the young pastor stopped watching television in the evenings, instead dedicating himself to hours of prayer. He proceeded to place an ad in the newspaper for his television set and prayed that someone would buy it by noon the next day. As the family sat waiting nervously, a man finally arrived at 11:59 a.m. to purchase the set, no questions asked.

There in the farm country of central Pennsylvania David Wilkerson poured out his soul to God, seeking a better understanding of the Lord's will. He studied the Word with a new-found zeal and made copious notes. More and more he experienced what he would call "an anguish of soul." He began to understand the import of God's truth. It was more than a head knowledge. Increasingly, he began to feel the heart of God expressed by the prophets, the apostles, and the Lord Himself.

David Wilkerson prayed for a gift which he called a "faith for souls."[6] Beyond just physical healings, what he really wanted to see was spiritual healings. He wanted a hope and a faith that the Holy Spirit was working and would work to draw new converts to Christ. He wanted to introduce lost souls to Jesus. He wanted to see the power of the Holy Spirit working within.

Little did David know that a year earlier a Presbyterian pastor named Dick Simmons of the Brooklyn Presbyterian Church had gone through a similar experience. One morning in 1957 Pastor Dick stepped out of his house to see the police hauling away two teenage gang members on stretchers. Apparently one of the boys had attempted to meet with the pastor but had been intercepted by another gang member. A knife fight ensued, in which both young men were severely wounded. Later Dick Simmons said, "[The episode] provoked me to begin getting up very early in the morning and going to the church to pray. The Spirit of God came on me, and I found myself praying all day long—eight, ten, even sixteen hours."[7] Three years later the Lord would bring Dick Simmons together with David Wilkerson in the inner-city work of Teen Challenge.

It was a pen drawing in *Life* magazine, however, that changed the direction of David's life. The article featured seven teen gang members in New York City who had assaulted and murdered a defenseless, disabled boy named Michael Farmer. The story was covered by every national news agency and spawned a countrywide outrage, but Wilkerson's response was different. He sat looking into the faces of the boys staring at him off the picture in *Life* magazine as tears ran down his face.

This country pastor wasn't ignoring the importance of God's justice or the terrible hurt inflicted on the victim's family. But he saw in the faces of those youth a larger problem, a deeper issue, and a crying spiritual need. He could feel the need in the faces of millions of young people, and his heart literally ached for them. "Wave after wave" of holy anguish swept over him.[8]

The next week, the pastor took up a collection from his church to cover gas money for the trip and, in company with his youth pastor, he made his first trip in to New York City. The two men attended the trial of the seven young gang members. However, when David tried to meet with the judge, he was thrown out of the courtroom. The newspaper photographers took full advantage of the little drama and instantly David Wilkerson's face was recognized all over New York City. As God directed the events that followed, David was never able to meet with the young murder suspects. However, this was the beginning of an inner-city ministry. For four months he made weekly trips into New York and wandered the streets, speaking to lost boys and girls in the gangs. He met with teens in drug dens; he slept in his car at night and then made his way back to his Pennsylvania home on Saturdays. His approach with the young gang members was always a quiet boldness, an open reception, and a deep concern for their souls.

For God has not given us a spirit of fear, but of power and of love and of a sound mind. (2 Timothy 1:7)

It was the Spirit of power, love, and a sound mind that filled David Wilkerson when he met Nicky Cruz, the most feared teen gang leader in New

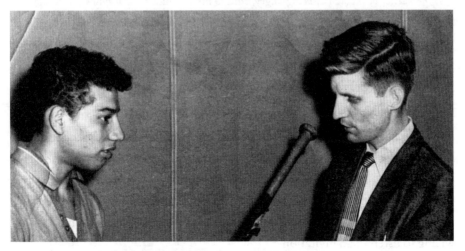

David Wilkerson and Nicky Cruz

York City. Cruz was known for his sadism, his readiness to wreak vengeance on his enemies, and his skillful use of the switchblade. When he threatened to cut David into a thousand pieces and throw him in the street, David responded, "You cut me into a thousand pieces, and every little piece of me will still be saying, 'I love you! Jesus loves you!'"[9] Cruz later confessed, "That was when Wilkerson beat the devil right there. And he got me."[10]

Mission to the Highways and Byways

Now when one of those who sat at the table with [Jesus] heard these things, he said to Him, "Blessed is he who shall eat bread in the kingdom of God!" Then He said to him, "A certain man gave a great supper and invited many, and sent his servant at supper time to say to those who were invited, 'Come, for all things are now ready.' But they all with one accord began to make excuses. The first said to him, 'I have bought a piece of ground, and I must go and see it. I ask you to have me excused.' And another said, 'I have bought five yoke of oxen, and I am going to test them. I ask you to have me excused.' Still another said, 'I have married a wife, and therefore I cannot come.' So that servant came and reported these things to his master. Then the master of the house, being angry, said to his servant, 'Go out quickly into the streets and lanes of the city, and bring in here the poor and the maimed and the lame and the blind.' And the servant said, 'Master, it is done as you commanded, and still there is room.' Then the master said to the servant, 'Go out into the highways and hedges, and compel them to come in, that my house may be filled.'" (Luke 14:15-23)

When the preaching of the Word within churches increasingly falls on deaf ears and hardened hearts, what does a preacher do? It is a quandary faced by many a pastor in churches and nations that are abandoning the faith. This passage from our Lord in Luke 14 gives the answer in no uncertain terms. The Christian laborer never sits fallow. He must always go out and find those who are walking in the highways and the byways—the down and outers who may still be willing to listen to an invitation.

Thus, Christian pastors in America and Europe have increasingly been forced into the highways and byways. They have ministered to immigrants, prisoners, drug addicts, and others. It was men like David Wilkerson who gained a heart for this ministry and acted on it. They followed the leading of the Holy Spirit into new fields.

In July 1958 David took a significant faith risk on the urging of churches around New York City. He called a meeting for the city's many rival gangs to gather at St. Nicholas Arena. The risk of such a gathering was all-out gang war, and the first nights of the crusade did not go well. Nobody was listening. "The place was ready to explode," as one gang leader put it.[11] It was the last five minutes of the last night of the crusade however, when the Holy Spirit came. A great change came over the preacher. He spoke of Christ's crucifixion and resurrection. Then he said, "And he's here in this place right now."[12] Nicky Cruz was radically converted that night. He remembers Dave "crying for me" as Cruz professed faith in the Lord Jesus Christ.[13] A year later, Nicky Cruz was enrolled in Bible college. He would later return to help with the ministry in New York City.

It was nothing short of revival breaking out in the slums of New York City as gang members, drug addicts, and those caught in sexual dissipation turned to Jesus. By 1960 Wilkerson formed his first Teen Challenge office in Brooklyn's most dangerous neighborhood. Sonny Arguinzoni was one of the first drug addicts whose life was radically transformed almost overnight. A Jewish mother drove up to the Teen Challenge office and pushed her drug-addicted son out of the car, dressed in nothing but an undershirt and boxers. Harvey Kuflik was hopelessly addicted to heroin. His mother told the staff, "I don't believe in Jesus Christ. But whatever you can do with Harvey, he's yours."[14] It wasn't long before Harvey was converted and drug free, and he became an evangelist to other young teens in the city.

For about a year David Wilkerson lived by himself in an apartment in Staten Island, equipped with a cot and an electric burner to warm up his food. His family lived at Gwen's family's home in Pittsburgh while the ministry was getting started. David worked himself to exhaustion and, whenever he collapsed, his friends would take him to the hospital to recover.

The staff at the center, largely populated by young people from Christian colleges and seminaries, met every day for prayer and the Word. Then they hit

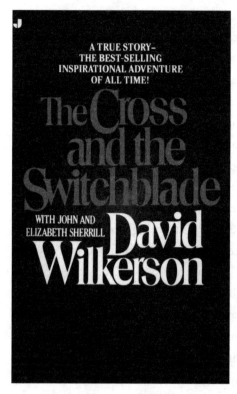

A TRUE STORY—
THE BEST-SELLING
INSPIRATIONAL ADVENTURE
OF ALL TIME!

The Cross
and the
Switchblade

WITH JOHN AND
ELIZABETH SHERRILL David
Wilkerson

*Cover of the original The Cross
and the Switchblade*

the streets to minister to more gangs and drug addicts in New York City. This introduced the evangelical world to caring for the poor and bringing the gospel message to those in the highways and byways.

It wasn't long before other Pentecostals, Presbyterians, and Dutch Reformed pastors and churches began joining the work. Leonard Ravenhill, the revivalist from England, came to help—and here he witnessed the revival he was looking for. In some cases drug addicts were completely cured of their addictions in thirty seconds. Later studies would find that David Wilkerson's Teen Challenge program sustained an 87% cure rate seven years after the addicts had left the program.[15]

It was in these early years that David Wilkerson wrote his first book, with the help of John and Elizabeth Sherrill—*The Cross and the Switchblade*. It sold 16 million copies and inspired a movie in which a well-known actor/singer Pat Boone played the part of David Wilkerson.

Ever since Jesus broke down the middle wall of separation between Jew and Gentile, the true church has always had a cross-cultural flavor to it. This is what developed in the 1960s through the work of men like David Wilkerson. The inner city church made up of men and women who were radically transformed by the gospel of Christ would turn out to be an international church. Cultural differences were of minor consequence when it came to the work of the Holy Spirit in the hearts of men and women. The mainline denominations were already dying in the 1970s and virtually dead by the 2000s. Yet, the Holy Spirit was not inactive on the frontiers of the immigration explosion in the big urban centers. The gospel-transformed inner-city churches made up of men and women hungry for the Word were just getting started in the 1960s and 1970s. David's son Gary grew up in Brooklyn and played basketball with Puerto Ricans, Hispanics, Anglos, and African Americans. His best friends were other boys of color.

The Jesus Movement and the Youth Crusades

Oh, that You would rend the heavens! That You would come down! That the mountains might shake at Your presence—As fire burns brushwood, as fire causes water to boil—to make Your name known to Your adversaries, that the nations may tremble at Your presence! When You did awesome things for which we did not look, You came down, the mountains shook at Your presence. For since the beginning of the world men have not heard nor perceived by the ear, nor has the eye seen any God besides You, who acts for the one who waits for Him. (Isaiah 64:1-4)

In the later 1960s, with revival strong in the air, David Wilkerson traveled with his son Gary on the crusade route. They visited hundreds of cities and villages across America, holding preaching meetings mainly targeting youth. Wilkerson preached to thousands, sometimes tens of thousands at a time. Hundreds, sometimes thousands of young people would crowd into the front of the meeting halls each night for counsel and prayer. During these years, the ministry always covered its own travel expenses and never asked for fees. They sold their books for 5 cents apiece wholesale. In the summer of 1970 the Wilkerson family moved to California where they participated in the growing "Jesus Movement." Having worked for years with young people who had sexual problems and drug addictions, David had an immediate connection with the crowds. Even David's daughters helped in the ministry—"singing choruses, sharing their testimonies, and leading other teenagers to Christ."[16]

On the crusade trail, David's messages were frank, transparent, and direct with the teens. He never shied away from talking the tough topics, always issuing a call to repentance. Although there were a few others like Chuck Smith of Calvary Chapel who participated in the revivals of the 1960s and 1970s, David Wilkerson will be remembered as standing in the forefront of this amazing movement of God. He was also a mentor for well-known Christian musician Keith Green in those early years.

Although the Jesus Movement was not characterized by extraordinary works of God's providence, a miracle did occur during a crusade service conducted in Brazil. Tens of thousands gathered to hear Brother Dave preach. While he was evangelizing ten thousand people in the city of Campinas, several hundred responded to a call to repentance. David told them to look up and smile if they were trusting in Christ. However, one young man did not look up. David told the interpreter to tell the young man to look up. The interpreter responded, "He says he has nothing to smile about; he was born blind."[17]

Dave responded even more emphatically, "You tell him to lift up his head and smile." The interpreter translated the message, and the young man began to raise his head. As he did so, he cried out, "I can see! I can see!" David Patterson witnessed the event and later wrote, "Both of his eyes were opened by the power of God! There had been no preaching about miracles or healing in the crusade service. We watched a sovereign miracle take place." [18]

The Shock of Cultural Apostasy

Yes, and all who desire to live godly in Christ Jesus will suffer persecution. But evil men and impostors will grow worse and worse, deceiving and being deceived. But you must continue in the things which you have learned and been assured of, knowing from whom you have learned them, and that from childhood you have known the Holy Scriptures, which are able to make you wise for salvation through faith which is in Christ Jesus. All Scripture is given by inspiration of God, and is profitable for doctrine, for reproof, for correction, for instruction in righteousness, that the man of God may be complete, thoroughly equipped for every good work. I charge you therefore before God and the Lord Jesus Christ, who will judge the living and the dead at His appearing and His kingdom: Preach the word! Be ready in season and out of season. Convince, rebuke, exhort, with all longsuffering and teaching. For the time will come when they will not endure sound doctrine, but according to their own desires, because they have itching ears, they will heap up for themselves teachers. (2 Timothy 3:12-4:3)

David Wilkerson was not just an evangelist. He had a gift of spiritual discernment, an uncanny sense for the spiritual condition of the world around him. It is best described as a special sensitivity to what was happening to America as a nation. Through the 1970s he began writing books and articles describing the trajectory of the nation. He could see the terrible rise of pornography, drugs, and homosexuality. He suggested that religious freedom in America would be severely curtailed. He thought marijuana would become legalized. He projected that churches would receive homosexuality and lesbianism as morally acceptable. He wrote of a "super church" or a "mega church" where religious leaders would "set out to comfort mankind in their sins."[19]

These insights were far too radical, too controversial, and too pessimistic for many American Christian to receive. Few believed that the situation could be "that bad." His popularity gained from *The Cross and the Switchblade* days began to fade.

There was a downside to David Wilkerson's commitment to address the sins of the nation as he took on a "prophetic role." The cultural decline seemed to fuel a pessimism about the future. His view of the end times was informed at this time by a rising interest in apocalyptic predictions and end times fever. He was influenced by premillennial Christian writers who believed that the Antichrist was soon to come and that the Great Tribulation would follow.

In some ways, however, Brother David Wilkerson's spiritual insights concerning the decline of the Western world were accurate. History vindicates this rather unpopular "Jeremiah," as he predicted the further softening of the church, the persecution of true Christians, and the rapid decline of national morality. Yet his focus on these issues threw a wet blanket over his ministry for a while.

Many Christians have a tendency to want to move into a segregated Christian community when the cultural outlook is negative and apocalyptic. However, the calling on David's life to disciple the nations and to preach the gospel was much stronger than the impulse to withdraw or run away. David moved his ministry to a rural area near Tyler, Texas in the early 1980s. Whether it was an impulse to sit and wait for the pre-tribulation rapture or some other motive, it is hard to say. Various people in the Jesus Movement wound up living in the community for a while, but it turned out to be too much salt in one pile.

David continued his ministry, preaching in prisons regularly. He brought the hard message to conferences with 10,000 ministers gathered, even at the risk of never being invited back. He always preached as if each sermon were his last. In his son Gary's words, "To Dad, the moment in the pulpit was the hour of life or death for those in the audience. The power of God had to move through him to bring them to repentance and salvation, and for that reason, he had to be utterly prepared—and emptied."[20]

The Turnaround

Who shall separate us from the love of Christ? Shall tribulation, or distress, or persecution, or famine, or nakedness, or peril, or sword? As it is written, "For Your sake we are killed all day long; we are accounted as sheep for the slaughter." Yet in all these things we are more than conquerors through Him who loved us. For I am persuaded that neither death nor life, nor angels nor principalities nor powers, nor things present nor things to come, nor height nor depth, nor any other created thing, shall be able to separate us from the love of God which is in Christ Jesus our Lord. (Romans 8:36-39)

From his early history in ministry, it is clear that the Lord used David Wilkerson to take a basic message of the gospel, faith, and repentance, to millions in America and around the world. David certainly faced his own limitations. He wasn't well-honed in doctrinal precision. His son Gary admits that he was plagued by a "performance-driven faith"[21] and a focus on externals (dress, hairstyles, the use of alcohol, etc.).[22]

Yet Wilkerson was still tortured by what he saw as a backsliding evangelical faith. The evidence was in the lack of fruit. In the mid-1980s he attended a Christian rock concert with its intense exhibition of loud noise, bright lights, and performance. His son writes of the experience, "He began to groan. He rose up from his seat and found himself running down the aisle, waving his arms and shouting, 'Ichabod! Ichabod! The glory of the Lord has departed!'"[23]

It was about this time that David shut down his crusade ministry. The mighty wave of the Jesus Movement seemed to have spent its force. The youth were not interested in evangelistic preaching anymore. This was a time of tremendous grief for him as he felt the religious temperature of the nation cooling.

The Lord chose this time to bring about an important theological turnaround in the thinking of David Wilkerson. During one of his last crusades, the staff bus was pulling out of the parking lot when the English revivalist, Leonard Ravenhill pulled up alongside in his car. Ravenhill had a sack of books for David. Leonard told him, "This is your future. Read it, and it will change your life."[24]

As the bus sped off, David chucked the bag of books to the floor with a thud. But, during the trip to the next city, he began reading the books—most of them old classic works written by Puritans. These books would transform David's life and ministry.

The doctrine they taught was more God-centered, in contrast with the man-centered religion that had so consumed American evangelicalism. David was captured by the message of the holiness of God and the beauties of Christ so well displayed in these Puritan writings. Their words were a fitting correction to his tendency to legalism.

In October 1987 David received a call to plant a church in Times Square, New York City. Once more he was called back into the highways and byways to find the bride of Christ. Like a magnet he was drawn again into the most troubled areas. "It is in the darkest places that God shows himself strongest" was his motto.[25]

Moreover, for David Wilkerson the kingdom was no longer Ameri-centric or Western-centric. The church had become international. This is how the Holy Spirit was moving in the Western church at the turn of the 20th century. At fifty-six years of age, David heeded the call to serve as pastor of a multi-national inner-city church. This congregation was made up of "rich and poor, middle class, all nationalities."[26] Famous politicians and actors could be seen in prayer circles alongside street people and drug addicts. It was a Jesus-type of church, pastored by a disciple of Jesus.

On October 18, 1987 David stopped his sermon mid-sentence. Turning to his co-pastor, he said, "There's going to be a crisis on Wall Street tomorrow . . . I want you to go there with me."[27] The next morning the stock market crashed. David Wilkerson and Bob Phillips were there to pray with the traders on the worst day since the stock market crash of 1929.

In the pastorate David learned how to weave the message of grace in and around a message concerning sin. He couldn't just preach judgment and repentance, and the message of the cross became more central. Conflicts in the church brought a whole new set of challenges for this itinerant preacher. The pain, the suffering, and the constant spiritual warfare that attends pastoring became very real to him.

In the end, it was the Puritans who helped him through. He learned of covenant grace. He consumed the great Christian classics written by men like John Owen, John Calvin, Charles Spurgeon, and Thomas Brooks. He finally realized the truth, "I can't please God no matter what I do. I've already pleased him in Christ."[28] He found comfort in the truth that he was adopted into the family of God. There was no more meriting God's favor. He was fully accepted in the sight of God. Such revelations released him from "a rigid pentecost that produces almost an eggshell walk."[29] As his views changed, David's ministry turned more from condemnation to reconciliation. He called up old friends who were estranged and asked for their forgiveness. A great peace descended on his ministry from then on.

David Wilkerson didn't like a Christian faith that yielded no fruit. But, on the other hand, he had come to realize the weakness of a faith or a salvation that could be lost. He realized that repentance could not be reduced to a merit system in which a person could never quite repent enough. God's sovereign, powerful grace was the answer. Finally, he came to understand that we believe in a powerful grace that is able to keep us and work in us before we work out our salvation in fear and trembling. God's will, God's preserving grace and His covenantal love must be stronger than our willpower and commitment to Him. We persevere *because* God's hand is under us preserving us.

> *Therefore, my beloved, as you have always obeyed, not as in my presence only, but now much more in my absence, work out your own salvation with fear and trembling; for it is God who works in you both to will and to do for His good pleasure. (Philippians 2:12-13)*

As his health failed after 2010, David Wilkerson continued to immerse himself in the Puritans. Towards the end of his life he began to read John Calvin, particularly on the subject of God's grace and the completeness of Christ's work in us.

In his final sermon given in his 80th year, David preached on the love of God, with these closing words:

> *This is foundational. You have to be convinced that no matter what you're going through, you are loved. I've seen a lot and been through a lot, and the one thing I know, the thing that has kept me over all these years, is that no matter what is thrown at me, God loves me.*[30]

Brother David Wilkerson died in an automobile accident near his home in Tyler, Texas on April 27, 2011.

Blessed are They that Mourn

> *Blessed are the poor in spirit, for theirs is the kingdom of heaven. Blessed are those who mourn, for they shall be comforted. (Matthew 5:2-3)*

The life of David Wilkerson is itself a picture of revival and reformation in an age of Christian apostasy. Every life is a journey and David traversed a good path. Undoubtedly God used him to reach millions with a basic gospel message. As the old evangelical and mainline denominations (both conservative and liberal) declined, a church in new wineskins developed. The church appeared in the highways and byways and became more and more characterized by the "every tribe and nation" plan of our Savior. The Lord used David Wilkerson, for one, to lead the way. It is an encouragement to know that the Holy Spirit of God is active and working even during the decline of Western Christianity.

On September 15, 2002 David Wilkerson preached his most famous sermon at Times Square Church, entitled "A Call to Anguish." Once again, the aging man of God spoke out strongly to a nation that continued to celebrate immorality heading towards a state of indescribable ruin. The theme of the sermon was based upon Jesus's simple words, "Blessed are those who mourn, for they shall be comforted" (Matt. 5:4). Preaching from Nehemiah 1, Wilkerson declared:

> *You search the scripture and you'll find that when God determined to recover a*
> *ruined situation, he would seek out a praying man, and he'd take him down into the*
> *waters of anguish. He would share his own anguish for what God saw happening to*
> *his church and to his people, and he would find a praying man, and he would take*
> *that man and literally baptize him in anguish.*[31]

David Wilkerson was an unusual man of God for his day. He was both famous and infamous. He would not allow fame to lure him into people-pleasing, and he would not allow criticism to silence him. He strongly resisted Pat Boone's suggestion to produce a movie based on *The Cross and the Switchblade*. Twice he turned down invitations to meet with US Presidents (Gerald Ford and Jimmy Carter). He was more interested in the state of the church than the state of politics, believing that as the church goes, so goes the nation.

While Brother David was not afraid of offending people, he still loved people with a powerful passion. His son Gary wrote of his father: "His flamboyance would become innovation. His natural restlessness would become a holy hunger. His self-judgment would become a spiritual discontent."[32]

David had a powerful preaching style. His sentences were short and direct. His audiences were always riveted from beginning to end, hanging on every word. His manner was serious and sincere, yet also loving, as when he looked at the violent gang member and said, "You cut me into a thousand pieces, and

Times Square Church, New York City, founded by David Wilkerson

every piece of my body will cry out 'I love you!'" Gary Wilkerson boils down his father's disposition as one who loved God, and was always in awe of what God was doing:

> He was awed by the powerful work of the Gospel by the Holy Spirit of God in hundreds and thousands of drug addicts. He saw it. He saw lives radically transformed, families reconciled, the poor lifted out of despair, and the captives set free. He really saw it, and he gloried in the power of the Gospel of the Lord Jesus Christ.[33]

That powerful message is even more relevant and more needed today than it was 50-60 years ago when Wilkerson brought it to the streets of New York City. The problem of drug addiction is far worse today than it was in 1957.[34] Almost 10% of Americans currently use illegal drugs. Only about 0.4% of New York City engaged in drug use in 1957. Pornography and homosexuality are perhaps a hundred times more rampant and more accessible and more encouraged today than they were when David began his ministry. Sadly, America on the whole has not listened to the servants of God like Wilkerson.

There are only a few weak cries for revival emerging out of a post-Christian America. Where is the powerful work of God, and where are the people waiting expectantly for it? Commenting on his friend David Wilkerson in the preface of his recently released biography, Jim Cymbala writes, "All the statistics prove that, by every measurable parameter, the Christian church is sinking. Part of the problem is what we've been fed for the last ten, fifteen, twenty years—the focus on church growth, on being user-friendly, seeker-sensitive. All that has opened the door to unbiblical teaching, just shallow nonsense. It's resulted in getting away from prayer, away from the gospel, away from loving all people of all races, away from dependence on the Holy Spirit . . . Where are the Tozers, the David Wilkersons who'll say, 'In all love, that is wrong'?"[35]

Yet the church of the Lord Jesus Christ will continue. It must be a church that is committed to the discipleship of every tribe and nation. The church must continue to serve as a powerful beacon of light and gospel proclamation in a dark and hopeless world. And the more hopeless the world presents itself, the more hope the gospel message will offer. The darker the night, the more promising the light. That was the heart vision of David Wilkerson.

> *My speech and my preaching were not with persuasive words of man's wisdom, but in demonstration of the Spirit and power, that your faith should not be in the wisdom of men, but in the power of God. (1 Corinthians 2:4-5)*

America: A Rich Christian Heritage

A merica. It was a unique experiment in faith and freedom in the history of the world. There is no denying the country's rich Christian heritage and the longstanding influence of that heritage for centuries. Without a doubt, the long shadow of Jesus Christ reached down into the lives of George Washington, Daniel Boone, John Quincy Adams, George Washington Carver, and William McKinley. This nation retained the influence of Christ for hundreds of years. The whole world has benefited by this beautiful experiment in Christian virtue and liberty. It is a story that must be told until the return of Christ. To obscure the story would be to leave the world without a good report. Refusing to recognize the work of Christ and His influence upon the nations would be to dishonor His royal reign. While certainly we must not ignore the rampant increase in abortion, euthanasia, godlessness, divorce, drug addiction, homosexuality, socialism, debt, and Christian persecution during the decline of the nation, the heritage never completely disappears.

As America entered the 21st century, it became clear that not much could be fixed by politics. Efforts made by conservatives to slow down abortion rates, socialism, and big government debt were largely thwarted by the courts and an increasingly immoral people. Unless there is reformation and revival in the church, there will be no fixing the broken families, the destruction of sexuality, the imploding birth rates, and the rising debt-to-GDP ratio. Without reformation and revival, there is no fixing the rising national disunity between political factions. Today in 2019, America is a nation in the balance. Will God have mercy on this nation? Will her people humble themselves, or will they mainly be concerned with making America great again?

Will the church begin to mourn? Will the church realize its spiritual poverty? Will there be meek and humble people in the church who will inherit the earth?

What America needs at the beginning of the 21st century is:

- humble scientists like George Washington Carver,
- humble repenting statesmen like John Quincy Adams,
- humble men of mourning like David Wilkerson,
- humble poets like Anne Bradstreet and Phillis Wheatley,
- humble husbands like William McKinley,
- humble generals like George Washington,
- humble missionaries like Adoniram Judson, and
- humble, sacrificial leaders like John Winthrop.

Will these come from the rising generation? Will God have mercy upon this nation again and raise up humble men and women of the faith to preserve a nation and leave another legacy? May it be so.

If My people who are called by My name will humble themselves, and pray and seek My face, and turn from their wicked ways, then I will hear from heaven, and will forgive their sin and heal their land. (2 Chronicles 7:14)

Endnotes

1. John Winthrop: America's Founding Father

1   Francis J. Bremer, *John Winthrop: America's Forgotten Founding Father* (New York: Oxford University Press, 2003), 5

2   Ibid., 70.

3   Ibid., 76.

4   Westminster Confession of Faith, 3.1.

5   Bremer, 79.

6   Ibid.

7   Ibid.

8   Ibid., 91.,

9   Ibid., 96.

10 Ibid.

11 Ibid., 97.

12 Ibid., 101.

13 Quoted in Peter Marshall and David Manuel, *The Light and the Glory* (Grand Rapids: Revell, 2009), 187.

14 Edmund S. Morgan, *The Puritan Dilemma: The Story of John Winthrop* (Boston: Little, Brown, 1958), 13.

15 Bremer, 228.

16 Ibid., 116.

17 Ibid.

18 Morgan, 13.

19 Bremer, 117.

20 Ibid.

21 Ibid., 138.

22 Ibid., 149.

23 Quoted in Morgan, 40.

24 Quoted in Morgan, 40.

25 Ibid.

26 Ibid., 158.

27 Ibid., 155.

28 Ibid., 169.

29 Quoted in ibid., 178.

30 Ibid.

31 Ibid.

32 Ibid.

33 Ibid.

34 Ibid.

35 Ibid., 192.

36 Morgan, 62.

37 Bremer, 195.

38 Ibid.

39 Morgan, 97.

40 Quoted in Edmund J. Carpenter, *Roger Williams: A Study of the Life, Times, and Character of a Political Pioneer* (New York: Grafton Press, 1909), 126.

41 Bremer, 307.

42 Morgan, 168.

2. William Bradford: Governor of Plymouth

1   Gary D. Schmidt, *William Bradford: Plymouth's Faithful Pilgrim* (Grand Rapids, MI: Eerdmans, 1999), 4.

2   Quoted in Schmidt, 12.

3   William Bradford, *Of Plymouth Plantation: Bradford's History of the Plymouth Settlement, 1608-1650* (San Antonio: Vision Forum, 1998), 9.

4   Ibid., 14.

5   Ibid., 21.

6   Ibid.

7   Schmidt, 41.

8   Nathaniel Philbrick, *Mayflower: A Story of Courage, Community, and War* (New York: Penguin, 2006), 20-21.

9   Schmidt, 57.

10   Ibid., 59.

11   Philbrick, 20.

12   Bradford, 64.

13   Philbrick, 42.

14   Bradford, 75-76.

15   Daniel J. Ford, *In the name of God, Amen: Rediscovering Biblical and Historic Covenants* (St. Louis, MO: Lex Rex Publishing, 2003), 152.

16   Bradford, 77.

17   Ibid., 80.

18   Ibid., 83.

19   Philbrick, 117.

20   Ibid.

21   Ibid., 117-118.

22   Quoted in Schmidt, 109.

23   Bradford, 89.

24   Ibid., 90.

25   Ibid., 94-95.

26   Ibid., 105.

27   Ibid., 110.

28   Schmidt, 146-147.

29   Bradford., 115-116.

30   Ibid., 115.

31   Schmidt, 155.

32   Ibid., 180.

3. Anne Bradstreet: America's First Published Poet

1   Anne Bradstreet, "To My Dear Children," *The Works of Anne Bradstreet*, ed. Jeannine Hensley (Cambridge: Harvard University Press, 2010), 263.

2   Ibid.

3   Ibid.

4   Bradstreet, "Upon a Fit of Sickness," *The Works of Anne Bradstreet*, 240.

5   Bradstreet, "To My Dear Children," *The Works of Anne Bradstreet*, 264.

6   Bradstreet, "In Honour of Du Bartas," *The Works of Anne Bradstreet*, 205.

7   Bradstreet, "The Four Seasons of the Year," *The Works of Anne Bradstreet*, 77.

8   "Epistle to the Reader, by John Woodbridge," in *The Works of Anne Bradstreet*, 1.

9   Bradstreet, "The Author to Her Book," *The Works of Anne Bradstreet*, 238.

10   Bradstreet, "To My Dear and Loving Husband," *The Works of Anne Bradstreet*, 245.

11   Bradstreet, "Upon My Dear and Loving Husband His Going into England, Jan. 16, 1661," *The Works of Anne Bradstreet*, 288.

12   Ibid., 289.

13   Bradstreet, "In Reference to Her Children, 23 June, 1659," *The Works of Anne Bradstreet*, 253.

14   Ibid., 255-256.

15   Bradstreet, "Before the Birth of One of Her Children," *The Works of Anne Bradstreet*, 243.

16   Bradstreet, "In Memory of My Dear Grandchild Anne Bradstreet Who Deceased June 20, 1669, Being Three

Years and Seven Months Old," *The Works of Anne Bradstreet*, 258.

17 Bradstreet, "Here Follows Some Verses Upon the Burning of Our House July 10th, 1666. Copied Out of a Loose Paper," *The Works of Anne Bradstreet*, 318.

18 Ibid., 319-320.

19 Heidi L. Nichols, *Anne Bradstreet: A Guided Tour of the Life and Thought of a Puritan Poet* (Phillipsburg, NJ: P&R, 2006), 82.

20 Bradstreet, "A Dialogue between Old England and New; Concerning Their Present Troubles, Anno, 1642," *The Works of Anne Bradstreet*, 191.

21 Ibid., 194.

4. John Eliot: America's First Missionary

1 William Bradford, *Of Plymouth Plantation: Bradford's History of the Plymouth Settlement*, 1608-1650 (San Antonio: Vision Forum, 1998), 21.

2 Quoted in Nehemiah Adams, *The Life of John Eliot* (Boston: Massachusetts Sabbath School Society, 1847), 46.

3 Ibid., 47.

4 Ibid., 67.

5 Ibid., 55.

6 Quoted in Convers Francis, *Life of John Eliot: Apostle to the Indians* (New York: Harper & Brothers, 1840), 319.

7 Adams, 19.

8 Quoted in Francis, 45.

9 Quoted in Adams, 92.

10 Quoted in Francis, 157.

11 Quoted in Adams, 132.

12 Quoted in Francis, 144.

13 Quoted in Daniel Gookin, *Historical Collections in New England* (Boston: Belknap and Hall, 1792), 41.

14 Quoted in Francis, 167.

15 Quoted in Adams, 139.

16 Ibid., 196-197.

17 Ibid., 270-271.

18 Ibid., 49.

19 Ibid.

20 Quoted in Francis, 335.

21 Ibid.

22 Ibid., 337.

5. Increase Mather: Rooting a Nation in Faith

1 Franklin B. Dexter, "Estimates of Population in the American Colonies," in *Proceedings of the American Antiquarian Society* (Worcester, MA: American Antiquarian Society, 1889), 5:22-50.

2 William Bradford, "Verses by Governor Bradford," in *Proceedings of the Massachusetts Historical Society* (Boston: Massachusetts

Historical Society, 1871), 11:477.

3 Philip Doddridge, *A Plain and Serious Address to the Master of the Family on the Important Subject of Family-Religion* (London: T. Longman, et al, 17947) 35.

4 Matthew Henry, Sermon Concerning Family-Religion (London: Bible and Three Crowns, 1704), 19.

5 Edmund S. Morgan, *The Puritan*

Family (New York: Harper & Row, 1966), 88-98.

6   William Brigham, *The Compact with the Charter and Laws of the Colony of New Plymouth* (Boston: Dutton and Wentworth, 1836), 270-271.

7   Quoted in Morgan, *The Puritan Family*, 84.

8   Michael G. Hall, *The Last American Puritan: The Life of Increase Mather* (Hanover, NH: Wesleyan University Press, 1988), 130.

9   Ibid., 107-108.

10 George M. Waller, ed., *Puritanism in Early America* (Lexington, MA: D.C. Heath, 1973), 116.

11 Quoted in Hall, *The Last American Puritan*, 41.

12 Ibid.,, 142.

13 Ibid., 143.

14 Ibid., 290.

15 "The Harvard Charter of 1650," *Harvard Library*, March 31, 1650, https://emeritus.library.harvard.edu/university-archives/using-the-collections/online-resources/charter-of-1650.

16 "Shield and 'Veritas' History," *Harvard GSAS Christian Community*, http://www.hcs.harvard.edu/~gsascf/shield-and-veritas-history/.

17 Hall, 199.

18 Ibid., 272.

19 Ibid.

20 Ibid., 167.

21 Ibid., 304.

22 Ibid., 285.

23 Increase Mather, "Ichabod. Or, A discourse, shewing what cause there is to fear that the glory of the Lord, is departing from New-England," 1702, https://quod.lib.umich.edu/e/evans/N00897.0001.001?view=toc.

24 Hall, 188.

25 Ibid., 204.

26 Ibid., 251.

27 Ibid., 252.

28 Cotton Mather, *Magnalia Christi Americana*, vol. 1, (Hartford, CT: Silas Andrus & Son, 1855), 204.

29 Hall, 205.

30 Ibid.

31 Rebecca B. Brooks, "Reverend Samuel Parris: Was He to Blame for the Salem Witch Trials?" *Massachusetts History Blog*, September 8, 2015, http://historyofmassachusetts.org/reverend-samuel-parris/.

32 Quoted in ibid.

33 Richard Middlekauff, *The Mathers: Three Generations of Puritan Intellectuals, 1596-1728* (Berkeley: University of California Press, 1999), 160.

34 Jerome S. Handler, "Slave Medicine and Obeah in Barbados, circa 1650 to 1834," NWIG: New West Indian Guide / Nieuwe West-Indische Gids 74, no. 1/2 (2000): 57-90, http://www.jstor.org/stable/41850026.

6. David Brainerd: A Life on the Altar

1   Quoted in Nehemiah Adams, *The Life of John Eliot* (Boston: Massachusetts Sabbath School Society, 1847), 10.

2   Quoted in John Gillies, *Historical Collections*, vol. 2 (Glasgow: Robert and Andrew Foulis, 1754), 29.

3   Quoted in John A. Dreisbach, "David Brainerd," *GFA Missions*, May 26, 1997, https://gfamissions.org/pages/learn-and-promote/detail/3/21/.

4   Ibid.

5   Ibid.

6   Quoted in Vance Christie, *David Brainerd: A Flame for God* (Fearn, UK: Christian Focus, 2009), 22.

7   Ibid., 43.

8   Ibid., 44.

9   Ibid., 52.

10 Ibid.

11 Ibid., 75.

12 Ibid., 86-87.

13 Ibid., 105.

14 Ibid., 104.

15 Ibid., 122.

16 Ibid., 153-154.

17 Ibid., 156.

18 Ibid., 161.

19 Ibid.

20 *The Life and Diary of David Brainerd*, ed. Jonathan Edwards (Peabody, MA: Hendrickson, 2006), 282-283.

21 Christie, 174.

22 Ibid., 177.

23 Ibid., 191.

24 Ibid., 245.

25 Ibid., 218.

26 Ibid., 283.

27 Ibid., 304.

28 Ibid., 308.

29 Ibid., 67.

30 Ibid., 238-239.

31 Ibid., 167.

32 Ibid., 143.

7. *Jonathan Edwards: A Passion for God's Glory*

1   Steven J. Lawson, *The Unwavering Resolve of Jonathan Edwards* (Orlando: Reformation Trust, 2008), 3.

2   Quoted in ibid., 35.

3   Quoted in Iain H. Murray, *Jonathan Edwards: A New Biography* (Edinburgh: Banner of Truth, 1987), 25.

4   Quoted in ibid., 31.

5   Jonathan Edwards, "The Spider Letter," in *A Jonathan Edwards Reader*, ed. John E. Smith, Harry S. Stout, and Kenneth P. Minkema (New Haven, CT: Yale University Press, 1995), 1.

6   Ibid., 5.

7   Ibid., 8.

8   Jonathan Edwards, "Personal Narrative, 1739," in *A Jonathan Edwards Reader*, 288.

9   Quoted in Lawson, 8.

10 Ibid., 29-30.

11 Jonathan Edwards, "Resolutions," *Jonathan Edwards Center at Yale University*.

12 Ibid., "Resolution 1."

13 Ibid., "Resolution 5."

14 Ibid., "Resolution 7."

15 Ibid., "Resolution 13."

16 Ibid., "Resolution 17."

17 Ibid., "Resolution 28."

18 Ibid., "Resolution 30."

19 Ibid., "Resolution 56."

20 Jonathan Edwards, "Apostrophe to Sarah Pierpont (c. 1723)," in *A*

Jonathan Edwards Reader, 281.

21 Quoted in Noël Piper, "Sarah Edwards: Jonathan's Home and Haven," in *A God Entranced Vision of All Things: The Legacy of Jonathan Edwards*, ed. John Piper and Justin Taylor (Wheaton, IL: Crossway, 2004), 67.

22 Quoted in Murray, 95.

23 Jonathan Edwards, "A Narrative of Surprising Conversions," in *Jonathan Edwards on Revival* (Edinburgh: Banner of Truth, 1965), 13-14.

24 Jonathan Edwards, "Sinners in the Hands of an Angry God," in *A Jonathan Edwards Reader*, 90-91.

25 Ibid., 104-105.

26 Murray, 226.

27 Quoted in Stephen J. Nichols, *Jonathan Edwards: A Guided Tour of His Life and Thought* (Phillipsburg, NJ: Presbyterian & Reformed, 2001), 124.

28 Quoted in Murray, 137.

29 Ibid., 342.

30 Ibid.

31 Ibid., 16.

32 Murray, 392.

33 Jonathan Edwards, in John Piper, *God's Passion for His Glory: Living the Vision of Jonathan Edwards, with the Complete Text of The End for Which God Created the World* (Wheaton, IL: Crossway, 1998), 183.

34 Quoted in Murray, 441.

35 Quoted in ibid., 442.

36 Edwards, "Resolution 4."

8. Patrick Henry: Lighting the Flame for Liberty

1 Henry Mayer, *A Son of Thunder: Patrick Henry and the American Republic* (New York: Grove Press, 2001), 38.

2 David J. Vaughan, *Give Me Liberty: The Uncompromising Statesmanship of Patrick Henry* (Nashville: Cumberland House, 1997), 39.

3 Mayer, 40.

4 William Wirt Henry, ed., *Patrick Henry: Life, Correspondence, and Speeches* (Harrisonburg, PA: Sprinkle Publications, 1993), 1:38-39.

5 Ibid., 1:41.

6 Ibid., 1:86.

7 Quoted in Mark Couvillon, ed., *The Demosthenes of His Age – Accounts of Patrick Henry's Oratory by His Contemporaries* (Red Hill, VA: Patrick Henry Memorial Foundation, 2013), 31.

8 Quoted in Edmund S. Morgan, *The Birth of the Republic, 1763-89* (Chicago: University of Chicago Press, 1956), 111.

9 Quoted in Henry, 1:264-266.

10 Quoted in Harrow G. Unger, *Lion of Liberty: Patrick Henry and the Call to a New Nation* (Cambridge, MA: Da Capo Press, 2010), 268.

11 Quoted in Norman Hapgood, *George Washington* (New York: Macmillan, 1901), 313-314.

12 Quoted in Jonathan Elliot, ed., *The Debates in the Several State Conventions on the Adoption of the Federal Constitution*, vol. 3, 2nd ed. (New York: Burt Franklin, 1888), 146.

13 Ibid., 54.

14 Quoted in Norine D. Campbell, *Patrick Henry: Patriot and Statesman* (New York: Devon-Adair, 1969), 352.

15 Quoted in ibid., 350.

16 Quote in ibid, 355.

17 Walter Williams, *Washington Times*, June 10, 1992, G1.

18 Quoted in Henry, 1:265.

19 Quoted in Patrick Daily, *Patrick Henry: The Last Years, 1789-1799* (Dexter, MI: Thomson-Shore Inc., 2013), 170.

20 Ibid.

21 Ibid.

22 George Morgan, *The True Patrick Henry* (Philadelphia: J.P. Lippencott, Co., 1907), 403.

23 Daily, 173.

24 Morgan, 402.

25 Daily, 174.

26 Letter to Mrs. Anne Christian, May 15th, 1786, in *Henry*, 2:287.

27 Henry, 2:631.

28 Quoted in Moses Coit Tyler, *Patrick Henry* (New York: Houghton Mifflin and Co., 1897), 377.

9. Samuel Adams: Founding Father of American Independence

1 Samuel Checkley, "A day of darkness. A sermon preach'd before His Excellency William Shirley, Esq; the Honorable His Majesty's Council, and House of Representatives, of the province of the Massachusetts-Bay, in New-England," *Evans Early American Imprint Collection*, May 28, 1755, https://quod.lib.umich.edu/cgi/t/text/text-idx?c=evans;idno=N05814.0001.001.

2 George W. Harper, *A People So Favored of God: Boston's Congregational Churches and their Pastors, 1710-1760* (Eugene, OR: Wipf and Stock, 2007), 101.

3 Ibid.

4 Quoted in Mark D. Puls, *Samuel Adams: Father of the American Revolution* (New York: Macmillan, 2006), 32.

5 Quoted in Dennis B. Fradin, *Samuel Adams: The Father of American Independence* (New York: Clarion Books, 1998), 142.

6 Quoted in John K. Alexander, *Samuel Adams: America's Revolutionary Politician* (Lanham, MD: Rowman & Littlefield, 1992), 241.

7 Quoted in J.L. Bell, "You Won't Believe How Samuel Adams Recruited Sons of Liberty," *Journal of the American Revolution*, February 5, 2014, https://allthingsliberty.com/2014/02/you-wont-believe-how-samuel-adams-recruited-sons-of-liberty/.

8 Ibid.

9 Ibid.

10 Puls, 40.

11 Fradin, 25.

12 Puls, 51.

13 Fradin, 52.

14 Samuel Adams, *The Writings of Samuel Adams,* vol. 1, *1764-1769* (New York: G.P. Putnam's Sons, 1904), 201-212.

15 Ibid, 27.

16 Ibid.

17 Samuel Adams, "Oration Delivered at the Philadelphia State House, August

1, 1776" in *The Life and Public Services of Samuel Adams*, ed. William V. Wells (Boston: Little, Brown, 1865), 3:419.

18 Quoted in "Correspondence to and from Samuel Adams on the Gaspee Incident," *Gaspee Virtual Archives*, http://www.gaspee.org/SamAdams.html.

19 Wells, 3:415.

20 https://history.hanover.edu/texts/adamss.html. Samuel Adams, "The Rights of the Colonists, The Report of the Committee of Correspondence to the Boston Town Meeting," Nov. 20, 1772, Old South Leaflets no. 173 (Boston: Directors of the Old South Work, 1906) 7:417-428.

21 Fradin, 68.

22 Quoted in *Proceedings of the New England Historical Genealogical Society*, January 1, 1873 (Boston: New England Historical and Genealogical Register, 1873), 11.

23 Quoted in William J. Jackman,

History of the American Nation, vol. 8 (Chicago: Western Press Association, 1917), 2389.

24 Quoted in David Hackett Fischer, *Paul Revere's Ride* (New York: Oxford University Press, 1994), 109.

25 Fradin, 111.

26 Alexander, 196.

27 Samuel Adams, *The Writings of Samuel Adams*, ed. Harry A. Cushing, vol. 3, *1773-1777* (New York: G. Putnam's Sons, 1907), 228.

28 Wells, 2:423.

29 Ibid., 3:408.

30 Alexander, 176.

31 Wells, 1:22.

32 Alexander, 311.

33 Wells, 3:347.

34 Ibid., 3:301.

35 Ibid., 3:327.

36 Ibid., 3:379.

37 Ibid., 3:365-366.

10. Phillis Wheatley: First African-American Writer

1 Henry Louis Gates Jr., *The Trials of Phillis Wheatley: America's First Black Poet and Her Encounter with the Founding Fathers* (New York: Basic Civitas Books, 2003), 18.

2 Vincent Caretta, *Phillis Wheatley: Biography of a Genius in Bondage* (Athens, GA: The University of Georgia Press, 2011), 2.

3 Phillis Wheatley, "On the Death of the Rev. Mr. George Whitefield. 1770," in *Complete Writings*, ed. Vincent Caretta (New York: Penguin, 2001), 15.

4 Quoted in Phillis Wheatley, *Complete Writings*, ed. Vincent Caretta

(New York: Penguin, 2001), 7

5 Quoted in ibid., 8.

6 Caretta, 141.

7 Quoted in Ibid., 143.

8 Caretta, 172.

9 Phillis Wheatley, "On Being Brought from Africa to America," *Complete Writings*, 13.

10 Wheatley, "Thoughts on the Works of Providence," *Complete Writings*, 26.

11 Ibid., 29.

12 Wheatley, "Atheism," *Complete Writings*, 67.

13 Quoted in Gates, 23.

14 Quoted in ibid., 24.

15 Quoted in ibid., 25.

16 Quoted in ibid., 42.

17 Quoted in ibid., 42-43.

11. *George Washington: The President Who Feared God*

1 Quoted in Nat Hillborn and Sam Hillborn, *Battleground of Freedom: South Carolina in the Revolution* (Columbia, SC: Sandlapper, 1970), 145-155.

2 Ibid.

3 Stephen Mansfield and George Grant, *Faithful Volunteers: The History of Religion in Tennessee* (Nashville: Cumberland House, 1997), 38.

4 Rodd Gragg, *By the Hand of Providence: How Faith Shaped the American Revolution* (New York: Simon & Schuster, 2011), 169.

5 Quoted in Claude H. Van Tyne, *The American Revolution 1776-1783* (New York: Harper, 1905), 323.

6 Quoted in Gragg, 171.

7 Ibid.

8 Quoted in Benjamin F. Morris, *The Christian Life and Character of the Civil Institutions of the United States* (Philadelphia: George W. Childs, 1864), 299.

9 Matthew Hale, *The Works Moral and Religious of Sir Matthew Hale* (London: R. Wilks, 1805), 54.

10 Quoted in Peter Lillback, *George Washington's Sacred Fire* (Bryn Mawr, PA: Providence Forum Press, 2006), 128.

11 David McCullough, *1776* (New York: Simon & Schuster, 2005), 48.

12 Quoted in John Marshall, *The Life of George Washington* (Philadelphia: Crissy & Markley, 1854), 1:11.

13 Quoted in Jared Sparks, *The Life of George Washington* (Boston: Little, Brown, 1853), 63.

14 Quoted in George Washington Parke Custis, *Recollections and Private Memoirs of Washington* (New York: Derby & Jackson, 1860), 304.

15 George Washington, *The Writings of George Washington from the Original Manuscript Sources 1745-1799*, ed. John C. Fitzpatrick (Washington DC: US Government Printing, 1931), 1:152.

16 Ibid., 1:153.

17 Ibid., 4:243.

18 Ibid., 4:441-442.

19 Quoted in Mark Beliles and Stephen McDowell, *America's Providential History* (Charlottesville, VA: Providence Foundation, 1989), 160-161

20 George Washington, "General Orders, 26 September 1780," *National Archives*, https://founders.archives.gov/documents/Washington/99-01-02-03388.

21 George Washington, "From George Washington to John Rodgers, 11 June 1783," *National Archives*, https://founders.archives.gov/documents/Washington/99-01-02-11434.

22 Quoted in Benson J. Lossing, *Mount Vernon and Its Associations* (New York: W. A. Townsend & Co., 1859), 134.

23 Quoted in Caroline Kirkland, *Memoirs of Washington* (New York: D. Appleton, 1857), 370.

24 Quoted in Lillback, 254.

25   Ibid.

26   Quoted in Sparks, 407.

27   Quoted in Ron Chernow, *Washington: A Life* (New York: Penguin, 2010), 690.

28   Quoted in ibid., 695.

29   George Washington's Papers, 28-408.

30   George Washington, "George Washington's Last Will and Testament, 9 July 1799," *National Archives*, https://founders. archives.gov/documents/ Washington/06-04-02-0404-0001.

31   Ibid.

32   Quoted in Chernow, 135.

33   George Washington, "Speech to the Delaware Indian Chiefs, May 12, 1779," ed. John Rhodehamel, in *George Washington: Writings* (New York: The Library of America, 1997), 351.

34   George Washington, "From George Washington to Lafayette, 25 July 1785," *National Archives*, https:// founders.archives.gov/documents/

Washington/04-03-02-0143.

35   George Washington's Papers, 3:7-16-1775, and 4:3-6-1776.

36   George Washington's Papers, 3-492.

37   George Washington, "From George Washington to Burwell Bassett, 28 August 1762," *National Archives*, https://founders. archives.gov/documents/ Washington/02-07-02-0092.

38   Quoted in E.C. M'Guire, *The Religious Opinions and Character of Washington* (New York: Harper, 1836), 138.

39   Quoted in Sparks, 523.

40   Custis, 508.

41   Quoted in Lillback, 939.

42   Quoted in Custis, 398.

43   Quoted in Frank E. Grizzard, *George Washington: A Biographical Companion* (Santa Barbara, CA: ABC-CLIO, 2002), 76.

44   Quoted in Sparks, 539.

12. Noah Webster: Christian Educator and American Patriot

1   K. Alan Snyder, *Defining Noah Webster: A Spiritual Biography* (Fairfax, VA: Allegiance Press, 2002), 21.

2   Quoted in Harlow Giles Unger, Noah Webster: *The Life and Times of An American Patriot* (New York: Wiley, 1998), 57.

3   Snyder, 23.

4   Ibid., 32.

5   Ibid., 33.

6   Unger, 36.

7   Quoted in Snyder, 40.

8   Ibid., 45.

9   Ibid., 46.

10   Unger, 45.

11   Snyder, 51-53.

12   Quoted in ibid., 54.

13   Quoted in ibid., 56.

14   Unger, 71.

15   Snyder, 66.

16   Unger, 83.

17   Ibid., 98.

18   Quoted in Snyder, 101.

19   Ibid., 169.

20   Quoted in ibid., 170.

21   Quoted in ibid., 175.

22   Quoted in ibid., 176.

23 Ibid., 177.

24 Quoted in ibid., 215.

25 Noah Webster, "Educate," *An American Dictionary of the English Language* (New York: S. Converse, 1828).

26 Quoted in Snyder, 223.

27 Quoted in ibid., 227.

28 Ibid., 232-233.

29 Webster, "Christian," *American Dictionary*.

30 Ibid., "love," *American Dictionary*.

31 Ibid., "meritorious," *American Dictionary*.

32 Quoted in ibid., 248.

33 Quoted in Unger, 274.

34 Ibid., "Preface," *American Dictionary*.

13. Daniel Boone: American Pioneer

1 John Bakeless, *Daniel Boone: Master of the Wilderness* (New York: William Morrow & Co., 1939), 11.

2 John Filson, *The Discovery, Settlement and Present State of Kentucke* (1784) (Lincoln, NE: Zea Books, 2017), 40.

3 Ibid., 41.

4 Ibid., 43-44.

5 Ibid., 44.

6 Account from Rev. James Welch, quoted in Bakeless, 368.

7 Letters from Dr. Felix Robertson (James Robertson's son) to Lyman Draper, quoted in William Curry Harlee, *Kinfolks: A Genealogical and Biographical Record*, 3 vols. (New Orleans: Searcy & Pfaff, 1935-37), 3:2500, 2513.

8 *My Father, Daniel Boone: The Draper Interviews with Nathan Boone*, ed. Neal O. Hammon (Lexington, KY: The University Press of Kentucky, 1999), 139.

9 Filson, 45.

10 Quoted in Bakeless, 369.

11 Filson, 39.

12 Lyman C. Draper, *The Life of Daniel Boone*, ed. Ted. F. Belue (Mechanicsburg, PA: Stackpole Books, 1998), 478.

13 Meredith Mason Brown, *Frontiersman: Daniel Boone and the Making of America* (Baton Rouge, LA: Louisiana State University Press, 2008), 2.

14 John Mason Peck, *Life of Daniel Boone: The Pioneer of Kentucky* (New York: The University Society, 1904), 137.

Unit 3 Introduction

1 Mark Noll, *A History of Christianity in the United States and Canada* (Grand Rapids: Eerdmans, 1992), 163.

14. John Quincy Adams: Keeping Faith During the Decline

1 Quoted in Gary Scott Smith, *Religion in the Oval Office: The Religious Lives of American Presidents* (New York: Oxford University Press, 2015), 19.

2 Ibid.

3   Quoted in Fred Kaplan, *John Quincy Adams: American Visionary* (New York: Harper Collins, 2014), 20.

4   Ibid., 30.

5   Ibid., 62.

6   Ibid., 107-108.

7   Ibid., 129.

8   Ibid.,165.

9   John Quincy Adams, "John Quincy Adams diary 24, 1 March 1795 - 31 December 1802, page 314," *Massachusetts Historical Society*,

10   Ibid.

11   Quoted in Kaplan, 173.

12   Ibid., 221.

13   Quoted in William W. Birdsall and Rufus M. Jones, eds., *Famous Authors and the Best Literature of England and America* (Philadelphia: American Book & Bible House, 1897), 552.

14   Quoted in Michael P. Ricaards, *The Ferocious Engine of Democracy: A History of the American Presidency* (Lanham, MD: Madison Books, 1995), 108.

15   Quoted in Kaplan, 545.

16   Quoted in David Waldstreicher & Matthew Mason, *John Quincy Adams and the Politics of Slavery: Selections from the Diary* (New York: Oxford University Press, 2017), 169.

17   Kaplan, 522.

18   John Quincy Adams, *Argument of John Quincy Adams Before the Supreme Court of the United States in the Case of the United States vs. Cinque and Others, Africans* (New York: S.W. Benedict, 1841), 9, 126.

19   Quoted in Kaplan, 525.

20   Quoted in John F. Kennedy, *Profiles in Courage* (New York: Harper and Brothers, 1955), 43.

21   Quoted in Kaplan 552.

22   Quoted in ibid., 313.

23   Smith, 122.

24   Quoted in ibid., 101-102.

25   Quoted in Paul C. Nagel, *John Quincy Adams: A Public Life, a Private Life* (New York: Alfred A. Knopf, 1997), 407.

26   Kaplan, 515.

15. Adoniram Judson: A Living Sacrifice

1   Quoted in Vance Christie, *Adoniram Judson: Devoted for Life* (Fearn, UK: Christian Focus, 2013), 15.

2   Quoted in ibid., 23.

3   Quoted in ibid.

4   Quoted in ibid., 24.

5   Quoted in ibid.

6   Quoted in ibid.

7   Quoted in ibid., 28-29.

8   Henry K. Rowe, *History of Andover Theological Seminary* (Newton, MA: Thomas Todd Company, 1933), 26.

9   Quoted in ibid., 38-39.

10   Quoted in Courtney Anderson, *To the Golden Shore: The Life of Adoniram Judson* (Valley Forge, PA: Judson Press, 1987), 83.

11   Quoted in ibid., 84.

12   Quoted in Christie, 101.

13   Quoted in ibid., 113.

14   Quoted in ibid., 131.

15   Quoted in ibid., 217-218.

16   Ibid., 191.

17 Sharon James, *My Heart in His Hands: Ann Judson of Burma, A Life with Selections from her Memoir and Letters* (Darlington: Evangelical Press, 1998), 157-158 .

18 Ibid, 163-164.

19 Anderson, *To the Golden Shore*, pp. 380-381

20 Quoted in ibid., 296.

21 Quoted in ibid., 312.

22 Jason Mandryk, *Operation World: The Definitive Prayer Guide to Every Nation*, 7th ed. (Downers Grove, IL: IVP, 2010), 610.

23 Quoted in Edward Judson, *The Life of Adoniram Judson* (New York: Anson D.F. Randolph & Co., 1883), 157.

24 Quoted in ibid., 253.

16. Asahel Nettleton: America's Forgotten Evangelist

1 Bennett Tyler, *Memoir of the Life and Character of Rev. Asahel Nettleton* (Boston: Doctrinal Tract and Book Society, 1852), 22.

2 Bennett Tyler and Andrew A. Bonar, Asahel Nettleton: *His Life and Labours* (Edinburgh: Banner of Truth, 1996), 34.

3 Quoted in Michael Farris, *American Commencement: Graduation Speeches that Inspired a New Nation* (Nashville: B&H, 2011), 78.

4 Lyman Beecher, *Autobiography of Lyman Beecher*, ed. Charles Beecher, vol. 1 (London: Sampson Low, Son & Marston, 1863), 30.

5 Quoted in Collin Hanson and John Woodbridge, *A God-Sized Vision: Revival Stories that Stretch and Stir* (Grand Rapids, MI: Zondervan, 2010), 68.

6 Quoted in John F. Thornbury, *God Sent Revival: The Story of Asahel Nettleton and the Second Great Awakening* (Durham, UK: Evangelical Press, 1988), 59.

7 Ibid., 81.

8 Ibid., 80-81.

9 Ibid., 107.

10 Tyler and Bonar, *Asahel Nettleton*, 179-180.

11 Thornbury, *God Sent Revival*, 103.

12 Ibid., 71.

13 Ibid., 76.

14 Tyler, *Memoir of the Life and Character of Rev. Asahel Nettleton*, 90.

15 Charles G. Finney, *Memoirs of Rev. Charles G. Finney* (New York: Fleming H. Revell Co., 1876), 63.

16 Charles G. Finney, *Sermons on Important Subjects* (New York: John S. Taylor, 1836), 37.

17 Charles G. Finney, *Lectures on Revivals of Religion* (New York: Leavitt, Lord & Co., 1835), 167-168.

18 Ibid., 293.

19 Iain H. Murray, *Revival and Revivalism: The Making and Marring of American Evangelicalism*, 1750-1858 (Edinburgh: Banner of Truth, 1994), 246.

20 For a more detailed critique of Revivalism see Iain H. Murray, *Revival and Revivalism: The Making and Marring of American Evangelicalism*, 1750-1858 (Edinburgh: Banner of Truth, 1994).

21 Quoted in Murray, *Revival and Revivalism*, 285.

22 Ibid., 289.

23 Quoted in Thornbury,
    God Sent Revival, 223.

24 Ibid.

25 Ibid.

26 Ibid., 55.

17. Lemuel Haynes: First African-American Minister

1   Quoted in John Saillant, *Black Puritan, Black Republican: The Life and Thought of Lemuel Haynes, 1753-1833* (New York: Oxford, 2003), 9.

2   Quoted in Timothy Mather Cooley, *Sketches of the Life and Character of the Rev. Lemuel Haynes* (New York: John S. Taylor, 1839), 30.

3   Thabiti M. Anyabwile, *May We Meet in the Heavenly World: The Piety of Lemuel Haynes* (Grand Rapids, MI: Reformation Heritage Books, 2009), 2-3.

4   Ibid., 36-37.

5   Quoted in Cooley, 53.

6   Quoted in ibid., 48.

7   Anyabwile, 4.

8   Ibid., 6.

9   Cooley, 66-67.

10 Ibid., 67-68.

11 Ibid., 89.

12 Quoted in ibid., 90.

13 Quoted in ibid., 90-91.

14 Ibid., 91.

15 Quoted in ibid., 103.

16 Anyabwile, 10.

17 Lemuel Haynes, "The Gospel and Slave-Keeping," in Anyabwile, *May We Meet in the Heavenly World*, 21.

18 Ibid., 22.

19 Ibid., 24.

20 Ibid., 25.

21 Quoted in Saillant, 15.

22 Lemuel Haynes, "Government and Religion Stand Together," in Anyabwile, *May We Meet in the Heavenly World*, 67.

23 Ibid., 68.

24 Lemuel Haynes, "The Gospel Ministry and Politics," in Anyabwile, *May We Meet in the Heavenly World*, 101-102.

25 Ibid., 103.

26 Lemuel Haynes, "Suffering and Glory," in Anyabwile, *May We Meet in the Heavenly World*, 113.

27 Quoted in Cooley, 304.

28 Quoted in ibid., 312.

18. Jedediah Smith: The Best Explorer of the American West

1   Hampton Sides, *Blood and Thunder: An Epic of the American West* (New York: Random House, 2006), 694.

2   Stephen Ambrose, *Undaunted Courage: Meriwether Lewis, Thomas Jefferson, and the Opening of the American West* (New York: Simon and Schuster, 2002), 254.

3   Ibid., 324-325.

4   Sides, 80-81, 86.

5   Dale L. Morgan, *Jedediah Smith and the Opening of the West* (Lincoln:

University of Nebraska Press, 1964), 8.

6   Ibid.

7   Ibid., 46.

8   Quoted in Larry E. Morris, *The Fate of the Corps: What Became of the Lewis and Clark Explorers After the Expedition* (New Haven: Yale

University Press, 2004), 243.

9   Charles L. Camp, ed. *James Clyman, Frontiersman, 1792-1881: The Adventures of a Trapper and Covered-Wagon Emigrant as Told in His Own Reminiscences and Diaries* (San Francisco: California Historical Society, 1928), 25-26.

10 Ibid., 26.

11 Quoted in Morgan, 241.

12 Ibid., 350-351.

13 Ibid., 359.

14 Ibid., 354.

15 Ibid..

16 Ibid., 312.

17 Ibid., 324.

18 Ibid., 326.

19 Ibid., 363.

20 Ibid., 330.

19. Thomas "Stonewall" Jackson: A Godly Soldier

1   Abraham Lincoln, "First Inaugural Address of Abraham Lincoln," *Yale Law School*, March 4, 1861, http://avalon.law.yale.edu/19th_century/lincoln1.asp.

2   Robert L. Dabney, *Life and Campaigns of Lieutenant General Thomas J. Stonewall Jackson* (Harrisonburg, VA: Sprinkle Publications, 1983), 20.

3   Ibid., 26.

4   Byron Farwell, *Stonewall: A Biography of General Thomas J. Jackson* (New York: W.W. Norton & Co., 1992), 14.

5   Ibid., 140.

6   Quoted in S.C. Gwynne, *Rebel Yell: The Violence, Passion, and Redemption of Stonewall Jackson* (New York: Simon & Schuster, 2014), 14.

7   Ibid., 105.

8   Ibid., 106.

9   Jackson, Letter to Laura, October 26, 1847, quoted in Gwynne, 107.

10 Ibid.

11 Jackson, Letter to Laura, April 1, 1853, quoted in Gwynne, 141.

12 Elizabeth Preston Allan, *Life and Letters of Margaret Junkin Preston* (Boston: Houghton Mifflin, 1903), 61.

13 James Power Smith, "The Religious Character of Stonewall Jackson," in *The Union Seminary Review*, vol. 25 (Richmond, VA: Union Theological Seminary, 1898), 273.

14 Quoted in Mary Anna Jackson, *Memoirs of Stonewall Jackson* (Louisville, KY: Prentice Press, 1895), 73.

15 Quoted in Farwell, 126.

16 Quoted in Gwynne, 157.

17 Quoted in Mary Anna Jackson, 141.

18 Ibid.

19 Quoted in Gwynne, 18.

20 Quoted in ibid., 29.

21 Quoted in J. Steven Wilkins, *All Things For God: The Steadfast Fidelity*

of Stonewall Jackson (Nashville: Cumberland House, 2004), 94-95.

22 Quoted in Ibid., 94.

23 Quoted in Clint Johnson, *Civil War Blunders* (Winston-Salem, NC: John F. Blair, 1997), 26.

24 Quoted in Gwynne, 91.

25 Quoted in Mary Anna Jackson, 182.

26 Quoted in Gwynne, 164.

27 Ibid., 490.

28 Ibid., 54.

29 Ibid.

30 John Williamson Palmer, "Stonewall Jackson's Way," in Elihu S. Riley, *Stonewall Jackson: A Thesaurus of Incidents and Anecdotes in the Life of Lieut-General Thomas Jonathan Jackson, C.S.A.* (Annapolis,

MD: n.p., 1920), 202-203.

31 Quoted in Gwynne, 486.

32 Quoted in Dabney, 108.

33 Ibid., 587.

34 Quoted in George F.R. Henderson, *Stonewall Jackson and the American Civil War* (London: Longmans, Green, & Co., 1898), 2:348.

35 Quoted in Gwynne, 544.

36 Quoted in Farwell, 521.

37 Quoted in Gwynne, 549.

38 Ibid.

39 Ibid., 551.

40 Ibid., 558.

41 Ibid.

42 Ibid.

43 Quoted in Henderson, 1:200.

20. Charles Hodge: Contending for the Truth

1 Quoted in W. Andrew Hoffecker, *Charles Hodge: The Pride of Princeton* (Phillipsburg, NJ: Presbyterian & Reformed, 2011), 37.

2 Quoted in ibid., 43.

3 Ibid., 50.

4 Quoted in ibid., 53.

5 Quoted in ibid., 73.

6 Quoted in ibid., 81.

7 Quoted in ibid., 84.

8 Ibid.

9 Quoted in ibid., 103.

10 Quoted in ibid., 115. Emphasis added.

11 Quoted in ibid., 115. Emphasis added.

12 Quoted in A.A. Hodge, *The Life of*

Charles Hodge (New York: Charles Scribner's Sons, 1880), 591.

13 Quoted in Hoffecker, 352.

14 Quoted in ibid., 168.

15 Quoted in ibid., 318.

16 Quoted in ibid., 319.

17 A.A. Hodge, *The Life of Charles Hodge*, 22.

18 Charles Hodge, *What is Darwinism?* (New York: Charles Scribner's Sons, 1874), 177.

19 Charles Hodge, *Systematic Theology*, 3 vols. (Grand Rapids: Eerdmans, 1872, reprinted 1982), 1:570.

20 Ibid., 1:570-571.

21. George Washington Carver: A Scientist in Awe of God

1 Quoted in Gary R. Kremer, ed., *George Washington Carver in His Own Words*, 2nd ed. (Columbia, MO: University of Missouri Press, 2017), 162.

2 Letter to Isabelle Coleman, July 24, 1931, in Kremer, 146.

3 Harriet C. Frazier, *Lynchings in Kansas*, 1850s-1932 (Jefferson, NC: McFarland & Co, 2015), 75-77.

4 Quoted in John Perry, *George Washington Carver* (Nashville: Thomas Nelson, 2011), 15.

5 Quoted in ibid., 21.

6 Louis R. Harlan, ed., *The Booker T. Washington Papers*, vol. 3: 1889-95 (Champaign, IL: University of Illinois Press, 1974), 93.

7 Book T. Washington, *Putting the Most into Life* (NY: Thomas Y. Crowell & Co., 1906), 23-25.

8 Quoted in Perry, 63.

9 Quoted in Kremer, 162.

10 Quoted in Christina Vella, *George Washington Carver: A Life* (Baton Rouge: Louisiana State University Press, 2015) 211.

11 Quoted in Perry, 87.

12 Quoted in ibid., 89.

13 William J. Federer, *George Washington Carver: His Life & Faith in His Own Words* (St. Louis, MO: Amerisearch, 2002), 36.

14 Quoted in Perry, 141.

15 Ibid., 62.

16 Quoted in Vella, 195.

17 Ibid.

18 Quoted in Perry, 107.

19 Quoted in ibid., 94.

20 Quoted in Federer, 35-36.

21 Quoted in Perry, 128.

22 Quoted in ibid.

23 Lawrence Elliott, *George Washington Carver: the Man Who Overcame* (Englewood Cliffs, NJ: Prentice-Hall Inc., 1966), 162.

24 Quoted in Vella, 327.

22. Dwight L. Moody: Evangelist and Entrepreneur

1 Mark A. Noll, *A History of Christianity in the United States and Canada* (Grand Rapids, MI: Eerdmans, 1992), 288.

2 Kevin Belmonte, *D.L. Moody, A Life: Innovator, Evangelist, World-Changer* (Chicago: Moody Publishers, 2014), 21.

3 Quoted in ibid.

4 Ibid., 22.

5 Quoted in Tim Challies, *Devoted, Great Men and Their Godly Moms* (Cruciform Press, 2018),109.

6 Quoted in ibid., 113-114.

7 Quoted in Belmonte, 27.

8 Quoted in ibid., 28-29.

9 Ibid., 29.

10 Quoted in ibid., 36.

11 Quoted in ibid., 41.

12 Quoted in ibid.

13 Quoted in ibid., 42.

14 Ibid., 47.

15 Quoted in ibid., 49.

16 Quoted in ibid., 64.

17 Ibid. 69.

18 Quoted in ibid., 77.

19 Quoted in ibid., 78.

20 Quoted in ibid., 101.

21 Quoted in Lyle W. Dorsett, *A Passion for Souls: The Life of D.L. Moody* (Chicago: Moody, 1997), 161.

22 Quoted in ibid.

23 Quoted in ibid.

24 Ibid., 179.

25 Stanley N. Gundry, *Love Them In: The Life and Theology of D.L. Moody* (Chicago: Moody, 1976), 90.

26 Ibid., 169.

27 Quoted in ibid., 171.

28 Quoted in Belmonte, 144.

29 Quoted in ibid.

30 Quoted in ibid., 152.

31 Quoted in ibid.

32 Quoted in ibid., 183.

33 Quoted in ibid., 184.

34 Quoted in ibid., 185.

35 Quoted in ibid., 186.

36 Quoted in ibid., 187.

37 Ibid., 191.

38 Ibid., 197.

39 Quoted in Dorsett, 379.

40 Quoted in ibid., 381.

41 Quoted in ibid.

23. William McKinley: Humble President, Faithful Husband

1 Quoted in Gary Scott Smith, *Religion in the Oval Office: The Religious Lives of American Presidents* (New York: Oxford University Press, 2015), 162.

2 Quoted in ibid.

3 Quoted in ibid., 160.

4 Robert W. Merry, *President McKinley: Architect of the American Century* (New York: Simon & Schuster, 2017), 18

5 Quoted in ibid., 23.

6 Ibid., 38.

7 Ibid., 39.

8 Ibid., 77.

9 Smith, 162.

10 William McKinley, "First Inaugural Address of William McKinley,"

The Avalon Project, March 4, 1897, http://avalon.law.yale.edu/19th_century/mckin1.asp.

11 Quoted in Smith, 173.

12 General James Rusling, "Interview with President William McKinley," *The Christian Advocate*, January 22, 1903, 17. Reprinted in Daniel Schirmer and Stephen Rosskamm Shalom, eds., *The Philippines Reader* (Boston: South End Press, 1987), 22–23.

13 Quoted in Smith, 189.

14 Quoted in Merry, 482.

15 Sarah Flower Adams, "Nearer, My God, To Thee"

16 Quoted in Smith, 163.

17 McKinley, "First Inaugural Address."

24. J. Gresham Machen: Valiant for Truth

1 Ned B. Stonehouse, *J. Gresham Machen: A Biographical Memoir* (Willow Grove, PA: The Committee for the Historian of the Orthodox Presbyterian Church, repr. 2004), 23.

2 Ibid., 25.

3 Stephen J. Nichols, *J. Gresham Machen: A Guided Tour of His Life and Thought* (Phillipsburg, NJ: P&R, 2004), 27.

4 Stonehouse, 38.

5 Quoted in ibid., 40.

6 Ibid., 124.

7 Quoted in ibid., 136.

8 Quoted in ibid., 131.

9 Ibid.

10 *Federal Reserve Bulletin*, February 1921 (Washington, DC: Government Printing Office, 1921), 184, https://fraser.stlouisfed.org/files/docs/publications/FRB/pages/1920-1924/23262_1920-1924.pdf.

11 Ibid., 220.

12 Ibid., 223.

13 North, 187.

14 W. Barksdale Maynard, *Woodrow Wilson, Princeton to the Presidency* (New Haven, CT: Yale University, 2008), 147.

15 Woodrow Wilson, *The Constitutional Government of the United States*, (New York: Columbia University Press, [1908] 1961), 54-57.

16 Quoted in Nichols, 87-88.

17 Quoted in Stonehouse, 295.

18 Quoted in ibid., 325-326.

19 J. Gresham Machen, *Christianity and Liberalism* (Grand Rapids, MI: Eerdmans, 1923, repr. 2009), 82.

20 Quoted in Stonehouse, 417.

21 Quoted in ibid., 418.

22 Quoted in ibid., 419.

23 Quoted in ibid., 450.

24 Ibid.

25 Quoted in ibid., 451.

25. Elisabeth Elliot: A Life of Gospel Sacrifice

1 Tertullian, *Apology*, 50.

2 Quoted in Janet and Geoff Benge, *Elisabeth Elliot: Joyful Surrender* (Seattle: YWAM Publishing, 2010), 43.

3 Elisabeth Elliot, *Through Gates of Splendor* (Carol Stream, IL: Tyndale Momentum, 1996), 4.

4 Benge, 66.

5 Ibid., 111.

6 Quoted in ibid., 129.

7 Quoted in ibid., 131.

8 Elliot, 50.

9 Quoted in Elliot, 57.

10 Quoted in ibid., 89.

11 Ibid., 94.

12 Ibid., 170.

13 Quoted in ibid., 190.

14 Ibid., 248.

15 Ibid., 265-266.

16 Quoted in ibid., 15.

17 Ibid., 253.

18 Quoted in Benge, 221.

19 Elliot, 264.

26. Henry Morris: Father of Modern Creation Science

1 Westminster Confession of Faith, 4.1.

2 Charles Hodge, *What is Darwinism?* (New York: Charles Scribner's Sons, 1874), 177.

3 Clarence Darrow, *Why I Am an Agnostic* (Girard, KS: Haldeman-Julius, 1929), 40.

4 Quoted in Rebecca M. Barber, *Henry M. Morris: Father of Modern Creationism* (Dallas, TX: Institute for Creation Research, 2017), 29-30.

5 Ibid., 168.

6 Ibid., 134.

7 Ibid., 134-135.

8 Henry M. Morris, *History of Modern Creationism* (Santee, CA: Institute for Creation Research,

9 Ibid., 1-2.

10 John C. Whitcomb and Henry M. Morris, *The Genesis Flood: The Biblical Record and its Scientific Implications* (Phillipsburg, NJ: Presbyterian & Reformed, 1961), 1-2.

11 Ibid., 118.

12 Quoted in Barber, 182.

27. David Wilkerson: Spiritual Revival During an Age of Apostasy

1 Leonard Ravenhill, "Quotes of Leonard Ravenhill," *gospeltruth. net*, https://www.gospeltruth. net/ravenhill.htm

2 Gary Wilkerson, *David Wilkerson: The Cross, the Switchblade, and the Man Who Believed* (Grand Rapids: Zondervan, 2014), 58.

3 Ibid., 63.

4 Ibid.

5 Ibid., 75.

6 Ibid., 189-190.

7 Ibid., 66.

8 Ibid., 77.

9 Ibid., 91.

10 Ibid.

11 Ibid., 91.

12 Ibid.

13 Ibid., 92.

14 Ibid., 98.

15 Ibid., 126.

16 Ibid., 156.

17 Ibid., 166

18 Ibid.

19 David Wilkerson, *The Vision* (New York: Pyramid Books, 1974), 79.

20 Gary Wilkerson, 187.

21 Ibid., 276.

22 Ibid., 169.

23 Ibid., 244.

24 Ibid.

25 Ibid., 258.

26 Ibid., 264.

27 Ibid., 260.

28 Ibid., 276.

29 Ibid.

30 Ibid., 291.

31 David Wilkerson, "A Call to Anguish," *SermonIndex.net*, September 15, 2002, http://www.sermonindex. net/modules/articles/index. php?view=article&aid=32622.

32 Gary Wilkerson, 75.

33 Ibid., 299.

34 https://www.drugabuse. gov/publications/drugfacts/ nationwide-trends

35 Gary Wilkerson, 298.

List of Images

Chapter 1

John Winthrop Portrait | iStock.com

William Tyndale | Wikimedia
  Commons | Public Domain

Portrait of Henry VIII | Wikimedia
  Commons | Public Domain

Trinity College | iStock.com

King James I | Wikimedia
  Commons | Public Domain

Massachusetts Bay | Wikimedia
  Commons | Public Domain

Portrait of Cotton Mather | iStock.com

Chapter 2

William Bradford Portrait | Wikimedia
  Commons | Public Domain

Mayflower in Plymouth | Wikimedia
  Commons | Public Domain

Signing of the Mayflower Compact
  | Wikimedia Commons
  | Public Domain

The First Thanksgiving | Wikimedia
  Commons | Public Domain

Miles Standish | Wikimedia
  Commons | Public Domain

Modern recreation of Plymouth
  Plantation | iStock.com

Chapter 3

Anne Bradstreet Portrait | Wikimedia
  Commons | Public Domain

King Charles I | Wikimedia
  Commons | Public Domain

Title page of The Tenth Muse
  | Wikimedia Commons
  | Public Domain

Simon Bradstreet | iStock.com

Chapter 4

John Eliot Portrait | iStock.com

John Eliot's home | Wikimedia
  Commons | Public Domain

Cambridge University | iStock.com

Martha's Vineyard | iStock.com

Marker for Indian Meeting House
  | Wikimedia Commons
  | Public Domain

Title page of Algonquin Bible | Wikimedia
  Commons | Public Domain

Chapter 5

Increase Mather Portrait | iStock.com

Peter Minuit | Wikimedia Commons | Public Domain

Richard Baxter | Wikimedia Commons | Public Domain

James II of England | Wikimedia Commons | Public Domain

Salem Witch Trials | Wikimedia Commons | Public Domain

Chapter 6

David Brainerd Portrait (attribution to Brainerd disputed) | Wikimedia Commons | Public Domain

Seal of the Massachusetts Bay Colony | Wikimedia Commons

| Public Domain

George Whitefield | Wikimedia Commons | Public Domain

Housatonic River | Wikimedia Commons | Public Domain

Chapter 7

Jonathan Edwards Portrait | Wikimedia Commons | Public Domain

View of the Connecticut River | iStock.com

Missions house in Stockbridge | Wikimedia Commons | Public Domain

Chapter 8

Patrick Henry Portrait | iStock.com

Samuel Davies | Wikimedia Commons | Public Domain

St. John's Church | iStock.com

The Governor's Palace | iStock.com

The Constitutional Convention | Wikimedia Commons | Public Domain

Chapter 9

Samuel Adams Portrait | iStock.com

British ships arriving | Wikimedia
    Commons | Public Domain

The Boston Tea Party | iStock.com

Independence Hall | iStock.com

Paul Revere's Ride | iStock.com

Chapter 10

Phillis Wheatley Portrait | iStock.com

George Whitefield | iStock.com

Title page of Poems on Various

Subjects | Wikimedia
    Commons | Public Domain

Thomas Jefferson | iStock.com

Chapter 11

George Washington Portrait | iStock.com

Washington crossing the Delaware
    | Wikimedia Commons

| Public Domain

Washington at Valley Forge | iStock.com

Mt. Vernon | iStock.com

Chapter 12

Noah Webster Portrait | iStock.com

West Hartford | iStock.com

Noah Webster's wife | Wikimedia

Commons | Public Domain

Webster's home | Wikimedia
    Commons | Public Domain

Chapter 13

Daniel Boone Portrait | iStock.com

Cumberland Gap | Wikimedia

Commons | Public Domain

Daniel Boone National Forest | iStock.com

Chapter 14

John Quincy Adams Portrait | iStock.com

John Adams | Wikimedia Commons | Public Domain

Abigail Adams | Wikimedia

Commons | Public Domain

John Quincy Adams at Age 29 | Wikimedia Commons | Public Domain

Chapter 15

Adoniram Judson Portrait | Wikimedia Commons | Public Domain

Ann Hasseltine Judson | Wikimedia Commons | Public Domain

Shwe Dagon Pagoda | iStock.com

Judson Memorial Church | Wikimedia Commons | Public Domain

Chapter 16

Asahel Nettleton Portrait | Wikimedia Commons | Public Domain

Lyman Beecher | Wikimedia

Commons | Public Domain

Charles Grandison Finney | Wikimedia Commons | Public Domain

Chapter 17

Lemuel Haynes Portrait | Wikimedia Commons | Public Domain

Fort Ticonderoga | Wikimedia

Commons | Public Domain

Home of Lemuel Haynes | Wikimedia Commons | Public Domain

Chapter 18

Jedediah Smith Portrait | Wikimedia Commons | Public Domain

Meriwether Lewis and William Clark | Wikimedia Commons

| Public Domain

Great Salt Lake, Utah | iStock.com

Mission San Jose | Wikimedia Commons | Public Domain

Chapter 19

Thomas Jackson Portrait | iStock.com

John Brown | Wikimedia Commons
| Public Domain

West Point | Wikimedia Commons
| Public Domain

Battle of Bull Run | iStock.com

Chapter 20

Charles Hodge Portrait | Wikimedia
Commons | Public Domain

Nassau Hall | Wikimedia Commons

| Public Domain

Charles Darwin | Wikimedia
Commons | Public Domain

Chapter 21

George Washington Carver Portrait
| Wikimedia Commons
| Public Domain

Booker T. Washington | Wikimedia
Commons | Public Domain

George Washington Carver with

colleagues | Wikimedia
Commons | Public Domain

Tuskegee Institute | Wikimedia
Commons | Public Domain

US World War II Poster | Wikimedia
Commons | Public Domain

Chapter 22

Dwight L. Moody Portrait | iStock.com

Railroad station | Wikimedia
Commons | Public Domain

Plaque | Wikimedia Commons
| Public Domain

The Great Fire of Chicago | Wikimedia
Commons | Public Domain

The Chicago World Fair | Wikimedia
Commons | Public Domain

Chapter 23

William McKinley Portrait | Wikimedia
Commons | Public Domain

Rutherford B. Hayes | Wikimedia
Commons | Public Domain

Ida Saxton McKinley | Wikimedia
Commons | Public Domain

Roosevelt's Rough Riders | Wikimedia
Commons | Public Domain

The Battle of San Juan Hill | Wikimedia
Commons | Public Domain

1900 re-election poster | Wikimedia
Commons | Public Domain

Chapter 24

J. Gresham Machen Portrait | Wikimedia
Commons | Public Domain

Baltimore, Maryland | iStock.com

Trench Warfare | Wikimedia
Commons | Public Domain

Faculty of Westminster Theological
Seminary | The Gospel Coalition

Chapter 25

Elisabeth Elliot Portrait | Wikimedia
Commons | Public Domain

Blanchard Hall | Wikimedia
Commons | Public Domain

Quito, Ecuador | iStock.com

Nate Saint | Wikimedia Commons
| Public Domain

Chapter 26

Henry Morris Portrait | Wikimedia
Commons | Public Domain

Thomas Huxley | iStock.com

The Genesis Flood | P&R Publishing

Farm in Texas | Wikimedia
Commons | Public Domain

Chapter 27

David Wilkerson Portrait | Wikimedia
Commons | Public Domain

David Wilkerson and Nicky Cruz
| Wikimedia Commons
| Public Domain

The Cross and the Switchblade
| Jove Books

Times Square Church | Wikimedia
Commons | Public Domain